CINEMA AND MODERNITY

CINEMA AND MODERNITY

EDITED BY MURRAY POMERANCE

RUTGERS
UNIVERSITY
PRESS

NEW BRUNSWICK,
NEW JERSEY,
AND LONDON

*61027515

Library of Congress Cataloging-in-Publication Data

Cinema and modernity / edited by Murray Pomerance.

    p. cm.

  Includes bibliographical references and index.

  ISBN-13: 978−0−8135−3815−0 (hardcover : alk. paper)

  ISBN-13: 978−0−8135−3816−7 (pbk. : alk. paper)

1. Motion pictures. 2. Motion pictures−Social aspects. I. Pomerance, Murray, 1946−

PN1994.C4885 2006

  791.43−dc22   2005020076

A British Cataloging-in-Publication record for this book is available from the British Library.

Book design by Adam B. Bohannon

Manufactured in the United States of America

For Abraham Kaplan
1918–1993
who taught me to think of beauty
and showed me anyone

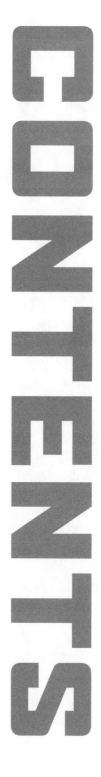

ACKNOWLEDGMENTS

For assistance, road directions, and generosity of many kinds on the long route to this publication, I am grateful to Scott Bukatman, Bruce Elder, Lester Friedman, Eve Goldin, Krin Gabbard, Barry Keith Grant, Nathan Holmes, Matt Justice, David Kerr, Ann Martin, Susan Oxtoby, Katina Saunders, Vivian Sobchack, Martijn van den Broek, and Chuck Wolfe.

My colleagues and friends at Rutgers University Press, who live in these pages, have been a constant pleasure as collaborators: specifically Molly Baab, Arlene Bacher, Adam B. Bohannon, Gary Fitzgerald, Alison Hack, Kenya Henderson, Adi Hovav, Suzanne Kellam, and Jessica Pellien. But I cannot say enough of thanks to Leslie Mitchner for patience, wisdom, true friendship, and constant critical taste, and to Marilyn Campbell, for a thousand minuscule attentions exercised with the greatest literary care.

To Carla Cassidy, I extend special thanks for thoughtful and substantial support.

Nellie Perret and Ariel Pomerance are, in all things, more of a help than I deserve and the very best companions for a happy exploration.

Murray Pomerance
Toronto
December 2005

He had also become the man to suit the image.

—ROBERT MUSIL

CINEMA AND MODERNITY

INTRODUCTION
Murray Pomerance

The Great Machine

Surely the book you are about to read, like modernity itself, had many origins, but the most memorable for me, because I can still see it as freshly today as I did for the first time more than thirty years ago, is a strange photograph that was part of a 1968 exhibition called "The Machine," at the old (and irreplaceable) Museum of Modern Art. This image was reproduced in a strange and wonderful catalogue of the same title, by K. G. Pontus-Hultén, that caught my eye on the bookshelves of my soon-to-be parents-in-law, George Albert and Claironel Foster Perret (who, seeing my desperate interest, very generously gave it over to me). The book has metallic covers and opens upon hinges, already a motive for my desire; but on page 175, not far past the classical vision of Charlie Chaplin trapped inside those mammoth gears from *Modern Times,* is a photograph by Ed van der Elsken called "Nigeria 1960." In a corner of what may well be a factory room, next to an expansive window admitting a blinding shaft of daylight, a young African man in colonial dress (short-sleeved white shirt and knee-length shorts) bends to tend a huge hissing boiler that is covered over with meters and knobs, pipes and release valves and flanges. Pipes, indeed, are coming off in all directions and filling the picture, and the eye is snagged by these and by the light reflected from the many well-polished pieces of metal that house the gauges and knobs. The worker is beside the machine, seen in profile, reaching forward to it with extended hands. He looks something like a hieroglyph.

What of modernity and its shocking confrontation with the past; of power, powerlessness, and design; of illumination overcoming the traditions of darkness; of strangeness (because the man and the machine in this photograph are still clearly not friends); of the horizon of urbanization; of systematization and control; and of magical possibility, is not invoked here! There is even a ghostly presence of cinema, because the huge machine with its ribbed pipes and dials vaguely resembles a theatrical projection apparatus with its many ducts for venting heat. We could be witness to a secret scene in a great projection room, and the light that had once seemed to be flooding *in through* the window may instead be emerging from the device and streaming *outward* to illuminate some faraway intoxicating screen.

If this African worker or manager—it is impossible to know which—is a tribal subject of the great machine, one whose life is committed to servicing it, he is also technological, which is to say, modern. Thus the photograph presents a paradox: is this not just as much *his* machine as a machine imposed upon him; has this device, as we see it here, not been his creation as much as his fate? Are we not just as much witnessing the birthing of this great machine out of Africa—so little does, and can, this image tell us of the sociological facts of the case—as the domination of African culture by Western technology: is this not just as likely the creation of the modern world out of what the Eurocentric must call the distance, the distance and the darkness? If the machine world that is this man's world is also our world, how very distant can he possibly be, given that he has embraced—is embracing—the same transformative apparatus as we do in every aspect of our lives? If this boiler is boiling images—and why may it not be?—there seems but a tiny step from here to the global cinema as contemporary machine, Quentin Tarantino digested in Africa and Idrissa Ouedraogo and Souleymane Cissé and Ousmane Sembene devoured in New York. If, as we have all come to suspect, cinema is modern life, the globalization of cinema is the wave of modernity spread all the way west to the east.

Modernity, of course, can hardly be spoken of outside of cinema, any more than I can speak of this single static image without animating it with my suspicion, my imagination, and my wonder. All of the sixteen essays in this volume make a similar attempt—to understand

4

the modern experience in light of cinema, and cinema in light of the modern experience. If not this image itself, then what this image can make us wonder about surely lies underneath them all.

The Shape of the Book

To box the strange intellectual compass of modernity in film, this book comes in four parts, followed by some "Modern Thoughts." First, "Dark Utopia" presents analyses of the shock, pain, and excitement of modernity as seen onscreen, from the electrified city to the moral equivocation of cinema noir, from the horrors of the concentration camp to the lingering traces of fascism in postwar America. Elsewhere, Will Straw has identified film noir's treatment of the "jazzy, nocturnal, vice-ridden American city" as being essentially "lurid" (1997, 123). This "dark city" is the focus of Lucy Fischer's discussion of cinema in the electric age. She is particularly interested in the "shock" value of film and its link to the birth of the modern city, where electricity was used "for extravagant effects." Examining the development of urban lighting and then the use of light in cinematography, Fischer notes electricity as an early theme in films such as *Electrocuting an Elephant, Electric Treatment, The Electric Girl,* and *Love and Electricity;* proceeds to a discussion of Keaton's *Electric House;* and then gives considerable attention to King Vidor's *The Crowd* and F. W. Murnau's *Sunrise,* two important films that reveal the complex social and aesthetic impacts of city life. Then, writing about film noir as an "ultimate" modernist style, Wheeler Winston Dixon plunges into a discussion of this urban topos in *Stranger on the Third Floor, The Big Clock, They Won't Believe Me, Kiss Me Deadly, Split Second,* and numerous other noirs of the 1940s and 1950s. For Dixon, noir systematically shows how if we are all connected in the urban scene we are also profoundly isolated from one another; hope is illusory; and the cinematic vision is nihilist. The "desperate, shabby, and unrelentingly bleak" noir is a perfect response to the economic uncertainty of the interwar period and to the social unrest and anxiety that followed World War II. Further, the bleakest and most authentic of the noirs came not from the major studios but from Poverty Row production houses like Producers Releasing Corporation; there, the actors and production personnel were themselves living on the dark side of life.

Much of modern cinema is a reaction to the trauma of World War II. Steven Alan Carr introduces the notion of the "alienated gaze" as central in understanding the production and reception of Holocaust imagery in American film. The "look that sees itself looking" offers a possibility for a disengaged, critical view that is essential, given the primacy of Holocaust imagery in "the struggle to negotiate subsequent standards for what constitutes atrocity, moral outrage, and ultimately military intervention." In this light, Carr considers *Night and Fog,* works of the NO!art collective (*Eichmann Remember* and *Lolita*), *The Great Dictator, To Be or Not to Be,* and various works of Alfred Hitchcock—including his little-known contribution to *Memory of the Camps*—highlighting ways in which all of these films come to play a role in establishing what Walter Benjamin called the "liberatory function" of images. An analysis of Hitchcock's role in cinema's modernity is extended through Walter Metz's discussion of that director in relation to Fritz Lang and to modernity's crisis in truth, with specific elaboration on *The Big Heat, Hangmen Also Die, Beyond a Reasonable Doubt, North by Northwest, Shadow of a Doubt, Vertigo,* and *Psycho.* Although, for Metz, the anti-fascist and European emigrant theoretizations of Benjamin, Max Horkheimer, Theodor Adorno, and Siegfried Kracauer are useful in reading Lang's despondent vision of a world where fascism lingers, Hitchcock's "classical realism" is best read through the prism of such American sociologists as Daniel Bell, William H. Whyte, and David Riesman. If Lang allegorizes the "lasting traumatic effects of World War II," finding it impossible to retreat in his films from the horrors of modern urban existence, Hitchcock shows, problematically for Metz, that accommodation to modernity is possible.

The section "Capital Advances" examines various aspects of the relation between modern culture and high capitalism as reflected onscreen. Modernity invoked a culture that favored the garrulous, tenacious, and, as Thorstein Veblen called it, "predatory" personality, able to circulate wildly and adapt in any kind of circumstance. Writing in particular about *Baby Face, Marked Woman,* and *Stella Dallas,* and especially about the performances of Barbara Stanwyck, Gwendolyn Audrey Foster explores class-passing, the "disrupting" of the notion of class identity, and shows how "class, like gender, may be construed as a socially constructed and regulated series of performed acts and

gestures." For Foster, the Depression-era maternal melodrama provided special opportunities for viewers to observe class as performative; in such films, class-passing is a "dangerous but possible act," and
dramatizations of it show the "noble display and noble erasure" of
women's social self. As it provided ground for this new image of
women, capitalism also demanded a new kind of hero. Rebecca Bell-
Metereau is concerned with the new capitalist heroic individual as
portrayed in science fiction film from *Things to Come* through *Island
of Lost Souls*, to *The War of the Worlds* and *The Day the Earth Stood
Still*. All of these films perpetuate "a model of progress and consumption that serves to promote the system that gives them life." This perpetuation, however, can be shown in science fiction film as embedded
in an optimistic display of radical design and apparently novel social
form, a skin of futurism that blinds viewers to the conservative forces
at play onscreen, which, for example, "familiarize and domesticate
nuclear power." The failure of film more generally, indeed, to provide
rigorous and subversive social critique, notwithstanding its persist-
ing promise to do so, characterizes a number of the postmodern
films discussed by Christopher Sharrett. In his critique of cinema as
inadequate and disingenuous, he ranges widely, from *Rebel Without
a Cause* and *Peyton Place* to *The Ice Storm, Elephant, Meet Me in
St. Louis*, and *Donnie Darko*. The possibilities for real critique, and
film's abject failure to approach it, get fuller discussion in relation to
The Rules of the Game, Eyes Wide Shut, and the work of Luchino
Visconti.

Georg Simmel showed how a central feature of modern social life
involves confrontation with the stranger. In a world of constant social
circulation and high social and geographic mobility, where travel and
transportation of goods, images, and people is the central mainstay of
the world economy, local community is fragmented and strangeness
becomes a pervasive feature of everyday life. To begin the third section
of the book, "Strange Personality," Krin Gabbard writes about the jazz
great Miles Davis as a contributor to modern film. Davis's work, and
jazz more broadly, take on the aspect of strangeness in terms of the
way filmmakers have attempted to co-opt or misrepresent it in a wide
variety of films, including *Elevator to the Gallows, Street Smart, The
Hot Spot, Runaway Bride, The Talented Mr. Ripley*, and *Pleasantville*. If
dislocation and misrepresentation are characteristic of the modern

encounter with the stranger, so are terror and withdrawal, discussed at length by William Luhr and Peter Lehman in a discourse upon Blake Edwards's *Experiment in Terror*. Of particular interest here is the director's use of the public space of the sports stadium as a setting in which the stranger's penetration of civilized life becomes both especially threatening and especially uncontrollable. Luhr and Lehman suggest that "postwar anxieties about the fragmentation of identity" often tended to characterize the relation of individuals to the state, and they show that Edwards's film is a thoroughgoing exploration of this theme. The fragmentation of identity is a tool of power. In that light, David Sterritt provides a Foucauldian exploration of Sam Fuller's *Shock Corridor*. As he shows, modernity implies a systematic takeover of personal life by state bureaucracy, an assault on individual memory, and a confrontation with "insane" discourses. Survival involves Foucault's "counter-memory," a state of active forgetting exemplified by the protagonist of Fuller's film. To conclude the section, my analysis of the central character in Steven Spielberg's *Catch Me If You Can* in relation to the protagonist of Lang's *Dr. Mabuse, the Gambler* examines the centrality of dramaturgical manipulation in modern life.

The section called "On the Move" brings together essays that examine aspects of modernity's obsessive and rhythmic pulsion, its linkage to systems of transportation, its abnegation of stasis, stolidity, permanence, and placement in favor of what Wolfgang Schivelbusch, writing about the development of railway travel, called "panoramic perception." Patrice Petro's focus is trained on the legacies of Weimar cinema, specifically a cluster of performers, genres, and images that circulated across Berlin, Hollywood, and the international community in the 1920s and beyond and reflected in a particularly sophisticated way on states of impermanence in modernity. *Blonde Venus* is considered as a "trace of an international urban culture" where the German Marlene Dietrich's Helen Farraday can originate in sources such as the American Josephine Baker's all-black revue; and *The Blue Angel* is examined as a showcase for Dietrich's genderless, cynical performance style. Dietrich's Berlin was, for Petro, a "node within a network of global cities"; and by way of this network, both images and performers "traveled across temporal and cultural boundaries to emerge as part of a new ensemble" that took form in Hollywood in the 1920s. While unemotional and misogynist erotic violence has long characterized

Weimar modernity for many critics, Petro sees "another Weimar legacy," involving women, that profoundly affected Hollywood. Tom Conley is interested in thinking through cinema's modernity in terms of its ability to map narrative spaces, and examines the "locational power" of the screen as part of the history of cartography. He discusses, in particular, the experience and sense of being lost in relation to the waterways mapped out in Jean Vigo's classic, *L'Atalante,* with reference to the importance of cartography in establishing the condition of modernity and the strategic use of a map in a culminating sequence of this film. Joe McElhaney writes about the speed of language and narrative development in the films of Preston Sturges, who developed the slapstick technique of speeding action in a form appropriate for talkies. Overlapping dialogue, speech rhythm, and dialogue as a pure sound element are all discussed in relation to numerous Sturges films, but especially *Sullivan's Travels, The Lady Eve, The Palm Beach Story,* and *Christmas in July.* The racing language in Sturges exemplifies the modern character's "drive toward social and economic success."

And finally, under the rubric of "Modern Thoughts," are two concluding essays. Tom Gunning notes that for early cinema artists, "the rise of the machine, its transformation of the human environment, as well as the rise of the masses, carried both apocalyptic and millennial possibilities," this to such a degree that "cinema metaphorised modernity." Here, considering Benjamin's "culture of shocks" against the context of such practices as "the new factory system, the establishment of worldwide standard time, and Taylorism," Gunning rethinks and rebalances his account of modernity to address not only the disruption of the social order but also the underside of this, "a systematic process of rational and scientific planning." For him, accounting for modernism, especially in relation to cinema, requires the idea of a pattern of shocks and flows. William Rothman follows with an exploration of the relation between film and modernity as conceived by the philosopher Stanley Cavell. For Cavell, writes Rothman, the true shock of modernity lies in the condition of our being displaced from the world, not in an explosion of technological progress. But the contribution of cinema to culture lies in the way it makes us feel that displacement as natural. The foundation of Cavell's approach to film is his conviction that film is both philosophical and modern in essence.

The modernism of film, indeed, leads it "not to repudiate" its own history but "to keep faith with that history in a situation in which doing so requires radically new forms and procedures."

Cinema and Modernity

Many origins. Modernity, let us argue, began in 1853, when Henri Le Secq photographed, and thus communicated, the Parisian demolitions that were preparing the way for the vast urban renovations of Baron Georges-Eugène Haussmann, Prefect of the Seine (see Rice 1997, 8–24). What had been, before the Haussmannization of Paris, an array of festering and intimate warrens, localized neighborhoods out of which many *citoyens* never managed to wander their whole lives, became a web of extensive avenues and stretching prospects, both an object of vision and a promise of mobility, evidence of its architect's "passion for exact spatial coordination" (Harvey 2003, 122).

Or let us say modernity began in 1839, when Edgar Allan Poe published in *Burton's Gentleman's Magazine* a story called "The Man of the Crowd," in which he introduced what would later come to be called, memorably, by Baudelaire the *flâneur*, prototype of the contemporary shopper, to be sure. This type wandered away from his local precincts and discovered the circulating strangers in the city, observing carefully their styles and traits, detecting their identities and backgrounds from exteriorized symptoms of class and attitude. "With some little difficulty I at length came within sight of him, approached, and followed him closely, yet cautiously, so as not to attract his attention," Poe's narrator confides to us. "I had now a good opportunity of examining his person" (Poe 1998, 88).

It began in 1829, we might say as well, when Louis-Jacques-Mandé Daguerre first fixed light in a photographic image. Now it was possible for the natural world that surrounded an observer to be stilled, caught, packaged, and itself transported, so that not only persons engaged in experience but also experience itself could move from place to place. Given the daguerreotype, Poe's "man of the crowd" was thinkable; and given Poe's "man of the crowd," it made sense for Haussmann to capitalize on the potential of the moving experience and the moving thought by removing the physical obstacles to motion and projection that had cluttered the city.

By the middle of the nineteenth century, as the "modern" world took form with numerous developments in numerous places reflecting new ways of thinking about numerous aspects of human endeavor, public illumination characterized every social change, marking, in a way, the artificiality and limitless possibility of the photographic act and also the desire to move into unknown territories and see the hitherto invisible, only imaginable, realities of life. "Any artificially lit area out of doors is experienced as an interior because it is marked off from the surrounding darkness as if by walls," Schivelbusch writes, reflecting on Emma von Niendorf's description of the Boulevard des Italiens illuminated at night (1995, 149). By 1845, Jules Michelet was already remarking on the astonishing progress of public illumination that had been achieved through the nineteenth century when he wrote, of the introduction of gaslight to factories, that the new illumination would "torture eyes accustomed to darker quarters. Here there is no darkness, into which thought can withdraw" (qtd. in Schivelbusch 1995, 134).

That darkness, into which thought had withdrawn, was the feudal, medieval, scholastic darkness, to be sure. Modernity, the era of public illumination, brought a new sense of exteriority: what had once been privately imagined was now dramatically depicted, broadcast, systematized for all to read and know. The city was not only a topos of intense navigation and movement, a stuttering form, but also the setting for an unending circulation of talents, purposes, attitudes, and personalities. If brightness was a torture because it vanquished meditation, so was it a blessing because it vanquished what festered and decayed. It promised the cure; it revealed the workings of the mystery as complex and beautiful and strange. Modernity saw the birth of the department store, the great avenues, the railway, the telegraph, later the telephone and audio recording, not to mention the proliferation of photographs to such an extent that an entire world of images took shape in journalism and in libraries. For images to be made of it, however, the world had to appear, more than simply exist. Pose, attitude, alignment, relationship—all these came to be signaled openly to the observing stranger with the special eye. Advertising and media followed, capitalizing on the postures and appearances we had all learned to interpret at first glance.

And into this sphere of light, where the darkness was made visible and the dream displayed, where experience was relentlessly externalized and made legible, came motion pictures, glimmering and also transparent, promising and also nostalgic, yet above all designed to capture and reveal, far beyond the shape of things, the rhythm by which the world moved and changed. Certainly by invoking modernity one has not said everything there is to say about cinema, any more than by invoking cinema it is possible to say everything there is to say about modernity. Yet without cinema, modernity is unthinkable; and without modernity, cinema would not exist. Cinema offered a vision of ongoing and unfolding eventuality, instantaneous linkage, happening, as when, at the end of his *City Lights* (1931), Chaplin's face is remade onscreen when he sees that the blind girl whose sight he has helped repair recognizes him, penetrates and discovers him, accepts him for what he is. Even as film made possible that viewers would witness action and gesture as such, that is, take note of the actual flow from certain signs and spatial arrangements to others, it also reflected modernity's contraction of experience from the timeless to the momentary. In modernity, commitments of attention and obligation could henceforward be situational, provisional, terminable, replaceable, and malleable in a routine way, and fixed relations could become negotiable as a result of chance encounters or collisions in the intensive circulation that was everyday life. This pervasive and energetic movement, on the basis of which a new social order was organized, made possible and normal, therefore, not only timetabling and interconnection, not only arrangement by long distance (such as Dr. Mabuse enacts in the robbery sequence at the beginning of *Der Spieler*), not only the revolutionary "panoramic perception" and "upholstered" experience described by Schivelbusch (1986, 122–23) but also a new and severe delimitation of the field of engagement through which people came to meet and work with one another. Talents and abilities separated themselves from personalities. Intentions could be guarded and hidden. Identity could be fabricated.

What film could reflect was all the rich confusion of: light and electric stimulation (thus, scientific development), temporary and impenetrable relationship (thus, social mobility and the omnipresence of strangers), alienation of labor from biography and history (thus, the pervasive organization of capitalism and its form of exploitation), and onwardly rushing movement (movement in many directions at once, so that collision, and then war, were inevitable)—the hallmarks of the modern world. In the workplace, in the marketplace, in the tearoom, in the theater, on the street, "invention is itself fetishized," as Fredric Jameson writes, "and . . . some older situation is somehow 'revolutionized' by the very presence of the new existent" (2002, 124). Cinema could perfectly symbolize modernity, and then could become modernity. The modern city, full of strangeness and illumination, always changing, conflicted and radiantly beautiful all at once, could be on the screen—and then could *be* the screen.

Consider, for an example of cinema's reflection of modern life, that sci-fi passion play, Ishiro Honda's *Godzilla* (1954), in which an awkward and menacing giant atavism from the ocean depths rises to threaten the shimmering scape of the busy city. He cannot be vanquished through the agency of science and high technology until he has stomped through massive towers bearing high-tension lines, dismantled and crumpled the television broadcasting tower, inspired countless panicky police and security agents to jabber hysterically on their telephones, and snacked upon a car lifted out of a train wreck. Invoked in this tale of nature gone amok in the space of modernity, then, are trains and vehicles generally, the system of broadcasting and telecommunication, and a widely diffused electrical grid. *Godzilla* is about a beast of superhuman proportions encountering the human world, but it is inconceivable without the appurtenances of modernity. Or consider the presence of the revolving door at a signal moment in F. W. Murnau's *Die Letzte Mann* (1924), when an old doorman, somewhat pompous in the uniform he treasures so much, and certainly taking his long-standing position at a grand hotel somewhat for granted, walks in from the street at the same time as another uniformed man walks out. It is the charm of the revolving door that pedestrians may go in opposite directions simultaneously without obstructing one another, indeed, without particularly taking cognizance of one another, this fact a profound irony here because the other man is the old fellow's replacement and the old fellow does not know it yet. Not only do persons criss-cross in this technologically marvelous door; so do occupations trade places, and even lives. One man's fortune goes up as another's goes down, in the same place, at the same moment. James Buzard describes Murnau's revolving door as being both a dehumanizing machine and a wheel of fortune (2001). The power lines that catch up Godzilla—power lines and electrical poles and towers dominate both the urban and island settings of the tale—and the revolving door that catches up the doorman: in both cases, spirit is trapped in a device for facilitating movement, transformation, speed, and radical change. And in both films, the old world is destroyed by the mechanism of the new. The old doorman has made the mistake of identifying his devotion and sensibility with his bureaucratic position (a feudal loyalty now out of place). The giant reptile has brought a Cretaceous sensibility to bear in a modernist utopia. He cannot survive there, but neither can any old wisdom or old culture thrive in this world of klieg lights, fighter aircraft, commuter trains, power grids, and Oxygen Destroyer beams: significantly, in rushing off to confront Godzilla, one of the heroes leaves behind tickets to the Budapest String Quartet.

In this book, which attempts neither to define modernity nor to exhaust, through any theory or collection of theories, the investigation of cinema's relationship to it, the contributors set themselves, each, to the study of some particular incidence of cinema and modernity in such a way as to see the subject in itself and for itself, yet at the same time in a field where it is known that all the others are simultaneously working, with similar energies and sensitivities but in other directions. Although some of the authors do draw a line around what "modernity" seems to be to them, the salient fact, I believe, is that they draw this line differently, that they have quite different conceptions of modernity (and modernism). We must not imagine that modernity is a single phenomenon; indeed, one of its features is the multiplicity of perspective that comes from movement, fracture, the encounter with strangeness, the rapidity of social and technological change. Through the variegation of treatment here, through the modulation of voice, we understand something of a unified approach to a multiplied subject! And the unification is precisely in the absence of uniformity. This book itself, then, is, I hope, characterized by precisely the sort of circulation—of ideas and implications—that qualifies modernity. These scholars are trained in different academic fields. There are adepts of literature and religion, sociologists, cultural theorists, historians, and political theorists, all of whom share a passion for the cinema and a keen desire to think through the implications of modern experience on cinematic history and form—but to think it through both with and apart from one another. Necessarily and desirably, too, the book is, in the most profound sense of the word, incomplete. It is meant to sketch and suggest lines of connection, not to establish boundaries and claim territory. Finally, it is addressed to anyone equally passionate about cinema and equally curious to explore the modern world, whether this reader is a professional scholar or student or an accountant, construction worker, or spy.

"Modernity" and "cinema" are not sacred words to be used only in secret council among a holy elite. They are invocations of our shared public lives together. After mechanization, after the intermittent device that made possible the opening and closing of the camera's and projector's apertures, after the widespread availability of electrical illumination, after the city filled with strangers, after the systematic commodification of labor, after the jump cut, after the trolley, after the modern war—modernity is in and around all of us, and cinema embodies, reflects, and recharges that modernity everywhere.

DARK UTOPIA

"THE SHOCK OF THE NEW"
ELECTRIFICATION, ILLUMINATION, URBANIZATION, AND THE CINEMA
Lucy Fischer

> A technology is not merely a system of machines with certain functions: it is
> part of a social world.
>
> DAVID E. NYE, *ELECTRIFYING AMERICA*

The Technological Sublime[1]

It has become reflexive to associate modernity with the startling, to speak (as Robert Hughes would have it) of the "shock" of the new. Hence, when we consider the 1920s, we think of such cultural "jolts" as the era's progressive morality, its feminist advances, its innovative assembly line, its metropolitan lifestyle, its arts of the spectacle. In general, when the notion of "shock" has been voiced by social commentators it has been used figuratively. Thus, Walter Benjamin (in speaking of Charles Baudelaire) asserts that the poet "placed the *shock* experience at the very center of his artistic work" (1997, 163; my emphasis). Extending this insight, Benjamin notes how Baudelaire links shock with the modern urban space: "Moving through [metropolitan] traffic involves the individual in a series of *shocks,* and collisions. At dangerous intersections, nervous impulses flow through him in rapid succession, like the *energy from a battery*. Baudelaire speaks of a man who plunges into the crowd as into a *reservoir of electric energy*" (1997,

175; my emphasis). Eventually, transcending Baudelaire's observations, Benjamin offers his own views on the connections linking shock, modernity, and "mechanical reproduction." Speaking of still photography he observes how, with "a touch of the finger . . . the camera [gives] the moment a posthumous *shock*." Then, musing on how "technology has subjected the human sensorium to a complex kind of training," he asserts that "a new and urgent need for stimuli was met by the film" where "perception in the form of *shocks*, was established as a formal principle" (1997, 175; my emphases).

While appreciative of the "circuit" of metaphors that have enlivened such discussions of modernity, I want to literalize these references by taking the word "shock" at face value in its direct affiliation with electricity. For that technology was simultaneously a crucial tie to the birth of the modern city and to the cinematic medium. Thus, as David Nye notes, "Electrification [was] not an implacable force moving through history, but a social process" (1990, ix).

Most historians date the inception of the electric age with the 1831 discovery of the law of electromagnetic induction by the English scientist Michael Faraday. This principle was later used in generating electricity to power motors and other machines (www.filmsite.org). By 1880, electricity was functionally "under human control," and in 1882 the first commercial power station opened on Pearl Street in lower Manhattan (www.inventors.about.com; Kyvig 2002, 45). As evidence of the growing importance of the science, world fairs of the era featured electrical displays as central attractions, and approximately one-third of the American population first experienced the technology at such events (Nye 1990, 34). At these exhibitions, electricity was used for extravagant effects. As Nye remarks:

> Spectacular lighting was dramatic, nonutilitarian, abstract, and universalizing. It provided a brilliant canopy, connecting the many exhibits, statues, fountains, and pools in one design that was at once refined, ethereal and stunning. Electrical displays also embodied the latest in science, lending the exposition its prestige by association. After 1881, all fairs emphasized dramatic lighting and many made illuminated towers their symbols. . . . Electricity became more than the theme for a major exhibit building; it provided a visible correlative for the ideology of progress. (1990, 35)

Among such fairs was the Pan-American Exposition of 1901 held in Buffalo, New York. The "crowning centerpiece" of the event was a 375-foot-tall Electric Tower (designed by Howard Cobb), lit nightly by thousands of colored bulbs and floodlights.[2] Electrically powered elevators carried visitors to the tower's many floors, which housed a roof garden, restaurant, and viewing pavilion. The fair's campus also included the Electricity Building (designed by Edward Brodhead Green and William Sydney Wicks), where power generated by Niagara Falls was transformed into a voltage appropriate to the fair's appliances (www.buffalohistoryworks.com). A Palace of Electricity was also part of the 1904 Louisiana Purchase Exposition in St. Louis. A guidebook describes its contents:

> The exhibits in the Palace of Electricity will make it a center of attraction for all who are concerned in electrical progress. The remarkable advance in electrical engineering and the new discoveries of the science during the last ten years made possible the most comprehensive exhibit ever assembled. Dynamos and motors of many kinds and new electrical machinery for a multiple of uses may be seen in operation. Definite progress has been made during recent years in the use of electricity in the treatment of diseases. How it is thus used is illustrated with X-ray apparatus and the famous Finsen light. The progress in electric lighting and the use of electric power is shown. Small but powerful electric locomotives for mining purposes make an interesting exhibit. The wonders of electro-chemistry are illustrated. (http://washingtonmo.com/1904/12.htm)

Significantly, at the end of the film *Meet Me in St. Louis* (1944), when the Smith family finally attends the famous turn-of-the-century exposition, it is the view of the fairgrounds illuminated at night that excites them and makes them realize how lucky they are to be residents of their American hometown.

Beyond enlivening celebratory expositions, the major way in which electricity changed daily life in Western society was through its powering of quotidian light sources. Thomas Edison did not "invent" the electric light bulb; rather, he purchased other scientists' patents and, in 1879, produced the first commercially viable version of the product—specifically, a 16-watt prototype with a carbonized filament that could burn for some 1200–1500 hours (www.the-history-of.net). Furthermore, it was "practical, safe and economical" in comparison to previous forms of illumination (www.inventors.about.com). During the early part of the twentieth century, the price of electricity fell, making it more available for widespread use (Kyvig 2002, 46).

At first, electric current was utilized primarily in the public arena, for street lighting, urban transit, skyscraper elevators, and industrial machinery. For example, the British town of Sheffield experimented with lighting a football arena in 1878, and the town of Godalming in Surrey was the first to boast electric street lamps in 1881 (Weightman 2003, 22). But the years following World War I saw applications of the technology that affected people's personal and private lives (Kyvig 2002, 43). As Nye points out, it was the electric light that "served as an entering wedge, opening up the home to other electrical devices" (1990, 16). It dramatically transformed the urban, middle-class, domestic scene. Whereas gas illumination had been dim, grimy, risky, and pungent, electric lighting was bright, clean, safe, and odorless. These advantages led to changes in home design. Gas-lit buildings required that individual rooms be shut off for periodic airing, but the electric home could be built according to the "open" plan, whereby living room, dining room, and kitchen "flowed together." Furthermore, while the Victorian abode had been decorated with dark curtains and drab upholstery to hide the omnipresent soil, the modern dwelling could employ a fairer color scheme (Kyvig 2002, 47).

Electric lighting also had a profound influence on the timetable of daily living.[3] As David Kyvig comments: "Bright light able to banish the night's darkness and lengthen the day was the earliest and in many ways most significant consequence of electrification. . . . [It] literally empowered [people] to redesign the basic schedule of their daily existence" (2002, 44). On the one hand, it encouraged reading (a solitary, sometimes educational activity) because light was available after sundown. On the other hand, "electrified society gained more opportunity to devote time to nonproductive, pleasurable pursuits" (Kyvig 2002, 45). As Nye explains, "Lighting engineers created a new experience of night space . . . including new kinds of public spectacles" (1990, x). Among these were amusement parks, brightened by the same kinds of stunning light displays found on world fair midways.

Often these parks were located at the edge of town, "overflow[ing] the bounds of the city and its immediate environs" (Carpenter 1932, 250) and accessible to most people only by an "electric streetcar," a form of transportation that had, by the 1880s, begun to replace the horse and buggy. Coincidentally, as the trolley brought city residents to the suburbs (and some citizens even took rides there in the summer just to feel the "trolley breeze"), it also brought rural dwellers into town, especially for recreation at the new electrified amusement sites and for shopping at the illuminated department stores (Nye 1990, 11).

One reason the city so attracted country folk was that electrification of the provinces lagged far behind. In the era of World War I, some farms had electric generators, but most did not. Thus, "nothing more rapidly and notably differentiated urban from rural life" in this period than technology (Kyvig 2002, 45, 55). In the interwar period, the number of electrified American homes grew dramatically, from just over 24 million in 1920 to just under 35 million in 1940. However, "almost all of this enormous increase occurred in urban areas" (Kyvig 2002, 56). Starting in the 1920s, electrical appliances began to appear on the consumer market: sewing and washing machines, vacuum cleaners, toasters, and refrigerators. At first they were considered luxury items, but by the 1930s their prices had dropped and mass production had made them available to the middle-class customer. In sum, in the early decades of the twentieth century Americans came to consider the acquisition of electricity to be more important than obtaining other domestic conveniences. "Electricity had become a necessity before central heating, hot running water, and indoor toilets" (Kyvig 2002, 56).

The Electric Arts
Although the ties between electricity and the cinema should be obvious, they are rarely discussed in any detail. I have studied the medium for some thirty years, but until I began to work on this project I was not entirely sure which early machines were hand-cranked and which were electrically powered, which optical devices were illuminated by the electric bulb and which were lit by one of its predecessors (sunlight, candlelight, oil burner, limelight, or Argand lamp [Waine 1995, 1–2]).[4] In some cases, the name of the machine gives it away, as with

the Electrograph or the Royal Electric Bioscope, both British cameras.[5] Yet one would not necessarily know from the name that both Edison's Kinetograph (formally introduced in October 1892) and his Kinetoscope (publicly exhibited in 1896) had electric motors and that the latter used a light bulb for illumination (www.filmsite.org; www.acmi.net.au). Ultimately, hand-cranked cameras (like the Lumière brothers' Cinématographe of 1895)[6] gained popularity because they were much lighter to operate and because "they did not depend on the multitude of different electrical sources in American cities of the time" (Gomery 1992, 14). Thus, non-electrified models prevailed through the 1920s.[7]

Many of the first reviews of film showings nevertheless stressed the medium's use of electricity. In an article about an Edison Kinetograph presentation in Auckland, New Zealand, in November 1897, the writer enthused, "the pictures were shown by means of the electric light, which was a great improvement and presented the views with wonderful distinctness" (www.geocities.com). Similarly, a piece in the *New Zealand Herald* of January 1897 describes a Cinématographe demonstration: after "an electric knob [was] touched . . . where all was darkness there appear[ed] illumination." The scenes projected (including *Sandow the Strongman*) were "depicted with an almost uncanny lifelike verisimilitude" (www.geocities.com). Thus, it was not only motion that created the sense of realism in the cinema (in comparison to the static, pre-electric magic lantern), but also its bright, radiant image.

Interestingly, electricity not only facilitated cinema's machinery, but also featured as a subject of the medium's early content. One film, *General Electric Flash Light* (1902) both documents and advertises the new technology. Other films record its presence at world fairs, as in documentaries shot at the Pan-American Exposition of 1901: *Circular Panorama of the Base of the Electric Tower Ending Looking Down the Mall, Circular Panorama of the Esplanade with the Electric Tower in the Background,* and *Panoramic View of an Electric Tower from a Balloon.* Some films record new means of transportation (*Sprague Electric Train* [1897]), while others register views from those conveyances (*Panoramic View of Boston Subway from an Electric Car* [1901]). Still other films give evidence of novel, though troubling, applications of the new science, as in *Electrocuting an Elephant* (1903).[8] Electricity also served as a plot device in early dramas, trick films, and comedies from England, Spain, France, and America, as in *Electric Treatment* (1903), *The Electric Hotel* (1905), *Electric Goose* (1905), *Le Théâtre de petit Bob* (1906), *Professor Puddenhead's Patents: The Electric Enlarger* (1909), *The Electric Servant* (1910), *Electric Insoles* (1910), *The Electric Vitalizer* (1910), *Invigorating Electricity* (1910), *The Electrified Pig* (1911), *The Electric Girl* (1914), *Love and Electricity* (1914), *The Electric Doll* (1914), *The Electric Alarm* (1915), and *Bobby Bumps Eellectric Launch* (1919).

By the 1920s, with electricity an established part of the American scene, the topic worked its way into the fabric of more extended and sophisticated cinematic narratives. Sometimes it constituted the entire focus of a movie's scenario. In 1922, for example, Buster Keaton made *The Electric House,* whose very title indicates the importance of technology to his comedy. It concerns a recent college graduate (Keaton) who receives the wrong degree, that of "electrical engineer"—clearly a new type of profession in the era. Instead, he should have received a certificate in the field of "botanical and allied sciences." At the same convocation, the real electrical engineer is granted a degree in "manicure and beauty culture," obviously (given the period's sexism) a certificate meant for the girl sitting next to him during the ceremony. On the basis of these administrative errors, Buster is hired by a homeowner who wishes to electrify his luxurious estate. As the man and his family depart for a holiday, a daughter hands Buster a book: *Electricity Made Easy*. Signaling a temporal ellipsis, an intertitle next informs us that the family is returning home, "impatient to see all the surprise electrical devices" that Buster has installed in the interim.

Obviously, the film will draw upon Keaton's persona of mechanical wizard, a quality that Noël Carroll (1976) has examined in films like *The General* (1927), which concerns the earlier technology of the steam engine. *The Electric House* proceeds to offer scenes that demonstrate the various gadgets that Keaton has contrived. In one sequence, he shows the homeowner his new electric stairs, which operate like an escalator. By turning another switch, Buster exhibits how an electrified "arm" delivers a particular volume from the bookshelf. In another presentation, Buster flips a switch that causes a bathtub to move from the lavatory to the bedroom and, in the same episode, displays an electrified Murphy bed that automatically appears from, and disappears into, the wall. Among the other electrical wonders of the home are: pocket doors that open and close automatically, a swimming pool that fills and drains on its own, a conveyor belt that carries billiard balls to the gaming table, a "train" that delivers food from the kitchen to the dining room, a lazy Susan that spins around unassisted, and chairs that move into and away from the dining table without effort by the occupant. Despite a few mishaps during Buster's demonstration of these devices, by and large, things go well.

Later in the film, however, the real electrical engineer appears on the scene and is enraged that Buster has unfairly usurped his position. He sneaks into the newly electrified mansion to get his revenge by wreaking havoc with the wiring just as the homeowner is showing off his contraptions to friends. Predictably, all ehll breaks loose. The electric stairs move too quickly and jettison someone out a window. The bathtub emerges from the lavatory without warning and knocks someone over. The owner's daughter becomes trapped in the Murphy bed as it uncontrollably folds into the wall. Just as a title informs us that "the fun heats up," guests are moved willy-nilly toward and away from the dining table, and Buster is mercilessly twirled on the lazy Susan. A man gets hit in the head by the electrified bookcase arm, and pocket doors close upon Buster's head.

Interestingly, only one sequence invokes electric lighting per se, most likely because it had become so ordinary by 1922 that it was not, anymore, the basis for inventive humor. This sight gag goes as follows: after the real engineer has scrambled the home's wiring, the switches for the chandelier become reversed, and lights turn on when they are meant to turn off and vice versa. Finally, Buster realizes what is happening and decides to "trea[t] his enemy to a little refined torture." He throws pots and pans at the man (who is inside the utility room), causing electrical sparks to fly. As the film closes, both Buster and his nemesis are banished from the dwelling.

Nye has observed how, for Americans, "'electrifying' was both a process and an attribute," and people "understood the new technology in both ways. They regularly shifted from seeing electricity in terms of technical change to a metaphorical level where it meant novelty, excitement, [and] modernity" (1990, x). Clearly, in *The Electric House* the comedy addresses the public's sense of a new, cutting-edge technology that has the dual potential to solve and to create household problems. But the film also evinces the figurative sense of the word, since, as Nye remarks, "Anything 'electric' was saturated with energy, and the nation came to admire 'live wires,' 'human dynamos' and 'electrifying performances'" (1990, x). Certainly, these three epithets all attach to Keaton in his capacity as both screen actor and comic character.

Tripping the Light Fantastic

Although the setting of *The Electric House* is vague and nondescript, the locales of other films of the 1920s are decidedly urban. In these works, the issue of electric technology pertains more to public than to private space. *The Crowd* (1928), a silent film directed by King Vidor, tells the story of Johnny Sims (James Murray), a small-town American boy born on July 4, 1900, into a family that strongly believes in the American dream. His father predicts that someday his son will be "someone big." By the age of twenty-one, Johnny has moved to New York City, where a stranger informs him that he must "be good to beat the crowd." Such words of advice are accompanied by intimidating shots of cars, buses, subways, skyscrapers, and pedestrians. As Niles Carpenter observed in *The Sociology of City Life*, "social psychologists are not altogether agreed as to the precise way in which participation in a crowd affects the individual . . . [but] they are all unanimous . . . in stating that such participation constitutes a profoundly disturbing experience" (1932, 215). In an image worthy of Sergei Eisenstein, Johnny is seen at work in a huge office where scores of identical men toil at similar desks. His is distinguished only by the number 137. Here we are reminded of Georg Simmel's observation in "The Metropolis and Mental Life" (1905) that the city is ruled by a commercial "money economy" where "man is reckoned with like a number" (2004, 13–14).

At the stroke of 5:00 p.m., the alienated white-collar labor force quickly disperses to take up the delights of metropolitan nightlife. We learn that it is the July 4 weekend, a special time of recreation for the American public (and Johnny's birth date as an all-American guy). When a colleague asks him to go on a double date to Coney Island, Johnny agrees and is introduced to Mary (Eleanor Boardman), with whom he is immediately smitten. As the two ride the top tier of a double-decker bus, Johnny mocks the crowd below for being stuck "in the same rut." Clearly, he assumes that he will be an exception to the rule.

The scene and mood shift dramatically when the group arrives at Coney Island. The lackluster workaday universe is left behind and immediately replaced by the dazzling, electrically illuminated realm of the amusement park—a site that functions like a permanent "world's fair." The couples enjoy numerous motor-driven rides: a rotating cylinder, a spinning disk, a carousel, and a "tunnel of love." As the tunnel ride draws to a close, a light suddenly goes on and a curtain is raised so that the crowd outside can see which couples have been necking during their trip through the dark. At the end of the evening, Johnny and Mary return home on the subway, yet another electrical vehicle. The rest of the film traces their subsequent marriage, parenthood, loss of a child, employment problems, economic struggles, interpersonal strife, and temporary separation. Although Johnny Sims began the narrative as a young man who saw himself above the crowd, he ends it as a far more humble and cynical individual with grave doubts about himself and America's Horatio Alger myth. Significantly, the final scene of the film depicts Johnny and Mary sitting in a vaudeville theater evading their troubles by watching a stage comedy. Now they are part of a distracted, laughing mob.

From our perspective, what is most significant about *The Crowd* is its association of the joys of urban life of the 1920s with electricity. (Significantly, in an Austrian film of 1927, which features Marlene Dietrich, the night spot where risqué youths congregate is called the Electric Café.)[9] In *The Crowd* and other American films of the era, young people go to electrically powered amusement parks, locales associated with modernity, innovation, spontaneity, hedonism, and romance. Both the light show provided by these sites and the mechanical thrills they offer account for their attraction and appeal. Here, Carpenter's words are again relevant. He noted that, in the urban world, recreation is generally "used for emotional release and escape from reality," because "the restlessness and sophistication . . . characteristic of urban populations cause new forms of recreation to be continually sought after" (1932, 250). In some quarters, however, such pursuits have problematic overtones. Carpenter cites the amusement park as a "demoralizing recreational enterprise" culturally associated with "vice." Once more, he links such places with the upheaval of modernity. As he remarks, the urban dweller "can hardly keep from undergoing a degree of personality *shock* that is in some measure proportionate to the potency of the instinctive drives to which organized vice makes its appeal" (1932, 216; my emphasis). Ironically, Wolfgang Schivelbusch sees certain aspects of "recreational" electricity as, perhaps, contributing to the kind of isolation that *The Crowd* rails against. As he notes, "The power of artificial light to create its own reality only reveals itself in darkness. . . . The spectator sitting in the dark and looking at an illuminated image . . . is alone with himself and the illuminated image, because social connections cease to exist in the dark" (1995, 221).

Lonesome (1928), a Universal Picture directed by Paul Fejos, is another urban drama. It tells the tale of two young, working-class New Yorkers who experience isolation in the big city. Significantly, both are employed in industries powered by electricity. Mary (Barbara Kent) is a telephone operator, a profession that stands for "modern times." In the first scene of the film we see her awaken in her one-room apartment on a hot summer day and hurriedly prepare for work. In a parallel sequence, we encounter Jim (Glenn Tryon) in his flat; he is a machinist who operates a punch press on an assembly line. Again, we witness his hasty morning routine: dressing, eating at a diner, and making his way to the factory on the subway. In the manner of an experimental "city symphony" (using superimpositions and the like), the film follows both characters throughout the work day, showing Mary endlessly plugging and unplugging phone lines and Jim operating mechanical equipment. Often the face of a clock is layered over these images, implying that contemporary life proceeds at a frantic and grueling pace.

As in *The Crowd,* the laborers rapidly scurry from work at day's end, as though released from prison. Again in parallel scenarios, Mary and Jim, lacking plans for the evening, seem dejected as they watch friends depart on dates. Both return to their solitary rooms. The fact that it is a holiday weekend—significantly, July 4 once again—makes their loneliness all the more poignant. At one point, Jim looks out his window and sees an advertisement for the beach. Similarly, Mary views a poster hawking trips to Coney Island. Both decide to take a van to the amusement park and, coincidentally, meet each other on board (after Mary has rebuffed a "masher" in an encounter that indicates the travails that exist for women alone). When Mary and Jim arrive at Coney

Island in late afternoon, they are greeted by a carnival atmosphere: crowds of smiling faces, confetti-filled air, midway games, swimmers, and sunbathers. As they spend time together, their solitude evaporates and they begin to fall in love. Night comes, and we see gorgeous views of an electrically lit Ferris wheel as well as other illuminated rides. Like Mary and Johnny in *The Crowd,* Mary and Jim frolic on spinning disks, revolving tunnels, and corridors of distorted mirrors. For souvenirs, they each pose in a photography booth, which prints a portrait on a button; they exchange these as tokens of their growing ardor.

After dancing for a while (and relishing the popular love song "Always"), they decide to ride the "Jack Rabbit" roller coaster; but as they attempt to board it, another man pushes ahead of Jim and sits next to Mary in the two-seat car. As the coaster is propelled along the tracks (and as, viewing, we experience a kind of "phantom ride"), Jim sees a fire break out in Mary's car. In the chaotic mêlée that follows the coaster's evacuation, Jim and Mary are parted and spend the rest of the evening futilely trying to find each other amid the mob, showing one stranger after another their photographic buttons. To make matters worse, a storm breaks out and lightning bolts fill the sky, contrasting "natural" and "synthetic" modes of power and illumination.

Finally, Jim and Mary return home to their respective apartments. Depressed, Jim plays his phonograph recording of "Always" to conjure Mary's presence. In the next shot, we see Mary with the image of a phonograph record superimposed upon her face, as though to signify that she, too, is listening to it. She becomes so frustrated and dispirited that she angrily flails against the walls, ostensibly making a racket. The scene then returns to Jim's room, where he seems annoyed at some noise coming from elsewhere in the building. When he leaves his apartment in search of the ruckus, he is shocked to come upon Mary in her room, and the two realize that they have lived in the same building all along. Here again, Simmel's observations on urban life are relevant. He asserts that in the city, where "reserve" triumphs over personal connection, people "frequently do not know by sight those who have been [their] neighbours for years" (2004, 16). Likewise, Carpenter finds that "a striking characteristic of city life is its anonymity" (1932, 240). Thus, once more, *Lonesome* comments upon the *anomie* of contemporary metropolitan existence, although, ultimately, in a less bleak fashion than does *The Crowd.* In both works, however, the exciting electrified space of the municipal amusement park represents, in part, a social site where alienation is suspended, where electricity is used (at least for guests) for play instead of work, providing an atmosphere in which people can bond with one another. However, its exuberance can lead to chaos—as when Mary and Jim are split apart.

It is significant that a phonograph record plays a role in *Lonesome*'s narrative. The film premiered as a silent on June 20, 1928, but then was re-released as a "part-talking" film on September 30 of the same year. The "coming of sound" had, of course, arrived in the United States two years earlier, with the opening in August 1926 of Warner Bros.'s *Don Juan*, which touted a synchronized musical score performed by the New York Philharmonic Orchestra. Directed by Alan Crosland, the film appeared more than a year before his watershed work, *The Jazz Singer* (released in October 1927). *Lonesome*'s sound sequences were recorded by Western Electric, whose very name attests to the continuing role of that science in the evolution of film technology—with microphones now introduced onto the set.

Apropos of the record player, it is significant that the first sound films were made by Edison in a machine (the Kinetophone) that combined his Kinetograph with his phonograph. In fact, it is a common assumption that Edison was primarily interested in the motion picture as merely a means to "illustrate" his record player. Although individual Kinetophone viewers and auditors could listen to a one-minute synchronized sound movie at the turn of the century, it took almost three decades before the electrified Audion tube (pioneered by Lee de Forest) made theatrical amplification feasible. Thus electricity factored not only into the subject matter of *Lonesome* (in the form of the protagonists' work and play spaces) but into its technological history as well.

The Sun Also Rises Electrically

Another film of the 1920s thematically related to *The Crowd* and *Lonesome* is *Sunrise: A Song of Two Humans* (*Sunrise* [1927]), directed in the United States by German filmmaker F. W. Murnau. Like *Lonesome* (also made by a European-born artist), *Sunrise* was produced during the "transition to sound," and after being released as a silent, it was re-released in 1928 with a synchronized score by Hugo Reisenfeld. Unlike

31

the subjects of *The Crowd* and *Lonesome,* the main protagonists of this film are country folk, a farmer and his spouse (called The Man [George O'Brien] and The Wife [Janet Gaynor]). However, the story begins with shots of a nearby metropolis in summertime, a period in which, we are told, people take pastoral vacations. As Carpenter remarked, a seasonal "flight from the city" was common in urbanized countries. "The holiday season," he noted, "finds thousands of city people seeking rest and relaxation in small towns and . . . the country" (1932, 259).

Among the refugees from the city (as depicted in *Sunrise*) is a young flapper (the so-called Woman from the City [Margaret Livingston]), who arrives in the farmer's town to spend her summer in bucolic surroundings. We also learn that she has seduced him. In an early scene, we see the City Woman whistle to the farmer from outside his cabin, whereupon, like a creature under some spell, he deserts his wife to meet his lover in the moonlit marshes. There, dressed in her stylish chemise, she shimmies before him to the imagined sounds of jazz music and urges him to end his marriage by murdering his wife and joining her in the city. As she proposes this course of action, pictures of urban modernity (lights, illuminated signs, searchlights) are matted into the frame, reminiscent of those we have seen in the opening sequence.

Ultimately, The Man complies with the City Woman's wishes and lures his wife on a boat ride to the city with secret plans to drown her. As he attempts the heinous act, he falters, and his wife (already aware of his adultery) becomes cognizant of his monstrous motives. He halts in his tracks and shamefully rows them both to shore. When they reach land, his wife runs away. Still terrified of his homicidal impulses, she jumps on a passing trolley to the city. He jumps aboard after her and they ride morosely, with distressed expressions on their faces. As we have seen, the trolley was an important electric vehicle of the era and one that conjoined suburban and rural spaces (though never quite as dramatically as depicted in *Sunrise*).[10]

Once we find ourselves in the metropolis, the contrast with provincial existence is blatantly clear. The farm couple faces a confusing jumble of pedestrians, automobiles, and trolleys—and they are overwhelmed by the traffic. Here, we are reminded of the words of Simmel, who wrote that "with each crossing of the street, with the tempo and multiplicity of economic, occupational and social life, the city sets up a deep contrast with small town and rural life with reference to the sensory foundations of psychic life" (2004, 13). Similarly, Carpenter talks about the "shock-effect of city life" for those who visit it from remote areas (1932, 217).

When The Wife runs into a fancy restaurant The Man follows her, and as they eat, we begin to sense some rapprochement between them. They next wander into a church and witness a marriage ceremony and gradually find themselves spiritually reunited. When they emerge, they act like a bride and groom. It is at this point that the symbolic valence of the city is transformed. While previously it had represented a space of danger and seduction (the latter tied to the femme fatale), it now becomes a site of connubial pleasure and harmony.

To mark their reconciliation, The Wife pleads to have a professional photograph taken, and, in preparation, The Man gets a shave at a chic salon. Clearly, sitting for such a portrait is a sign of modernity: portrait studios are available only in the metropolis. What this photographic sequence (and a similar one in The Crowd) reminds us of is another tie between the cinema and electricity: in the initial years of film production, sunlight was used to illuminate sets (often filtered through glass roofs), but as early as 1905, electrical arc floodlights were being utilized (Salt 1983, 74). Pioneer director D. W. Griffith first used them at Biograph Studios in 1909 in making The Drunkard's Reformation, and the first film to employ them exclusively was Vitagraph's Conscience (1912) (Salt 1983, 89, 98). Between 1914 and 1919, electrical spotlights also began to be employed, and in 1915 the first evening scenes were actually shot at night, lit by electrical lamps rather than filmed in daylight and printed on tinted blue stock. But there was a difference, in this regard, between filmmaking in the United States and abroad. Whereas in the 1920s "all American studio filming was . . . being done on totally blacked-out stages," Barry Salt notes that "this was not the case in Europe, as can be seen in the many films in which it is obvious that on the sets of large-scale interiors a good deal of the light is old-fashioned diffused sunlight coming through the studio roof." Here, significantly, Salt cites "F. W. Murnau's early films" (1983, 182–83).

After the husband and wife have their photograph taken, night falls, and they return to Luna Park—a site, ostensibly, much like the real one that existed on Coney Island at the time.[11] The sequence opens with a beautiful, hypnotic, electrically illuminated spinning wheel. We also see decorative lights in a restaurant and in the midway area. In actuality, the real Luna Park was lit by 122,000 electric lights at the time of its debut. (Although many people thought that the park's name referred to its illumination, it was in fact named for the sister of one of the founders.) Upon visiting the park, Russian writer Maxim Gorki commented on its impressive visual appeal: "Thousands of ruddy sparks glimmer in the darkness, limning in fine, sensitive outline on the black background of the sky. . . . Golden gossamer threads tremble in the air. They intertwine in Transparent flaming patterns. . . . Fabulous beyond conceiving, ineffably beautiful, is this fiery scintillation" (qtd. in Pilat and Ranson 1941, 148). *Sunrise* concentrates on the farm couple's experience at old-fashioned game booths (like those that involve hitting a target with a ball, or ringing a bell by swinging a hammer) and does not show them on modern rides like the roller coaster. Perhaps the film wanted to avoid the kind of condescending comic portrayals of "country bumpkins" that had typified shorts like *Rube and Mandy at Coney Island* (1903).

After a night of fun in the city and a renewal of mutual affection, the farm couple leaves to return home in the small craft in which they originally set sail. A storm, however, has been brewing and strikes with full force once they depart. Lightning bolts pierce the sky (as they did in *The Crowd*), and rising waves overturn the vessel, throwing both passengers into the water. The Man finds himself beached on the shore and realizes that he has been separated from his wife. He looks for her but is distraught to find that she is nowhere in sight. Clearly, a huge irony is involved here. Although he meant to drown her earlier, he is now anguished at the thought that she might have perished in the waters to which he brought her. Ultimately, she is found and the sun rises as the couple is reconciled.

Elsewhere, I have discussed *Sunrise* in a variety of contexts: city versus country, good girl versus bad, European versus American film, silence versus sound (Fischer 1998). The film is a resonant masterpiece, and placing it within a new framework leads to fresh interpretations. As seen from the perspective I have sketched in this essay, *Sunrise* becomes a complex treatise on illumination (a fact that seems suddenly obvious from its title). First, the film offers us the light associated with the femme fatale—that of the moon—a frequent symbol of female sexuality and human madness. Although a natural source, within the text it is a dangerous one, ensnaring The Man in a web of deceit, depression, and destruction. Moonlight has this denotation not only in the marsh scene but also on the final sail home, when The Man's homicidal lunacy comes back to haunt him. It is also associated with Luna Park, a site to which he takes his wife only because his attempt at murder has been followed by an unplanned trip to the city. And the film also invokes artificial light. In the farm setting, it takes the form of the lantern, still tied to the primitive power of the flame. But we also have the electric lights of the city, a space in which the hard-working farm couple finds excitement, enjoyment, and fun—all emotions unavailable to them in their austere rural existence. Specifically, the city offers the joy of the night, made possible by modern electrification. As noted earlier, such power did not come to rural America until decades later. Perhaps this is why the farm couple (in dress, characterization, and abode) appears to date more from the eighteenth or nineteenth century than from the twentieth. Finally, the film concludes on an image of light, with the picture of a sunrise. Here, the solar icon seems to unify both natural and synthetic illumination, because it is registered not by an actual shot of the sky but by a drawn, Art Deco sunray motif, like that which would later top the Chrysler Building. Significantly, according to Schivelbusch, "The introduction of [electric] arc lighting for the first time made good the metaphorical description of street lanterns as artificial suns. The arc-light was, in fact, a small sun and the light it cast had a spectrum similar to that of daylight" (1995, 118).

Interestingly, the subjects of electrification, urbanization, illumination, and the cinema, which we have discussed here in terms of comic and dramatic films of the 1920s, were also raised in documentaries, a coincidence that makes clear how fiction can address central cultural issues. In Walter Ruttmann's *Berlin, Symphony of a Great City* (1927) many of the topics we have analyzed are introduced—two years earlier than in Dziga Vertov's *The Man with the Movie Camera* (1929). The Berlin that Ruttmann advances is an electrified universe of trolleys, traffic lights, street signs, and illuminated shop windows, all made emphatically visible at night when they are reflected in the rain-soaked pavement. The same modern, electricity-based professions represented in *Lonesome* (telephone operator and machinist) are also depicted in *Berlin,* and on multiple occasions movie theaters (the Ritz and the Berliner Kino) can be glimpsed. As in *The Crowd,* the image of a clock face punctuates the film, highlighting the division of the modern day into regulated segments.

Finally, although *Berlin* does not show us an overview of an amusement park or fair ground, Ruttmann does, in an experimental fashion, periodically incorporate such sites into the film's text. At moments, in a disjunctive, avant-garde fashion, first-person point-of-view shots taken from within a rapidly ascending and descending roller coaster car are intercut into the mix, sometimes followed by a rotating spiral graphic (as in *Anemic Cinema* [1926]) or a rapidly panning camera. That such a ride symbolizes disruptive modernity is signaled by the fact that the sequence is sandwiched between a dramatization of a suicide and (as in *Lonesome* and *Sunrise*) the onset of a storm. Clearly, the roller coaster is meant to suggest the kind of dizzying, frenetic vortex that the electrified urban landscape of the 1920s engenders, one that is "shocking" in both a positive and a negative sense. It is both energizing and enervating, like the technology that powers it.

As Vertov (an enthusiast of electricity) once intoned, "We compose film epics of electric power plants . . . [and] we delight in the . . . gestures of searchlights that dazzle the stars" (1984, 8). Significantly, *Berlin* ends with the image of a searchlight above the city—simultaneously an emblem of electricity, illumination, and the cinema itself.

Notes

1. Leo Marx (1964) uses the phrase "technological sublime."
2. Schivelbusch (1995, 12) discusses how electric street lighting originally seemed too "dazzling" and could not be looked at directly. Therefore, lights were often mounted quite high in a kind of tower effect.
3. On this and other themes related to the domestication of electricity, see Schivelbusch (1995).
4. The Argand lamp was designed by Swiss scientist Aimé Argand in the eighteenth century (http://www.terrypepper.com/lights/closeups/illumination/argand/lewis-lamp.htm).
5. These devices are mentioned in *Early Photography: Camera and Moving Pictures* (MPI Home Video, 1991).

6. The Cinématographe was a combination camera, printer, and projector in the same housing and could be hand-cranked (www.filmsite.org).

7. Barry Salt says that "the American Society of Cinematographers claimed in 1925 that its members were still cranking at 16 frames per second!" (1983, 203). Elsewhere, he notes that "individual cameramen's cranking speeds differ[ed] with respect to the averages" (204). Thus, one assumes that cameras were generally hand-cranked rather than electrically motored.

8. A helpful discussion of this film in relation to the development of electricity is given in Doane (2002, 145–50).

9. The film, *Café Electric,* was directed by Gustav Ucicky.

10. The region in which the farmer and his wife live looks not "suburban" but fully rural, heightening the contrast with the city. Further, it seems more like an eighteenth-century European village than anything ever found in the United States.

11. Luna Park opened on May 16, 1903 (http://naid.sppsr.ucla.edu/coneyisland/articles/1920.htm).

THE ENDLESS EMBRACE OF HELL
HOPELESSNESS AND BETRAYAL IN FILM NOIR
Wheeler Winston Dixon

> There ain't no answer.
>
> There ain't never going to be an answer.
>
> There never has been an answer.
>
> *That's* the answer.
>
> GERTRUDE STEIN (QTD. IN MCFADDEN 1996, 9)

Film noir, it can be argued, constitutes the ultimate modernist style. It sees the future and doesn't like it one bit. It exists in a state of perpetual future shock, stunned by suddenness of change, uneasy at the passing of tradition, yet constantly alert in a state of near paranoia to any and all cultural displacements. Noir is modernist because it embraces the disposability of modern culture right down to its rotten roots. We live in an eternal now, curving around the bend in ways that we can't see, foretelling a future riddled with rupture, uncertainty, and deceit. In the late 1940s, in the newly falling shadow of the nuclear bomb, noir was born, and with it an essence of cinematic modernism: the sense that the past was closed off forever. Noir speaks only to the future, if there is one. It exists only in the present, which exists in a state of constant mutability. Nothing from yesterday can help us; there is only the present to guide us until tomorrow. As Lemmy Caution observes in Jean-Luc Godard's classic noir/science fiction film *Alphaville* (1968), "No one has lived in the past. No one will live in the future."

Readings of such films as *Stranger on the Third Floor* (1940), *Leave Her to Heaven* (1945), *Roadblock* (1951), *Bodyguard* (1948), *Fall Guy* (1947), *The Big Clock* (1948), *The Big Combo* (1955), *Black Angel* (1946), *In a Lonely Place* (1950), *Detour* (1945), *They Won't Believe Me* (1947), *Apology for Murder* (1945), *The Blue Dahlia* (1946), *Crossfire* (1947), *Kiss Me Deadly* (1955), *The Mysterious Mr. Valentine* (1946), *Decoy* (1946), and *Split Second* (1953) uncover the subterranean world of true film noir, behind the surface of such popular, canonical, classic examples of the genre as *The Big Sleep* (1945) and *The Maltese Falcon* (1941)—two films among many that have subsumed other, more authentic noirs. Created in such Poverty Row studios as Producers Releasing Corporation (PRC; perhaps the ultimate noir studio), Allied Artists, and Monogram, these ultra-cheap visions of paranoid uncertainty more authentically portrayed the inherent sense of personal failure, betrayal, and hopelessness that informs the structure of the best noirs.

The film noir movement was a modernist tidal wave of cinematic despair and anger, a response at first to the uncertainty of the late Depression and later to the horrific end of World War II, which ushered in the threat of instant annihilation with the atomic bomb. Women, earning paychecks for the first time in defense plants during the war, were not eager to relinquish their newfound personal and financial freedom, and as a result social roles were changing. Men returned from the war to a new and hostile social landscape with a postwar inflationary economy, in which all the values they left behind were suddenly being called into question. Racial equality, women's rights, the inability of ex-soldiers to fit into postwar society: all of these factors contributed to the general unease and distrust that created the world of film noir.

Smaller, cheaper films more accurately reflected this nihilistic worldview, in ways that the major studios could only flirt with in their A pictures where nothing was really at risk. In A films, personal redemption or heterotopic romance was allowed to shape the narrative drive of the film. Billy Wilder's *Double Indemnity* (1944), for example, suffers in comparison with Sam Newfield's *Apology for Murder* simply because Newfield's film is more desperate, more marginal, and hence more authentic. In cheaper productions, the making of the film itself involved risk for the producers, directors, and actors, who, stuck in the depths of Poverty Row, were creating visions of their own personal hell for public consumption. It is these stories that constitute the true legacy of noir, one that has been obliterated by the exigencies of canon, and one that is only now being brought to light. We should embrace these fugitive low-budget visions and examine them as a response to social and economic conditions, while noting how the major studios adopted the genre (with modifications) once it had become popular.

Stranger on the Third Floor is often cited as one of the first film noirs, and, given its unrelentingly bleak and hallucinogenic structure, it is easy to see why. Made on a shoestring budget by RKO's B unit, *Stranger* tells the tale of a young newsman, Mike Ward (John McGuire), who fingers a taxi cab driver, Joe Briggs (Elisha Cook Jr.), for a particularly brutal murder. Briggs, however, is innocent; the real killer is the psychotic Peter Lorre, billed only as "the Stranger" in the film's credits. At the last minute, the Stranger's guilt is discovered almost by accident, and Briggs is set free.

Director Boris Ingster, forgotten today, would go on later in his career to produce the highly successful escapist teleseries "The Man from U.N.C.L.E." In this film, in contrast, he creates a nightmarish vision of urban life set in a city of perpetual night. Lorre's part, almost wordless, is that of a restless psychopath, driven to kill by forces he is unable to control. As Briggs, Elisha Cook Jr., filmdom's perennial fall guy, is made to order to step off for the murder, and no one, not the police, the jurors, or reporter Ward, is inclined to believe his whimpering protestations of innocence. The obligatory "happy ending," in which Briggs offers the services of his taxi to Ward and his new wife, Jane (Margaret Tallichet), apparently without any rancor for his false conviction through Ward's testimony, is a mere sop to the demands of the Production Code. In the real world we live in, *Stranger on the Third Floor* darkly suggests, Lorre will continue to kill blithely, Briggs will go to the chair, and justice will utterly fail all the film's protagonists. Shot on a few cheap sets by the gifted cameraman Nick Musuraca, whose work defined the RKO B look throughout the 1940s, *Stranger* offers a world without hope, escape, or even the illusion of a future.

The diffuse despair of the postwar world gave a distinctive flavor to the experience of modernity, especially as it appeared in Hollywood screen visions. In *Split Second,* one of Dick Powell's few directorial efforts, a sadistic criminal holds a group of prisoners hostage in a deserted Nevada town, which also functions as a test site for atomic bomb experiments. As with most noir films, the action here is confined to a few cheap, claustrophobic sets, and the characters are all too eager to betray one another in order to escape. Shot in gritty black and white, *Split Second* is an 85-minute Mexican standoff, in which escape into the desert only increases one's personal risk. In Harold Daniel's *Roadblock,* another RKO noir with cinematography by Nick Musuraca, corrupt investigator Joe Peters (Charles McGraw) falls prey to a complex web of blackmail and deceit and is shot down by the police in the Los Angeles sewers. *Bodyguard,* from an original story co-written by Robert Altman (later to become a major director in his own right), Harry Essex, George W. George, and Fred Niblo Jr., presents Lawrence Tierney as Mike Carter, a brutal cop suspended from the police force for his strong-arm tactics. Hired as a bodyguard to a rich woman who owns a meatpacking plant, Carter soon discovers he's being framed for murder. Pushing his way through the brief 62-minute film with violent assurance, Tierney's Carter has to unmask the real killer in a world where no one can be trusted and all appearances are merely that—surface impressions without any real depth or veracity. Contemptuous of authority ("One side, Dracula," he barks at an astonished butler who tries to block his entry into a particularly palatial estate), Carter regards the world around him with perpetual, justified suspicion. At the film's end, he discovers that the murder he must solve merely covered up another crime; the owners of the meatpacking plant are spiking their beef with salt water to increase the package weight. This corporate greed becomes murder, and only Carter's lack of faith in humanity prevents him from becoming the fall guy for it.

Indeed, Reginald LeBorg's *Fall Guy,* an especially cheap B film, is emblematic of one of the central concerns of the noir: misplaced blame. In this brief, 64-minute programmer, a young man named Tom Cochrane (Clifford Penn) is arrested for murder solely on circumstantial evidence: a young woman has been brutally stabbed to death, but Tom has no memory of the evening of the murder, and thus is unable to defend himself. In a typically convoluted narrative, he discovers that he has been drugged and then framed for the murder;

the real killer is revealed as a distinguished member of the community. Based on the short story "Cocaine" by Cornell Woolrich, *Fall Guy* is cheap and shoddy in every respect, and was shot in a mere six days on standby sets at Monogram Pictures, one of the most impoverished Hollywood studios. But although the technical execution of the film suffers from haste and lack of money, in many ways *Fall Guy* is the perfect noir: desperate, shabby, and unrelentingly bleak.

Even cheaper, of course, is Edgar G. Ulmer's legendary film *Detour*, made for PRC—without a doubt the most marginal studio in Hollywood history. Shot for $20,000 in six days on a few threadbare sets and a car parked in front of an omnipresent rear projection screen, *Detour* tells the tale of Al Roberts (Tom Neal), who hitchhikes to California to marry his girlfriend Sue (Claudia Drake). Along the way, he is picked up by a fast-talking salesman named Haskell (Edmund MacDonald), who suffers from a heart condition. When Haskell suddenly dies, Roberts assumes his identity, convinced that otherwise the cops will pin Haskell's murder on him, and appropriates the dead man's money and car. But, in a masterful plot twist, Roberts, posing as Haskell, picks up Vera (Ann Savage), a young woman to whom the real Haskell had given a ride the day before. Vera blackmails Roberts into selling the car and splitting the money, and then tries to convince him to pose as Haskell for Haskell's dying father, so that the two of them can collect Haskell's inheritance. Roberts recognizes that the idea is insane, but Vera, in a drunken stupor, threatens to expose him unless he plays along. In the film's climax, Roberts accidentally strangles Vera with a telephone cord and, now truly a murderer, disappears into the night. In a nod to the Production Code, Roberts is picked up outside a cheap roadside diner at the end of the film, presumably to face the death penalty for Vera's murder. In the modern world, this film seems to suggest with hopelessness, all of life is a detour from the more stable world that is by now long gone.

In his excellent book, *Dark City Dames* (2001), Eddie Muller recounts in detail the production history of *Detour* as part of an interview with Ann Savage, the only surviving cast member of the film. "If Edgar was under any pressure from the short shooting schedule," she told him, "he never showed it. He was fast, decisive, and unflappable. You just couldn't make a mistake—there simply wasn't the time or money to do things over" (2001, 162). Having only 15,000 feet of raw stock to work with, Ulmer directed Savage to speed up the tempo of her delivery to a machine-gun pace: "faster! faster! he really wanted me to spit out the lines" (Savage, in Muller 2001, 162). Because the film was a PRC production, Ulmer had to move through Savage's scenes with lighting speed, and her "work on the film lasted a mere three frantic days—barely thirty hours of total work" (Muller 2001, 164). Three days later, the entire film was complete. But as with all true noirs, the ferociously tight budget and compressed schedule of the filming do nothing to detract from *Detour;* rather, they reify the film's atmosphere of an endless embrace of hell. Just as no character will escape the dark confines of the story, so no one working in this film will ever escape the shabby PRC sound stages; Roberts's car is on a journey to nowhere (its movement achieved through obvious rear projection), both inside the story and out.

What emerges is a stark charcoal sketch of a film, with rough edges, flimsy props, grinding music, and a relentlessly nihilistic scenario. A film like *Detour* would never have been made at the majors, and it would have suffered, rather than benefited, from a cast of A stars and a decent budget. The domain of perdition is poorly lit and eerily inescapable; once an actor appeared in a PRC film, he or she seldom went on to the majors. PRC was itself a noir construct, the last stop before the gutter for a host of once-famous Hollywood stars now working for a fraction of their former salaries in films that were inherently compromised by their conspicuous lack of production values. Ulmer was PRC's most gifted director but hardly its most productive one. The studio's main house director, Sam Newfield, was so prolific that even PRC was ashamed of his prodigious output, forcing him to adopt two aliases (Peter Stewart and Sherman Scott) to cover his tracks. Newfield, in fact, directed Ann Savage in her only other PRC feature, *Apology for Murder,* a typically low-rent riff on Billy Wilder's Paramount Pictures production of *Double Indemnity,* in which Hugh Beaumont stands in for Fred MacMurray, and Savage for Barbara Stanwyck.

Not surprisingly, Paramount took a dim view of *Apology for Murder* (for a time, PRC had actually considered calling the film *Single Indemnity* [Muller 2001, 167]), and the film played only two days at Grauman's Chinese Theatre before PRC pulled it in response to a threatened lawsuit. More than half a century later, *Apology for Murder* is still in legal limbo, although a clandestine screening of the film in 2002 at the Los Angeles Cinematheque demonstrated that *Apology,* although a much cheaper film, is in many ways more authentic than Wilder's original. In PRC films, the protagonists really *need* the money, as do the directors, actors, grips, cameramen, and other technical personnel who are working to dramatize them. By keeping costs down to a minimum, for example, Newfield shot some of his PRC westerns for as little as $5,000 in two days, relying on a library of recycled stock footage and a skimpy plot line punctuated by frequent fights. For film workers, after PRC there was nothing left but oblivion, and everybody knew it. PRC, in contrast to the more established studios, offered absolutely *no* security to any of its employees. When a film was finished, PRC simply moved another low-budget project into production, like an assembly line.

Republic Pictures, most famous for its Saturday morning serials, churned out a long series of 60-minute programmers in a variety of genres. Among the most interesting, and certainly the most curious, of these brief films is Philip Ford's *The Mysterious Mr. Valentine.* The first ten minutes of this film are so crammed with narrative coincidence as to virtually defy description. While driving home on a lonely road late at night, a young woman, Janet Spencer (Linda Stirling), has a flat tire. Walking along the dimly lit road, she sights a chemical factory. Janet enters the building and discovers research chemist John Armstrong (Tristram Coffin), of whom she asks permission to use the telephone to call a garage. Unbeknownst to Janet, John Armstrong has just murdered his partner and left the body in the back room. While she is on the phone trying to get help, he returns to the back room to discover that . . . the body of his victim has disappeared!

To relax his nerves, Armstrong suggests to Janet that they both have a drink. Moments later, Armstrong's wife and a police photographer break into the factory and photograph Janet and Armstrong in a seemingly compromising position. Janet flees, stealing Armstrong's wife's car. Driving away at high speed, Janet is blinded by the glare of oncoming headlights and accidentally runs down a pedestrian. The driver of the other car emerges with an associate and offers to dispose of the body at the local hospital, telling Janet to go home and forget the whole thing. Frantic, she drives wildly through the streets in the stolen vehicle, sideswiping the car of private eye Steve Morgan

(William Henry). Returning home at last, Janet discovers the first of a series of blackmail notes from a "Mr. Valentine," demanding $25,000 for not implicating her in the hit-and-run fatality.

That's just the first 6 minutes of this 56-minute wonder, which grows more complex with each passing second. In a quest to extricate herself from the blackmail plot, Janet enlists the help of Morgan, who has followed her home to collect on the damages to his car. However, he operates on the thinnest edge of the law, playing off the protagonists against each other in a series of jaw-dropping triple crosses. These deceptions are all the more disturbing because of the breezy self-assurance with which he lies to each character to preserve his own interests. As Morgan weaves his way through the increasingly byzantine case, he repeatedly informs his prospective victims, "You know, I could *use* you . . . I mean, as a client." At last, after numerous plot twists, insurance agent Sam Priestley (Kenne Duncan) is unmasked as the mysterious Mr. Valentine; the whole affair has been an elaborate insurance scam. In a final moment of what can only be described as heterotopic insanity, Janet agrees to marry Morgan, despite the fact that he has been working against her interests (or, perhaps more accurately, only in his own interests) throughout the entire film.

Unlike PRC, the Republic lot occasionally served as a production facility for John Ford, Fritz Lang, and other A list directors, but the bulk of the studio's output consisted of Roy Rogers and Gene Autry westerns, the aforementioned children's serials, and a modest series of program pictures. Yet the superior production capabilities of Republic lent a sheen to even their most pedestrian work, while at the same time robbing their noir films of the true fatalism inherent in the genre. If nothing else, Republic's noirs are a curiosity, a peculiar mixture of violence (fistfights and spectacular car crashes and/or explosions were the studio's specialty) and assembly-line perfection. Republic's films always had a sleek, professional polish, no matter how cheaply they were made, and the studio's low budgets and short shooting schedule ensured that directors and scenarists would be left alone on the set, so long as they adhered to the draconian cost-consciousness for which Republic was famous.

In contrast, when the major studios (Paramount, Fox, MGM, Universal, and the like) tackled noir, the results were often glossy, like a picture postcard version of hell. John M. Stahl's *Leave Her to Heaven* is chiefly memorable for the inscrutably psychotic presence of the pathologically jealous Gene Tierney, who will do anything to retain the affections of her husband, Richard Harland (played by a young Cornel Wilde). Throwing herself down a flight of stairs to abort an unwanted child, purposefully allowing her husband's crippled younger brother to die in a swimming accident, and penultimately fatally poisoning herself to frame her half-sister for her murder, Tierney's Ellen Berent is an unstoppable agency of human destruction, an inexhaustible reservoir of deceit and betrayal. Yet the film is sumptuously mounted, designed with swank color coordination, and photographed in three-strip Technicolor by the great Leon Shamroy; more, Alfred Newman's perpetually ominous score pounds home every fresh treachery with tiresome insistence. As a melodrama the film is admirably successful, but as a noir its intensity is compromised by 20th Century Fox's obsessively lush production values. How can anyone be *truly* desperate in such transparently luxurious surroundings?

The same can be said of John Farrow's *The Big Clock*, a Paramount noir in which George Stroud (Ray Milland), brash young editor of a national crime magazine, is framed for a murder actually committed by his employer, publishing tycoon Earl Janoth (Charles Laughton). Unaware of his boss's guilt and assigned by Janoth to "catch the killer," Stroud must conceal himself from the police, even as he tries to discover the real murderer's identity. The narrative structure of *The Big Clock* is interesting in that the audience knows more than Stroud (we see Janoth commit the murder of his mistress, Pauline [Rita Johnson]), but the editor doesn't discover Janoth's secret until the final minutes of the film. At the same time, Janoth is unaware that the man he is trying to frame for the murder is his own star employee, the inventive George Stroud. His crime at last discovered, Janoth runs from the authorities and plunges to a well-deserved death in an elevator shaft.

The levels of deception and betrayal in *The Big Clock* are numerous. Only Stroud's long-suffering wife, Georgette (Maureen O'Sullivan), stands by him during his ordeal, while Janoth is aided by his sexually ambiguous underling Steve Hagen (veteran heavy George Macready). The physical look of *The Big Clock* is Art Deco modern, and Farrow makes good use of the antiseptic premises of the Janoth Organization as the site of ritual corporate back-stabbing, lies, and deceptions, but in the end the film is more of a mystery than a noir. We know that Milland's George Stroud is innocent, and conventional narrative closure demands that he be cleared of the crime. Similarly, Gene Tierney's Ellen Berent in *Leave Her to Heaven* is so spectacularly mendacious and devious that she *exists* to be vanquished; the outcome of the long courtroom trial that concludes the film is never really in doubt. Cornel Wilde will certainly escape her machinations, no matter how intricate they are. The same cannot be said of the protagonists of *Detour*, *Bodyguard*, *Roadblock*, *Apology for Murder*, *Stranger on the Third Floor*, and the other films examined here thus far. Working at the margins of the industry, the protagonists of true noirs are doomed from the start; for them there will be no happy endings, no certainty of escape. Actors like Tom Neal and Ann Savage in *Detour* are expendable commodities. No one cares what happens to them; they belong to the truly damned.

Roy William Neill's *Black Angel* is another noir film in which appearances are deliberately deceiving. As in *Fall Guy*, another film based on a Cornell Woolrich story, the central character, Martin Blair (Dan Duryea), is unaware that he is the murderer of his wife, Marvis Marlowe (Constance Dowling). As with *Fall Guy*, alcohol and/or drugs cloud the consciousness of the film's protagonist, who searches vainly for his wife's killer, only to discover his own guilt at the end of the film. In an echo of *Stranger on the Third Floor*, another man is tried and convicted for the crime, once again on circumstantial evidence. Only Blair's recovery of his repressed memory saves an innocent man from the electric chair.

This central and peculiarly modern conceit of being unable to account for one's own actions informs numerous noirs in the 1940s, a period when psychoanalysis was just coming into vogue. Such films as Joseph H. Lewis's *So Dark the Night* (1946), in which French homicide detective Henri Cassin (Stephen Geray) is unaware that *he* is the murderer he seeks for a particularly vicious strangulation killing, speak to the essential mystery of the human psyche, capable of blocking itself off from interior knowledge that it finds disturbing or contradictory. Maxwell Shane's *Fear in the Night* (1947) and his remake, *Nightmare* (1956), Harold Clurman's *Deadline at Dawn* (1946), Jack Hively's *Street of Chance* (1942), and Arthur Ripley's *The Chase* (1946)—all five derived from source material by Cornell Woolrich—explore similar themes of mistaken culpability and self-deception. In Otto

Preminger's *Whirlpool* (1949), a corrupt psychoanalyst (Richard Conte) hypnotizes patient Gene Tierney into committing a series of crimes while under his influence. Edmund Goulding's *Nightmare Alley* (1947), a rare A noir from Fox, presents Tyrone Power as Stanton Carlisle, a sideshow barker with a gift for gab who bilks wealthy clients as a "spiritualist" with the help of an unscrupulous psychiatrist, Dr. Lilith Ritter (Helen Walker). Budd Boetticher's *Behind Locked Doors* (1948) is just one of many films that treat mental hospitals as little better than fraudulent enterprises designed to bilk patients out of their life savings; *Behind Locked Doors* was later remade by Samuel Fuller as *Shock Corridor* (1963), a late entry in the initial noir cycle. The public's distrust of conventional authority figures (doctors, policemen, psychiatrists), coupled with individuals' fear of their own internal mental landscape, propelled the noir to national prominence in the late 1940s, when returning soldiers who had fought and killed in battle sought to readjust to a superficially calm but deeply repressive postwar environment.

Another A noir, George Marshall's dark and sinister *The Blue Dahlia*, based on an original screenplay by Raymond Chandler, tackles the problem of "socializing" returning veterans. Johnny Morrison (Alan Ladd) and Buzz Wanchek (William Bendix) discover that Johnny's wife, Helen (Doris Downing), has been unfaithful during their enforced wartime separation. When Helen is murdered shortly thereafter, suspicion falls on Johnny, and then on Buzz, who has come home from the war with a steel plate in his head. Buzz is given to frequent headaches, bouts of amnesia, and violent, erratic behavior. In fact, Chandler had originally intended Buzz to be the murderer, but the War Office intervened, protesting that the proposed narrative conclusion unjustly maligned returning servicemen. Paramount immediately capitulated, and Chandler was left with the task of finding a new killer even as the film was being shot. At the last minute, he decided to pin the crime on a down-at-the-heels house detective, "Pop" Newell (Will Wright), seen skulking in the shadows throughout the film. The revised ending was hastily photographed in a single office set; Chandler was so upset with the final result that he wrote the last scenes of the film literally in a drunken stupor (see Houseman 1976, 7–23). *The Blue Dahlia* projects a world of utter hopelessness, treachery, deceit, and betrayal, in which, once again, one of the key protagonists can't recall his whereabouts at the time of the murder. The nominal romance between Johnny and nightclub singer Joyce Harwood (Veronica Lake) that brackets the film is merely a cynical reteaming of two of Paramount's biggest stars of the postwar era, fresh from their surprise box office hit *This Gun for Hire* (1942). The true center of *The Blue Dahlia* is a world of hopeless, terminal despair.

In the paranoid world of postwar film noir, even innocence is no defense against the misguided judgments of society; indeed, the entire fabric of conventional justice is called into question. Irving Pichel's *They Won't Believe Me,* from a screenplay by noir novelist Jonathan Latimer, tells the story of ne'er-do-well Larry Ballentine (Robert Young, interestingly cast against type as an amoral social climber), who has married his wife, Greta (Rita Johnson), solely for her wealth and position. Larry forthrightly admits that he has no love for Greta and conducts a series of tawdry affairs right under her nose, despite his wife's continued protestations of love for him. Desperate to salvage their marriage, Greta relocates Larry to a Los Angeles brokerage firm of which she is the principal shareholder. But there Larry immediately falls for his scheming secretary, Verna Carlson (Susan Hayward), and the two impulsively run off to Reno so that Larry can establish residency there, divorce Greta, and marry Verna.

On the way to Reno, however, the two are involved in a car crash, and Verna is killed. With the woman's body burned beyond recognition in the flaming wreck, Larry passes it off as Greta's and returns home to kill his wife for real, so he can inherit everything. But when he arrives at their ranch, he discovers that Greta has committed suicide, driven over the brink at last by his repeated infidelities. Fearful of being blamed for Greta's death, Larry hides the body at the bottom of a deep canyon on their property, hoping to pass off her death as a riding accident. But his "deception" is discovered, and Larry is put on trial for Greta's murder, a crime that he did *not,* in fact, commit.

The entire film is structured as a flashback, as Larry relates his story to a skeptical judge and jury from the witness box, and then disconsolately waits for the verdict. When the jury returns, Larry is convinced they have found him guilty of first-degree murder and jumps to his death from a courtroom window before the verdict can be read. But against all odds, the jury *has* believed Larry's story and acquitted him. The final shot is a close-up of the court clerk (Milton Parsons, who

usually specialized in playing ghouls, undertakers, or police inform-
ants) reading the verdict. *They Won't Believe Me*'s astoundingly bleak
scenario created considerable controversy at the time of its initial release. As Robert Porfirio notes, "Contemporary reviews suggested that
the popularity of Billy Wilder's adaptation of James M. Cain's *Double
Indemnity* had had a deleterious influence upon American films, as illustrated by *They Won't Believe Me*" (1988b, 286). Against such a backdrop of unrelenting fatalism and despair, there is no defense. One either capitulates to a new social order in which everything and
everyone is suspect, or one is dragged under its wheels.

Jack Bernhard's *Decoy* is an even more vicious and cynical film,
which for some reason has slipped between the cracks of film history.
Produced by Monogram Pictures, the film is cheap in every respect,
but is salvaged by the remarkable performance of British actress Jean
Gillie as the psychopathic Margot Shelby, a woman who will stop at
nothing to retrieve $400,000 in stolen bank funds hidden by her for-
mer boyfriend, Frankie Olins (Robert Armstrong), who is scheduled
to die in the gas chamber for the murder of a policeman. Olins refuses
to tell Margot where the money is hidden, so she concocts an elaborate
plan to revive him after his execution with the aid of a crooked prison
doctor, Lloyd Craig (Herbert Rudley). Olins's box, once located, contains only a single dollar bill and a note saying that he has left "the rest
of the money to the worms" (Porfirio 1988a, 87). Almost never shown,
even on television, and unavailable on VHS or DVD, *Decoy* is one of
the key noir films of the late 1940s.

As the noir genre entered the late 1940s and early 1950s, many of
the styles and strategies of the earlier productions were absorbed by
mainstream filmmakers, who adopted, with some modifications, what
had essentially been the style of "outlaw" filmmakers who worked for
the smaller studios on minuscule budgets. Edward Dmytryk's *Crossfire*
tackled the issue of postwar anti-Semitism in a police procedural with
strong noir overtones, as psychopathic racist ex-soldier Montgomery
(Robert Ryan) leads homicide detective Finlay (Robert Young)
through a myriad of blind alleys as Finlay attempts to solve the sense-
less murder of Joseph Samuels (Sam Levene), a Jew who invited a
group of returning World War II veterans back to his apartment
for drinks. In the original script, homophobia rather than religious intolerance motivated the killing, but RKO demanded that the sexual

orientation angle be dropped and replaced with something "less problematic" (see Porfirio 2002, 181–82). Dmytryk is more concerned with the social implications of *Crossfire* than with the creation of an insular atmosphere of paranoia and betrayal—one of the hallmarks of the essential noir style—but the tactic of lighting the film with only a few key lights minimizes the time taken for each camera setup and creates a convincingly gritty urban milieu. The modern world of noir was specifically a zone of diffuse happening, rawness, energy, and immediacy: distinctively missing were classical polish, baroque embellishment, sedate social and aesthetic graces, and the refinements of psychologically repressing etiquette. *Crossfire* brings the inner fires of loathing and resentment to the surface. Robert Ryan, always memorable in character roles, attacks the part of the psychotic veteran with his usual gusto, and the film emerges as a "message" picture that capitalizes upon and incorporates stylistic and thematic preoccupations of then-contemporary noir films.

Downbeat crime films, such as Joseph A. Lewis's *The Big Combo* and Robert Aldrich's *Kiss Me Deadly,* also embrace the dark, shadowy visual style of the most aggressive noirs, with remarkable results. *The Big Combo* is a seemingly run-of-the-mill syndicate saga redeemed by the excellent performances of Jean Peters, Cornel Wilde, and Richard Conte. Although the film is often cited for its uncompromisingly brutal treatment of the mechanisms of organized crime, it pales in comparison with two of the more personal projects of Lewis, who cut his teeth as a director in the 1940s in the Columbia B unit and won initial acclaim for his film *My Name Is Julia Ross* (1945). There, a young woman, the eponymous Julia Ross (Nina Foch), is kidnapped, drugged, and passed off to the world as the bride of a murderous psychopath, Ralph Hughes (George Macready), who lives under the thumb of his domineering mother (Dame May Whitty). Ralph has already murdered his first wife; to cover up the crime, Julia is to be next in line for an "accidental" death. Assigned twelve days to shoot the film, Lewis threatened to quit unless he was given eighteen days to complete his assignment. Over the strenuous objections of Columbia studio boss Harry Cohn, he was granted his wish, a nearly unprecedented occurrence for a B director (see Porfirio and Macek 2002, 67–68). This film bristles with visual invention, especially extreme close-ups to highlight Foch's growing sense of dread and isolation, and noir's signature high-key lighting. When released, *My Name Is Julia Ross* became a "sleeper" hit, and might have propelled Lewis to more ambitious projects within the studio. But as an indefatigable iconoclast, he preferred the role of industry outsider.

Noir aficionados have long hailed Lewis's *Gun Crazy* (1950) as the director's masterpiece. He was a kind of "pyrotechnical dandy" of the cinema, mounting cameras in eccentric spots to get points of view nobody else would seek. He excelled in deep-focus shots of the most extreme nature, for instance, from the top of a stairway all the way to the bottom. His close-ups were always angled up or down, and in general he used extremes in all his setups to suggest an extreme extravagance of visual style. *Gun Crazy* was shot on a nonexistent budget for the notorious King Brothers, who specialized in producing low-budget tales of violence. It tracks the codependent relationship of Annie Laurie Starr (Peggy Cummins) and Bart Tare (John Dall), both of whom have been obsessed with guns since childhood. The two first meet at a carnival, where Annie is performing a trick-shooting act, and Bart is immediately taken with her. Soon, they are the stars of the carnival, but are fired when the owner reveals that he has romantic designs on Annie. They hit the road and are soon robbing liquor stores and gas stations, and eventually banks. Perhaps the single most famous sequence in the film is a one-take bank robbery shot on location without the use of process screens or studio sets. It is described by Silver and Macek:

> The camera mounted in the backseat of their car begins by recording their nervousness and anxiety, like teenagers on their first date, on the outskirts of town. Their excitement mounts as they approach the savings and loan building: with Annie Laurie behind the wheel, they worry over whether things will go as planned, whether there will even be a place to park in front of the building. During the actual robbery, the camera remains in the car with Annie and only pans over to the sidewalk when she must slip out to distract a passing policeman by admiring his revolver. When Bart emerges, she clubs the policeman with her gun. Even after this climactic moment, the single shot and its visual tension are maintained as their vehicle races out of town. Annie Laurie glances back, short of breath, at the camera, while

leaning toward Bart as if to embrace him, and sees that they are not being followed. (1988, 118)

The couple's momentary idyll is shattered when a meatpacking plant robbery goes awry, and Annie senselessly guns down two employees. Hunted, the couple flees into the swamp, pursued by the police. As the authorities close in, Bart kills Annie with his gun and then shoots himself. The *Cahiers du cinéma* critics (particularly Jean-Luc Godard and François Truffaut) were astounded by the film when it first appeared, and Lewis became a darling of the *Nouvelle vague*. But despite the film's rapturous reception abroad, Lewis remained a maverick, and *The Big Combo* did little to advance his career. Lewis ended his career with a string of pedestrian westerns, but even in this genre the director's *outré* sense of the macabre never deserted him. His final film, *Terror in a Texas Town* (1958), features a final shootout in which George Hansen (Sterling Hayden) uses a whaling harpoon to vanquish his opponent. Lewis's affection for the rebel and the alienated outsider in all his films has made his works fertile ground for remakes; Arthur Penn's *Bonnie and Clyde* (1967) owes a distinct debt to *Gun Crazy,* as does Oliver Stone's *Natural Born Killers* (1994).

Robert Aldrich's *Kiss Me Deadly* features perhaps the most successful of the many screen adaptations of Mickey Spillane's fictional Mike Hammer, this time in the person of a decidedly sadistic Ralph Meeker, who is described by Alain Silver as "less heroic than he is egocentric, callous and brutal" (1988, 157), motivated strictly by revenge. As with *Decoy,* the central object of the film's quest is the recovery of a mysterious box, but here it contains radioactive isotopes that eventually kill the film's obligatory femme fatale, Lily Carver (Gaby Rogers). In a landscape of beatings, torture killings, extortion, and random violence, Meeker's Hammer operates as a totally unfettered angel of destruction, as he seeks to avenge the killing of a young woman, Christina (Cloris Leachman), to whom he offers a ride in the beginning of the film. Hammer, unlike most fictional private detectives, is not motivated by either personal gain or codes of honor or a sense of chivalry; what pushes him forward is a thirst for violence, which the film delivers in increasing doses. *Kiss Me Deadly* operates in a twilight world of deception and betrayal, a world—the dry rot of the modern city—that the film views as the real state in which we all exist, whether we know it or not. *Kiss Me Deadly* is the private eye film reborn as a noir, lost in a wilderness of urban pain and destruction, where only violence carries any genuine authority.

Moving Mike Hammer from his home town of New York City to Los Angeles for *Kiss Me Deadly* was an entirely appropriate strategy when one considers that the film industry, a business that traffics in images for mass consumption and instant-read icons, was arguably one of the most hypocritical and duplicitous corporate enterprises of the twentieth century. Nothing in the dominant cinema is real. All is illusion, and all "friendships" exist solely for mutual gain and/or exploitation. Few people have captured the hopelessness, emptiness, and despair of Hollywood as well as Nicholas Ray in his film *In A Lonely Place,* a suitable subject for concluding this brief survey of the noir.

Humphrey Bogart plays Dixon "Dix" Steele, a screenwriter who is down on his luck and given to violent outbursts of diffuse rage. In the opening moments of the film, Dix threatens to punch out a motorist who cuts into the wrong lane of traffic. Minutes later, at a film industry watering hole (modeled after Mike Romanoff's famous Hollywood restaurant; Romanoff himself has a bit part in the film), Dix nearly comes to blows with a patron over another trivial incident. His pattern for violence thus established, it seems reasonable that the police finger Dix for the brutal murder of a hatcheck girl, whom Dix brought back to his apartment for a story conference. Dix, it seems, is too lazy to read the novels he is assigned to adapt for the screen, and he cynically assumes that the young girl's summary of the hackneyed novel will be more than sufficient for his purposes. But a new neighbor, Laurel Gray (Gloria Grahame), comes to Dix's rescue with a phony alibi that momentarily clears him with the police. Intrigued by Laurel's nerve in deceiving the police on his behalf, Dix drifts into a romance with her and begins writing his first worthwhile screenplay in more than a decade. Soon they decide to marry, but Dix's repeated jealous rages drive them apart, and Laurel becomes convinced that he may, in fact, be the murderer the police thought him to be. When Laurel attempts to skip town on their wedding day, Dix flies into a towering rage and tries to strangle her. Just at that moment, the phone rings. The police have caught the real killer; it is the hatcheck girl's meek, well-mannered boyfriend. But the revelation is of little use to Dix and Laurel. Their relationship has been irreparably damaged, and they part, never to meet again.

In A Lonely Place is a remarkable project for a number of reasons, not the least of which is the fact that it was produced by Bogart's own production company, Santana, after the actor had departed from a long-term contract with his home studio, Warner Bros., because of his displeasure over being typecast in a series of predictable crime thrillers. On his own, Bogart hoped to make more personal films, none of which turned out to be major hits. To add to the production difficulties, Gloria Grahame and Nicholas Ray were in the throes of divorce during the shooting. Ray slept each night at the studio, while Grahame returned to their home. The onscreen tension between Bogart and Grahame thus mirrored the uneasiness between the director and his leading lady, who was about to leave him after a brief and troubled marriage (see Polan 1994 for a detailed analysis of this film).

The lighting and framing of *In a Lonely Place* is flat and uninviting, focusing our attention on the performers rather than on Ray's directorial style. But his quotidian strategy is entirely in tune with the spirit of the film, which paints the movie industry as a corrupt and vicious enterprise, the perfect backdrop for a sordid tale of murder and violence. Not surprisingly, *In a Lonely Place* was not particularly successful when first released; audiences craved the smooth exoticism of Michael Curtiz's *Casablanca* (1942) over Ray's garish vision of life in the trenches of the film business. And yet, as noir doubles back on itself in *In a Lonely Place*, we can see the face of fear, despair, and loneliness written large on the screen. Hollywood, the capital of cinematic dreams, created the noir in the first place, as a representation of the fears and desires of postwar America. Now, with the Korean War looming and the Cold War well underway, the noir began to reference itself and its *auteurs*. Soon the noir would give way to the Red Scare films of the early 1950s, as the "communist menace" turned into the HUAC/McCarthy witch-hunts, ending the careers of many who had created the genre in the first place. Bogart, for example, first spoke out against the new blacklist, but was forced to recant to save his career; others, such as Edward Dmytryk, were sentenced to jail for refusing to cooperate with the authorities, and resumed their careers only after appearing before HUAC and informing on their former associates.

In Dmytryk's case, his "testimony" resulted in his immediate return to the director's chair, where he created one of his most vicious and despairing films, *The Sniper* (1952), starring Arthur Franz as Eddie

Miller, a psychopath who kills women at random with a high-powered rifle. *The Sniper*'s vision of American life is vicious, cold, and clinical; people exist in the film only to be destroyed, and the police are seemingly powerless to stop the killer until the film's final moments. The film remains absolutely up-to-date today. Significantly, Franz's Eddie Miller repeatedly seeks help from the authorities, because he knows he's about to go over the edge, but none is forthcoming. Eddie falls through the cracks, until he reemerges as a figure of violent death. Yet as the 1940s gave way to the 1950s, our fear of the Other in our backyard was replaced by the fear of foreign invasion, and even atomic attack from an entirely new—and unanticipated—antagonist. After all, hadn't the Russians been our allies in World War II? The basic precepts of noir—to trust no one, to believe nothing as truth, to expect the worst in all possible situations, to realize that deception is an integral feature of social discourse—were all coming true as fundamental characteristics of modern life.

Whom, indeed, could we trust? No one. We could not even trust ourselves; a little pressure, and each of us could easily be made to implicate our friends and associates in whatever crime the authorities wished. What has been termed Neo-noir, in such films as Bryan Singer's *The Usual Suspects* (1995), John Dahl's *Red Rock West* (1993), and Larry and Andy Wachowski's *Bound* (1996), is little more than a stylistic homage to a genre whose authentic sense of menace and deception will never be equaled. Today, we have new fears to deal with, and a new set of escapist tools to transcend or confront them: video games, hyperviolent action films, Internet chat rooms, and interactive Web sites. We are all "connected," yet we have never been more isolated from one another. This was already the true message of noir sixty years ago: that today is horrible, and tomorrow will be worse, and hope is an illusion.

Once upon a time, we were adult enough to pay heed to this message. Now, we avoid the questions raised by film noir with the trivial pursuits of Neo-noir, searching cozily for something to pass the time.

MASS MURDER, MODERNITY, AND THE ALIENATED GAZE
Steven Alan Carr

The Battle over Holocaust Imagery

Modernity promises both utopia and dystopia. As utopian ideology, modernity celebrates linear progress, technological efficiency, scientific authority, and industrial achievement. As the Rosetta Stone for dystopian anxiety, modernity signifies massive social change, population shifts from rural to urban centers, the rise of consumerism and capitalism, increased industrialization, increased regimentation of daily lived experience, more sophisticated methods of concentrating social power and gaining popular consent, and, of course, more barbaric methods of deploying technology in the service of military aggression and fascist regimes.

Despite the presentation of a relatively coherent voice, the stylistic emphasis of modernism functions as a schizophrenic Greek chorus that both laments the more dystopic conditions of modernization and promotes the utopian teleology of individualism, humanism, and advancing scientific rationalism that itself helps generate and justify the conditions to which modernist styles often react. In *Practices of Looking: An Introduction to Visual Culture,* Marita Sturken and Lisa Cartwright define modernism as a set of aesthetic practices that sought to break away from conventional representations, emphasizing "form over content" and self-reflexivity (2001, 360). Reacting to perspectival realism and the assumptions of three-dimensional depth, modernist works sought to contradict assumptions of an "ideal spectator," instead offering a fractured but not necessarily fragmented view of the world. Rather than discount the possibility of a coherent observer, as much of the fragmentation that came to define postmodernism sought to do, modernism began with the assumption of a coherent individual who could access real phenomena through scientific methods, and ended with the individual subject alienated from a phenomenological reality that, while it did exist, remained too complex and contradictory for mere human consciousness to access. If the subject and even narrator of modernist fiction could prove unreliable, the notion of a coherent authorship deploying form over content as a way to comment upon the conditions of modernity and challenging traditional representations nonetheless remains intact, arguably even into the postmodern era.

Between modernism and postmodernism there is no clear break. This blur is the starting point for thinking about the construction of what we may call an *alienated gaze,* how it becomes encoded into popular culture, and how it functions as a stylistic response to the growing public emergence of the Holocaust and its visual record of atrocity. By this term, I mean to indicate a view that is at once conscious of itself and, to some degree therefore, in contradiction with itself; a look that, as it were, sees itself looking; a disengaged, and therefore potentially critical, view. I believe it is important to consider such a gaze in the context of the Holocaust and its attendant image of atrocity, a defining metaphor for the twentieth century against which all other images of atrocity stand in relation. Nothing of the photographed images of liberation—skeletal survivors crowded three or four to a bunk, ovens and showerheads, and piles of nude corpses being bulldozed into pits—inherently fixes the powerful and complex implications of these images as arbiters of atrocity. The images have been bestowed with two kinds of meaning, meaning that can be asserted but also meaning that gets pushed and pulled according to ideological struggle, and thus constitute together a battleground of myriad attempts of various social forces all seeking to maintain, negotiate, or ascend to legitimacy.

Given the primacy of Holocaust imagery in the struggle to negotiate subsequent standards for what constitutes atrocity, moral outrage, and ultimately military intervention, there has been surprisingly little public discussion—and even outright resistance to having a discussion—that moves beyond issues of propriety or the bogey of Holocaust denial to question the primacy of the visual in representing the Holocaust, or the consequences for an overreliance upon images to serve as arbiters for what constitutes an atrocity and what does not. To be sure, both art and analysis have decried the encroaching commercialism of Holocaust imagery. The reasons for the absence of this discussion are understandable. The most vociferous challenges to photographic images of atrocity often come from the ludicrously marginal Holocaust deniers, who deploy this challenge as part of a larger project to restore anti-Semitism to mainstream legitimacy. The images must be fake; none of this could possibly have really happened. Another position, however, is more problematic, adopting Holocaust images as absolute givens, total definitions of a truth. The criticism that faces any attempt to engage the consequences of using these images as the arbiter for what constitutes atrocity—instead of accepting them unconditionally as if they were, themselves, the Holocaust—points to the perils of having a discussion like this one. Sadly, the work of Zbigniew Libera or Alan Schechner—the latter raised a storm by interpolating himself into a photograph of a concentration camp bunkhouse, posing casually with a Diet Coke can—generates controversy because of a public unable or unwilling to distinguish between the increasingly commodified representation of the Holocaust on one hand and, on the other, artists who use their work to comment upon the consequences of this commodified representation, not to reinforce or hasten the commodification of Holocaust imagery.

Alienation and the Record

To begin an honest discussion of what I call the alienated gaze and its useful link to Holocaust and atrocity images, it helps to address the inherent alienation that is inspired by the direct encounter with the photographic record of atrocity. "Alienation," particularly in its Marxist connotation, need not be interpreted in the negative; to see the process of one's own seeing can ultimately promote a sense of critical engagement and awareness that is necessary to the functioning of a civil, pluralist, democratic society and can be, at the very least, appropriate when we encounter new levels of barbarism achieved in the name of modern progress. To find a deep-seated ambivalence, we need look no further than the inscription on the west wall of the U.S. Holocaust Memorial Museum in Washington, DC. Taken from a letter written by General Dwight D. Eisenhower to General George C. Marshall dated 15 April 1945, the passage testifies to both the horror of atrocity and an awareness of the skepticism that evidence of atrocity will surely meet: "The things I saw beggar description. . . . The visual evidence and the verbal testimony of starvation, cruelty and bestiality were . . . overpowering. . . . I made the visit deliberately in order to be in a position to give first-hand evidence of these things if ever, in the future, there develops a tendency to charge these allegations merely to 'propaganda.'" Despite its moral certainty, the inscription betrays a deep-seated ambivalence toward the gaze in modernity, namely, a lack of certainty concerning the act of looking and what its consequences might hold for future generations.

Why does Eisenhower insist upon positioning himself as a first-hand witness? Surely those critics predisposed to dismiss photographic evidence of atrocity as propaganda could easily explain away the testimony of a military general as part of a larger, ongoing effort to sustain anti-Nazi propaganda. Eisenhower understood that if his testimony were to have credibility, he would have to position himself in relation to the evidence of atrocity. Yet, as many from Walter Benjamin to John Berger and James Elkins have observed, the act of looking is neither passive nor one-sided. Rather, gazing is a relationship constructed between both material and imaginary conditions of existence. In reformulating Marxist conceptions of ideology, Louis Althusser suggests that the imagined relations indeed are far more complex, durable, and flexible than earlier notions of "false consciousness" had once assumed. For Althusser, ideology "hailed" the individual subject, but Elkins articulates the concept even more succinctly: in a visual society, our objects stare back. What, then, was Eisenhower's encounter with "starvation, cruelty and bestiality," and how were the images of these realities staring back at him?

The alienated gaze is not simply a passive activity; nor is it an activity initiated solely by human beings. Rather, it is a mutual relationship between animate subjects and inanimate, indexical traces of the real. That relationship has already been constructed and, through our ongoing participation, continues to be constructed, maintained, and repaired. We enter into this relationship, not necessarily knowingly and perhaps the less knowingly the more effectively the relationship binds us to it. Of course, none of this theory is particularly radical or new: feminist film scholarship had already addressed the ideological nature of the gaze by the 1970s, when it used Freudian tenets to dissect how sexism becomes encoded in visual meaning. Rather than explore the gaze as a gendered construction, however, this essay will explore the gaze as an ideological modern construction that is infused with an especially ambivalent and complex alienation when confronted with the image of atrocity.

Of course, overt visual and narrative motifs of alienation and alienated characters have received extensive attention in analyses of individual artistic creations, especially in the work of European art film directors such as Ingmar Bergman, Michelangelo Antonioni, and Federico Fellini. Here I shall argue that with some interpretive work, one can also find a complex appropriation of modernist strategies encoded in relatively middle-brow and mainstream Hollywood films. Despite the tremendous advance that critical theory offered by revising and rethinking Marxist notions of ideology and false consciousness, most discussions about the failure of popular culture to respond adequately to the Holocaust persist in presuming the same, now somewhat tired, Marxist notions of ideology that applied before the advent of critical theory. Therefore, rather than merely assume that Hollywood films avoided or trivialized the Holocaust, we might ask how Hollywood films appropriated a sophisticated, complex, and nuanced subject position consistent with a modernist response to atrocity, and how from this position these films implicitly but consistently questioned and interrogated the very practice of looking. One can locate the material practice of this position in the alienated gaze, articulated through visual elements such as camera angle, shot composition, and shot selection; but it can be seen as well through editing and even narrative. The practice emerged both in mainstream Hollywood and in newsreel footage of the camps, but documentary practice explicitly articulated the alienated gaze before it was appropriated by studio filmmaking. Admittedly a subtle response to the rise of Nazism and the Holocaust, the alienated gaze reveals the implications and consequences of looking at the unbearable.

Alienation and the Alienated Gaze

The archetypal criticism of popular culture comes from Theodor Adorno, whose famous maxim, "To write poetry after Auschwitz is barbaric," warned that any art—not just poetry—would be unthinkable after the horrors of the concentration camp. However, critic Lawrence Langer has offered a much-needed corrective to this oft-cited passage. As Langer observes, "Perhaps what Adorno really meant to say was that to write poems after Auschwitz the way we wrote poems before Auschwitz was barbaric" (2002, 78). What I am calling the alienated gaze is, following Langer, a new way of writing and responding to the visual poem. As a signifying practice of filmmaking, it does not solely seek to unmask the prewar suspension of disbelief as so much denial and pretense. Rather, it is a self-reflexive practice that makes the viewer aware of the artifice of looking and ethically implicates the viewer in troubling ways. The alienated gaze can be manifest narratively, in stories of mistaken identity and "plays within a play," but it is also a visual construction. Indeed, the two genres in which one finds it most prevalent are comedy and the psychological horror film. Through point of view, constructed via camera angle, shot composition, and shot/reverse shot, the alienated gaze makes the viewer aware of the process of looking—indeed, the viewer's own looking—even as it can uncomfortably align those who identify with morally ambiguous protagonists and antagonists.

I find the alienated gaze operating as the kind of "socially symbolic act" described by Fredric Jameson (1981, 81). It betrays broad, deepseated, and unresolved ideological tensions within the general narrative superstructure of our culture, tensions that can be taken as responses to the witnessing of modern-day atrocity. Consider that narratives distill the cultural forces, tensions, and contradictions of the day into easily recognizable symbols. Thus, whether any individual author of a text meant to respond or react to the Holocaust is irrelevant. In fact, the possibility that the alienated gaze might be an intentional device remains highly suspect. I see it as a symptom of a culture traumatized by its own looking. Just as, for Sigmund Freud, the narrative of the individual subject could be analyzed as a symptom, the gaze is symptomatic of a modernist schism, an utterance of the cultural meta-subject that reveals an unwitting attempt to reconcile the barbarism of the Holocaust with the teleological notions of progress and civilization.

That the alienated gaze "lets slip"—more than it intentionally artic-ulates—a symptomatic schism is crucial in terms of how it encodes alienation in modern life. To see that schism in strictly Marxist terms, one can certainly think of alienation, from the proletarian perspective, as "indignation" against the "depravity" of witnessing a contradiction between humanity and the "blatant, outright, and all-embracing de-nial" of that humanity (1978, 133–34). But although this definition might describe an immediate encounter with the photographic image of atrocity, Walter Benjamin's account of alienation in "The Work of Art in the Age of Mechanical Reproduction" builds upon a prescient understanding of fascist aesthetics and is closer to the kind of alien-ation reproduced in the alienated gaze. Benjamin understood that alienation from the aura and cult value of art was a necessary and in-evitable process. While alienation would destroy the aura surrounding a work, it inevitably would bring about greater critical awareness.

In the service of "politicizing art," alienation would be a powerful democratizing force. In the service of fascism, however, alienation could become a dangerous tool for mobilizing mass movements "on the largest scale" (1985, 693). Without the constraint of an overriding critical context, the relationship between art and authority could be used to centralize power and promote war rather than to politi-cize and democratize art. As Benjamin notes, "All efforts to render politics aesthetic culminate in one thing: war" (1985, 693). Seeking to give the masses "an expression while preserving property" relations, fascism's aesthetic glorification of war is the epitome of art for art's sake, a penultimate form of alienation that finds aesthetic pleasure in the destruction of human lives (1985, 694). Fascist pageantry capital-izes upon alienation from the aura and cult value of art, but asserts an authoritarian framework to structure how one experiences that alien-ation. Not necessarily a reaction to fascism, the alienated gaze none-theless articulates a greater degree of ambivalence toward looking than fascist pageantry, more along the lines of how Benjamin de-scribes the estrangement that one feels when encountering his or her own image on a screen. As he observes, the alienation one experiences is not just the estrangement one feels when looking into a mirror, but an estrangement from a reflected image that now "has become sep-arable, transportable" to the public. Independent of the person who is its source, the image has a currency of its own, and the alienated gaze shows us the image independently circulating with that currency.

As part of the political unconscious, the alienated gaze represents a similar estrangement, not from a particular image but from the very act of looking itself. The alienated gaze does not so much mirror a reflected image as it mirrors the very act of looking, as a relationship and as a process. Because the alienated gaze mirrors the act of looking, not the image, looking itself becomes separable and transportable, gains a currency. As Benjamin notes, discourses on photography long debated whether photography represented a triumph of science over human subjectivity, or a major quandary for traditional aesthetics. But what underscored these debates, without being explicitly acknowledged, was that the "science" of photography could newly encode (and popularize) the position of the dispassionate, objective observer. Just as photography could erode any sense of authorial ownership over the image, it could also reinforce a position of neutrality and present the image as a form of evidence. When Eisenhower spoke of "visual evidence" that "beggars description," he was maintaining that the antidote to charges of propaganda is to preserve a first-person account, both buttressed by material signifiers and ensconced within an institutional discourse that asserts its military authority. Even as the pictures become "real," the act of looking at them must be reasserted as engagement and authentication.

Recent Holocaust scholarship has focused upon the signifying practices of photography and documentary filmmaking during the liberation of the concentration camps, and how these practices evolved. As Barbie Zelizer notes, documenting "liberation" ultimately "depended on larger impulses to call the atrocities by name," and the photographic records of the camps were intended to be a form of "governmental persuasion." Although one might dismiss the intent and origination of Holocaust photographs as government-induced propaganda, Zelizer correctly observes that, unlike earlier forms of government propaganda that were selective in what they presented, the sheer weight of the photojournalistic record with regard to concentration camps eventually rendered untenable any charges that the atrocities of the concentration camps had not occurred. More important, though, was the way in which these photographs were able to shock "nations out of their skepticism" by "processing the unbelievable atrocity story into a plausible interpretive schema" (1998, 11–12). Whereas Zelizer sees the documenting of atrocity as the event that launches the signifying practice of news photography, Dagmar Barnouw interprets the photographing of the camps at the time of liberation—in both still and motion pictures—as an encoding of military authority and perspective. As Barnouw perceptively notes, the photographs showing German civilians confronting German atrocities are,

> by their very nature, visually self-conscious since their goal was to show what needed to be seen. Not surprisingly, the photographic spaces of these images are constructed around the topos of looking. Through the lens of his camera, the photographer looks at Germans looking at large numbers of piled-up or lined-up corpses, using the perspective of one or more American or British soldiers who are shown observing these prescribed acts of "viewing the atrocities." Positioned at different points of observation, the witnesses to these acts are themselves witnessed by the photographer, reaffirming the photographic evidence of the German population's obedience. (1997, 7)

Barnouw's stunning analysis of camp liberation images suggests that in addition to an emergent practice of news photography after the war, there was an emergent practice of framing atrocity through a military perspective. Such analysis demands more than looking at the image itself or treating the image as mirrored reflection. It demands that one consider a whole structure of looking as following a consistent pattern of meaning. Witnessing atrocity becomes a form of evidence in and of itself. In looking, the viewer says, "My reality as a viewer is confirmed by this reality I see," and also, "What I see is in fact a reality as it occurred." As Barnouw notes, it was military personnel who shot these photographs, the object of which was "to make clear that showing evidence of German atrocities will ensure German obedience in accepting, along with the new authorities, their new identity" (1997, 7).

Alienated Gaze as Modernist Visual Strategy
In and of itself the alienated gaze is neither fascist nor militaristic, but one would be foolish to deny links between the fascist appropriation of alienation observed by Benjamin and the Allies' encoding of

military authority within the visual record of atrocity. Although the alienated gaze is not an intentional or even explicit signifying practice, perhaps the most easily accessible example of structure comes from the highly self-conscious and stylized European art cinema. Alain Resnais's *Night and Fog* (*Nuit et brouillard* [1955]), for example, is rightly regarded as a classic modernist approach to the Holocaust. Critics often note the striking juxtaposition of color footage of an abandoned concentration camp with black-and-white documentary and newsreel footage depicting Nazi atrocities, and especially the way in which the film graphically matches these juxtapositions through editing: a tracking shot of fence posts in the abandoned camp cuts to black-and-white newsreel footage of Nazis marching in formation past the camera (Bordwell and Thompson 2004, 299). Then there is the laconic voiceover narration by Jean Cayrol, himself a survivor, which deploys ironic distance at key moments in the film, such as when Cayrol self-consciously uses a spectrum of architectural styles to describe the camps ("No specific style—that's left to the imagination: *style Alpin, style garage, style Japonais,* no style"). Perhaps the most tangible and most self-conscious invocation of an alienated gaze, however, is in the visual motifs revealed during the color footage. The film opens with a devastating series of tracking shots, each one starting with a vista of "a peaceful landscape" before being reframed to reveal barbed wire or the electrified fence of the camp. Later in the film, the tracking camera becomes a surrogate point of view for the arrival of the deportation train at the camp. Beginning with a tracking shot of the railroad ties, the camera tilts up to reveal the camp entry. The motif of dramatic change through camera movement underscores a sense of alienation. Placed before the camp gates, we witness this moment from the abandoned tracks via the distancing color footage and plainly cannot approximate the historical suffering of those who were actually on the boxcars and sent to the camps. How easy it is to overlook the subtle and complex visual meanings of these shots—perhaps because so many of the once-radical cinematic techniques employed in *Night and Fog* have been subsumed within a popular visual lexicon.

In terms of representing the Holocaust, such practices were hardly new or unique to film, given the cinematographic records made by the Allies at the end of World War II. One has to wonder, then, what all the fuss was, in the very late twentieth century, over an exhibition mounted at the Jewish Museum in New York City nearly forty years earlier (yet considerably after *Night and Fog*), when the NO!art collective group was employing similar distancing and alienating techniques in Sam Goodman's *Eichmann Remember* (1961) or Boris Lurie's *Lolita* (1962). Politicizing Pop Art, and in some ways reacting to it, the NO!art collective used radical collage to shock the viewer out of complacency in the wake of Auschwitz and Hiroshima. Both Goodman's and Lurie's works sought to engage what Hannah Arendt would later dub the "banality of evil" in her 1963 *New Yorker* articles and later book manuscript, *Eichmann in Jerusalem*, an account of the trial of Adolf Eichmann, a high-level Nazi official complicit in the Final Solution and apprehended and put on trial by the Israelis in televised proceedings in 1961. As Estera Milman notes, both Goodman's and Lurie's works are obsessed with Eichmann's inability, or perhaps stubborn refusal, to grasp the ramifications of his having to answer for war crimes (Milman 2001, 24). At his trial, Eichmann could or would not recall the seminal role he played in the Wannsee Conference, the 1942 meeting of high-level Nazi officials to discuss various methods of mass execution that could be used to exterminate Jews. Constructed as a triptych, Goodman's *Eichmann Remember* helps prod memory through a ghastly collage of photographic evidence of atrocities committed by the Nazis, with the central panel featuring various photographs of Eichmann himself, his glasses shattered and the phrase "6,000,000 DEAD" scrawled across his face.

Even though Goodman does little to mask his indignation, the piece politicizes alienation through the central metaphor of Eichmann's *not* seeing, or refusing to see. Lurie's work, however, is even more confrontational in that it juxtaposes a fragment from a movie poster for the MGM adaptation of Vladimir Nabokov's *Lolita* (1962) with a photograph from the Gardelegen massacre, where the Nazis locked an estimated one thousand or more concentration camp slave laborers in a barn and then burned them alive. Less than a month after American troops came upon the massacre, *Life* published the series of photos (7 May 1945). Given that both images had achieved popular currency in their time—actress Sue Lyon in heart-shaped sunglasses, sucking on a lollipop; and a charred corpse partly visible underneath a barn wall after apparently trying to escape the building by digging with bare hands—the juxtaposition is shocking. Perhaps this shock is achieved because the synthesis of these images offers no stable subject position from which to view them. The only gaze that approaches stability when confronted by this work is one that is informed by the knowledge that Eichmann had refused a copy of Nabokov's novel after finding it "unwholesome" (Milman 2001, 24–25).

The instability of the subject position in viewing both *Night and Fog* and the works of the NO!art collective suggests that the notion of an alienated gaze was addressed most confrontationally and explicitly at the levels of art and art cinema. However, one need not look far to find less explicit engagement with the alienated gaze within popular culture. Indeed, much of NO!art draws from and comments upon commercialization and popular culture. And even though *Night and Fog* uses its techniques to destabilize how one views the concentration camp today, similar distancing techniques arguably were present in earlier documentaries immediately after the war, and even in Hollywood feature films before 1945.

Alienated Gaze as Narrative Strategy

The most pronounced form of the alienated gaze in mainstream cinema before the United States entered World War II is to be found in a number of different genres, in films that address, however elliptically, the early ramifications of the Holocaust. The two films that most notably engage this subject, both from United Artists, are Charlie Chaplin's *The Great Dictator* (1940) and Ernst Lubitsch's *To Be or Not to Be* (1942). Although these films lack the visual flair of the European art cinema or NO!art photo collages, their narratives of mistaken identity, performance, and the tenuous balance between fiction and reality foretell the visual motifs of alienation that appear in subsequent mainstream films. In *The Great Dictator,* Chaplin plays a dual role: both a thinly disguised caricature of Adolf Hitler, Adenoid Hynkel, and a Jewish barber. The dual narrative serves both to satirize fascism through the depiction of Hynkel and to elicit sympathy for the plight of Jews through the appearance of the Little Tramp–like barber. Only in the final fifteen minutes of the film do both narratives coincide, as the barber's resemblance to Hynkel precipitates the capture and arrest of the actual Hynkel while the barber gets to speak to an audience of millions. Chaplin then steps out of character to deliver a monologue in a direct address to the camera, creating a third "character" who seems to exist at the margins of both diegetic and non-diegetic narrative space.

Mistaken identities and doppelgängers were nothing new at the time. But *The Great Dictator* represented a departure from Chaplin's other films and was seen as less entertaining, in part because of its infusion of politics into his art. The film does represent a substantial distancing from the persona of the Little Tramp in such earlier films as *City Lights* (1931) and *Modern Times* (1936). Where the earlier narrative films presented a coherent character, Chaplin fractured his onscreen persona in *The Great Dictator* not once but twice—first between Hynkel and the barber, and again when the barber turns into a version of Chaplin himself. Although the barber seemed to be a holdover from Chaplin's earlier films—so much so that many viewers mistakenly believed Chaplin himself to be Jewish—Hynkel is the antithesis of the Little Tramp. Chaplin used to recall how so many people had commented upon his physical resemblance to Hitler, yet in his performance he seems to call attention to the artifice of Hynkel in his own right: the grandiose sets, the exaggerated use of nonsense language mixed with English, the anthropomorphized props (such as the bendable microphone). Such comic exaggeration would seem to underscore the difference between Chaplin and Hitler, rather than the similarity between the two. The ultimate alienation effect, however, occurs when the barber addresses the crowds who expect to hear Hynkel. At this point, Chaplin completely breaks the artifice of the scene, playing neither Hynkel nor the barber but a third character who directly addresses the camera and calls for an end to violence, war, and fascism. Although neither as polished nor as efficient as *To Be or Not to Be,* the climactic soliloquy does work as a kind of ultimate alienation that ends up rupturing the narrative and provides only minimal narrative resolution.

If *The Great Dictator* ends with narrative rupture, *To Be or Not to Be* begins with it, imagining what would happen if Hitler visited the Warsaw Ghetto in 1939 Poland. The film immediately sets up its own conceit, revealing that the "visitor" is actually an actor impersonating Hitler on the stage of a theater, at one point improvising and issuing an anticlimactic "Heil myself!" Distancing the audience through this bit of trickery—revealing the artifice of the actor's performance by showing that within this film "the play's the thing"—*To Be or Not to Be* sets up a chain of subsequent scenes that call into question the nature of seeing and performance: Maria Tura's (Carole Lombard) divalike insistence that her stage character wear an evening gown for a scene to be played in a concentration camp; the assassination of the pro-Nazi agent Professor Alexander Siletsky (Stanley Ridges) on the stage of a theater, of all places, after members of the theatrical troupe fail to maintain their disguise as military officers (in order to help a colleague prevent the Nazis from gaining sensitive information concerning the Polish underground); the confrontation of Joseph Tura (Jack Benny), head of the acting company, who is impersonating Siletsky, with Siletsky's actual corpse; and Greenberg's (Felix Bressart) performance of Shylock's "Hath not a Jew eyes" soliloquy before German soldiers to stall them from an ensuing chase.

Such instances of dual, appropriated, and mistaken identity establish the formation of the alienated gaze, because these plot devices ultimately reference the non-diegetic aspects of performance. By featuring staged "diegetic performances" within the (diegetically performed) narrative, the film heightens the viewer's awareness of performance itself. In this manner, one can understand a film like *To Be or Not to Be* as countering the fascist embrace of spectacle in such a film as *Triumph of the Will* (*Triumph des Willens* [1934]), which although Benjamin does not mention it would certainly conform to the kind of estrangement from humanity that he attacks. The estrangement from performance is similar to the estrangement Benjamin describes when an actor in role encounters his or her own image. Estrangement in these films, whether intentional or not, appears to function as a form of politicizing art by encouraging viewers to take a skeptical view of Nazi pageantry.

The Alienated Gaze in Popular Culture

The encounter with fascism may acquire a certain degree of politicization through an alienation from fascism, but the encounter with atrocity requires an alienation from the gaze itself. A number of films and newsreels documented the atrocities and liberation of the camps, many of them made under the auspices of the Allied military command. In May 1985, the PBS documentary series "Frontline" aired an unreleased documentary entitled *Memory of the Camps,* which was long thought to have been lost. A joint production of the United States and Britain, the film was reconstructed from a fine cut, a shot list, and a narrator's script. Trevor Howard was employed to read the narration.

Although there is some dispute as to how much of a role director Alfred Hitchcock played in editing the footage, interviews reveal that he was involved as a creative adviser at some point in the production of the original film. Peter Tanner, one of the editors at the time, recalled in an interview with Elizabeth Sussex that Hitchcock was very concerned with preventing people from "thinking that any of this was faked, which of course none of it was." Hitchcock's strategy, according to Tanner, was to use footage that was "never cut. It was all in one shot. And this I *know* was one of Hitchcock's ideas, and it was very effective. There was *no way* for somebody seeing it that it could have been faked" (Sussex 1984, 96). Indeed, in the sequence depicting the liberation of Dachau, there are haunting uncut tracking shots of crowds of inmates staring back at the camera as it surveys them.

More intriguing, however, is the way in which the editing functions in this documentary to question not the veracity of evidence but the nature of looking. In the longest sequence of the film, a record of what the Allies found at Bergen-Belsen, the first scene presents pastoral views of the town before cutting to a wide shot of the camp. The editing suggests a disturbing veneer of normalcy camouflaging the horrible, not unlike the narrative conceit of Hitchcock's earlier *Shadow of a Doubt* (1943) or subsequent *Strangers on a Train* (1950). The motif also occurs in the narration, which often ironically wonders how a German could have failed to know what was taking place. Toward the end of the sequence devoted to this camp, a scene shows two chaplains delivering last rites to a pit full of corpses. The scene is intercut with reaction shots of prisoners witnessing the event and shots of a bulldozer pushing dirt over the bodies. The first shots of the chaplains are framed to exclude the pit, but the following ones show them above it. The next shot is a close-up of dirt being bulldozed into the pit. The camera slowly pans left to reveal the corpses.

The sequence betrays a concern for the believability of such images of atrocity that echoes throughout Hitchcock's subsequent work, particularly through the 1950s. I am not suggesting that Hitchcock's films are about the Holocaust, but their narratives frequently convey at least as much concern for whether events will be believed as does the editing of *Memory of the Camps* in its concern with skepticism. Both *Rear Window* (1954) and *Vertigo* (1958) address issues of the gaze. Of course, these films are not about looking at the Holocaust, but they are about the ethics of looking at horrible crimes. The unseen and seen murders in these films arguably serve as narrative surrogates for atrocities, and the way in which both films implicitly call into question the spectator's gaze seems most relevant in terms of what we know from the film *Memory of the Camps* and Hitchcock's participation in it. *Rear Window* is a film about looking, and the central metaphor for fear in *Vertigo* is the famous special visual effect of the camera pulling back as the lens zooms in. Both are films that one can appreciate on a purely narrative level. Yet both films also accommodate a more metavisual reading that encompasses the role and function of the camera as the central position for the spectator.

This concern for looking becomes most apparent immediately before the shower scene in *Psycho* (1960). As Marion Crane (Janet Leigh) disrobes to take a shower, Norman Bates (Anthony Perkins) removes a framed picture from a wall to view her through a peephole. An extreme close-up of Bates's eye anticipates the later shot of Marion's eye as she stares blankly into the camera after having been murdered. By showing both Norman's eye and the spectacle of her disrobing that he sees, Hitchcock highlights and calls into question the act of watching: Norman watching Marion, the camera (and us) watching Norman watching, and the act of watching the film itself. The audience occupies the same gaze as a Peeping Tom. Later, a similar alienation occurs after Marion's murder. She stares lifelessly into the camera, but there is no reaction shot to reveal what can be seen from the point of view of her eye. The camera tracks over to a newspaper that is hiding the money she had embezzled, but there is no subjectivity to ground this visual flourish. Through the use of this technique, Hitchcock implicates the viewer in the narrative of the film: now, only the viewer—and none of the characters—knows the significance of this camera movement and what it shows.

Arguably, the filmic moments I have been describing here could do more to politicize meaning along the lines that Benjamin proposes. In terms of viewing the Holocaust not as a discrete historical moment but as one with repercussions at both the overt and implicit levels, such moments can reveal a political unconscious at work. It is hard to imagine that the impact of the visual witness to atrocity would not have made some kind of impression, especially for those Hollywood personnel actively engaged in documenting atrocity for both military and civilian audiences. I have tried to suggest that the concern raised by images of atrocity can lead to a heightened awareness of the ethics and politics of looking, and that not just European art films but even Hollywood feature films can encode within their meaning the ambivalence present in the alienated gaze. Such ambivalence may or may not lead to a heightened politicization, but the presence of the alienated gaze would seem to reinforce Benjamin's initial observations about the inherently liberatory function of images. Although it is certainly not insulated from co-optation by authoritarian forces, even popular culture can encode complex and charged visual subjectivities with which the most dominating systems of control must reckon.

Note

I wish to thank Murray Pomerance for his editorial assistance, and Daniel J. Silverstein for bringing the NO!art movement to my attention. This essay was made possible through the generous support of the U.S. Holocaust Memorial Museum Center for Advanced Holocaust Studies, the National Endowment for the Humanities, and Indiana University–Purdue University Fort Wayne. A very different version of this essay appeared in *Proceedings of La Mémoire des Villes/Memory of the Cities*, ed. Yves Clavaron and Bernard Dieterle (Saint-Etienne: University of Saint-Etienne, 2003).

MODERNITY AND THE CRISIS IN TRUTH
ALFRED HITCHCOCK AND FRITZ LANG
Walter Metz

When at first I came to think of writing about "falseness and the instability of knowledge," I had been dabbling in the application of Walter
Benjamin's writings to the films of Fritz Lang but was by no means expert in the critical theory of modernity. Nevertheless, I strove to think
about the crisis in truth in Lang's later films, especially *Beyond a Reasonable Doubt* (1956), a film with which I had recently compared *The
Life of David Gale* (2003) as the opening volley in an attempt to re-
invigorate a kind of "middle-ground" (not too theoretical, not too
populist) film criticism (see Metz 2004). And then, as the months
wore on, I began to notice that much of what I teach and think about
regarding the cinema hesitates at the nexus of cinema and modernity.
The project of defining modernity anew, as we talk about film history,
is desperately needed. However, in the wake of Tom Gunning's book,
The Films of Fritz Lang: Allegories of Vision and Modernity (2000),
which offers such a wide-ranging analysis of modernity as it is expressed in Lang's cinema (an analysis, indeed, connected to an acute
understanding of German critical theories of modernity, mostly via
Miriam Hansen and the other important thinkers of the New German
Critique school), what more could one say about the topic?

But then it struck me that piecemeal observations about the culture of modernity—themselves very different in attitude, in focus, and in tone from Gunning's rigorously organized work—might offer some real illumination of Lang's filmmaking. Indeed, through something of a chaotic encounter with the films of Fritz Lang and Alfred Hitchcock seen against one another, modernity might be apprehended by its fragmentary shards, not just through a systematic method. Such fragmentary moments occur, outside of Lang, in a late golden-age silent film, King Vidor's *The Crowd* (1928), near the opening when Johnny Sims (James Murray) rides a ferry into Manhattan, convinced that he can fulfill his dead father's dream by becoming someone important, like Abraham Lincoln. The film suddenly, and oddly, leaves Johnny behind and instead gives us fragmentary images of Manhattan, boats swirling into the harbor, trains and cars forming geometric patterns, chaotic streets filled with people scurrying about. These images, drawn in particular from the modernist, avant-garde depiction of the city in *Manhatta* (1927), yet also from the 1920s experimental cinema in general—similar shots of the chaotic city appear at the beginning of René Clair's *Entr'Acte* (1924), for example, as we float downward from high atop a building toward the street with a piece of paper blowing in the wind—mark a crucial moment in the representation of the city. It makes sense, following such a cinematic and cultural moment, to locate the onset of modernity in the cinema around 1930, a date that may at first seem completely bizarre.

After all, as an instrument of mechanical reproducibility, hasn't cinema itself, since 1895, been a marker of modernity, technologically and socially? When the train arrives at the station of La Ciotat, aren't we witnessing the onset of filmed modernity? And when in the earliest years of the twentieth century Georges Méliès uses his camera's magic tricks, which we know today as editing, aren't we witnessing the cinema's articulation of modernity as well?

Yes, and no. The culture of modernity invents a language for representing itself, and this language develops over time into a critical practice that is quite different from its initial "tricks." Méliès's tricks on the one hand, and a critical representation of them on the other, are two very different things. Cinema's modernity is not fully tangible in *Ex-*

traordinary Illusions (*Illusions funambulesques* [1903]), but it is by the time we get to the end of Clair's *Entr'Acte*, when the film's magician uses Méliès's editing tricks in front of the coffin from which he has recently stood up to make first the other characters, and then himself, disappear. However, editing is not the only trick up his sleeve. Instead, he suddenly falls through the "Fin" title card and has to be kicked in the head to get back into the film. It is the fragmentary nature of representation itself that is fully present by the late 1920s, and this representational system was, and is, fully compatible with a classical Hollywood representational style.

Marking the fragmentary representation of the city in such late 1920s films as *The Crowd* opens to observation the strangely under-theorized nature of the relationship between modernism (an artistic movement) and modernity (a social descriptor). Much debate raged among the German critical thinkers on this point: consider Benjamin's complex defense of the cinema as a popular modern art form in his famous essay on mechanical reproduction (1985) as opposed to Theodor Adorno and Max Horkheimer's embrace of modernism as the proper corrective to the fascist potential of modernity in their "culture industry" essay (1972). Our understanding of textual, cinematic modernity is based to some degree on the latter. For example, Alfred Hitchcock's *Rear Window* (1954) is often seen as a superior critical engagement with postwar modernity because it relies on the reflexive technique of treating Jeff Jeffries's view of his neighbors as an analogy to the cinema itself.

Classical Modernity: Of Apes and Men

Such modernist interpretations of modernity need not drive our entire understanding of modernity and cinema between 1930 and 1960. A very different definition of modernity is offered in Tom McGurl's excellent essay, "Making It Big: Picturing the Radio Age in *King Kong*" (1996). McGurl analyzes the significance of the Empire State Building as an early 1930s marker of modernity, one that RKO was able to hybridize in both its corporate logo (a giant radio tower that dwarfs the earth) and the plot of its first major success, *King Kong* (1933), a film about a gorilla who is ripped from his cave and taken by an impresario filmmaker to New York City to be turned into a media celebrity. When the new "star" doesn't take kindly to flash photography, he seeks out the solace of the closest substitute to his mountain aerie, climbing to the top of the Empire State Building. However, a beast's triumph over a skyscraper cannot be allowed by *King Kong*'s filmmakers, so another icon of modernity, the airplane equipped with a machine-gun—invented during World War I—is deployed against him, resulting in his bullet-ridden fall from the world's highest artificial peak.

Modernity can be articulated using the language of fragmentation. For instance, *King Kong* is a film not just about the skyscraper but also about filmmaking and the airplane. That all of these are key descriptors of modernity illustrates the fact that 1933 marks one important, and very culturally coherent, historical moment in our study of modernity as a lived experience, even if it is a moment presented through fragmentation. The skyscraper as an important cultural site for the analysis of modernity can also be pursued in relationship to the films of Lang and Hitchcock. There's a moment in Fritz Lang's *The Big Heat* (1953) that allegorizes his cinematic vision of modernity. When Mike Lagana (Alexander Scourby), the film's criminal, puts "the big heat" on the city, he intends to immolate it unless the city bows to his will. Lang frames Lagana's attack not directly but through fragments, images that continue to haunt us as critics of the film: for example, disabled Selma Parker (Edith Evanson), the woman who first helps Detective Dave Bannion (Glenn Ford), limping near a cold chain link fence at a junkyard filled with the debris of Western civilization. One might see the film as an allegory for a much larger experience of modernity, the nuclear age as the (il)logical extension of the Age of Reason (see Metz 1997).

In the first act of *The Big Heat*, Lagana's henchmen have been stalling Bannion's investigation into the violent murder of a woman. Bannion returns home, discouraged. He stands at the doorway of his young daughter's room, where she is playing with building blocks. A proud father, Bannion tells her, "That's the most beautiful castle in the whole world." She runs to give him a hug, but corrects him: "It's a police station, just like you." Bannion's desire for his daughter to exist outside the realm of his corrupted world, his hope that she is living in a world of fantasy castles, is not tenable. She cares about her daddy, and thus uses her blocks to build a police station to keep him safe.

However, it is not some small-town police station; it is in fact a high-rise version that houses the police force for an entire city. Now his daughter asks him to help build the roof. As Bannion places blocks on the top of the structure, his wife, Katie (Jocelyn Brando), asks him about his day. Bannion snaps answers to her questions, then immediately apologizes. She is understanding, telling him he should "let off steam." However, Bannion cannot find it in himself to pollute his home with the world's corruption, and under the tension of such repression his hand shakes, causing the wooden blocks to tumble at his daughter's feet. She runs crying to her mother, while Bannion hangs his head in shame. Katie reassures her, "Daddy will help you to build even a bigger one."

However, Bannion will never get that chance. The next time the family is together in this room, Bannion puts his daughter to bed while Katie goes to the car to get some ice cream for dessert. We see a white flash in the window as Lagana's car bomb kills her. Bannion abandons the domestic space, deposits his daughter with friends, and spends the rest of the film on a mad quest for vengeance. The images in this film grapple as much with Hiroshima—the white flash of the car bomb mirroring that of an atomic blast—as with the conventions of the police procedural. In Axel Madsen's essay on Lang, he provides a framework for understanding this connection culturally: "To [Lang], the twentieth century is Dachau and Hiroshima more than it is Einstein, acceleration of knowledge and humanitarianism through abundance" (1967, 109).

In a seeming slip, Bannion's daughter tells him that the wood-block police station is "just like you," not "just like where you work." She reduces her father's status to that of a city building. In fact, the rest of the film proves her formulation to be exactly correct. Without the support of his wife, Bannion is reducible exactly to his function as a police detective. He no longer has time for his daughter or for a relationship with Debby (Gloria Grahame), the film's femme fatale and the potential new object for his domestic love.

The depiction of the Bannion household fully allegorizes the shifting gender relations implied by modernity. In feminist criticism, this is commonly articulated in terms of the shift from "true" to "new" womanhood. Under the discourse of True Womanhood, late-nineteenth-century Victorian women stayed at home while their husbands went out to work. This arrangement was appropriate because women were morally pure and could regenerate their husbands upon their return home from the dirty, corrupt industrial world. By the 1920s in the United States, the flapper and other images of New Women were competing with this gender discourse. Significantly, *The Big Heat* reveals that even as late as 1952 Katie's status as a strong, New Woman— she is unafraid to speak her mind—was still mostly grounded in the material realities of True Womanhood. Katie's job is to give Bannion room to "let off steam," something that his daughter doesn't quite understand when his "steam" results in the destruction of her beloved toy police station. We, on the other hand, *will* understand all too clearly when the real steam of Lagana's bomb kills Katie and blows the lid off Bannion's civilized repression.

An allegorical reading of *The Big Heat* as an atomic thriller and an engagement with postwar nuclear trauma raises other questions about how modernity comes to be defined as a particular historical mode of experience. Most famously explored by the historian Michel Foucault, modernity becomes the devastating failure of the Enlightenment. For Foucault, modern institutions are the result of vicious constraints on human freedom. Thus, the madhouse is an Enlightenment attempt to contain the "insane" and keep them away from the "normal" sane people; Jeremy Bentham's panopticon prison building is a rational system of surveillance where the lookers take power over the looked at; and medical discourse produces a binary division between normal heterosexuality and a "deviant" homosexuality. For Foucault, modernity is produced out of an arrogant belief in rationalism. But Lang's films study people's lives in an irrational world. After all, the atomic bomb is a most powerful marker of modernity, perhaps the "great" end product of the Enlightenment, whose only purpose is the extinction of humanity.

Alfred Hitchcock's *North by Northwest* (1959) is a very different kind of film. During the 1950s, Hitchcock made suspense thrillers that did not need to rely on allegory. Instead, they harnessed the cultural moment of the Cold War national security state to stories of individual Americans caught up in the hysteria. Thus, *North by Northwest* concerns not a police detective but an ordinary businessman, Roger Thornhill (Cary Grant), who gets caught up in a plot by foreign agents to smuggle vital microfilm out of the United States.

Like *The Big Heat, North by Northwest* is centered on city life at its beginning. Indeed, the opening credits are displayed against the front of a high-rise skyscraper, on the diagonal lines etched on the building's floors. The film pursues a reference to Shakespeare. Hamlet's comment to his friend Horatio that he is "but mad north-north-west, / When the wind blows southerly I know a hawk from a handsaw" suggests that he can distinguish nature from manmade artifice. Similarly, Thornhill's leaving behind the twentieth century's modernity, his skyscraper life in New York, for the world north-northwest of it, an America of cornfields and traditional marriage, shows that he can escape the world of deception in a way that Hamlet cannot. As the narrative begins, we see Thornhill riding in a cab with his secretary. He is a bachelor who cares more about his mother than his sex partners. (As many contemporary Hitchcock critics have suggested, perhaps most cogently Steven Cohan, the project of the film is to cure Thornhill of this infantile, Oedipal psychological state.) Thus, after Roger falls in love with Eve Kendall (Eva Marie Saint) he is angered when he discovers she is a spy; but he recovers from this betrayal, matures, and helps her defeat the foreign agents. In the film's infamous last sequence, Roger moves away from the north-by-northwest diagonals of the film's credit sequence by lifting Eve vertically from the façade of Mount Rushmore into their train compartment's honeymoon bed. Hitchcock jokingly cuts to the phallic train penetrating a receptive mountain tunnel.

Crucially, the movement between New York City and the film's later settings is from urban to rural. In the middle of the film, Thornhill is attacked in a Midwestern cornfield. And the film's ending takes place in South Dakota, which is *literally* north-by-northwest from Manhattan. However, *symbolically*, the film proposes that Mount Rushmore is the place where wholesome Americans will defend their national security (an idea best articulated by Robert Corber [1993]). *North by Northwest* treats the skyscraper itself as an image of pathology, thus indicting the culture of modernity, the shift from rural to urban that characterized the effects of the Industrial Revolution.

The Big Heat, however, is beyond imagining something outside of the city. In this intensive, centripetal film noir, the city is the only foundation on which an abusive modernity can be built. For Thornhill, there is a possibility of escape into suburban conventionality. *The*

Big Heat, a much more radical film, murders off that conventionality at the first turning point, and instead becomes a study in how humanity might struggle to continue under these irrevocably altered circumstances.

Modernity and World War II

Oddly, whereas typically Lang is the allegorical filmmaker and Hitchcock the populist, narrative-driven one, the opposite is true of their wartime films. The basic falseness of modernity is more thematically developed in Hitchcock's *Shadow of a Doubt* (1943) than it is in Lang's more literal, realist anti-Nazi film, *Hangmen Also Die* (1943).

Here I assume that the impact of World War II on human civilization is the central hallmark of modernity. If the impact of the Industrial Revolution of the late eighteenth and nineteenth centuries produced the clearest experiences of a new form of living that we know as modernity—large cities with ghettos, industrial pollution, a destructive form of warfare capable of using mechanical reproduction to produce mass forms of death—then World War II is the ultimate articulation of the negative impact of modernity. Its moment finds a way to purge those cities, sometimes of their ghettos, using Fordist modes of efficiency in its concentration camps, but more generally with firebombs or, later, atomic ones. It invents industrial pollution with—from the point of view of human experience—an infinite half-life, in the form of nuclear waste. And finally, the atomic bomb takes the mechanical operation of the Browning automatic rifle (bursts of death, which the "machine-gun" is able to replicate quickly) and reproduces it at the atomic level, in the guise of the chain reaction. The cinema, at least, merely used the machine-gun technology to repeat abusive *images.*

World War II produces a geographic fragmentation in the experience of modernity. Both European countries and the United States perpetrated abuses of modernity—dropping the bomb on Hiroshima, firebombing Dresden, building and using the concentration camps—but the United States was never modernity's victim. Thus, a careful definition of World War II as the articulation of modernity would need to define the United States as a protected site from which a postmodernity would be reborn in the postwar period. In terms of individual artists' lived experiences, travel from Europe to America in the 1930s could be seen as a journey away from modernity.

This last point is an important link between Alfred Hitchcock, who arrived in 1939 to make films with David O. Selznick, and Fritz Lang, who arrived in 1936 in exile from the Nazis. Each of these artists, partially because of his different reasons for coming to America, but partly for much more profound reasons, responded differently to geographical dislocation. Hitchcock became a public celebrity and a well-respected filmmaker, among both the public and the critics. Lang was also esteemed among certain critics but never achieved Hitchcock's public celebrity. Although Hitchcock made movies into the 1970s in New Hollywood, Lang's flight back to Europe (and then unproductive return to Hollywood to die) was initiated by the collapse of classical Hollywood, perhaps best seen in the demise of RKO in the mid-1950s, to which he contributed, but also allegorized in films such as *While the City Sleeps* (1956) and *Beyond a Reasonable Doubt*.

Hitchcock came from Britain on the strength of a set of prewar films about international espionage in which a vague Germanic threat looms over Britain: *The Man Who Knew Too Much* (1934), *The 39 Steps* (1935), *Secret Agent* (1936), *Sabotage* (1936), and *The Lady Vanishes* (1938). After the war, Hitchcock would go on to create a set of equally direct films about the significance of World War II, including *Notorious* (1946), about postwar Nazis in hiding, and *I Confess* (1953), a film about a Canadian soldier who becomes a priest to atone for his sins and who later finds himself framed by a German refugee whom he had befriended. During the war, however, Hitchcock's films are strikingly disconnected from current events. Having mastered the American filmmaking idiom immediately, Hitchcock's wartime films rely on allegorical abstraction and experimentation, the most famous example of which is *Lifeboat* (1944). At first glance, *Saboteur* (1942) might be reduced to an uninteresting application of British cinema's anti-Nazi suspense thriller method to the American milieu, but its outsider's representation of the American condition, this time via a bizarre flight through the American Southwest, is quite remarkable.

However, it is *Shadow of a Doubt* that best defines Hitchcock's wartime depiction of modernity. The film concerns a psychotic who murders women for their money and is on the run. He comes to the small town of Santa Rosa, California, to hide from the police with the family of his beloved niece. Both the killer and the niece are named Charlie, much to the delight of psychoanalytic critics, who read the film brilliantly as a metaphor for incest. I am more interested, however, in a central moment in the film, where young Charlie (Teresa Wright) confronts her Uncle Charlie (Joseph Cotten) about her suspicions. He takes her by the arm and, during a busy time at night downtown, steers her into a sleazy nightclub. There, surrounded by American soldiers carousing, Uncle Charlie scornfully tells her:

> You go through your ordinary little day, and at night you sleep your untroubled, ordinary little sleep, filled with peaceful, stupid dreams. And I brought you nightmares. Or did I, or was it a silly, inexpert, little lie? You live in a dream. You're a sleepwalker, blind. How do you know what the world is like? Do you know the world is a foul sty? Do you know if you ripped the fronts off houses, you'd find swine. The world's a hell. What does it matter what happens in it? Wake up, Charlie. Use your wits. Learn something.

Young Charlie storms out, pursued by Uncle Charlie. He will be punished in the end, pushed off a train and run over for his murderous transgressions, but this small-town comedy turned nightmare reveals its allegorical substrate at this one fascinating moment. Uncle Charlie rips the front off of young Charlie's world, exposing the horrors of World War II, which is everywhere else in this film repressed. The appearance of the carousing soldiers at the beginning and end of the sequence indicates that Hitchcock is in on the satire as well.

Uncle Charlie's ripping of fronts from houses is, of course, the theatrical method of Naturalism, the theater's primary late-nineteenth-century shift to modernity. In 1879, Henrik Ibsen's *A Doll House* brought modernity into the high theater. In that play, we see the inner workings of an outwardly normal middle-class household: Torvald is a successful banker, and his wife, Nora, flits about the household like a bird, directing servants to take care of the children. Ibsen's Naturalist method, like Uncle Charlie's, uses the artifice of fourth-wall realism to show us the swine behind the illusion. For Torvald is a hypocrite, and punishes Nora for having violated in the backstory the contract of True Womanhood to get the money necessary for him to recover from a life-threatening illness. When this repressed past returns in the form of Krogstad, a blackmailer, Torvald is revealed to be a coward. Nora, seeing the truth of her life for the first time, leaves her husband, headed for parts unknown. In the famous last moment of the play, Nora leaves and slams the door on Torvald.

For all practical purposes, *Shadow of a Doubt,* via Uncle Charlie's speech in the 'Til Two Club, presents itself as a World War II allegory that relies on the theatrical birth of modernity. In order to represent the truth, one needs to rip off the fronts of houses and study the swine scientifically. *Shadow of a Doubt* is not sure whether to indict or applaud its Krogstad, Uncle Charlie, because in the midst of a global apocalypse, it is not at all clear that Uncle Charlie is wrong in his immoral assessment. And for all practical purposes, this is the modernity in which we live. In a world of the atomic bomb, in which individual leaders can extinguish life on the planet as a result of modernity's major triumph, technology, what is our proper moral stance? In no minor way, this dilemma is why modernity produces a major crisis in falseness and the instability of knowledge.

During World War II, Hitchcock captured the allegorical significance of this crisis in ways that Lang's films did not. As Gunning argues, the German modernist émigré Lang was forced to smuggle an allegorical method into the Hollywood cinema, both before the war (1938's *You and Me,* a Brechtian musical about criminals) and after it (1953's *Rancho Notorious,* a Brechtian western about revenge). During the war, however, he made the most direct—that is to say, the least modernist and least allegorical—film of his career, *Hangmen Also Die,* ironically with the fount of theatrical modernism, Bertolt Brecht himself, as his screenwriter. *Hangmen Also Die* is, on paper, the most important film ever made concerning cinema and modernity, with a highly allegorical filmmaker in charge of a script by the most important modernist playwright. And yet, for whatever reason, *Hangmen Also Die* is an astonishingly conventional film, without any of the thematic complexity of Uncle Charlie's "swine" speech.

The film begins with a literal engagement with the horrors of Nazi modernity and the simplicity of simple folk. Gestapo agents arrest a working-class Czech taxi driver for letting his motor run while waiting for a fare (and thus wasting precious Nazi gasoline). It turns out that the taxi driver is the escape driver for a Resistance operation. The

Resistance, however, quickly enlists the aid of a horse carriage driver who also works for them. This driver succeeds in keeping the film's central female protagonist out of the hands of the Nazis.

Here we have the World War II equivalent of 1909's *The Lonely Villa,* a Victorian D. W. Griffith film. As famously analyzed by Gunning in "Heard Over the Phone" (1991), technology in that film is an evil that fails consistently. When a man drives away from his wife and children, tramps attack the house and quickly take the bullets out of the wife's gun. She is able to alert the husband by telephone, but the tramps then cut the phone line. Predictably, the husband's car breaks down, forcing him to enlist the aid of a gypsy's horse, which he rides to a successful last-minute rescue. The conflation between two registers of modernity, the crisis over True Womanhood and the fallibility of technology, is repeated in *Hangmen Also Die.* The female resistance fighter is aided by a network of men protecting her from Nazis, who are clearly evil because they are obsessed with gasoline to fuel their blitzkrieg. Conversely, the Resistance relies on horses because they represent the Polish cavalry that the blitzkrieg tried unsuccessfully to immolate.

The European "Shop Guys" Make the Movies

Quite a different picture of modernity emerges in a comparison between Hitchcock's *Vertigo* (1958) and Lang's *Beyond a Reasonable Doubt.* In *Vertigo* the instability of knowledge is famously housed within the narrative structure. When Hitchcock cuts to the flashback midway through the film, revealing that Judy Barton (Kim Novak) is in fact Madeleine Elster and that the first half of the film was lying to us, a major disruption has occurred to the classical Hollywood cinema, something that might account for both the film's initial failure and its subsequent importance in academic film studies. However, Lang's film is even more systematically radical: a heroic anti–death penalty crusader is revealed in the last moments of the film to have actually committed a murder and is thus sentenced to death. Catherine Russell (1995) finds the anti-Aristotelian twist in Lang's last American film to be significant, and she builds a critical method for understanding classical Hollywood cinema's linkage to modernist European art cinema. Coining the term, "narrative mortality," to describe this process, Russell argues that the method of *Beyond a Reasonable Doubt*—like the more familiar modernisms of the New Wave cinemas of Godard and Oshima—"mortifies" classical representation, exposing a radical crisis, an inability to achieve certainty in epistemological systems such as filmic representation.

Ultimately, Lang's allegorical and Hitchcock's classical realist languages are at odds and offer two distinct strategies for a filmic critique of American culture. We must connect such representational practices in American cinema to a larger intellectual climate of the 1950s, one fueled by the devastation of World War II and of particular importance to European émigrés.

As demonstrated by Gunning, an appropriate theoretical grid for reading Lang's allegorical cinematic strategy is the German sociological work of figures like Walter Benjamin and Siegfried Kracauer. We can seek to link the work of cultural theorists to film practitioners, to ask whether the differential immigrant experiences of Frankfurt School successes like Adorno and of those who never quite found their niche in American culture like Kracauer offer a productive grid for assessing Hitchcock's successful negotiation of American film culture and Lang's unsuccessful attempt to convert allegorical filmmaking into economic success. In the latter half of his career Lang bitterly detested the success afforded to Hitchcock and denied to him.

Out of this historical reality, and out of this bitterness, Lang invented an allegorical method that defines differently the experience of modernity. In his Benjaminian reading, Gunning positions Lang's films as allegories of modernity: these films allegorize the criminals (Dr. Mabuse in *Dr. Mabuse, der Spieler* [1922], the serial killer in *M* [1931]), who terrorize the city, as figures standing for the human experience of modernity more generally. Hitchcock's method relies far more on classical realism. *The Wrong Man* (1956), a pseudo-documentary, places us in the deeply unsettling position of a man who is falsely accused of robbery and can do little to clear his name. This paranoiac experience certainly relates to Lang films like *M* and *Beyond a Reasonable Doubt*. *The Wrong Man*, however, still relies on straightforward narrative structure and film style to tell its story (complete with an end-of-the-film title card to inform us that this wrong man was eventually released from prison). *Beyond a Reasonable Doubt*, on the other hand, shatters its contract with us: when the film destroys our paranoiac identification with its hero, revealing that he really is the murderer we were assured he was not, we are left with a modern filmic experience that is unstable and untrustworthy.

A comparison of these two directors demands an examination of the British and American careers of Hitchcock on the one hand and the German and American careers of Lang on the other. Indeed, for each director such a comparative approach has been one of the dominant modes of criticism of their work. But Lang's and Hitchcock's response to dislocation is descriptive of a larger cultural movement. In particular, the difference between their experiences cross-checks profitably with certain critics of modernity: for Lang, members of the Frankfurt School, including Adorno, Benjamin, Kracauer, and Horkheimer; for Hitchcock, the American sociologists of postwar America, such as Daniel Bell (author of *The End of Ideology*), David Riesman (co-author of *The Lonely Crowd*), and William H. Whyte (author of *The Organization Man*). The connection between Alfred Hitchcock and 1950s American sociology has been fairly well established in film literature. Corber, for instance, builds a devastating critique of the homophobia and political centrism of both the "Cold War Liberals" (such as Bell and Riesman) and such Hitchcock films as *Strangers on a Train* (1950) and *Vertigo*. Steven Cohan (1997) connects *North by Northwest* and *The Man in the Grey Flannel Suit* (1956), using Whyte's book. The connection is established more generally in Peter Biskind's *Seeing Is Believing* (1983), which uses Cold War Liberalism to formulate a grid for American film politics, pitting the centrists against the extremists. Remarkably, Hitchcock's films are glaringly absent in Biskind's scheme, showing up only with the collapse of 1950s ideology in his conclusion, a study of *Psycho* (1960). Lang is also barely present in Biskind's analysis of the conservative vigilantism of *The Big Heat*. Astonishingly, writing outside of the film studies tradition, Biskind treats both Lang and Hitchcock as conservatives.

Cohan's wry use of *The Man in the Grey Flannel Suit* to read *North by Northwest*—a film about "the spy in the grey flannel suit"—posits Hitchcock's cinema as being in tune with the Cold War Liberal sociologists, as opposed to the Frankfurt School critics, who were obsessed with the lasting and permanent traumas of World War II. Like Lang, Adorno and Horkheimer were only partially successful in America, but like him, too, they significantly returned to Europe in the late

1950s; Benjamin tragically never made it to America; Kracauer, like Lang, struggled when he did. On the other hand, both Hitchcock and the postwar American sociologists found a quite different America, one in which the "end of ideology," to use Daniel Bell's parodic anti-Marxist phrase, was within grasp, an America flawed by capitalism but ultimately redeemable via centrist intellectualism. Adorno and Horkheimer's famous treatise on the "Dialectic of Enlightenment" offers a response to their sorrowful discovery that the abuses of fascism are present in yet another form in American capitalism. Awakened to the same sad vision, Lang's films are allegorical presentations of the lasting traumatic effects of World War II. Lang criticism has gravitated toward theorists like Benjamin for understanding the filmmaker's project. For his part, Hitchcock offered a more hopeful and less theoretically bleak vision of 1950s American culture.

The Horror, the Horror

Lang bitterly resented his postwar position in Hollywood as the inventor of the thriller but its current second-banana B-level practitioner. *While the City Sleeps* represents the mid-1950s Oedipal drama in its baldest form. At the beginning of the film, a serial killer enters the apartment of a beautiful woman taking a bath and murders her. When detectives come to investigate, they find that the psychopath has written on a bathtub tile, "Ask Mother." A similar allusion riddles *Psycho,* the film that serves as the crucial break between classical Hollywood and New Hollywood cinema. The traditional horror film was about a threatening Europe (the castles of Dracula and Frankenstein), whereas *Psycho* shows that horror lies in the American home, with a small-town boy who murders his mother and stuffs her, using his skills as a taxidermist.

The legacy of this mode of filmmaking is clear enough. It would be impossible to imagine 1970s slasher films, whose psychodynamics are so well studied by Carol Clover in *Men, Women and Chainsaws* (1992), without *Psycho* as their intertextual source. *Halloween* (1978) is a textbook reconstruction of it, as is Stanley Kubrick's *The Shining* (1980). And yet this comparison between *While the City Sleeps* and *Psycho* also reveals more about the nature of modernity in the films of Lang and Hitchcock. The slasher film retreats into suburban locations

(*A Nightmare on Elm Street* [1984]) and rural ones (*The Texas Chain-saw Massacre* [1974]), locations that are predicated on Marion Crane's retreat from the city of Phoenix to the rural Bates Motel. For Lang, however, there is never any possibility of retreat from the city. The Mabuse films (*Der Spieler; The Testament of Dr. Mabuse* [1933]; *The Thousand Eyes of Dr. Mabuse* [1960]) all the way through to *While the City Sleeps* offer a definitional treatment of modernity that is dominated by the city as the only form of social life possible after industrialization. It may seem strange that Lang, living almost as long as Hitchcock did, stopped making films after 1960; but *Psycho*'s influence helps to show that Hitchcock was able to adapt to the new Hollywood, whereas for Lang there was no space left. Modernity in a Lang film is Dachau (after all, a brand-new city built in a rural area to accommodate the multitudes kidnapped from urban ghettos) and Hiroshima, on a personal scale, and by 1960 we had ceased being able to face this troubling fact.

This conclusion seems especially tragic in light of cinema and culture at the beginning of the twenty-first century. McGurl's study of *King Kong*, written in the late 1990s, ends with a fascinating application to the first World Trade Center attack as well as the Oklahoma City bombing. He conceives of these assaults on skyscrapers as iconic attacks on modernity, by disaffected Arabs and working-class paranoid Americans, respectively. Thus, our postmodernity turns out to be driven by questions, irresolutions, and vectors of mid-century modernity, as faced in different ways by the films of Hitchcock and Lang. Modernity's crisis in knowledge partly stems from its inability to see what devastation it has caused. As the government has returned to an updated style of World War II warfare, Hollywood cinema has returned to classical genre stability, leaving responses to—indictments of—modernity behind. Lang's cinema, but not Hitchcock's, I think, stands as the antidote for this madness.

CAPITAL ADVANCES

PERFORMING MODERNITY AND GENDER IN THE 1930s
Gwendolyn Audrey Foster

In many films of the 1930s and 1940s, signs of class difference (poverty and opulence) are exhibited, performed, and foregrounded in women who pass across barriers or make melodramatic sacrifices in order that their children might effectively "class-pass." Especially typical are *Forbidden* (1932), *The Sin of Madelon Claudet* (1931), *Baby Face* (1933), *Marked Woman* (1937), and *Stella Dallas* (1937). In these films, performing gender and performing a "classed" modernism are inextricably linked to the narrative, to the characters, and to the world they inhabit. Indeed, one might argue that modernism is itself defined (through the sets and costumes) as elite, classed, and sleekly designed as well as gendered in these films. We find women having "designs" upon wealth, and harboring the Modernist American dream of moving up in class status. Modernist principles of mechanization are implied in myriad ritualized acts of self-stylization performed against a backdrop of sleek, classically designed period costumes and accessories, as much as they are juxtaposed against the opposing constructs of realism, sexism, and classism.

Crossing class boundaries was itself problematic to the censors of the day. As Lea Jacobs writes, "The M[otion] P[icture] P[roducers and] D[irectors] A[ssociation] repeatedly warned producers that the heroine's rise in class, particularly in *Back Street* (1932), would make a film vulnerable to public criticism" (1987, 108). The motion picture Production Code, as enforced in the mid-1930s, seemed to be more than obsessed with the power of motion pictures to appeal to and perhaps disrupt the masses or multitudes of every class. Interesting is how the code sidesteps labels such as lower, middle, and upper class. Instead, the framers (notably Will Hays) divide the class structure into three categories: "mature/immature, developed/undeveloped and law-abiding/criminal" (Doherty 1999, 349). In a special section of an appendix to the MPPDA code, the writers take up the "special moral obligations" for motion pictures in the area of class, given their undifferentiated audience. This section repeatedly emphasizes the mobility of film, its ability to reach "every class" and to influence "places unpenetrated by other forms of art," and the difficulty of producing films "intended for only certain classes of people." It continues (italics in the original document):

The motion picture has special *Moral obligations*:
(A) Most arts appeal to the mature. This art appeals at once *to every class*—mature, immature, developed, undeveloped, law-abiding, criminal. Music has its grades for different classes; so has literature and drama. This art of the motion picture, combining as it does the two fundamental appeals of looking at a picture and listening to a story, at once reaches every class of society.
(B) Because of the mobility of a film and the ease of picture distribution, and because of the possibility of duplicating positives in large quantities, this art *reaches places* unpenetrated by other forms of art.
(C) Because of these two facts, it is difficult to produce films intended for only *certain classes of people*. The exhibitor's theatres are built for the masses, for the cultivated and the rude, mature and immature, self-restrained and inflammatory, young and old, law-respecting and criminal. Films, unlike books and music, can with difficulty be confined to certain selected groups.

(D) The latitude given to film material cannot, in consequence,
      be as wide as the latitude given to *book material*.
(Production Code, qtd. in Doherty 1999, 349)

Thus, the code alludes to the power of modern cinema to break with traditions designed to preserve the constituency of the leisure classes by admitting even the immature, undeveloped, and criminal element into their world. As Thorstein Veblen argued in 1899, class-passing before widespread film exhibition was meant to occur only by selective admission:

> The constituency of the leisure class is kept up by a continual selective process, whereby the individuals and lines of descent that are eminently fitted for an aggressive pecuniary competition are withdrawn from the lower classes. In order to reach the upper levels the aspirant must have, not only a fair average complement of the pecuniary aptitudes, but he must have these gifts in such an eminent degree as to overcome very material difficulties that stand in the way of his ascent. Barring accidents, the *nouveaux arrivés* are a picked body. (1994, 144)

But, as Veblen also noted, "tenacity and consistency of aim" were also distinguished qualities of the "successful predatory barbarian" (1994, 145) or class-passer.

Class-Passing and Predation

Veblen's description was never truer than in the modern era. Perhaps no one in the cinema has quite as much tenacity, single-mindedness, and consistency of aim as the main character of *Baby Face*, Lily, played brilliantly by Barbara Stanwyck. *Baby Face* concerns a "gold-digging" young woman from a small town who moves up the economic ladder by using her brains and her sexuality. As the film's tag line notes, "She climbed the ladder of success—wrong by wrong." Thomas Doherty dubs the film "the most notorious of the sex-in-the-workplace vice films of the pre-Code era" (1999, 134). Jeanine Basinger sees *Baby Face* as "a classic example of a movie in which a woman climbs over men to the top" (1993, 266). Most readings of the film understandably emphasize Lily's use of *sexuality* to overcome obstacles and rise to the top, but what assures her success is her blatant embrace of *modernism,* evident in her brazen capitalist predatory zeal. In addition, Stanwyck takes to the role with a gusto that is contagious; she enjoys herself thoroughly, and isn't the slightest bit ashamed of the human mechanics behind Lily's rise to power. The audience easily identifies with her struggle to get ahead in the midst of the Depression, particularly when she beds, and then discards, a young John Wayne (in the role of mid-level executive Jimmy McCoy Jr.) on her way to the top of the corporate ladder.

Lily embraces the "hardening process" of the big city, a consequence alluded to in the MPPDA censorship code: "Small communities, remote from sophistication and from the hardening process which often takes place in the ethical and moral standards of larger cities, are easily and readily reached by any sort of film" (qtd. in Doherty 1999, 350). Lily not only seduces men on her way to the top; she seems literally to conquer the modern city skyscraper floor by floor: the camera cuts to an exterior of the Art Deco "Gotham Trust Company" each time she successfully manages to get a better job through seduction, flirtation, and changed appearance, all in an embrace of American modernism. Lily is embodied by the modern skyscraper; it is in turn emblematic of her hardening process, her quick-change class-passing from a woman trapped with trampy, old-fashioned clothing and hair to the dazzling, bleached blonde, Deco-gowned modern woman she becomes. In forging her identity, Lily in turn embodies the problematic emphasis on capitalism, luxury, and Art Deco we find in modernity. As Mike O'Mahoney writes, "Despite this utopian emphasis on luxury, Art Deco emerged in an era of economic slumps and depressions, social strife, hunger marches and the political battle between Communism and Fascism. It was against this troubled and traumatic backdrop that Art Deco forged its own identity" (2000, 6).

Lily's traumatic and troubled backstory includes being forced to turn tricks by her father, who runs a speakeasy. No wonder she has no interest in the past. She moves forward with the passion and tenacity of a luxury freight train. She makes fun of the snobbery of the old-fashioned Emily Post. She's only interested in the future, her future. Her friend Adolf Cragg (Alphonse Ethier), a German mentor, encourages her to read Friedrich Nietzsche. "You must be a master, not a slave," he tells her. But her embrace of the future betrays her class origins, for, as Paul Fussell reminds us, "Classy people never deal with the future. That's for vulgarians like traffic engineers, planners and inventors" (1992, 72). Instead, old money characters are interested in what Veblen terms "veneration of the archaic" (1994, 72).

Lily has *no* interest in studying Nietzsche as if he were a classical antiquity; instead, she parlays his ideas into modernist capitalist ideology. Her class-passing is dependent upon trampling over anyone in her way. Indeed, it was perhaps her single-minded aspiration for wealth and luxury that was most highly problematic to the censors. It was in reference to *Baby Face* that the MPPDA was concerned about the heroine's rise in class and public criticism. According to Lea Jacobs, the administrator of the Production Code, Joseph I. Breen, in particular "seems to have agreed with his predecessors that class rise presented a problem for the [film] industry" (1987, 108). But Jacobs soon dismisses her own evidence, concluding that "from the perspective of the MPPDA, showing a character become rich was not, in and of itself, a point of difficulty" (1987, 109). Instead, she highlights as problematic the inherent attractiveness of the immoral gold-digger, "insofar as her movement in class united a certain image of money and power with illicit sexuality" (1987, 109). Nevertheless, given the language and ideology of the code, it seems to me plausible to emphasize the censors' class jitters with regard to a script and a film that is preoccupied with class rise.

Class opposition, breaking the borders of class, whether in gangster films or gold-digging films, brings about the specter of modernist possibilities for mobility and, at the very least, a critique of the class/gender system. As Chuck Kleinhans writes: "When we look at the emergence of the modern melodrama about 250 years ago (the bourgeois domestic melodrama, to be more precise), today everyone can clearly understand its class nature as drama of and for a specific class, poised against another class: a cultural-ideological weapon in a political and economic struggle that changed history forever" (1991, 198). Not all critics agree. Charles Eckert, who sees class position as only temporal or fleeting in films such as *Marked Woman*, calls into relief the sharp delineation of the spectacle of class opposition: "The city with its pent-houses and limousines can function as reified capitalism; wittiness can be allied to the manipulations of financiers; all of this can be given high resolution by the use of visual coding—skyscrapers, tuxedos, one-hundred-dollar bills; but every thrust of class or economic protest is sufficiently blunted to avoid breaking the skin" (1991, 217).

I disagree. *Marked Woman* is a perfect example of outright puncturing of the skin of class. This feminist classic is centered around the struggles of a group of prostitutes led by the central figure, Mary Dwight (Bette Davis), who works in a sleazy clip joint in order to send her sister, Betty (Jane Bryan), to boarding school. Betty, who is completely unaware of her sister's occupation and her own complicity in the situation, arrives unannounced for a visit. At Mary's insistence, her roommates pretend to be fashion models. But Betty ends up class-passing downward when she goes to a party and is drawn to the allure of the nightlife of gangsters. She wears one of the girls' swanky Deco dresses and is impressed by the Deco nightclub and penthouse of Johnny Vanning (Eduardo Cianelli), a vicious mob lord based on Charles "Lucky" Luciano, the Depression-era mafioso who ruled by terrorism. Meanwhile, as Betty gets sucked into the glamour of the nightlife, Mary agrees to testify against Vanning. Betty finally figures out that her sister is really a clip joint B-girl and part-time prostitute. She is suspended between class statuses when the newspapers carry the story and she feels unable to return to school. In her anger and despair Betty lashes out at her sister and goes off to a party, where she is killed by Vanning as she struggles to evade his sexual advances. It is her downward class-passing that brings about her murder: Vanning accuses her of putting on airs when she does not submit to his come-ons. He punches her for "putting on an act," and she falls down a short flight of stairs to her death. When Mary learns of her sister's death, she vows to get Vanning. She confronts him, his thugs beat her, and she is marked with a horrible gash on her face in the form of an "X," a sign that she is the boss's enemy.

Without her beauty, viciously beaten and recovering in the hospital, Mary finally decides to cooperate with the district attorney, David Graham (Humphrey Bogart). She vows to testify against Vanning and persuades her roommates to testify as well. After Vanning is convicted, Graham, who has demonstrated an interest in Mary, approaches her on the courtroom stairs. One might expect an impossibly happy ending: Bogart and Davis sharing a romantic kiss and a wedding proposal. But this pre-Code film gives us a realistic ending, one that clearly raises the specter of class difference. After Mary congratulates him on his victory in court, Graham responds:

Graham: You're the one who should be getting the congratulations, not me.

Mary: Uh uh—I don't want them.

Graham: But where will you go?

Mary: Places.

Graham: But what will you do?

Mary: Oh, I'll get along, I always have.

Graham: Mary, I'd like to help you.

Mary: (*curious . . . and interested*) Why?

Graham: Why . . . because I . . . because I think you've got a break comin' to you.

Mary: (*still curious*) And?

Graham: And I'd like to see that you get it.

Mary: (*suddenly dejected*) What's the use of stalling? We both live in different worlds, and that's the way we've got to leave it.

Graham: I don't want to leave it that way. I once said to you that if you ever started helping yourself I'd be the first one to go to bat for you, and that still goes. No matter what you do or where you go, we'll meet again.

Mary: Goodbye, Graham. I'll be seeing you.

In declaring that she and Graham live in different worlds, Mary recognizes that for the fallen woman class-passing is nearly impossible. After the conversation, Mary joins the other women who have testified. Blues swell on the soundtrack as they are surrounded by mist from studio fog machines. The bravery and sisterhood with which they face the world is truly compelling. Eckert calls *Marked Woman* "vintage *cinéma brut*"; but, as mentioned above, he regards the film's class opposition as limited. I assert instead that the film's ending is powerful *agit-prop*. Just because the women accept their fate, it does not necessarily follow that the audience will accept it as well. In fact, this grim ending, which starkly points to the realities of gender and class in the Depression era, is more likely to provoke the audience to call for change to the status quo than a falsely romantic heterotopic union might do.

Marked Woman takes aim at the exploitative capitalist patriarchal system as it also takes aim at modernism. If modernism comes at the expense of human life, what is the point of fast cars, huge Deco penthouses, luxurious gowns, champagne, and progress? There are no easy answers to this question. Instead, the film insists that the burden of class struggle lies at the feet of the audience, who must speak out just as did the women who testified against Vanning.

Marked Woman, like *Baby Face*, is a damning film. It damns the audience and manifestly identifies, in the spirit of Theodor Adorno, the manner in which the masses are oppressed by the culture industry. "If the masses have been unjustly reviled from above as masses," Adorno writes, "the culture industry is not among the least responsible for making them into masses and then despising them, while obstructing the emancipation for which human beings are as ripe as the productive forces of the epoch permit" (2003, 60).

Films like *Baby Face* and *Marked Woman* do not abide by the code of the culture industry. They emphasize the *trauma* implicit in the modernist paradigm, a trauma steeped in economic strife, classism, sexism, ageism, and the perils of class-passing, set against the two-sided backdrop of squalor versus luxury and glamour. Fallen-women films of the pre-Code era exposed the dangers of glamour and luxury. This is not to suggest that there is not a certain ambivalence running through these films in their sociopolitical messages. *Baby Face*, for example, suffers from a tacked-on ending that conforms to Production Code pressure: in an about-face, Lily instantly abandons her selfish ways when she hears of her lover's financial ruin, and runs to his side to offer him her jewels and thus save him from bankruptcy. It is such an unbelievable Hollywood ending that some female spectators simply refuse to accept, remember, or acknowledge it. Betsy Israel, writing in *Bachelor Girl: The Secret History of Single Women in the Twentieth Century*, omits it in her summary of the film:

In *Baby Face* (1933), a heartless-woman masterpiece, Barbara Stanwyck, a speakeasy bartender, puts on a decent dress and works her way up within a corporation, starting on the first floor as a filing clerk. We know immediately that she's an operator. She casually asks a colleague how she got *such* a great perm. She asks another one where she got the *fabulous* shoes. She shows up with the perm and identical shoes the next day. Soon she's headed up the corporate skyscraper. On each new floor (accounting, mortgages, et cetera) she's transformed: better clothes and hairstyles, an entirely new professional manner. At each stop she lures then abruptly drops at least one ardent lover, although one man she keeps around—a strategist and booster, who's advised her and helped finance her climb. Finally we see her at the top, draped in one of those sparkly floor-length gowns so many thirties heroines wear just to swish around the house. In this key scene, the lover and friend charges into her office. He needs cash. He's desperate. And he asks her point blank for some jewels he once helped her buy. She stares at him. Thinks. And then she delivers a heartless-woman manifesto: "I have to think of myself. I've gone through a lot to get those things. My life has been bitter and hard. I'm not like other women. All the gentleness and kindness in me has been killed. All I've got is those things. Without them, I'd be nothing. . . . I'd have to go back to what I was! No! I won't do it, I tell you, I won't." And she doesn't. (2002, 157)

But in truth, she does. As Basinger accurately points out, "Throughout this film, there has been no indication that Stanwyck is the woman she becomes in the final five minutes" (1993, 270). Basinger is perplexed, as audiences must have been, by the abrupt departure:

What we have seen and the way we are asked to view it are not completely matched. In the end, of course, Stanwyck becomes a "real woman." She has wept, given back the jewelry, and accepted her position of slave, not master. Love will not be her career. The ultimate irony of this astonishing movie is the very ending. Brent and Stanwyck are back in Erie, Pennsylvania, in the same factory slums she began in. The final image of the movie is the identical skyline of the coalfields that was visible in the first moments of the film. Stanwyck has progressed exactly nowhere. (1993, 270)

Perhaps Israel can be forgiven her lapse of accuracy, given the tacked-on nature of the end. More important, however, is that Israel's more feminist rendering could easily have been the favored method of spectatorship of the film when it was released. Audiences co-produce the meanings of a text, and women audiences are perfectly capable of constructing (or reconstituting) their own endings. When I show this film to my classes at the University of Nebraska, they, too, have a way of disposing with the ending, easily linking it to censorship. In paper after paper, students say they simply prefer to disregard the false "happy" ending, just as they embrace the ending of *Marked Woman* as a strong feminist critique of gender and class, and disagree with Charles Eckert's estimation of the film as politically benign displaced opposition.

Mothers at War

When it comes to moral complexity, feminist ambiguity, and messages of class-passing, contemporary students are most frustrated by the maternal melodrama. This absolutely twisted genre manages to both value and devalue women, particularly mothers. As Linda Williams asserts, "The device of devaluing and debasing the actual figure of the mother while sanctifying the institution of motherhood is typical of the 'woman's film' in general and the subgenre of the maternal melodrama in particular" (1991, 308). Christian Viviani suggests that the maternal melodrama can be experienced on different planes: "In sum, the maternal melo plays—sometimes with a certain cunning—on two levels. It seems outwardly attached to the old moral code by making the mother pay for her 'sin.' But it implicitly condemns the old system of values represented by a sterile or unhappy couple, which is obliged to adopt the bastard child in order to offer up the image of a traditional family" (1987, 94). Jeanine Basinger, however, sees the possibility for a more radical and certainly more subversive reading of the maternal melodrama:

> A movie plot in which a woman has to give up her child provided a two-way street of response for viewers who were mothers, perhaps feeling burdened with the difficulties of raising their own children. A woman on film who sacrifices a child suffers and

is ultimately punished, reassuring the women watching. At the same time, the woman on film who gives up a child suddenly has freedom. Often, she finds a better life of riches, success, adventure, and, in the end, even an opportunity for love with another man or the same man who caused her problem in the first place. The viewer could watch a woman get free of the burden of mothering without having to feel guilty about it. (1993, 395)

Amazingly formulaic, the maternal melodrama is nevertheless effective. The list of remarkable maternal melos includes *Forbidden,* in which Barbara Stanwyck falls for an unhappily married attorney (Adolph Menjou). She gives birth to his child and allows his wife to adopt it, thus ensuring the child will effectively class-pass into a world of wealth and security. Similarly, in Edgar Selwyn's *The Sin of Madelon Claudet,* Helen Hayes is an unwed mother forced into prostitution to raise her son. Kay Francis covers for her daughter Margaret Lindsay, who accidentally kills a man, in Robert Florey's *House on 56th Street* (1933). She similarly gives up her life for her child Sybil Jason in Mervyn LeRoy's *I Found Stella Parrish* (1935). Ruth Chatterton and Gladys George make a similar sacrifice in different versions of *Madame X* (1929, 1937); unaware that she is his mother, the son ultimately defends the heroine in court. In *Frisco Jenny* (1932) Chatterton allows herself to be executed rather than jeopardize her son's social status as district attorney (he convicts her and allows the execution). And as the eponymous Stella Dallas, Barbara Stanwyck gives up all rights to her daughter Laurel (Anne Shirley) so that Laurel can experience the privileges of status and social class.

All these mothers wage war on the class system. They are strong role models of martyrdom and valiant heroes with whom women could identify. Because they suffer, many feminist critics and contemporary audiences cannot stomach their martyrdom. But it is in their suffering that they transcend gender roles as a class. If we compare their suffering with that of male heroes in war movies, for example, these mothers acquit themselves equally as figures to be admired, if not emulated. If we can but suspend our own moral outrage at their endless and complete suffering, we can find examples of some of the strongest women on celluloid. We must not doubly punish them because of their gender. I insist that if men had comparable roles, they would be celebrated and held up as exemplars of archetypal heroism. The actions of these women condemn the old system of values that gender discrimination and class oppression depend upon. It is not so much that I enjoy watching them in their child-free states, enjoying bachelor adventures aboard luxury liners or skirting the boundaries of expected female norms of behavior. Rather, I value their iconic status as strong role models who outwit the system in the best ways they can. Most pointedly, they attack and subvert the social class system, and if we read them within a different context, by their own terms, *they win*.

Stella Dallas is triumphant when she walks away from her child as she weds into a socially connected family. Min (Marie Dressler) is similarly triumphant in *Min and Bill* (1930) when she walks away, bound for prison, knowing that she has beaten the system. Her adopted daughter Nancy (Dorothy Jordan) will never know that her real mother was a drunken prostitute, and that Min murdered her to protect Nancy. Ruth Chatterton's attorney son Dan Reynolds (Donald Cook) will never know that his mother in *Frisco Jenny* chooses not to fight a murder charge in order to protect his innocence and thus assure his prospects for mayoral office. Barbara Stanwyck is a tower of strength as she walks away from her child in *Forbidden*. When Vergie Winters (Ann Harding) falls in love with a married politician, John Shadwell (John Boles), in *The Life of Vergie Winters* (1934), she refuses to hinder his career, even when she becomes pregnant. Vergie is content with a backstreet romance, while their class-passing daughter, Joan, grows up in ignorance of her birth mother's true identity. The class-passing children of Madelon Claudet, Stella Parish, Vergie Winters, Madame Blanche, Madame X, and all the Madames X will not ever have to face the grinding mill of poverty, sexual abuse, neglect, and race, gender, and class oppression suffered by their mothers. Neither will they ever really know how their mothers triumphed as heroines in the American class system of oppression, but audiences will and do.

On a more symbolic level, while aware of the triumph of these celluloid mothers, the audience also becomes distinctly aware of the realities of the class system and its supporting structures, such as racism, gender discrimination, and the marriage system. Depression-era escapist fare offered the proletariat a diversion from thinking about disturbing political issues. bell hooks notes that consumer culture does the cultural work of silencing discussion about class. But class does matter, as she insists:

> Consumer culture silences working people and the middle classes. They are busy buying or planning to buy. Although their fragile hold on economic self-sufficiency is slipping, they still cling to the dream of a class-free society where everyone can make it to the top. They are afraid to face the significance of dwindling resources, the high cost of education, housing, and health care. They are afraid to think too deeply about class. At the end of the day the threat of class warfare, of class struggle, is just too dangerous to face. (2000, 6)

The children who successfully class-pass in 1930s melodramas prove Rita Felski's observation that "[a] person from a lower-class background who has acquired education and money might be said to pass as middle or upper class in the same way as a gay man or lesbian can pass as straight" (2000, 38). As I have written elsewhere, "Class-passing is in some ways like race-passing, gender-passing, or straight/gay-passing, but class-passing, like whiteness, is not often noticed or examined. It is essentially viewed as normative behavior, especially in America, where one is expected to do as much class-passing as possible, regardless of one's race, gender, or economic circumstances" (2003, 102). Class-passing has much in common with gender- and race-passing and is also related to drag and cross-dressing. Indeed, successful class-passing, even when dependent on the sacrificial mother figure, *proves* that class is a *fabrication*.

To borrow from Judith Butler's work on the performative nature of gender, I think it would be profitable to revisit her most important and revolutionary work: the chapter on "Subversive Bodily Acts" in *Gender Trouble*. In the following passage, I have substituted the word "class" for the word "gender" in order to emphasize how Butler's methodology, when applied to class, disrupts the notion of coherence and stability just as it did when she used it to overturn the discursive origin of gender constitution. "If the inner truth of [class] is a fabrication and if true [class] is a fantasy instituted and inscribed on the surface of bodies, then it seems that [classes] can be neither true nor false, but are only produced as the truth effects of a discourse of primary and stable identity. . . . In imitating [class], drag implicitly reveals the imitative structure of [class] itself—as well as its contingency" (1999, 174–75). Thus, where Butler overhauls the idea of original or true gender identity, I have used her words to disrupt the notion of class identity. Class, like gender, may be construed as a socially constructed and regulated series of performed acts and gestures. One might claim, then, that actual wealth is required for a performance of class, but that's not always necessarily true, just as it's not always necessary to enact gender through biological evidence. Following Butler, we can conclude that class norms are in many ways a fiction disguised as a truth and that the perimeters of class are patrolled just as regularly as those of gender.

The maternal melodramas of the Depression era allowed viewers a peek into, or even a roadmap to, the performative nature of class. The films' finales highlight the effectiveness of class drag and class-passing, usually through the marriage system or the education system. Min and Bill step aside, for example, as their adopted wharf-rat of a girl learns how to class-pass. She stops chewing gum and shouting. She learns to speak differently and to dress better. She goes away to boarding school and acquires manners and other proper behavior. She meets a young man of the aristocracy who marries her. But class-passing, like gender- and race-passing, can be painful and shatter families. When Nancy comes home to visit Min and Bill, Min breaks all ties with the girl, bringing into sharp relief the pain and hardship that both the class-passer and the facilitating mother figure must endure. The pain is registered indelibly on the face of Marie Dressler, who won an Academy Award for her performance. Min, who has a chance to escape from a murder charge, remains on the scene just long enough to see her adopted daughter marry up, but marrying up is not painted as an entirely positive step on the ladder of class-passing.

There is a price for the child's upward mobility, and both the parent and the child pay it: the pain of permanent separation. Nancy, like many other child class-passers, is not well delineated as a full character. As my students have pointed out to me, the children in maternal melos are more like concepts of personalities, not fully fleshed out, and in that way they also provide glimpses of class drag. Their incomplete personalities are like modernist paintings of light and shadow, dapples of color that barely connect as fully human beings, especially when contrasted with the more richly characterized mother figures.

Perhaps these class-passing children best exemplify the fragmented and incomplete identities of the self, redefined in modernist literature as "frail, brittle, fractured, fragmented . . . a conception probably the preeminent outlook in current discussions of the self and modernity" (Giddens 1991, 169).

Similarly, Barbara Stanwyck's daughter Laurel in *Stella Dallas* becomes less interesting, less complex, and less a full character the higher the class status she attains. The social climber is increasingly bored by her mother's behavior. When Stella comes to visit after Laurel has gone to live with her rich father and his upper-class wife, the daughter is permitted some bit of character, that of a selfish little snob who is increasingly embarrassed by her real mother's gaudy wardrobe. Indeed, *Stella Dallas* is interesting in the maternal melo cycle in that Stella does not simply make a quick disappearance. Instead, she hangs around the edges of the picture, acting inappropriately, being made fun of by the rich kids at the club, and embarrassing her daughter.

In a devastating scene of class rupture, mother and daughter are returning home on a train. In her compartment, Stella overhears the rich young aesthetes making fun of her—"Laurel's horrible mother." Laurel, torn in two by class, climbs into her mother's compartment to console her and display her loyalty. Later, Stella pretends to be a hopeless drunk in an instance of downward class-passing in order to push her daughter away. She "performs" lower-class drag in even more outlandish and cheap clothing, and pretends to smoke, gamble, and sleep with a shabby bum (Alan Hale).

Stella Dallas is a bigger and better figure than anyone in the film. Laurel's new father (John Boles) is cold, awkward, and unfeeling. Interestingly, his wife, Helen (Barbara O'Neil), is a more fleshed-out and sympathetic character. At first portrayed as barren, rich, and idle, Helen learns morality from Stella and makes sure that Stella can watch Laurel's marriage by carefully opening a curtain. The wedding takes place in the picture window of a mansion, highlighting Laurel's effective class-passing for the audience. The image of Barbara Stanwyck is indelibly stamped on the audience's psyche as she stands in her shabby clothes, a tear in her eye, and a cop asks her to move on. But she is a triumphant woman, a complete hero. Her sacrifice is as great, or greater, than that of any male hero of the day. Even my most resistant male student, tired of the maternal melo formula, fell for this film.

Laurel is left to wonder why her mother has not shown up for the wedding. She and Min and Bill's adopted daughter Nancy share the pain and legacy of class-passing through the marriage system. Other children who successfully class-pass as a result of maternal efforts in melodramas manage their ascent via education, typically for law or medicine. It's always interesting to note that the male figures are clueless about class politics. Again, there is something fragmented and modernist about them: they are not full characters. The wooden performance of Donald Cook as the son Dan in *Frisco Jenny* is a good case in point. Pregnant and alone, Jenny loses her fiancé and her father during the San Francisco earthquake. She tries to survive by working as a prostitute and allows her son Dan to be adopted by a "good family." Soon Jenny is one of the leading madames in the rackets. When she sees that her son, who does not know her, has a chance to become a successful district attorney, she turns in the crooks around her. One of them threatens to expose her identity as Dan's mother, and she shoots him. On the witness stand she offers no explanation. The viewer is torn with the desire for her to speak up and save herself. But here, in William Wellman's cold retelling of the *Madame X* formula, Jenny never reveals her identity and goes to the electric chair so that her son may successfully class-pass. Once again, effective class-passing is dependent upon the erasure of the strong-willed, sacrificing mother.

Helen Hayes plays an almost identical role as Madelon Claudet, who sacrifices all for her illegitimate son, played by the stiff cardboard cutout Robert Young. Hayes won an Oscar for her portrayal of a suffering mother reduced to a haggard streetwalker. Gladys George turns in another remarkably strong performance in *Madame X* (1937). Her husband (Warren William), who has thrown her out of the house, is unable to forgive her one infidelity. She ends up on the streets and gets mixed up in a murder. She is threatened by the snarling Lerocle (Henry Daniell), who tries to blackmail her into owning up to her identity as the mother of Raymond Fleuriot (John Beal), a promising young lawyer. Raymond, stiff and hollow, ends up trying to defend her on a murder charge, but she never reveals her true identity to her son. She is saved from the gallows only by a fatal heart attack in the judge's chambers, just before sentence is passed.

Perhaps it is important that the class-passing child is not fully characterized or knowledgeable, because any commitment to the lower class and any excess emotion betrays one's humble background. Maternal melodramas give us a blank character, perfect for class drag because he or she has so little to hide. The burden of hiding class-passing is placed firmly on the shoulders of the mother. She can be read as the victim, but I see her as the ultimate hero of modernism. She embraces change, she embraces the future, and by enabling class-passing for her children she embraces an end to oppression and darkness. Class-passing, finally, is shown as a dangerous but possible act in Depression-era films. It is celebrated and displayed, only to be ritually punished. In a gendered context, the class-passing subject is seen as a threat to the social order, even as her success within the film's narrative is celebrated. Issues of fragmentation and identity are not always easily glossed over. The class-passing identity can come apart easily if just one thread is pulled from the newly constructed self. In the modernist realm, the best way to class-pass effectively is through marriage or reproduction. The greatest sacrifice is to marry up, reproduce, and then disappear, leaving a motherless child who can fully class-pass, because of the total erasure of her lineage. Thus, melodramatic tales of class-passing permit the noble display and noble erasure of the female self.

THE CAPITAL SHAPE OF SCIENCE
FICTION HEROES TO COME
Rebecca Bell-Metereau

A standard feature of classic Hollywood narrative has been the positive depiction of a lone individual with fresh ideas, determined to rescue a decadent society. In early science fiction the daring protagonist usually thinks in new and modern ways, but at the same time this hero is often threatened, tainted, or damaged by association with modernity and its ethos of mechanization and capitalist exploitation. Fritz Lang's *Metropolis* (1927) is the most famous negative envisioning of a mechanized future, but even in comedies, modernity is viewed with some suspicion. For example, the first science fiction musical comedy, *Just Imagine* (David Butler, 1930), tells the story of a man accidentally preserved in suspended animation. He awakens in 1980 to find a world in which "food comes in pill form, manufacturing lines now make planes instead of automobiles (there are even gags about Henry Ford's notorious anti-Semitism—in the future all cars have Jewish names), even babies come out of slot machines. The jokes are fairly lame, some of the puns excruciating—although it, surprisingly for the era, manages to get away with a number of gay jokes" (Scheib 2003).

Richard Scheib's comment about the unexpected "gay jokes" reflects a common assumption among viewers today that older mainstream films, however modern, had little that was risqué or progressive about them. A review of older science fiction and horror films, however, reveals a daring quality in their depiction of women and gay men, as demonstrated in *Things to Come* (1936), *Island of Lost Souls* (1933), *The War of the Worlds* (1953), and *The Day the Earth Stood Still* (1951). These films present sophisticated visual and structural innovations as well as thematic novelty. Yet at the same time they constitute part of a larger project that very few films escape: the perpetuation of a model of progress and consumption that serves to promote the system that gives them life.

Past and Future Worlds

Things to Come, a British film that had a significant impact in the United States, considers progress in terms of modern warfare. Covering a time span from pre–World War II London through a war-devastated society, on to a future in which war is obsolete, the film depicts two key women as being more forward-thinking than the majority of men around them. In the second part of the film, savage survivors subsist in the ruins of London until an airman arrives to announce that civilization is alive and well (ironically, we might think) in Basra in the Persian Gulf. In *Island of Lost Souls* (based on H. G. Wells's *The Island of Doctor Moreau*) an innocent's encounter with the futuristic scientific experiments of a ruthless scientist ends in horror. The film follows a pattern that is apparent in *The Mysterious Island* (1929), *The Invisible Ray* (1936), and *Frankenstein* (1931), all of which depict the unintended ill effects of a maverick individual's scientific quest. Central characters from these early works contrast in some important ways with heroes of films from the 1950s, when science fiction came into its own as a genre in such works as *The Thing from Another World (The Thing)* (1951), *Invaders from Mars* (1953), *Them!* (1954), *This Island Earth* (1955), *Invasion of the Body Snatchers* (1956), *Invasion of the Saucer Men* (1957), and *The Blob* (1958).

None of these films would normally be associated with modernist studies, because science fiction as a popular "low" genre is usually considered antithetical to the aims and forms of modernist literature, art, film, and criticism. In the modernist pantheon, H. G. Wells would occupy a position as messenger at best, carrying bulletins from the aesthetic and antibourgeois heights of modern art to the popular audiences peeping over the fences on the outskirts of the intellectual playing field.

Nevertheless, it may be argued that several popular science fiction films reflect the classic modernist literary characteristic of "an avant-garde disengaged from bourgeois values" (Baldick 1991, 161), particularly in terms of narrative closure, individual heroic action, communitarian social models, and the role of unconventional modern women. Science fiction films can present scenarios in which the individual is a positive force in comparison with a corrupt or degraded dystopic society. Although the post–World War II depiction of the maverick hero, his fate, and his relation to modernity changed significantly from the prewar cinematic conception, with a wholesale shift toward antibourgeois heroes in a dystopic future, most heroes of science fiction films— regardless of the decade or filmmaker—embody a capitalist ethic, touting a model of progress and constant change as ultimately good for individuals and societies. More significantly, even when women take an unconventionally active role in science fiction narratives, they implicitly further the highly conventional and bourgeois project of consumer capitalism. These contradictions point to a more fundamental problem in examining the influence of modernism on film and vice versa.

Modernism covers a "wide range of experimental and avant-garde trends in the literature (and other arts) of the early 20th century. Modernist literature is characterized chiefly by a rejection of 19th-century traditions and of their consensus between author and reader: conventions of realism . . . or traditional meter" (Baldick 1991, 162). Modernist writers tended to see themselves as agents of change who "disturbed their readers by adopting complex and difficult new forms and styles" (Baldick 1991, 162). Most critics acknowledge that what we must examine are "modernisms" or the general notion of "modernity" in form, rather than a single coherent philosophical or aesthetic movement identified as "modernism." Although science fiction film generally employs traditional narrative forms, it sometimes partakes of the modernist method of collage, fragmentation of images, and allusive or symbolic structures in its fascination with the future.

Baldick notes that "modernist writing is predominantly cosmopolitan, and often expresses a sense of urban cultural dislocation, along with an awareness of new anthropological and psychological theories. Its favoured techniques of juxtaposition and multiple point of view challenge the reader to reestablish a coherence of meaning from fragmentary forms" (1991, 162).

The emphasis on formalism in much modernist criticism stands in sharp contrast to the sociological and political slant of cultural studies, a theoretical split analyzed by Rita Felski in "Modernist Studies and Cultural Studies: Reflections on Method." She notes the "lure of the word 'postmodern' and the concomitant association of 'modernity' in cultural studies with conservative politics, old hat metaphysics, and snobbish aesthetics" (2003, 501). Gill Branston's *Cinema and Cultural Modernity* rejects a strictly postmodernist stance; rather, he examines film "through an emphasis on its place in the formation of cultural modernity" (2000, 2). Dragan Milovanovic argues for the superiority of postmodern thought over the modernist ethos in "Dueling Paradigms: Modernist versus Postmodernist Thought" (1997). Both Branston and Milovanovic assert that admiration for individualism is a feature of modernist thought, and both address the issue of totalizing meta-narratives, generally associated with modernist literature and film, as opposed to the fragmentation of postmodernism. In *Empty Moments: Cinema, Modernity, and Drift,* Leo Charney looks at the cinema of modernity and the forces that created "a state of consciousness collapsed into a mode of re-presentation." Unable to grasp, understand, or regulate the emptiness found in modernity's desire to capture presence, cinema came "to mask the emptiness, to endlessly defer each present moment into the future. Meaning, identity, truth, and subject(ivity) were sought and lost simultaneously in the cinematic experience of the fleeting present" (1998, 83).

Felski comments on the unacknowledged similarities between the dueling cultural and modernist studies groups, noting that for both, "the idea of the avant-garde, according to Matei Calinescu, yokes a progressive and future-oriented vision of time to a cataclysmic splitting of the world into opposed camps. Assuming their own inevitable victory, avant-gardes define themselves against the tyranny of the past, the forces of stagnation, the benighted ignorance of old ways of thought. A parallel rhetoric runs through cultural studies" (2003, 503). She recommends mapping out two useful avenues through the morass of cultural studies: the sociology of literature and what she identifies as "political formalism" (2003, 504). In so doing, she redeems such genres as melodrama and science fiction as legitimate objects of modernist studies, and she brings into play a number of neglected considerations of gender criticism. She notes how melodrama, for example, "captured the paradoxical nature of femaleness at a pivotal phase of modernity, celebrating the excitement of women's new mobility outside the home, while also depicting lurid scenarios of assaults, abductions, intimated rape, and torture arising from their movement in the mixed-sex, mixed-class, and mixed-ethnicity chaos of the modern urban milieu" (2003, 509). Science fiction places females in similar scenarios. But perhaps even more than melodrama, some of the most influential science fiction films depict women as agents of change.

Scott Bukatman argues for the inclusion of science fiction in the canon of modernist art, claiming that "the stock scripts and relatively wooden performances of science fiction cinema shouldn't distract one from the articulations of meaning located in the mise-en-scène as well as the state-of-the-art technological spectacle on display" (2001, 209). Bukatman observes that the attempt of science fiction to represent or hint at the sublime is accomplished in such films as *2001: A Space Odyssey* (1968) and *Blade Runner* (1982) not through dialogue but through representation of eerie landscapes or of a natural landscape replaced by such technological wonders as a field of oil refineries, made strangely new and beautiful by the use of lighting and effects.

Indeed, science fiction film is not the only genre to be neglected in the modernist canon, nor is it the only venue for transgressive and forward-thinking heroines. Toril Moi (2004) makes a plea for the legitimacy of popular works of art that have been omitted from the modernist canon, noting that theatrical works, particularly those of Henrik Ibsen, have not received notice from modernist scholars in spite of their revolutionary heroines and their numerous potential ties to modernist values.

The presence of unconventional characters as primary agents of change signals a film's freshness and forecasts the work's inclusion in the pantheon of cult films, many of which feature either an aggressive woman or a man who is coded as "gay" as a minor figure with major importance. These films create subtextual elements that violate bourgeois social norms and account, at least in part, for their persistence as objects of fascination and analysis. In the 1930s, such films as *Things to Come* and *Island of Lost Souls* broke new ground in predicting the arrival of World War II and modern genetic engineering. In 1951, *The Day the Earth Stood Still* undermined the standard anti-alien propaganda later associated with the majority of Hollywood science fiction films by configuring its extraterrestrials as a neutral, largely benevolent force, depicting the dead-end future of warfare, and advocating a relatively pacifist message even as the United States was engaged in the Korean War. *The War of the Worlds* presents a contrasting view of aliens as ruthlessly competing with humanity. H. G. Wells had intended his tale to demonstrate his atheistic belief in Darwinian survival of the fittest, but director Byron Haskin attaches a religious message to the aliens' defeat, hinting at a God-delivered solution to the invasion problem. The film nevertheless presents a strikingly prophetic vision of the possibility of germ warfare. The newness, the modernity of placing marginalized groups at the center of more or less traditional narratives helps to explain the enduring appeal of those films that managed to alter the popular genres of science fiction and horror.

What all of these films also have in common, in spite of their progressive elements, is admiration for capitalist motives and ideals. Moreover, the consumer mentality is often subtly embedded in feminine characters, sensibilities, and values. Paul Peppis examines the role of gender politics in the creation of the "modern" woman in "Rewriting Sex: Mina Loy, Marie Stopes, and Sexology." He notes that "the early years of modernism's development in England and America witness a lively public debate about sex in which women play a leading role" (2002, 561). Women as violators of the status quo certainly appear in mythology as far back as stories of Gilgamesh and the Garden of Eden, but more often than not, film narratives align women with tradition, conservation of family, and caution in the face of new developments. Presenting women as agents of change also has a contradictory and regressive effect on their depiction in film and on their real-life influences within society. When women see themselves as innovators, willing to try on new ideas (that is, buy new products), they more readily become the insatiable customers necessary to an economic system based on unlimited growth and conspicuous consumption. In a materialistic culture, the doctrine of modernity and newness dovetails nicely with the project of capitalism, which depends upon overproduction, constant change, and planned obsolescence. This pattern of women being open to change and instigators or supporters of "modernity" occurs in films that use violation of traditional gender boundaries as a central structural element of the narrative.

Women to Come

An early example of this proto-feminist pattern appears in the film adaptation of H. G. Wells's *Things to Come* (released in the United Kingdom as *The Shape of Things to Come*), which covers a time period that ranges from 1940 in a country that very much resembles Great Britain to 2036 in a futuristic world of multistoried living complexes, wall-sized television screens, and space travel. Opening on Christmas Eve, the film begins with discussions of an imminent war, with John Cabal (Raymond Massey) suggesting that war will devastate civilization. His predictions come true, and after a montage of war scenes the next setting is that of a civilization reduced to rubble and a primitive village culture resembling medieval society. The scene recalls Albert Einstein's prediction that World War IV would be fought with sticks and stones. The government is run by a warlord, The Boss (Ralph Richardson), who must fend off the power grabs of other warlords and even his own compatriots. This leader must decide how to deal with the landing of a pilot from a more advanced civilization, Oswald Cabal (Raymond Massey).

The Boss's woman, Rowena (Margueretta Scott), goes to Cabal's room and tells him of her desire to go beyond the bounds of her provincial village, to leave her "small, limited world" and see the "greater world of camps and factories." Her interest in Cabal recalls the depiction of woman as a vessel of evolution, bringing to mind George Bernard Shaw's concept of the Life Force, which uses women as instruments of natural selection who favor innovative, creative men. She talks of how she was attracted to the power and charisma of the warlord, but she also warns that he plans to "do something violent and foolish" unless she prevents him. Paradoxically, yet predictably, the film's pacifist message fits with the image of women as peacemaking benefactors at the core of material advances. Cabal, the man of progress, conquers the warlord when his cohorts, the "Wings Over the World" (a futuristic United Nations of Technology), spray "peace gas" on everyone, causing them to fall asleep (a moment reprised by Steven Spielberg in *Close Encounters of the Third Kind* [1977]).

Despite the film's disturbing proto-fascist social implications, *Things to Come* offers a montage of technological imagery that J. P. Telotte argues is relatively rare during the 1930s, except in pulp fiction and film serials: "When we look at what Hollywood (or, for that matter, the rest of world cinema) produced in the 1930s, we find remarkably little evidence of this technological fascination" (94). A number of critics have compared the film's formal aspects to works as varied as *Metropolis,* Leni Riefenstahl's films, and the intellectual montages of Sergei Eisenstein. Glenn Erickson (2003) notes that "the opening musical montage of the Christmas jitters and the later air raid on Everytown are truly successful examples of Eisensteinian montage, juxtaposing images of 'peace' and 'war.'" In such scenarios, as Bukatman argues, "If technology is seen as a dehumanizing force that leads to an impoverishment of spirit, then utopian technologies will permit a new emergence of spirituality and cosmic connectedness" (2001, 222).

Within this technological world, female characters are influential figures who often form the emotional bridges between Apollonian and Dionysian worldviews. Two important archetypal female figures emerge in *Things to Come*. The "primitive" woman, as represented by Rowena, has the look of a gypsy, with long, dark, curly hair, dangling coins on her earrings, and draping Bohemian clothing. She is fiery, outspoken, and vigorous, and she immediately sees erotic potential in the flyer-hero Oswald Cabal. In contrast, the pilot's wife (Sophie Stewart) is blond, unemotional, and garbed in a surprisingly modern outfit that looks like a woman's business suit. Although Rowena is the more exciting of the two characters, she disappears from the narrative with little fanfare. These two figures are supplanted later in the film in similarly antithetical roles by Cabal's matter-of-fact, determined, scientific daughter (Pearl Argyle) and a dreamy granddaughter (Anne McClaren). Once again, the more emotional (and younger) female disappears from the narrative without explanation, while the woman of science and derring-do (associated with masculinity and modernity) travels to the stars, to be immortalized in a chain of future scientific developments.

Most striking, in terms of filmic innovation, is the montage depicting the construction of the new world of the future, which is reminiscent of Fernand Léger's *Ballet mécanique* (1924). Rapidly edited clips create a collage of abstract shapes formed by test tubes, factory lines, industrial machines, and numbers, all dissolving into one another as Arthur Bliss's musical score trumpets the march of progress. The triumphal and lyrical quality of the music signals that these developments are to be viewed as "progress" rather than as a nightmarish scene of relentless mechanization, as we see in Charlie Chaplin's *Modern Times* (1936) or Lang's *Metropolis*. The montage ends with the introduction of the world of 2036, a futuristic cityscape set below ground in a brightly lit multiplex of clean architectural lines, large potted plants, simple built-in furniture, and floor-to-ceiling television screens. Bukatman's description of *Silent Running* (1971) also captures the essence of designer-director William Cameron Menzies's intertwining of mise-en-scène and thematic issues in *Things to Come*: "In the absence of nature's grandeur, technology constitutes a new ground for human definition and for our obsession with infinite power and possibility" (2001, 220).

The futuristic scene opens with a young girl talking with her grandfather (Charles Carson) about John Cabal and his progeny, who now lead their society. As her grandfather describes all the progress humanity has made, she tells him she hopes they just keep inventing new things in order to make life "lovelier and lovelier." Here, as earlier in the film, the role of woman—even a very young one—is to demand physical, consumerist manifestations of progress. The futuristic architecture, with its massive white expanses of walls, windows, and walkways, towering to an invisible heaven, suggests a vision of limitless and unending improvement in the material circumstances of human beings, a blueprint for an ever-brighter capitalist future.

Umberto Eco argues in "Eternal Fascism" that the "cult of heroism is strictly linked with the cult of death . . . . The Ur-Fascist hero craves heroic death, advertised as the best reward for a heroic life" (1995, 59). Eco goes on to explain the role of women and sexuality: "Since both permanent war and heroism are difficult games to play, the Ur-Fascist transfers his will to power to sexual matters. This is the origin of machismo (which implies both disdain for women and intolerance and condemnation of nonstandard sexual habits, from chastity to homosexuality)" (1995, 59). In *Things to Come,* H. G. Wells's anticapitalist ideal is tarnished not only by a consumerist model of progress but also by masculinist, fascist ideas about essentialism and genetic determinism that undermine his depiction of human strength and strong women in particular. The masses in *Things to Come* act as rampaging and ignorant hordes, ready to follow any demagogue and to destroy the scientists and intelligent *Übermenschen* who call for progress.

The film repeatedly emphasizes the importance of breeding and eugenics, and when it is time for someone to go on a space voyage, it is naturally the daughter of the upright insider Cabal and the son of his friend Raymond Passworthy (Edward Champion), another government official, who insist on sacrificing themselves to fulfill this opportunity. The ignorant masses unsuccessfully attempt to stop the takeoff, after which Cabal points to the sky and talks with the father of the young man who went to the moon with his daughter. Passworthy asks if the object of life is not simply happy living, and Cabal replies, with sententious gravity, that the "best of life lies closest to the edge of death." He closes the film by stating that individuals have a choice between being human or being animals, for it is "all of the universe or nothing: Which shall it be?"

Manufacturing Modern Men

Biological determinism and hierarchical models of society, countered by the motif of woman as savior, reappear in yet another film based on an H. G. Wells story, *Island of Lost Souls.* Although it is usually categorized as horror rather than science fiction, this film nevertheless appeals by predicting future scientific developments. Wells's story took cinematic shape initially in an uncredited film made in France in 1913, and was later incarnated in both the uncredited 1959 film made in the Philippines, *Terror Is a Man,* and *The Island of Dr. Moreau,* made in the United States in 1977 and remade in 1996. Although Wells was reportedly not pleased with *Island,* it may be argued that the "literate script by Philip Wylie, the science fiction author who also co-wrote the book that became *When Worlds Collide* (1951) as well as the film adaptation of Wells's *The Invisible Man* (1933)" (Scheib 2001) actually improved on the original novel, especially in terms of its depiction of gender issues. Wylie's script added two women, perhaps for ideological reasons, but more likely out of an understanding that most moviegoers in the 1930s were female.

The plot of Erle C. Kenton's *Island of Lost Souls* appeals to women and to other disenfranchised groups, from sexual to racial outcasts, as a locus of positive identification because it at least offers them screen exposure, albeit unflattering. Female and gay male viewers often respond positively to films that locate disempowered figures from the fringes of society as appealing alternatives, or additions, to traditional narratives of lone heroes. Depiction of the "monstrous other," embedded in a mainstream narrative, directly addresses viewers who consider themselves to be outsiders as well:

> A number of classic horror movies have spoken to gays and lesbians strongly about what it is to be queer in society without actually showing any same sex physical attraction. The top movies in this category are: *Frankenstein* (1931)—two men bring a "child" into the world; *Dracula* (1931)—a monster seduces and destroys the innocent; *Island of Lost Souls* (1933)—two men create "unnatural" life; *Dracula's Daughter* (1936)—we start to see the beginnings of the lesbian vampire; *Dr. Jekyll and Mr. Hyde* (1932)—a man has a secret life that no one must know about; *The Lodger* (1944)—*Jack the Ripper* (1959) with homosexual overtones; *King Kong* (1933)—a misunderstood "monster" in a cruel world. (Popcorn Q)

This queer reading of classic horror texts demonstrates how a conventional archetypal configuration may be interpreted in a new way incompatible with traditional monolithic nineteenth-century readings and virtually unrecognizable to mainstream audiences even while it is palpably present for marginalized viewers. For consideration of *Island of Lost Souls,* this kind of interpretation is compelling. Dr. Moreau (Charles Laughton, who was reputedly gay in real life) lives with a male companion and assistant, Montgomery (Arthur Hohl), on an island populated by their freakish "children" (that is, natives who have been experimented upon by the adventurously "scientific" doctor). When Moreau finds the brawny castaway Edward

Parker (Richard Arlen), he instantly wishes to see whether his lone female creation, Lota the Panther Woman (Kathleen Burke), will feel desire as a real woman would when exposed to a man, whether she has "normal" human sexual urges—a phenomenon he studies with a disturbing combination of sinister salaciousness and almost juvenile glee and naiveté. "Of course, you and I don't count," he tells Montgomery, suggesting they are not "real men." While arranging for Lota to meet Parker, Moreau warns her to reveal nothing about him or his "House of Pain." Moreau introduces the two, saying quite pointedly that Lota is "pure Polynesian" (perhaps a marker of Wells's famed racism), and then leaves them alone to let biology do the sort of natural magic that seems to be foreign to Moreau himself. A tight two-shot shows Parker questioning Lota intensely as he sits beside her. When he asks her to pardon him if he seems "too inquisitive," the camera flash-pans to a shot of Moreau behind the door, spying on them.

In this scene, a soft-focus lens captures Laughton's pale, moonlike face shining out of the shadows through the bars of the door as he plays the leering voyeur manipulating the couple's encounter. The bars act as more than a visually stunning device, for they also represent the barrier between Moreau's effete homosexual persona and the heterosexual interplay that he engineers. The next shot returns to a much tighter two-shot of the couple: Lota, leaning back, glances up seductively into Parker's eyes. This gaze is linked visually and psychologically with Moreau, who watches with hungry fascination as the two become more and more intimate. Parker absentmindedly strokes the cigarette he has neglected to light, a suggestive caress of his phallus substitute, as Lota tells him in her broken English that she wishes he would not go away. This tender scene is interrupted by the agonized screams of one of Moreau's experimental victims undergoing "treatment" in the House of Pain. Occurring in the context of Moreau's voyeuristic placement, these cries subliminally suggest both sexual climax and agonized envy. The film problematizes the dynamics of the gaze in a way that is distinctly modern and unconventional, first offering the point of view of the homosexual watching the heterosexual couple, and then offering the viewpoint of the sexually aggressive female, Lota.

Parker and Lota try to escape, but they are soon trapped at the edge of a cliff. Gathering around the couple, Moreau's creatures, the "natives," resemble a lynch mob, complete with torches and threatening demeanor, until Moreau appears and demands that they recite "the law." He accentuates each tenet with a crack of a whip. A cowering Sayer of the Law (Bela Lugosi) leads a chant about not running on all fours, eating meat, or spilling blood, and in response to each interdiction the hairy, apelike creatures shout in unison the famous rhetorical question, "Are we not men?" This line calls attention to modernist questions that are central to the narrative—the nature of humanity in the face of technological progress and the possibility for genetic engineering to produce and control evolution of animal species.

Parker is forced grudgingly to admit that he owes his life to the doctor. He defensively maintains that he sees now why Moreau and his island "stink from one side of the South Seas to the other." At this point, Moreau hands his gun to Parker in a symbolic surrender of his phallic power, softly telling him that he clearly means no harm. The tone of their interchange shifts dramatically at this point, as Moreau explains enthusiastically his work of condensing and accelerating the process of evolution in plants and animals. Impressed in spite of himself by Moreau's genius, Parker follows Moreau into the "House of Pain," this time with Lota lingering behind in the shadows to watch their conversation as jealous and fearful voyeur. Moreau lounges sideways on an examination table in his laboratory in a sort of Mata Hari pose, rakishly leaning on one elbow and crossing his legs effeminately at the ankles. The surreal image of Laughton in his white tropical suit, gleaming in the dusky shadows of the examination room, adds a note of campy hysteria to the scene. With the characteristically impish Laughton grin, Moreau purses his lips, rolls his eyes, smiles, and flirts with the hero by making the joke that he might even proceed to create a woman, a task that would, of course, be easier than making a man. This comment is ironic, given the fact that he has already "created" Lota; but more important, it highlights Moreau's misogyny. As they leave the room, Moreau appears to have won Parker over, even putting his arm around the burly young man's shoulder. "Do you know what it means to feel like God?" Moreau asks, as the camera looks up from a low angle that makes him appear powerful and sinister.

Moreau's menace is most apparent when he expresses his fascination with the possibility of mating Lota with Parker. In order to complete this experiment, he arranges for the destruction of the boat

Parker is about to use for his escape from the island. When Parker sees the half-sunken boat, Moreau blames the natives and winks at his companion, Montgomery. At one point the camera captures a reflected image of Lota walking alongside the artificial pond where Parker sits reading. Genetically altered flowers vaguely resembling giant female genitalia float in the water in the background, as she descends on him with feline stealth. He caresses her long curly hair the way one might stroke a kitten or a child, while she repeatedly implores him in a seductively mewing voice, "Talk to me." When Parker explains that he is reading a book that will help him build a short-wave radio to get away from the island, Lota throws the book into the pond. Once again, the camera captures the inverted reflection as the book splashes into the water. This scene suggests a triumph of the feminine and the natural, presented in Lota and the pond, over the technological and the "civilized," symbolized by the book. Even though Parker tells her that he is in love with someone else, Lota sits and rubs against him, combining bold feline sensuality and feral timidity. Despite her supposedly primitive status, she is in many ways the very type of the modern woman, a sexually aggressive flapper, complete with daring attire and Clara Bow eyes.

As Lota turns her back and arches against him, Parker succumbs to her literal animal magnetism, kissing her passionately. But when Lota embraces him, he is horrified to see her claws. Parker now threatens to expose Moreau's experiments. In a scene of confrontation, his revulsion toward Moreau takes on sexual overtones, as he strikes the mincing doctor, who holds his teacup with pinky finger delicately raised. Laughton's acting in this scene brilliantly combines a sly smirk of defiance, a refusal to react or reveal his pain, with the impassive indifference of the masochist who has achieved exactly the punishment for which he secretly longed. Lota ultimately defies Moreau and takes steps to keep Parker on the island. After Parker's rejection of her beastly body, Lota sits staring at her own visage, like a frustrated woman examining her wrinkles in a makeup commercial. Moreau arrives, looks at her hands, and tells Montgomery that the "stubborn beast flesh" keeps coming back. When Lota cries, Moreau is cheered by the fact that she can shed real tears. His triumphant declaration that this show of emotion proves she is human ironically serves to demonstrate that he has utterly lost his human empathy for the creatures he has cobbled together. Lota the Panther Woman finally dies. Sparing no ceremony over her demise, Parker and his friends escape. As in *Things to Come,* the "primitive woman" disappears from the narrative with little acknowledgment or concern.

Technology Saves

A rescue by a woman also occurs in the American cult favorite, Robert Wise's *The Day the Earth Stood Still.* But here, two decades after *Island of Lost Souls,* the female character is much more reactive and cautious. One of the most influential science fiction films of the 1950s, the film features an intellectual-looking alien named Klaatu (Michael Rennie), who lands on Earth with his robot Gort (Lock Martin) to convince humanity that it must abandon warfare or be destroyed by a superior alien civilization. Single mother Helen Benson (Patricia Neal) and her son Bobby (Billy Gray) befriend the visitor, who is calling himself John Carpenter. Helen represents a relatively unheralded phenomenon of the 1950s: a working mother with sole economic responsibility for her child. She may be widowed or divorced—the narrative does not clarify her status—but her son speaks about her occupation in a significant addition to the exposition about her character and social role. As Bobby explains to Klaatu, his mother works for the Secretary of Commerce, who "isn't a real secretary." Helen, on the other hand, *is* a real secretary, whose work delivers tangible results.

As much as the film stretches credibility in the details of the science fiction plot, it is uncommonly realistic in its depiction of class and gender issues. For example, it shows Helen, in need of childcare, accepting Carpenter's babysitting services with a hint of reservation that any mother might feel when hearing such an offer from a strange man. Klaatu/Carpenter represents a prototype of the sensitive New Age guy in his willingness to take over childcare as Helen goes out with her boyfriend (Hugh Marlowe), a man who eventually proves himself to be a callous cad. When Klaatu takes Billy to the Lincoln Memorial and then to visit Professor Barnhardt (Sam Jaffe), the film presents intellectuals in an unusually flattering light.

In the figure of Gort, technology is pictured as a solution to the ills generated by humanity's compulsion toward militarism and space travel. When trigger-happy soldiers shoot Klaatu, he tells Helen to find Gort and utter the now famous words, "Klaatu barada nikto," which will prevent the robot from destroying the entire planet. Although Helen makes a heroic stand and demonstrates foresight in accepting the alien, she is unlikely to be anyone's poster child for women's liberation. In the scene in which Gort approaches her, she fulfills a science fiction cliché of the hysterical fainting woman, with the director taking full advantage of her victimized position and body posture as she faces the metallic creature practically twice her size. She cowers and crouches, a look of horror transfiguring her face, appearing to freeze and forget the mantra she has been told to repeat. Finally, after agonizing seconds of uncertainty, she recites the famous phrase and then faints, as Gort lifts her and carries her effortlessly across the threshold of the giant gleaming ship like some cosmic bride. The giant also carries Klaatu's lifeless body and, once aboard the ship, manipulates machines until Klaatu comes back to life. Commanded by a woman, he is, as Vivian Sobchack observes, "a perverse visualization of the medieval knight in shining armor" (79). And the miraculously reborn Klaatu's final act before entering his space ship and leaving the planet is a salute of appreciation and acknowledgment to Helen, whose face is captured in a close-up reaction shot of rapt adoration and wonder.

What is left out of the film adaptation of Harry Bates's original story, "Farewell to the Master" (1940), is a key twist, the fact that the robot, not the humanoid Klaatu, is the master. But more important than this possibly negative interpretation of technology is the addition of the female character, significantly a single mother. Woman is here aligned with the alien and technology, an arrangement that dovetailed nicely with common advertising practices that featured American housewives eager to try out the latest modern conveniences that would make the drudgery of housework a little less tedious. The importance of women as consumers in the modern era was clear to merchandisers, and a large percentage of the advertisements for new technologies for the home was geared toward women. Bending the story so that Gort (under the right command) is an unalloyed force for good seems to link the film's take on modernity to such early modernists as Filippo Marinetti and Guillaume Apollinaire, who lauded technology as the force that would liberate humanity. *The Day the Earth Stood Still* creates an alliance between the soft woman and the hard machine, a marriage featured in 1950s ads of a beaming housewife post-orgasmically hugging her Hoover vacuum cleaner. Gort, indeed, is like a gleaming home appliance, big enough to clean the whole planet. The bourgeois romantic view of women was cast aside by modernists in favor of a sexist view of women as sexual playthings. But in the commercial world of film marketing, with real women working and becoming educated, popular culture demanded that women, in their change of status, become a veritable symbol for change itself.

In this film, woman is the mediator between domesticity and national totalitarianism. Early on, Helen is a paragon of level-headed reason, standing in sharp contrast to her greedy and unscrupulous boyfriend, who is ready to betray Klaatu in order to win the publicity and supposed reward to be gained from turning in the alien. *The Day the Earth Stood Still* depicts a skeptical attitude toward centralized government and law enforcement, and a sympathetic attitude toward the "other." Helen's acceptance of Klaatu and her rescue by the robot Gort combine anxiety, terror, awe of technology, and eventual reconciliation with that same potentially destructive power.

In light of the nation's then recent actions in dropping the atomic bombs on Hiroshima and Nagasaki, the film also stands as a neat allegory for modern warfare, and the mise-en-scène evokes images of the nascent nuclear age. When Helen witnesses the lifting of Gort's visor to reveal a blinding light emanating from the interior, she has an initial reaction of paralyzing fear. The scene is reminiscent of footage of the early testing of atomic explosions, for which witnesses wore protective eye visors. The final monologue also lends credibility to this interpretation. Klaatu explains matter-of-factly that his actions are based on necessity, for once the activities of humans on Earth pose a threat to their neighbors, they must be stopped, even if prevention means destroying the entire human race. Since the inception of the atomic bomb, this preemptive theory has been the rationale for modern nuclear warfare. Even though a number of critics view the film as carrying a pacifist message that critiques the nuclear arms race, it may also be interpreted as a justification for the actions of Americans during World War II, in bombing two "demonstration cities" of an enemy that the United States viewed as a threat to global stability. Like Klaatu's demonstration of bringing all technology on Earth to a halt for half an hour, the American bombing of Hiroshima and Nagasaki grabbed attention around the globe and established the United States as the new world's policing power.

Larger Forces

Made just two years later, Byron Haskin's *The War of the Worlds* stands in contrast to *The Day the Earth Stood Still* in its depiction of aliens as competitors in a fight for survival. In a visually modernist and lyrical opening sequence, the film offers a visual montage of different planets, accompanied by voiceover narration that explains how and why Earth is about to be invaded. The contrast between the calm voice and the shock of the alien invasion constitutes part of the film's appeal, as does the film's oddity. *The War of the Worlds* is unusual for the 1950s in that a Mexican American actor delivers lines and shows greater wisdom than his Anglo colleagues. He and his two friends are guarding a strange "meteor" that has landed. We crosscut to scenes of scientist Clayton Forrester (Gene Barry) and library science professor Sylvia Van Buren (Ann Robinson) at a square dance, and then back to the scene of what turns out to be a spaceship. When a metallic, cobralike alien head emerges from the ship, accompanied by a red glow and Bernard Herrmann's electronic pulsating score, the Mexican American observes, with delicious understatement, that maybe these are "not human, not like us." One of his Anglo companions replies, in typical liberal humanist fashion, "Everything human doesn't have to look like us." The second Anglo suggests that they should advance with a white flag to let the alien know they are friendly. When the Mexican American asks, "What are we going to say to them?" his buddy answers, in one of the cleverer lines of the film, "Welcome to California." They advance, protesting their friendship, and are answered by a blinding white light and instant pulverization. So much for the philosophy of trust, pacifism, and benevolent aliens, as put forward by *The Day the Earth Stood Still*. The shot of the alien attack burns out to a shot of a blackout at the square dance, where everyone realizes that all of their power sources have failed simultaneously.

As in *The Day the Earth Stood Still*, it takes this sort of violent interruption of technology to get people's attention. When Clayton goes to the landing site, nothing is left of the three guards except an imprint of their ashes on the ground, outlining their bodies. This image resembles the photographs that audiences may have seen of victims of Hiroshima and Nagasaki, which were not widely distributed until several years after the bombing. Sylvia's uncle, the Reverend Dr. Matthew Collins (Lewis Martin), suggests that they should try to communicate with the aliens before proceeding to shoot them. Once again, this supposedly reasonable advice proves to be a bad idea: walking out into a smoking field, Bible raised and reciting the Lord's Prayer, Uncle Matthew is instantaneously vaporized. Sylvia screams hysterically, and Clayton grabs her, shielding her from witnessing this horrific scene. The army fires with all its force, but, as Clayton explains, the Martians have an electromagnetic shield that makes their ships invulnerable. These battle scenes are predictive of the look of some early computer games, with sparkling rays that first turn the target red and then vaporize to green before entirely obliterating the object.

The depiction of Sylvia is a return to a retrogressive cliché for females. In most scenes she is the only female present, a solitude that befits her position as iconic female, an object to be protected rather than a real character to be explored. Clayton and Sylvia fly away from the area where the Martians have landed, and she whimpers and screams as they finally crash. The action cuts to shots of a general who resembles Dwight D. Eisenhower briefing government officials and news media, sandwiched between shots of Clayton and Sylvia and montages of stampeding animals. At first Clayton cradles Sylvia, who sleeps peacefully. Later, they find an abandoned farmhouse and eat, sharing a brief moment of domestic bliss. Immediately, however, an alien ship plows into the house and Sylvia must take care of Clayton, who has been knocked unconscious. As he wakes, he begins speaking enthusiastically of finding "one of them" for observation. In one of the most famous scenes from this cult favorite, an alien lays a three-fingered appendage on Sylvia's shoulder, at which point she breaks into hysterical screams. As Clayton stops her, he smiles approvingly, able to calm and control her as though she is a child or a frightened animal.

Scientists finally decide that they will need to use an atom bomb to destroy the enemy. Shots of the flying wing that will deliver the bomb feed viewers' hunger for displays of modern technology, and scenes showing Sylvia and Clayton wearing protective glasses and hunkering down with a group of soldiers help to familiarize and domesticate nuclear power while they also update Wells's original tale for 1950s viewers. The atomic solution proves ineffective, however, and chaos reigns as people desperately flee from the Martian attackers. Clayton clings to his belief in science, gathering his instruments for testing the biological functions of the aliens, but a frantic mob destroys his equipment and knocks him down. Finally, he searches for Sylvia in a series of three churches, until he sees her across a crowd of praying people. When they reach each other, they hug and close their eyes, as dust from explosions outside the church rains down on their heads.

Suddenly, silence falls, and everyone in the church looks skyward in wonder. The crowd goes outside to see an incapacitated Martian ship that has crashed in the street, its door open and a three-toed foot slipping feebly out as another Martian ship crashes into a building. Clayton touches the creature and declares it dead, after which Cedric Hardwicke's mournful voiceover explains that the Martians had no immunity to our bacteria, "the littlest things, which God in his wisdom had put upon this earth." Music swells, and the film ends with a choir singing a grateful "Amen." The religiosity of this ending violates the original intent of Wells's story, but the film version of *The War of the Worlds* epitomizes the sanctimonious attitudes of mainstream America during the 1950s.

Films that demonstrate the empowerment of marginalized or outsider groups, such as the four I have written about here, contain elements of modernity, regardless of genre. The role of gender in the development and influence of films that depict the future was certainly a concern of the Italian Futurists and of modernist avant-garde cinema, but it was an even more important factor in popular science fiction, a commercially driven medium. All the films considered here increased the importance and agency of female characters in the narrative. The addition of the active female reflects the modernity of these works and reflects, too, the influence of a capital-driven artistic medium that transformed itself to reflect the economic realities of its audience. It is a transformation that captures the essence of modernity.

FALSE CRITICISM
CINEMA, BOURGEOIS SOCIETY,
AND THE CONSERVATIVE COMPLAINT
Christopher Sharrett

As the most extraordinary art form of modernity, the cinema can
claim as its greatest accomplishments the subversive critique of various received truths, from conventional notions of sexuality to the operations of time and space, and the undermining of the very concept
of being in the age of relativity. As has been demonstrated elsewhere,
the cinema offers clear illustrations, often through its very nature, of
the powerful impact of Marx, Freud, and Einstein on dogmas associated with Western patriarchal capitalist civilization (see Vogel 1974).
Perhaps the greatest, even obsessive, locus of subversion on the part of
all cinemas—Hollywood, foreign, avant garde—is the debunking of
bourgeois life embodied in the community, the family, the heterosexual monogamous couple, and the larger political-economic system
they represent. Films with this concern present the couple and the
family not as the social bedrock that dominant civilization has portrayed, but as the conditioning structures that regulate desire, delimit
sexual roles (especially for the female), encourage competition and
deceit among individuals, and in short form the basis of the capitalist
state. What happens, however, when the modern critique is lost to us?

Cinematic subversion has produced a distinguished tradition: Jean Renoir's *Rules of the Game* (*La Règle du jeu* [1939]); Max Ophüls's *The Reckless Moment* (1949), *Letter from an Unknown Woman* (1948), and *Madame de . . .* (1953); the melodramas of Douglas Sirk; various films by Luis Buñuel, especially *The Discreet Charm of the Bourgeoisie* (*Le Charme discret de la bourgeoisie* [1972]), *That Obscure Object of Desire* (*Cet obscur objet du désir* [1977]), and *Belle de jour* (1967); and Pier Paolo Pasolini's remarkable *Teorema* (1968) and *Porcile* (1969), among many other films. We might count most or all of the major films of Alfred Hitchcock as sly social criticisms; Hitchcock may in fact be the representative figure of the classic Hollywood to critique bourgeois culture from a conservative position. Renoir, Buñuel, and Pasolini, as representative examples, helped create a major oppositional European cinema within a sometimes hostile cultural context. Further, the work of Ophüls, Sirk, and others who managed to work within the ideological interstices of late Hollywood seems especially remarkable when one contrasts it with the woeful inadequacies of the contemporary cinema of social criticism.

The postmodern moment saw a marked increase in "underside of suburbia" films that seem a response to the "morning in America"–style of reassuring platitudes offered by Ronald Reagan in the wake of the Vietnam / Watergate years, which had brought a serious challenge to the dominant social-economic order. The number of commercial films "critiquing" suburbia or family or gender relations produced in the 1990s and the first years of the twenty-first century is a bit overwhelming. A comprehensive list would have to include at least: *The Adjuster* (1991), *Safe* (1995), *Before and After, The Daytrippers* (both 1996), *The Ice Storm, The Sweet Hereafter* (both 1997), *Happiness, Pleasantville* (both 1998), *American Beauty, Election, The Virgin Suicides, Fight Club* (all 1999), *Ghost World* (2000), *L.I.E., Donnie Darko, In the Bedroom, The Deep End, Storytelling* (all 2001), *Far from Heaven, Laurel Canyon, One Hour Photo, Confessions of a Dangerous Mind, The Secret Lives of Dentists, Autofocus, The Good Girl, The Hours* (all 2002), and *Capturing the Friedmans, Elephant, Thirteen, In the Cut* (all 2003). Some of these films are exemplary, even devastating, critiques of middle-class life, but others are decidedly troublesome, their focus being almost exclusively the travails of the male and the presentation of desire, regardless of its ideological frame, as axiomatically perverse (*American Beauty, Autofocus, The Secret Lives of Dentists*). Still others (*Laurel Canyon, In the Cut, The Ice Storm, In the Bedroom*) are repugnant demonizations of the sexually adventurous or overbearing female.

A number of issues arise as to the meaning of this recurring preoccupation. If a few of these films are representative of a struggling, tentative oppositional cinema more or less lost amid the "blockbuster" fare of the New Hollywood, the great majority of them suggest a form of inoculation whereby the critical faculties of the audience are placed in service of gaining new legitimacy for the social order (see Barthes 1972). They offer rather calculated, obvious, clumsy observations of society, focusing (within a very delimited debate) on, for example, sexual frustration from the viewpoint of male privilege, while pretending that important social issues can be addressed within the confines of accepted notions of political economy. One's chief concern about many of the critical projects of these films is the disturbing vision they offer: a familiar criticism of capitalist culture from the right, its aim ultimately upon consolation and restoration through the destruction of some aberrant agent rather than challenges to a bankrupt, irredeemable social order.

Certain strains of the postmodern cinema, most obviously the films affected by forms of apocalypticism, remind the informed spectator of Georg Lukács's caution about large tendencies of artistic modernism—that, for example, alienation is thought located in immutable, metaphysical forces (Lukács 1963, 1983). Lukács has much instruction to offer as we note that at the heart of contemporary cinema's critique of society is a despair that accepts alienation as an inevitable state of being, in fact one that can be the subject of celebration, as religiosity and nihilism become complementary ideologies of this civilization. The work of Buñuel, Jean-Luc Godard, and Pasolini, or the horror film of the seventies, offered uncompromised accounts of the social catastrophe wrought by the basic assumptions of patriarchal capitalism and the culture flowing from it. These films suggested a specific apocalypticism (pointing to capitalist culture as the site of apocalypse), a diagnosis of a disease that could not be addressed by convenient palliatives. Nor did they suggest that the human subject could somehow slip past the crisis and survive. But numerous contemporary films, such as *Se7en* (1995) (and the endless serial killer films following it and *The Silence of the Lambs* [1991]), *Fight Club,* and the new suburban nightmare films, prove Lukács's point repeatedly: these films posit a distorted "fallen" world (the locus of horror is often metaphysical or ineffable) that cannot be helped, in which we are all somehow complicit (in what way is usually unclear), and in which political-economic remedy is generally off the table, with a new society based on an end to repression and social and economic injustice unthinkable (see Sharrett 2000).

In discussing the particular atheism affecting much artistic modernism, Lukács makes remarks applicable to the culture that has produced *Se7en* and an entire cycle of films that view metaphysical forces as determining the downfall of bourgeois society. For Lukács, modernist atheism is not an emblem of rebellion, but a "token of the 'God-forsakenness' of the world, its utter desolation and futility." He states: "Modern religious atheism is characterized, on the one hand, by the fact that unbelief has lost its revolutionary *élan*—the empty heavens are the projection of a world beyond redemption. On the other hand, religious atheism shows that the desire for salvation lives on with undiminished force in a world without God, worshipping the void created by God's absence" (1971, 44). A culture that wallows in the despair of a *Se7en* or the nonsensical solipsistic fantasies of a *Donnie Darko,* or the vicious nihilism of *Gummo* (1997) or any of the films of David Lynch, would profit from Lukács's thinking.

In considering the inadequacy of the new antibourgeois cinema, it is instructive to think of the achievements and the unsparing yet complex social vision of Renoir, Ophüls, and Sirk vis-à-vis the work of a filmmaker like David Fincher or, far worse, David Lynch—whose *Blue Velvet,* while seeming at the moment of its release in 1986 a provocation to the "retro culture" of Reaganism, proved under close examination to be anything but—indeed, an extremely reactionary film (see also Wood 2002, 43–49). Here as in his other works, including especially his television project "Twin Peaks," ostensibly a send-up of the American self-image as represented in the situation comedy, Lynch uses quirkiness as a substitute for critique. For him, the "oddities" of daily life, displayed particularly in characters representing sexual transgression, are the sum and substance of a social vision among the more poisonous but decidedly influential elements of which is a sense of moral superiority fused to nihilism.

1950s Hollywood Melodrama and the Inadequacy of Postmodern Antibourgeois Cinema

The Hollywood cinema of the 1950s is notorious for its critiques of civilization from a rightist perspective, even as the advertisements for its films screamed out controversy and in so doing set a certain negative standard, a "bad example" for the disingenuous social criticism of postmodernity. This cinema, which must be distinguished from numerous radical challenges, such as the work of Sirk, provides a model of explanation for understanding both the ideological contradictions of the commercial cinema and its conscious attempts at revivifying the elements of bourgeois life, increasingly a subject of doubt in the postwar years. It also points the way for the dissolution of oppositional cinema under the new corporate arrangements of the 1980s and after. Representative are Nicholas Ray's *Rebel Without a Cause* (1955) and, at a far lesser level of achievement, Mark Robson's *Peyton Place* (1957).

Ray's film is the most remarkable "teenpic" of its era, with all the disrespect for adolescent culture that the term has come to signify. The very title suggests that adolescents have no grounds for complaint, that their rebellion (which is little indeed) is based on emotional problems precipitated by parents not on proper duty. More particularly, the threats to society described by *Rebel* concern primarily the feminized, domesticated male, embodied in the protagonist's henpecked father (Jim Backus). The female and her culture are a source of woe. Jim Stark's (James Dean) frustration with a father who will not "knock mom cold" represents the film's dominant statement, one that tends to overwhelm the more subversive sequences of the narrative, including the building of an alternative family by Jim, Judy (Natalie Wood), and Plato (Sal Mineo), a triad with strong bisexual overtones, particularly as we see Plato's evolving hero worship of Jim and the obvious affection shared by the two men, both very feminine figures among the stars of the new postwar youth cinema. That Plato must be destroyed and Jim's bright red windbreaker replaced with the father's gray suit jacket are logical enough outcomes given the assumptions of the narrative. It is Dean's iconic presence that transcends and saves the film, offering an image of bisexuality that reigns eternal in poster shops ever since the star's early death (my reading of this film owes much to Biskind 1983, 200–217).

The undermining of potentially radical material by an opportunistic late studio system is most flagrant in Robson's *Peyton Place*. The Grace Metalious source novel, for all its crudity, might be seen today as the legitimate outcry against stifling postwar society of an emotionally isolated woman thoroughly alienated from a dreadful New England small-town culture—her alienation made all the more profound with the book's publication—that further propelled the writer's mental illness, alcoholism, and early death. *Peyton Place*, the novel, is a scathing condemnation of the small town as degraded, hypocritical, bigoted, and irredeemable. Aside from removing the more provocative sexual elements of the novel, the film, in exploiting its source, reprieves in the most intellectually dishonest way imaginable the material the book condemns. The film's conclusion is a wistful, unqualified valorization of small-town life despite all its vicissitudes.

However, the difficult contradictions of certain 1950s melodramas do not unduly undercut their sophistication when one sets them against the social criticism of films made in the last decade of the twentieth century and the first decade of the twenty-first. Ang Lee's *The Ice Storm* might be considered alongside 1950s melodrama, particularly for the issues it and similar contemporary melodramas find no longer worthy of examination. The suburban locale might be compared with that of Sirk's melodramas, noting here the failure to attend to the entrapment by the suburban domicile (for instance, the television, commodities, and accoutrements of *All That Heaven Allows* [1955]). The location and timeframe are instructive, the script by James Schamus telling us much about the current perspective toward both class and the perceived self-indulgence of 1960s and 1970s culture, especially the consequences of the feminist and sexual liberation movements. The film is a frequently compelling portrayal of the bankruptcy of family life as two families implode during the Watergate years—the Nixon scandals are mirrored in the duplicity and denial that are the fabric of daily life. The overcast dreariness of the film complements well the sense of isolation and emotional petrifaction encompassing all its characters. But *The Ice Storm* seems representative of a tendency of the new Hollywood cinema to focus on the travails facing the upper middle class, with the assumption that the working classes no longer exist except as a subject for romantic nostalgia or demonization. The homes of the new melodramas are comfortably appointed, often extravagant, the point being not so much an exposition of the decadence flowing from the emptiness of bourgeois creature comforts (a point made by Sirk) as the assumption that the new, upwardly mobile America has *indeed* made it, even if the price is a bit high.

Of greater concern are the sexual politics of the film, particularly because the focus is largely on sexually adventurous housewives (Sigourney Weaver and Joan Allen), whose provocative behavior, portrayed as depraved, dissolute, and ultimately destructive, is consequent to the muddle-headed behavior of weak males who, it would seem, are unable to provide cohesion to the family or community. A positive appraisal of the film might suggest that it speaks to the impossibility of the old image of male-as-provider and enabler of the continuation of bourgeois life, but the image of the sexualized female (Weaver's Janie Carver in particular) as a figure central to the community's doom, however related her malaise may be to general social disquiet, is typical of Hollywood's continued skepticism toward female sexuality. The portrayal of suburban "swinging" is at least as troubling: sexual transgression is ultimately associated with the death of a neglected child, and, more important, the pathological culture of infidelity and "cheating" is seen not merely as an extension of the lies of patriarchal civilization, with its insistence on monogamy, but also as a terrible effect of the 1960s sexual revolution "polluting" bourgeois life.

Jane Campion's *In the Cut* (2002), a film that depends for its sexual-political vision on *Klute* (1971) and *Looking for Mr. Goodbar* (1977), reminds the spectator yet again how little has been accomplished within the commercial cinema since the 1970s relative to a vision of alternative sexuality for the female, and how challenging a film such as *Goodbar* was despite all its inconsistencies. Frannie Avery (Meg Ryan) is a young college professor haunted by her father's desertion of her mother even as she dreams of their early romance in sepia-toned fantasies. She becomes embroiled in the pursuit of a serial killer of women, an investigation led by a sexually seductive and sexually adept detective named Malloy (Mark Ruffalo), who is able to satisfy

Frannie's needs even as he grows in her suspicions as the probable killer. Her sexual awakening by Malloy is linked to her need to accept the notion that he is a possible murderer and, more important, to the destruction of a potentially feminist culture by a male sexuality, which Frannie internalizes—she illustrates her lecture on Virginia Woolf's *To the Lighthouse* with an enormous, red, phallic building. Indeed, the film's denouement occurs at a red lighthouse where Frannie confronts and triumphs over the killer—but not, it seems, the ideology the killer represents. With the ending we learn that the killer is not Malloy but his sidekick, a doppelgänger in the police force who shares all of Malloy's traits down to identical tattoos. It is to Malloy that Frannie submissively, forlornly returns after a hellish, bloody struggle with the murderer. The suggestion is that she has been liberated from one version of romantic love (the dream of her parents' early life) only to submit to another, the brutal reality of contemporary patriarchy that replaces bogus gentility with a coarse genital sexuality offering the promise of pleasure to the female, provided that she can come to terms with its associations with the most gruesome oppression and violence.

Elephant, Minnelli, and the Twilight of America

I had the occasion not long ago to view Gus Van Sant's *Elephant* (2003) more or less back-to-back with Vincente Minnelli's *Meet Me in St. Louis* (1944). One's first impression is how these two films, both about the temperament of Middle America, seem utterly impossible outside of the respective periods of their production. One could hardly imagine Minnelli's film in 2004, and certainly not Van Sant's in the 1940s, Van Sant suggesting the endgame of American civilization, the total absurdity of restoring confidence in its so-called values and aspirations. *Elephant,* which attempts to respond in part to the 1995 Columbine High School shootings, depicts autumnal, overcast suburban America at the end of its road. Yet the apparently separate enterprises of the two films need consideration.

Although Judy Garland felt that Minnelli's quintessential tribute to small-town life—St. Louis very much figured as a small town to be preferred to the strange urban world of New York that threatens the Smith family—was so sugary and unrealistic it could only be played tongue-in-cheek, the idealized provincialism of *Meet Me in St. Louis* is already a send-up of American life, showing off its ideological cracks without resorting to camp.[1] The Halloween and snow-people scenes are well known and viewed as moments of the cinema that prefigure modern horror, especially as we see Tootie (Margaret O'Brien) the locus of instability and family discord even as she is the cute symbol of family cohesion.[2] Her little paean to drunkenness at the family sing-along, her fantasy of derailed trolley cars, and her gleeful mention of drowned bodies at an exhibit of the Louisiana Purchase Exposition complement Mr. Smith's (Leon Ames) discontent, especially his exasperated return from work to be confronted by a demanding (largely female—the film reminds one that male disempowerment and hysteria do not begin with the Angry White Male) family that deprives him of even a moment's peace. His statement in the penultimate scene that he will surrender career advancement and remain with his family in St. Louis "until we rot" emphasizes the current of morbidity running through the film as it attempts its comforting affirmations. Similar in this regard are the smiling faces of the bourgeois couple (Garland and Tom Drake), too mannered to be entirely believable in their enjoyment of the garish spectacle of the fair. The moment has obvious touches of sarcasm conveying a rejection of the fair's spectacle and the permanence of small-town provincialism ("Right here where we live, right here in St. Louis!"). The sarcasm is furthered by Tom's remark, "I liked it better when it was a swamp, and there was just the two of us!" The idealized vision of America that the film seems to advance is not taken at all seriously. Judy Garland's rendering of the hit song "Have Yourself a Merry Little Christmas," perhaps the grimmest of all Christmas songs, makes most explicit the film's sly critical project, which obviously runs counter to its promotion.

It seems to me that these points, far better developed by other critics (cf. Nowell-Smith 1977 and Britton 2004), make the distance between Minnelli's film and Van Sant's not all that great. The implicit criticism in *Meet Me in St. Louis* is more satisfying than the empty gestures of *Elephant* as it attempts to understand a decayed society. *Elephant*'s long, Kubrickian tracking shots (from behind, making the tired existential assertion that people are unknowable) following students down the long corridors of their high school too easily mark the emptiness of daily life—of the indoctrinating school system in particular—without any attempt at analyzing the reasons for this bankruptcy. The shots of the overcast sky with its encroaching storm clouds, again offering impending, apocalyptic doom as the only response to social crisis, are completely representative of the deficiencies of this form of social critique.

John's (John Robinson) trip to school with his alcoholic father (Timothy Bottoms)—the car careens down the leaf-strewn street—repeats the admonitions of *Rebel Without a Cause*: if children had better care, such things wouldn't happen—a notion made all the more puerile by the devil icon on the rearview mirror of Alex (Alex Frost) and Eric's (Eric Deulen) car as they head off to their slaughter at the school, with Satan again carrying the bag for all the ills of the world. Patriarchy's role in causing the crisis goes no further than John's trouble with his drunken dad, a minor berating by the principal, and a smarmy exchange between Eric and Alex's mother as she serves him pancakes. The film's "cosmic doom" theme is especially troublesome because Alex and Eric are gay, or at least experimenting sexually, a state of affairs that presumably accounts for the bullying they get at school or at least for their designation as "different." Alex's mastery of two difficult Beethoven sonatas, especially *Für Elise* (virtually the theme of the film, chosen perhaps because of its melancholy aspect), is another puzzling idea, made more troublesome when we see the boys watching a Nazi documentary on television. Does Van Sant, quite stupidly, want to associate fascism with the classics? Does he suggest that the best sensibilities are driven crazy by the current culture? Whatever may be the rationale, the rendering seems both underdeveloped and banal.

It might be noted that *Elephant* is no more satisfying on the topic of race than *Meet Me in St. Louis*. Bennie (Bennie Dixon), the black student introduced (like other characters merely through a title card) and then murdered by one of the killers, may be seen as a minority witness to archetypal white violence, but he is no more that than Minnelli's black footman statue, for many years a subject of disingenuous debate (painting these statues white seemed a substitution for public policy against racism), which stands in front of the Smith household. On the surface, *Elephant* seems a telling tone poem about the dissolution of American life and the fate awaiting the young, but its understanding of a social situation may be less thoughtful than that of Minnelli's film, a work not nearly so conscious or ambitious in approaching society.

Set against the richness of work such as Minnelli's, one cannot help but view the apparently scathing *Elephant* with great skepticism. And, like *Elephant*, Richard Kelly's *Donnie Darko*, which has become something of a youth cult film, is similarly involved in abandoning the obvious subject of its narrative—adolescent alienation and its foundations within middle-class assumptions—in favor of more cosmic malarkey, on the notion that any answer to social disorder under patriarchal capitalism must be absolutely personal. The imperviousness of the social system to radical change is treated as a given, even when the system is confronted by so highly perceptive a protagonist as Donnie (Jake Gyllenhaal). Thus, the core elements of what could be a fine satire, including the portrayal of mind-deadening high school life, a humorously dysfunctional family, predatory supervisors of the young, and the bankrupt culture offered adolescents, are all abandoned in favor of a science fiction story that is, according to the director, the real concern of the film.[3] And yet, even on this level the film cynically waffles, asking us to muse on whether or not Donnie is crazy, or if "strange things do happen in the universe"; and as we ponder these profundities, the awful family is sentimentalized and restored, the crude father seen as a bearer of common-sense wisdom.

Renoir and Kubrick

An understanding of the relationship of an authentic cinema of transgression to what is now accepted as contentious art adversarial to dominant culture might profit from a comparison of Renoir's *Rules of the Game* with Stanley Kubrick's *Eyes Wide Shut* (1999). It seems to me that such a comparison is not meretricious but useful as a model of explanation in examining, if very tentatively, the essential trajectory of the postmodern cinema, that is, in this instance, a cinema that has dispensed with modernist aspirations during a time of reaction and retrenchment. The two films share a number of elements: each, in its respective period, is concerned with an examination of the sexual mores of the upper classes, prewar France in *Rules of the Game*, contemporary America in *Eyes Wide Shut*; both are centered on the sexual and romantic fantasies of a relatively isolated wife, fantasies more romantic than sexual for Christine (Nora Grégor) in *Rules of the Game*, more sexual for Alice Harford (Nicole Kidman) in *Eyes Wide Shut*; both deal with the disempowerment of the male as a sexually charismatic, socially influential figure; they share a few devices, including especially a costumed ball that functions as a highly theatrical, rather unnerving set piece on which the rest of the drama turns; and both are derived from literary sources that seem at first glance rather out of place within the sensibilities of the films they engender, certainly in the case of *Eyes Wide Shut*. Finally, both films were made by canonized master filmmakers concerned for much of their careers with substantial social issues sometimes offered sleight-of-hand in works marketed as idle entertainments.

This brief discussion precludes any substantial examination of the relative value of Renoir as opposed to Kubrick. Suffice it to say that by comparing Kubrick with Renoir, I am not concerned with diminishing Kubrick (although I think him an almost marginal figure when set against the monumental Renoir). Rather, I want to indicate the failure—or dismissal—of an oppositional vision by a very competent director who demanded total control over his ostensibly critical works (so much so that his output became limited) and did not cave in to the occasional generic potboiler (although it has been argued that *The Shining* [1980] was precisely this, made to reclaim an audience lost in the wake of the failure of what may be his greatest achievement, *Barry Lyndon* [1975]). In other words, Kubrick's films represent some of the most highly regarded, ostensibly challenging work in cinema.

Although he is representative in some respects of Hollywood's ideological drift in the last thirty years, Kubrick is not *merely* representative. His ideology was fully developed before his final film, and long before *Blue Velvet* and *Fight Club* caught audience attention with their apparent challenges to the order of things. This ideology might be regarded as an extremely reductive naturalism, viewing humanity as monstrously bestial, a notion evidenced as least from *2001: A Space Odyssey* (1968). The point of view jibes well with Hollywood's false criticism, then and now, which prefers to place blame on a dubious concept of human nature rather than on political-economic frameworks, in fact, on anything but what is relevant to effectuate social change. Aside from *Paths of Glory* (1957) and, to a degree, *Barry Lyndon* and *The Shining,* which gesture in the direction of class criticism, all of Kubrick's productions, including especially what should be his most political film, *Full Metal Jacket* (1987), trade in an outlook that chooses an extreme cynicism toward humanity over an interrogation of the political systems that shape human action. In this sense, Kubrick's vision compares well with David Fincher's *Fight Club* and its like in preferring nihilism to a comprehensive (however tentative) social critique as a response to our civilization's various repressions. One might argue that Kubrick was not attempting in *Eyes Wide Shut* the devastating class critique of *Rules of the Game*.[4]

Yet the source material of the Arthur Schnitzler novella and the content of Kubrick's film suggest that the upper class is at least the central *subject;* the difficulty is the shallowness of Kubrick's approach to an understanding of class, his indifference to ideological foundations not rooted in some form of determinism. Certainly his film is inadequate as such a critique precisely because his focus is never on social systems, but rests on the cruel appetites of the sexes, especially that of the female. A few basic issues present themselves:

Female Sexuality and the Persecution of the Male. In *Eyes Wide Shut,* sexuality is wholly associated with a sexual paranoia that becomes a nightmare realm to such an explicit extent that it seems not unreasonable to call this a horror film, particularly because Kubrick draws heavily from Expressionism for most of his atmospherics. The horror is associated with Bill Harford's (Tom Cruise) descent into the after-hours New York sexual demimonde, precipitated by his wife Alice's rather pointless revelation to him of her sexual fantasies (that women have a fantasy life and unrequited sexual desires seems to shock Kubrick, who in turn thinks it shocks us). The film's horror flows from the notion, far more pronounced in the film than in Schnitzler, that sexual transgression is horrific, associated with madness, disease, death, and certainly paralyzing guilt, all notions Kubrick leaves uninterrogated. Although both Bill and Alice enjoy brief flirtations at Ziegler's (Sydney Pollack) party in the film's opening, Alice's verbal accusations and subsequent revelations (with Nicole Kidman rendering them at the most over-the-top hysterical register) seem totally unwarranted. Even during his postmortem examination of the nude, overdosed hooker in Ziegler's bathroom (one of the film's most awkwardly strained moments), Bill comes across as a well-scrubbed, straitlaced boy, a doctor quite as sexually incurious as he says he is to Alice during her accusatory tirade. It is Alice who opens a potentially deadly Pandora's box, igniting a jealous resentment in Bill that nearly drives him into the arms of the young hooker (who happens to have HIV); into sexual self-doubt as he is bullied by gay-bashers (on leaving the young hooker); into an awareness of sexual profligacy as purely repugnant, even crazed (when he returns his paraphernalia to the costume dealer and his daughter); and finally into the inferno of the masked ball, culminating in a castration threat as he is told to undress by a sinister, red-robed master of ceremonies. His rescue by a young nude woman, who may or may not be the hooker whose life he saved at Ziegler's, only propels him deeper into guilt for the nightmare consequences of sexual exploration. Bill's discovery, in a later scene accompanied by Mozart's *Requiem,* that the hooker was found dead of a drug overdose further compounds the general sense of sex equated unproblematically and absolutely with the death wish. Alice's discovery of Bill's costume mask—an unexplained device to underscore the revelation (for Kubrick, it seems) that "we all wear masks"—just before the final scene wherein the archetypal bourgeois couple is reconstituted sets the moment for their acknowledgment that "a dream is never just a dream" (so we need to be careful of wish fantasies?).

Throughout, the situation of the male as figurehead of a class system is never a topic of concern for Kubrick's narrative. Robert (Marcel Dalio) in *Rules of the Game* is presented as aware of his own social position, yet unaware of his entrapment by it (the audience is made *fully* aware). Bill Harford in *Eyes Wide Shut,* though obviously not a figure of the same class stature as the Marquis, does live in a controlling class (and does continually bring to mind the perpetual attempt to pretend class does not exist in the United States); he is a figure whose bourgeois social position is threatened not because of his class arrogance but merely because a sexual curiosity has gone haywire. And in the haywire behavior Bill is always reacting to the female, whether his own wife, the hookers at Ziegler's, the young street prostitute, or the nude woman at the masked orgy.

Any genuine interest in the female seems indiscernible in this film. The interest, such as it is, seems solely at the voyeuristic level: we are treated in the opening scene to a nude Alice, closely followed by an image of her urinating on the toilet. That there is no similar display of the male, while the female is relegated to the margins of the narrative, indicates where the scales are balanced in terms of sympathies for the sexual torment of one sex versus the other. The situation may be contrasted with *Rules of the Game,* where the woman, with the fixation of the narrative flowing from the men's utter misunderstanding and deception of her, is always at the center of the film. She is the Other on at least two counts (gender and nationality), but is in fact far from the cause of the debacle that slowly occurs—which is clearly portrayed as the product of the gender and class prejudices, and the self-deceptions, of an entire civilization. The masks worn by people in Renoir's film are no surprise for its director, who in turn assumes they are no surprise to his audience. The opposite must be said of Kubrick, for whom transgression is a terrible departure from an otherwise healthy norm of behavior.

The Masked Ball. The costumed ball that is the site of Bill's last episode of sexual investigation is an important moment to set against the comparable scene in *Rules of the Game.* The soirée in Renoir's film offers a complete description of social breakdown as well as of the social configuration of the story, with each character's façade dismantled during the costume ball's unraveling of the rules, and with its Dance of Death moment signifying the oncoming (temporary) collapse of this system and the advent of war. The *danse macabre* sequence becomes a moment when the ruling class is exposed and examined, not made into an ominous, impervious, vaguely metaphysical force as in the corresponding scene of *Eyes Wide Shut.* The ghosts' dance and the Saint-Saëns music gain their unnerving aspect from the association of the macabre with the ordinary features of life at the chateau, such as the daily routine, the preparation for the hunt, and so on. The false front of bourgeois life, with sexual jealousy its key emblem, finds its culmination in Schumacher's (Gaston Modot) murder of André (Roland Toutain), which may be read as the state enforcement apparatus (Schumacher as fascism, the embarrassing but useful instrument of the ruling class) attempting to restore the façade that the ruling class itself had partially demolished by its antics of sexual jealousy. But never in the scene of the costumed ball is there an association of sex itself with doom, which is very much the center of Kubrick's masked orgy.

Sex is portrayed in Kubrick's ball as dreadful, always mechanical and full of menace, always devoid of joy. It has been noted that Kubrick's is one of the most unerotic sex orgies ever rendered, the assumption in part being that group sex is axiomatically unpleasurable precisely because sex needs the secrecy of the bourgeois couple, the cause of the disaster in the first place. *Rules of the Game* turns such a notion upside-down, suggesting that each private moment produces new duplicity. The social world of La Colinière leads to the partial cracking open of the ruling class's contradictions, even if its members are so beyond redemption that their only recourse is to ignore contradiction and continue business as usual. Renoir's masked ball contains numerous *unmaskings,* as the pretensions and deadliness of class power, as well as the compulsive drives to conquer people sexually, come to the forefront. In Kubrick, there is little or no suggestion of the inner life of the ruling class, which remains a masked array of horrid gargoyles. The notion that they are driven solely by sexual predation itself seems undercut by his cast's typical somnambulism, the sense that those in the ruling class are walking corpses, an idea that would have some value were it not overridden by moments with pretenses toward drama, such as Harford's final confrontation with Ziegler at a blood-red pool table.

The Ruling Class. In a concluding scene of *Eyes Wide Shut,* Ziegler assures Bill that Bill "wouldn't want to know" the identities of the people at the masked orgy, the suggestion being that they represent formidable elements of power. We are presented, therefore, with a notion of the ruling class as a faceless cabal somewhat on the order of S.P.E.C.T.R.E. in the James Bond films. Assuming—against the advice of some critics who argue vehemently in the opposite direction—that the film is not "just a dream" and a projection solely of Bill Harford's anxieties, we are left to understand that the ruling class is separate from Bill himself, whose seemingly inexhaustible wallet and social clout have taken him through the evening's adventures. Bill's wealth and the assorted consumer goods in his home (we see Alice dutifully wrapping pricey Christmas presents) have an almost studied nonrelationship to the crisis of the Harford household. Andrew Britton has noted in a comment on *The Reckless Moment* that Christmas, the quintessential celebration of the bourgeois family, has had within the melodrama the function of underscoring family oppressiveness (2004, 79). In *Eyes Wide Shut* one gets the sense that Christmas, while omnipresent in the background with its gaudy trappings, is simply neglected by Bill, as if he had overlooked its "true meaning." On the other hand, one might read Christmas as an emblem of profligacy associated rather thoughtlessly with Bill's sexual profligacy, a form of excess that leads him, and perhaps the more "innocent" members of his class of whom he seems representative, to the edge of the abyss.

To help sort through the confusion, Bill's relationship to the material world should be compared with that of Robert in *Rules of the Game*. Although Robert's class status is higher than Bill's in their respective periods, the comparison is instructive. Robert's toys and various avocations, including his affair with Geneviève (Mila Parély), provide convenient means of avoiding anything close to confrontation with himself and his connections to class rule, although the narrative takes his authority as a given. Bill Harford seems to have no such connections to a larger ideology; his appurtenances are not connected to greater compulsions related to the effectuation of power. Although he, too, dons a cloak and mask at the orgy, he is unrelated to those whose identities he "wouldn't want to know." One might argue that in learning the extent of his entrapment by the whims of his class, Harford is taken aback; and the film does go out of its way to distance his sexual curiosity from rapaciousness. But to be sure, he is as rapacious as anyone at the party, or more, and so the film is disingenuous in trying to redeem Harford. We see the world of sex, obviously horribly evil and debased in the film's vision, as owned by a ruling class to which the essentially good-hearted Harford does not really belong. Such a reading would have Harford, the doctor, merely the servant of this class, running about to assist friends like Ziegler, a major player with inside knowledge of the nefarious orgy. This notion offers Harford as key supporter and enabler of a class that the film wants to distance from its hero. It seems to me that such a reading, while taking us no further in understanding Kubrick's class analysis, merely furthers a sense of *Eyes Wide Shut* as a ludicrously irresponsible and reactionary film.

For Visconti

Earlier I mentioned Buñuel, Pasolini, Renoir, Ophüls, Sirk, and Godard as among the great filmmakers of the last century whose vision of bourgeois life was unsparing and uncompromised. Although I hesitate in certain respects to distinguish Luchino Visconti from among this extraordinary group, chiefly because I do not in the slightest wish to undercut the others, this director, especially in his later films, seems to me an artist whose supple understanding of Western patriarchal capitalist civilization has importance for our present moment, especially in regard to his understanding of the various manifestations of this civilization and its attempts to restore itself. A comment on what he offers seems a suitable way to conclude these remarks.

Visconti's personal history as a semi-closeted gay man, an aristocrat who embraced Marxism, and a believer in many laudable (certainly not unproblematical) features of Western culture as important toward the salvation of humanity probably guarantees him a status within our present-day film culture even more marginal than the above-named European and American colleagues of his time. His work, especially several of his later films, centers on the disintegration of society owing to the social engine of the family and the construction of the bourgeois subject therein. Strongly influenced later in his career by Lukács (and Antonio Gramsci), Visconti made films that are a correlate to the nineteenth-century novel of which Lukács was a passionate advocate, although Visconti's films have a built-in critical project, their mode of realism not merely a reflection of a historical moment but a self-conscious interrogation of the realist mode and its tradition of interaction with history as described by Lukács.

The Leopard (*Il Gattopardo* [1963]), until very recently almost totally unavailable in the United States, has been celebrated in some quarters for its lavish representation of the era of the Risorgimento, especially its attention to the details of the Italian cultural identity figured in the home of the Prince. This view fixates, of course, solely on Visconti's attention to the period details used to underscore his essential point: the degree to which the ruling class engages in co-optation and preemption to preserve privilege ("For things to remain the same, everything must change"). The view that the Prince (Burt Lancaster) is a sympathetic figure who slowly fades into oblivion is offset by his close association with his nephew, the cunning Tancredi (Alain Delon), who is shown to be his mirror image, reflecting and finally displacing him as the younger man aligns himself with revolutionary change, then tries to destroy it by aligning with a bourgeois order that preserves class privilege. Visconti's intricate dissection of the world of class and the relationship of class to sexual privilege and the social instruments that ensure repression are interwoven throughout, beginning with the opening scene, which shows the Prince and family praying the rosary with the resident priest (the church as instrument of the ruling elite). This scene is soon followed by the Prince's rendezvous with a prostitute, in which the priest is complicit, and various scenes of the Prince's utterly miserable marriage (covered over by a public façade), which flows naturally from the powerless, marginal place of the female—one alternately aggrandized and dismissed—in the society of the narrative.

If *The Leopard* is an examination of the ruling-class family as emblem of the ruling order's transformations to preserve power, *The Damned*, about the complicity of a family of German industrialists in the rise of Nazism, details the murderous rampage of patriarchal capitalist civilization in its most venomous manifestation. By centering the film on the Essenbecks, Visconti is able to offer more than a political-economic thesis on the origins of the Nazi state; the story demands attention to family dynamics, sexual politics, and the uses thereof by state and private power. Visconti was frequently criticized upon this film's release—and for years afterward—for his fixation on sexual "decadence" and his apparent assumption that Nazism arose principally from the sexual excess and amorality of prewar German society. One critic argues that Visconti's Lukácsian Marxism is, in *The Damned*, "an overlay" only in "the most perfunctory way," that Visconti prefers a vague European humanism to political criticism (Nowell-Smith 2003, 155), a view that the entirety of the film in any close reading repudiates. His critics further argue that the Sturmabteilung gay orgy and subsequent bloodbath during the re-creation of the Night of the Long Knives display Visconti's self-hating homophobia. The drag act by Martin (Helmut Berger), the film's signature scene in which he impersonates Marlene Dietrich in *The Blue Angel* (*Der Blaue Engel* [1930]) during his grandfather Joachim's birthday party, is staged by Martin's angry, cunning mother Sophie (Ingrid Thulin) to humiliate both her son and the hypocritical patriarch (Albrecht Schoenhals).

In defending certain provocative statues of idealized Aryan male nudes, Goebbels reportedly once remarked, "We are not prudes," an idea more or less replicated in Ashenbach's (Helmut Griem) remark to Bruckmann (Dirk Bogarde), citing Hitler, "Personal morals are dead." A common reading of the Nazi state from a psychoanalytic perspective regards it as representing the "id unchained," a far too facile notion that *The Damned* demolishes. Certainly *The Damned* is about anything but Nazism's assault on repression; rather, it is about the transmutation of every sexual impulse into predation (figured most obviously in Martin's pedophilia), the drive for power, and finally the death wish (the fully Nazified Martin, in SS regalia, presiding over the marriage and subsequent forced suicide of Bruckmann and his mother Sophie, all within a nearly empty and rather gothic Essenbeck estate). The destruction of Konstantin (René Koldehoff) and the SA at the Night of the Long Knives represents a coherent interpretation not just of Hitler's consolidation of power in 1934, but also of the sexual politics at the heart of the horrendous coup. Ernst Rohm, the street-brawling leader of the SA brownshirts who brought Hitler to power during the bleak days of the Weimar economic calamity, was indeed gay; his SA cadres consisting of disaffected working-class men whose frustration took a rightist turn with the brutal suppression of the post–World War I leftist rebellion. Visconti's rendering of the prolonged gay orgy at Bad Wiesse, the key site of the Long Knives massacre, highlights in its hyperbole the sexual vitality of the SA brawlers for all their ludicrous, destructive camaraderie. Their dilemma is contained in the close shots of their drunken faces at the evening drag ball, as they suddenly stop their sexual antics and drinking songs to launch into patriotic hymns, their libido circumscribed by obligations to state. The sexual self, at a seemingly totally unfettered moment, is always contained by—and then destroyed by—the demands of state power.

And Visconti's delineation of all these events comes within his basic project of the study of family: its deformation of the human subject, and its role in furthering oppressive political structures. The bullying, abusive Konstantin mercilessly torments his sensitive, Bach-loving son Gunther (Renaud Verley), engendering a ferocious hatred that makes Gunther, the gentlest soul of the narrative, an instrument of state terror. The calculating Sophie feminizes and humiliates her son Martin, not merely because she is the phallic mother continuing the best "tradition" of the Essenbecks of degradation and subjugation, but because she rebels (within a society that knows nothing of rebellion), even with her malevolence, against the role of grieving widow imposed on her by the seemingly kind patriarch Joachim. Martin's eventual rage-driven rape of his mother is an act of incest drawn from classical sources (the use of *Oedipus Rex, Hamlet, Macbeth,* and *Die Götterdämmerung* strike me as supple and ingenious rather than heavy-handed, as Visconti's critics have often charged), an act that seems logical and lawful, a destruction of a poisoned sexuality constructed as explicitly so from the early moments of the film. Sophie's rape by her demented son—a creature, like herself, fully a product of patriarchy and its expectations—is the son's attempted destruction of the family in its essence. The family unit represented by the Essenbecks, especially Sophie, her son Martin, and her fiancé Bruckmann, seems in many respects archetypal, conforming to the norm—that is, the expectations of a monstrous social order.

Visconti's next film, *Death in Venice* (1971), is extraordinary for its focus not on the family, the Visconti preoccupation, but on the disintegration of the bourgeois self at the cusp of the murderous twentieth century. Venice, Aschenbach's (Dirk Bogarde) destination and the target of the archetypal Italian journey of the bourgeois artist seeking a wellspring of Western culture, a city that once revivified, becomes in this narrative its inverse, the site of the artist's—and the bourgeois subject's—destruction. Aschenbach's pursuit of the boy Tadzio (Bjørn Andresen) is the failure of a projected ego ideal that suggests the failure of idealist thought, the collapse of dramatic notions of being as the pursuit of a distorted self becomes a form of repetition compulsion. Aschenbach's inability to reconcile the material with the ideal, to come to a reasonable understanding of human interchange, creates a self-generated crisis, an internal apocalypse leading to his demise. If one sees him as an emblem of his class and his epoch—as seems reasonable, given the scope of the work and its many allusions to classical culture and the history of the West—this death in Venice is that of Western bourgeois civilization.

The work of Visconti and others will continue to provide progressive people with authentic consolation, that of hope for a progressive future in the knowledge that there exist in film art committed consciences, which the civilization of the early twenty-first century seems bent on trying to erase from our collective memory. We might take heart that these consolations, infinitely preferable to the false criticisms offered by Hollywood past and especially present, are for the moment still available to us.

Notes

1. Judy Garland's comments about the film are contained in the supplemental documentary to the two-disk DVD re-release of *Meet Me in St. Louis* (Warner Home Video, 2004).

2. Remarks about the film's relevance to the modern horror film are contained in, among other sources, Robin Wood (2003, 76, 158, 172).

3. See Richard Kelly's DVD commentary on *Donnie Darko* (Fox Home Entertainment, 2005).

4. I have yet to find a piece of writing on the film that confronts seriously both its sexual politics and its view of class. The most extensive work to date is by Michel Chion (2003), although his book strikes me as highly eccentric, especially in regard to its view of *Eyes Wide Shut* in relation to *2001: A Space Odyssey*.

STRANGE PERSONALITY

MILES DAVIS
AND THE SOUNDTRACK OF MODERNITY
Krin Gabbard

Jazz and high modernism are now part of the same package. In the 1960s, Philip Larkin ruefully made the case in his attack on Charlie Parker, granting him pride of place in his anticanon: "Parker, Pound, and Picasso" (1985, 22–23). For Larkin, Bird was one of those twentieth-century artists who pursued sterile technical flash while turning away from the large audience that had once taken so much pleasure in premodern poets, painters, and musicians. Forty years later, in the age of Ken Burns and Jazz at Lincoln Center, Alfred Appel Jr. made the same case in *Jazz Modernism: From Ellington and Armstrong to Matisse and Joyce*. Like Larkin, Appel linked musicians such as Parker to the great high modernists, but this time the goal was to promote jazz as the equivalent of the best art of the twentieth century.

Regardless of what agenda a critic brings to debates about modernism, jazz is a decidedly modernist enterprise. As far as American modernism is concerned, jazz may be the best, if not the most essential, exemplar. It is difficult to imagine the American beginnings of modernity without the Jazz Age. More important, consider the achievements of an artist like Louis Armstrong. In his 1930 recording of "Dinah," Armstrong played a solo that lasted only two choruses but borrowed short, easily recognizable phrases from Verdi's *Rigoletto,* "My Hero" from Oscar Straus's *The Chocolate Soldier,* Gershwin's "Oh Lady Be Good," the "National Emblem March," "Lover Come Back to Me," and that snake charmer's dance to which schoolchildren used to sing, "Oh, oh, down in France, where the naked women dance." Armstrong was motoring past the old academic notion of "serious" music, waving it bye-bye in his rearview mirror. And yet solos such as those in the 1930 "Dinah" flowed together seamlessly as formally elegant works of art. No definition of modernism can afford to exclude the work of a musician as original, as eclectic, as thoughtful, and as transgressive as Armstrong. Much the same can be said for Jelly Roll Morton, King Oliver, Duke Ellington, Charlie Parker, Thelonious Monk, Charles Mingus, Rahsaan Roland Kirk, and numerous others who transformed American popular music as surely as Eliot transformed lyric poetry.

The American modernist par excellence, however, may have been Miles Davis. No one else was so constantly engaged in musical and personal re-invention, the *sine qua non* of modernist art. Once, when he accompanied Cicely Tyson, his actress wife, to a tribute for Ray Charles at the White House, a female socialite asked Davis what he had done to be invited. In his famously raspy, bellicose voice, Davis replied, "Well, I've changed music four or five times. . . . What have you done of any importance other than be white?" (Szwed 2002, 374). Actually, Davis may have been too modest: he can legitimately claim to have changed music six or seven times. In fact, beginning in the mid-1940s, when he joined Charlie Parker and Dizzy Gillespie in creating the musical revolution known as bebop, Davis transformed jazz every five years. He was central to "The Birth of the Cool" in the late 1940s, the re-invigoration of jazz as "hard bop" in the mid-1950s, the dramatic turn toward freer, "modal" jazz in the late 1950s, and the radically, even nakedly expressive forms of improvisational art in the early 1960s. His most radical innovations may have come in the late 1960s, when he famously and infamously electrified the historically acoustic timbres of mainstream jazz. In addition, Davis may have been the first black jazz musician to insist, successfully, that he be recognized as an artist rather than as an entertainer. Although the great black novelist and essayist Ralph Ellison was no fan of Miles Davis, both artists were highly successful in their appropriations of African American culture. They transformed despised and denigrated material into high modernist works that were as heartfelt as they were structurally coherent.

Today, Miles Davis is comparable to Oprah Winfrey, James Earl Jones, and a very few other black Americans who no longer raise associations with African American culture in the minds of most white Americans. And yet, as a black man, Davis represents the fulfillment of what Eric Porter has called "critical ecumenism," the highly modernist project of black jazz artists in the 1940s who moved out of the jazz ghetto to pursue "a collective, worldly, African American intellectual orientation" (Porter 2002, xx).

As the twentieth century gives way to the twenty-first, Davis is more prominent than ever. Both his image and the sound of his trumpet have taken on new sets of meanings. He is still being re-invented. If Davis himself would scarcely have embraced most of these meanings, he continues to figure in both high and low discourses of modernity. *Kind of Blue,* his album from 1959, is the best-selling jazz record in history and is itself the subject of two books. His LPs have been repeatedly reissued, most recently in elaborately packaged collector's editions complete with the kind of unreleased material that once appealed only to obsessive-compulsive completists. Numerous movies have put Davis's music on the soundtrack, both before and after his death and with and without his cooperation. At least two novels, a fiction film, and several television documentaries have been devoted to him, not to mention at least five biographies. The image of no other artist is so omnipresent in the popular imagination, perhaps because Davis worked very hard at supervising how people saw him. Thanks in part to the interventions of Debbie Ishlom, a resourceful publicist at Columbia who helped construct an image for Davis in the 1950s, the trumpeter was as much involved with controlling his own visual identity as he was with controlling his music.

Toward the end of his life, however, Davis was less concerned with his image, even if he complained loudly that the photograph on the back cover of his autobiography showed him smiling too broadly. But Davis also began appearing in television commercials (in Japan), and took acting jobs in an episode of the television series "Miami Vice" and in *Dingo,* an Australian movie that appeared in theaters in 1992, a year after his death. He also made an appearance in *Scrooged* (1988), briefly joining several other musicians in a delicately hip version of "We Three Kings of Orient Are." The song was appropriate for a film that takes place on Christmas Eve, but Davis seems out of place performing on a street corner in Manhattan. As a soon-to-be-transformed miser based on Charles Dickens's Ebenezer Scrooge, Bill Murray ridicules the musicians, even shouting, "Great! Rip off the hicks, why dontcha? Did you learn that song yesterday?" With Davis are David Sanborn, Paul Shaffer, and Larry Carlton. The camera reveals a hand-lettered sign in Davis's trumpet case: "Help the starving musicians." Most viewers would instantly recognize Davis and his trumpet, and probably the three other musicians as well, so the joke is on the self-involved philistine played by Murray as well as on the extremely successful musicians, who, unlike many jazz artists, were certainly not starving. But meanings are not always so clear in the other films in which the trumpet of Miles Davis can be heard. There are major differences among (1) films in which Davis was in control of the music, (2) films for which he recorded music without knowing how the music would function, and (3) films in which someone else put an old recording by Davis on the soundtrack.

The white appropriation of "primitive" art is a modernist practice that goes back at least to the gone-native creations of Paul Gauguin. Black people in particular have been constructed as spontaneous, sexually liberated, and transgressive—prime desiderata for modernist artists. In effect, the modernists saw blacks as brimming with "authenticity." Although few other terms in the modernist lexicon are as easy to deconstruct, authenticity and the fantasies that surround it have been absolutely essential to white appropriations of black and "primitive" art, at least since the first minstrel shows in the 1830s. Gershwin's *Rhapsody in Blue* may have been the first modernist appropriation of black music by whites, although Dvorak's *New World Symphony* and Milhaud's *La Création du monde* may be even earlier examples. Duke Ellington perfectly understood the paradoxical attractions that African American art held for whites, ironically crafting a "jungle music" that was entirely cosmopolitan. Miles Davis arrived a generation after Duke Ellington and refused to be constrained—even ironically—by the same racist notions. Nevertheless, he too profited from the strange concatenation of fantasies that black music aroused in the minds of white listeners.

The purpose of this essay is to examine the ways in which filmmakers—all of them white—have made use of Miles Davis's music. It makes a great deal of difference when black musicians invisibly provide background for a film about white people, especially when the film may conceal a racial agenda of its own. Many American films have appropriated the music of the African American Davis while sidestepping any overt engagement with the racial issues that are essential to understanding Davis's history (and that of black musicians in America in general). Although it is possible to accept or even celebrate the film industry's modernist, laissez-faire lack of concern for the color of musicians playing on movie soundtracks, the constant use of black music in films about whites needs to be questioned if only because it is so seldom mentioned by film critics and other personnel from the American film industry.

Nightwalk

A touchstone film for assessing Davis's movie music comes from France: *Ascenseur pour l'échafaud,* usually translated as *Elevator to the Gallows* (*Lift to the Scaffold* in England; alternate American title: *Frantic* [1958]). Davis was invited to improvise a score for the film by its young French director, Louis Malle, an early exponent of the modernist movement in French cinema now known as the Nouvelle Vague. Davis improvised music for the film in a Paris studio with three French musicians (René Urtreger, piano; Barney Wilen, tenor saxophone; and Pierre Michelot, bass) and the American expatriate drummer Kenny Clarke. This group, with which Davis had been touring Europe for several months, was afforded the same privileges enjoyed by almost every film composer in mainstream movies since the 1930s: they were given a complete copy of the film and allowed to put their own music where they thought it worked best. The musicians actually improvised as they watched the film. The CD of the music for *Elevator to the Gallows,* reissued in 1988 with several alternate takes, reveals how many times Davis and his sidepeople went through the exercise until they knew they had it right. And in many ways, have it right they did. Thanks largely to the music, the film won the prestigious Prix Louis Dullac in 1957.

Nevertheless, *Elevator to the Gallows* contains a stern lesson for anyone seeking the perfect marriage of jazz and cinema. In only one scene does the music truly transform the images on the screen, specifically, the moment when the film's female protagonist, Florence (Jeanne Moreau), slowly walks through the Paris night while Davis and his quintet read her mind with their improvisations. Florence has conspired with her lover Julien (Maurice Ronet) to kill her husband, a wealthy industrialist. After Julien has carried out the carefully planned murder in the victim's own office, he prepares to drive away to meet Florence. But once he has arrived at his car, he looks up at the office building where the dead body remains undiscovered and sees that the rope he used for his surreptitious entry can still be seen from the street. Leaving the motor of his car running, he re-enters the building and is immediately trapped in the elevator when the custodian shuts down the power as the workday comes to an end. A young florist who works across the street and her petty thief boyfriend take the car for a joyride while Julien desperately searches for a way out of the elevator. A few blocks down the street, Florence sees the pair driving off in Julien's car, but she can only make out that a young woman is in the passenger seat. She suspects that the driver is Julien, but she cannot be certain.

The director has written a scene for Florence that perfectly accommodates the improvisations of a jazz group. (Louis Malle did not know that Davis would consent to provide the music until after the film was almost finished.) While the camera follows Florence for several minutes through the streets of Paris, there is no dialogue, only a series of looks at her face and body. As she wonders if her husband is dead, if Julien has betrayed her, and if she will ever see her lover again, Davis solos on his trumpet. Many critics have pointed out how jazz instrumentalists—especially African American ones—make their instruments sound like the human voice. On one memorable recording from 1961, for example, Charles Mingus and Eric Dolphy actually have a "conversation" on string bass and bass clarinet. Even without words, their intonations and emphases make clear what they are saying to each other. At one point, as Davis plays for Florence, his trumpet sounds almost as if it is singing in French. We could argue that Davis is engaging in a dialogue with the character, trying to find musical means for expressing what she feels. Moreau utters only one word of dialogue in this scene, when she sees a car that looks like Julien's. She calls out his name, only to see that the car is being driven by a man she does not know. At this point, Davis lays low, holding a long note as the man gets out of the car and the audience has a moment to sort out whether or not Florence has found her lover. Davis returns to his agitated but soulful improvisation when the heroine realizes that the driver is not Julien and continues her slow walk through the city. Davis obviously knew that music must not get in the way when the audience expects a crucial plot point.

But this is the problem with jazz in the cinema. If it's too good—if we actually find ourselves listening to the music—it's no good. Film theorists know this as well as the composers of movie music. Since the early days of cinema, film scores have been carefully relegated to the background, only swelling up for a moment or two when the audience is meant to feel what the characters are feeling. But even on these occasions, composers have prevented the music from calling attention to itself by making it sound like other movie music. The codes for film music were established early in the 1930s by a small group of composers, almost all of them schooled in the European music of the late romantic period. Max Steiner, Miklós Rózsa, and Erich Wolfgang Korngold transformed Mahler, Wagner, Richard Strauss, and Borodin for the cinema (Kalinak 1992). A large part of the film audience already knew this music from radio and from the piano in the parlor— they knew when the music was cuing them to be sad, to feel happy, or to fear the worst. With these sound codes in place, audiences did not need to think long about what they were hearing, especially when the codes were completely consistent with what was happening on the screen. Claudia Gorbman has described the standard film score as invisible and "inaudible" (1987, 73). In other words, the music is meant to be felt and not really listened to.

Many viewers who went to *Elevator to the Gallows* expecting to see a suspense story about two attractive people hoping to get away with murder may have sat through Jeanne Moreau's night walk without paying attention to the music. On one level, the music that Davis created for the film gestures toward the codes that were already well established in the history of film music. Few in the audience were baffled, wondering what the music was doing there behind the action. At the same time, the music is completely faithful to a modernist jazz idiom. Those who know the music can hear the improvised solos and the group interactions that only Miles Davis could create. But the sequence with Florence on the streets of Paris is the only scene in the film in which the band plays for more than a few minutes. Almost every other musical moment in *Elevator* is brief and unremarkable. We can admire a few nearly perfect minutes when jazz and the cinema elegantly complement each other, but we cannot expect this fortuitous symbiosis to work for more than those few minutes.

Ashley Kahn has suggested that the music for *Elevator to the Gallows* has the modal feel that Davis would use two years later in recordings such as "Flamenco Sketches" on *Kind of Blue* (2000, 65). I would argue that the practice of supplying music for specific moments in a film teaches the artist to avoid conventional gestures of beginning, middle, and end that go with the standard chord structure of a popular song. Working in films may have been partially responsible for Davis's idea of creating improvisations free of conventional song structures at the *Kind of Blue* session. I would also argue, *contra* the standard wisdom of the jazz purist, that the music for *Elevator to the Gallows* is best understood as part of a movie and not as stand-alone music. Davis was creating specific sounds to go with specific images. As an African American jazz artist, he is somewhat stereotypically associated with urban nightlife in the French film, but the filmmakers granted a great deal of control to Miles Davis, and the result is something much more than a racial stereotype. It is the unique statement of a black artist working well outside the boundaries that usually contain African American jazz musicians.

Easy Work

Thirty years after *Elevator to the Gallows,* Davis was again making music for a movie, but with much less involvement in the process. The results were not nearly as successful, and the film had very little to do with Davis's modernist projects. Working with keyboardist Robert Irving III on *Street Smart* (1987), directed by Jerry Schatzberg, Davis simply laid down a number of tracks in the studio and left it to Irving and music editor Emily Paine to put the music into the film. As a result, the music often seems extraneous, entirely unlike what is heard in *Elevator to the Gallows*. In one scene, Davis's music simply stops and gives way to a familiar recording by Aretha Franklin. Christopher Reeve, playing a newspaper reporter, is interviewing a prostitute played by Kathy Baker. Although it is not the reporter's intention, he ends up having sex with her as Franklin's "You Make Me Feel Like a Natural Woman" swells on the soundtrack, overwhelming the dialogue and Davis's doodling, which was already very much in the background.

The introduction of the Franklin song at a crucial romantic moment in *Street Smart* is an excellent example of the typically modernist practice of recruiting the music of black Americans to sexualize the lives of white Americans in Hollywood films. Think of the voice of Johnny Hartman enhancing the love scenes between Clint Eastwood and Meryl Streep in *The Bridges of Madison County* (1995), or Ray Charles and choir performing "You Don't Know Me" while Bill Murray and Andie McDowell fall in love in *Groundhog Day* (1993) (see my book *Black Magic* for many other examples). Although the situation would change again a few years later, in *Street Smart* a recording by Davis was considered inadequate for a love scene and replaced by the more accessible music of Aretha Franklin.

In 1990, working with composer Jack Nitzsche, Davis provided music for Dennis Hopper's *The Hot Spot*. In the liner notes for the soundtrack CD from the film, Hopper claims that Davis had once punched out Hopper's heroin dealer and then told Hopper that he would kill him if he ever did drugs again. It was Hopper's idea to create music for *The Hot Spot* by matching Davis's trumpet with the blues guitar and vocals of John Lee Hooker (who, like Nitzsche, died in 2000). Eventually, Hopper and Nitzsche brought in another blues singer and guitarist, Taj Mahal. Although he did not think that Davis would agree to work on Hopper's film, let alone with straight blues artists, Nitzsche dutifully asked Davis if he wanted the job. To his surprise, Davis said yes. John Lee Hooker showed up a day ahead of Davis, and when he was laying down tracks in the studio with Nitzsche, it became clear that Hooker, like many blues musicians, could play only three chords. Nitzsche called Davis in despair, saying, "Miles, John Lee Hooker only knows three chords. What are we going to do?" Davis replied, "Am I in your movie? How can that be bad?" (Brophy 2001).

Davis had no interest in watching *The Hot Spot* while he made music for it. As with *Street Smart*, he simply recorded some tracks and walked away, completely unlike what he had achieved with *Elevator to the Gallows*. He did not see the film until it was in general release, if at all. But Jack Nitzsche had a print of the film and knew exactly what should go where. One of the moments when the music is most noticeable is comparable to the scene in *Elevator to the Gallows* when Jeanne Moreau wanders through the night. Don Johnson plays Harry, a drifter who has arrived in a small Texas town for reasons that the film never bothers to establish. Although he has become involved with two women, one pure and innocent (Jennifer Connelly), the other a femme fatale (Virginia Madsen), Harry still has time to rob the local bank. His plan is to set fire to a building across the street to create a distraction while he empties the cash drawers. As in *Elevator to the Gallows,* Davis and the other musicians jam demurely during a long, dialogue-free sequence in which Harry carries out the bank job. Thanks to Nitzsche's editing, however, Davis's piquant solo suddenly stops when an elderly blind African American man wanders into the bank. Taj Mahal croons *a capella* while we wonder what the blind man is going to do. After Johnson tiptoes around the man and out of the bank with the stolen money, Davis's trumpet and Hooker's guitar kick in again. It is especially intriguing that the blind man is black. In fact, he's the only black person in the entire film. I associate his blindness with the invisibility of black musicians in so many American films about white people. The blindness of the audience toward blacks on the soundtrack is *displaced* onto the black man.

If in 1988 the creators of *Street Smart* did not regard Davis's music as appropriate for a sex scene, by 1999 the music supervisor for *Runaway Bride* considered him the most romantic of recording artists. The film also opened a new chapter in the modernist appropriation of Davis's music, associating it with films that Davis might not have embraced, even back in the days when he was content to lay down a few tracks in the studio and leave the matching of music and image to others. *Runaway Bride* was directed by Garry Marshall, who in 1991, the year of Miles Davis's death, had a huge hit with *Pretty Woman,* a film that starred Julia Roberts and Richard Gere and earned more than $450 million. In an effort to recapture some of that magic and some of that money, Marshall cast Roberts as a small-town girl who has abandoned three fiancés at the altar and Gere as a newspaper reporter from New York intent upon writing a story about her. Early on, the two characters are at war. Gere is digging deeply into her life history, and Roberts is sure that he is exploiting her. She even breaks into his hotel room to see what he is planning. Looking over his possessions, she sees a cassette tape with "Miles" written in large letters on the case. She puts the tape in her pocket, saying to herself, "I hope it's his favorite." But when she listens at home to Davis's intensely romantic 1954 recording of "It Never Entered My Mind," we know what will happen. Shortly after hearing Davis's music, Roberts gives Gere an old but well-preserved LP copy of *Kind of Blue*. This is clearly the moment when we know they are made for each other. *Runaway Bride* provides still another example of how invisible black music provides romance in a film in which no black people appear.

When Roberts holds the *Kind of Blue* LP, with its picture of Davis's face, we see an image that has gradually taken on meanings that have little to do with African American culture. The picture, along with the music, has been effectively detached from the real-life person Miles Davis. In fact, the LP in *Runaway Bride* seems to be there primarily to assure us that Richard Gere is a tolerant, sophisticated gentleman with a boyish enthusiasm for jazz. Because of Davis's special place in American culture, few viewers are likely to see any contradiction between Gere's character and the more disturbing aspects of Davis's life.

A White Negro Masquerade

The Talented Mr. Ripley (1999) finds more complex strains of eroticism in Davis's music. Directed by Anthony Minghella just after he won a Best Director Oscar for *The English Patient,* the film is similar to *Runaway Bride* in the modernist if racist practice of making black people almost completely absent even as it liberally borrows "authenticity" from African American culture.

In the 1950s, Tom Ripley (Matt Damon) meets the wealthy parents of Dickie Greenleaf (Jude Law) at a party on a terrace overlooking New York City's Central Park. Although he is employed as a washroom attendant and never went to college, Tom is an accomplished classical pianist. To accompany a singer at the party, he has borrowed a blazer with the insignia of Princeton University. When the Greenleafs ask him if he knew their son while he was at Princeton, Tom leaps at the opportunity to pose as an aristocrat. He soon accepts a thousand dollars from Greenleaf Sr. (James Rebhorn) to bring his son back from Italy, where Dickie lives in a seaside village with his girlfriend Marge (Gwyneth Paltrow). Instead of participating in his father's shipping business, Dickie has been indulging himself, playing jazz on his saxophone, sailing, swimming, and dallying with at least one of the attractive local women.

To enter Dickie's affluent world, Tom must, paradoxically, put aside his passion for classical music and learn jazz, the music that Dickie loves but that the elder Greenleaf calls "insolent noise." In early scenes Tom clings to conventional 1950s hierarchies of taste, practically holding his nose as he learns to recognize the playing styles of Charlie Parker, Dizzy Gillespie, Chet Baker, and the rest. In a comment that resonates with the homoerotic role that Baker's music plays later in the film, Tom says, "I can't tell if it's a man or a woman," as he listens to Baker singing "My Funny Valentine." Indeed, throughout much of the film, jazz marks Tom and Dickie almost as strongly in terms of race as in terms of sexuality. The modernist play with race and sexuality is immediately apparent when Tom first encounters Dickie and Marge on the beach near their house. When he approaches them in his bathing suit as they lounge in their beach chairs, the contrast between the perfectly tanned flesh of Dickie and Marge and the pale skin of Tom is so obvious that Dickie says, "You're so white!" Then to Marge, "Did you ever see a guy so white?" Tom makes the most of the situation, smilingly insisting that his color is just "primer" and an "undercoat," as if his whiteness were only temporary.

But like the pale-skinned protagonists in African American passing novels, such as *The Autobiography of an Ex-Colored Man, Plum Bun,* and *Passing,* as well as in such films as *Pinky* (1949), *Show Boat* (1936, 1951), and *Imitation of Life* (1934, 1959), Tom does not change color so easily. Later, he is suspected of being an imposter by Freddie Miles (Philip Seymour Hoffman), who senses immediately that Tom is not a member of the moneyed classes and certainly not someone with the contempt for upper-class decorum that Dickie exhibits in his bohemian passion for jazz. If *The Talented Mr. Ripley* borrows the modernist passing narrative from African American culture, it relies even more heavily on black music to develop the character of Dickie. On several occasions Dickie plays boppish solos on his saxophone, and after the local woman with whom he had been having an affair becomes pregnant and drowns herself, he consoles himself by playing "You Don't Know What Love Is," a favored song among African American vocalists and musicians. The film endows Dickie with natural grace and a talent for expressing himself through music, qualities that many Americans associate with black people. When Tom and Dickie first meet, Tom is indeed the whitest person on the beach. Dickie, by contrast, is the hip American whose passion for jazz is consistent with the cool, nonchalant comportment borrowed from African Americans.

As the film progresses, it becomes clear that Tom is not just an aspiring aristocrat posing as a white Negro in order to get close to Dickie Greenleaf; he is also a gay man passing as a heterosexual. *The Talented Mr. Ripley* is based on Patricia Highsmith's novel of the same title. Published in 1955, the novel includes a brief suggestion that Tom's interest in Dickie might be more than friendly when Marge asks Dickie if he thinks Tom is gay. Highsmith herself was a lesbian, and several of her novels directly address the homosexuality of her characters. But in the four novels that Highsmith wrote to continue the story of Tom Ripley, the antihero lives in a small village near Paris in a comfortable if passionless marriage with a French woman. In the first Ripley novel, Tom kills both Dickie and Freddie, escapes detection, and ultimately succeeds in inheriting all of Dickie's money by forging a will. Minghella's film departs radically from the novel's conclusion when Tom recklessly kills his new gay lover on a cruise ship and faces certain capture when the boat lands.

Minghella enlarged the novel's gay subtext in subtle as well as obvious ways. Among the less overt references to gayness is the film's fascination with jazz trumpeter/vocalist Chet Baker and the Richard Rodgers/Lorenz Hart song "My Funny Valentine," which Baker recorded and performed throughout his career. In the 1950s Baker won the hearts and minds of an audience that was large even by non-jazz standards. Some responded to his youthful beauty (he was regularly compared with James Dean); some heard depths of emotion and sensitivity in his understated singing and trumpet playing (his music epitomized the West Coast or "cool" school of postwar jazz); and sadly, some cast him as jazz's Great White Hope, the anointed heir of Bix Beiderbecke and a paragon of the more sedate, less threatening, white modernist strains of the jazz trumpet that have always coexisted alongside the more intense music associated with African Americans.

One of those charming sociopaths accustomed to having everything their own way, Baker suggests a comparison with Jude Law's Dickie Greenleaf in the film version of *The Talented Mr. Ripley*. Like Baker, Dickie possesses youthful beauty and natural grace, and unselfconsciously carries great appeal for men as well as women. Also like Baker, Dickie is accustomed to being adored and does little to repay the love he receives. To make an early, positive impression on Dickie, Tom pretends that several jazz LPs, including a copy of *Chet Baker Sings,* have accidentally dropped out of his briefcase. When Dickie picks up the Chet Baker LP, he says, "This is the best." Minghella may or may not have known Baker's biography well enough to see how much the trumpeter shares with the Dickie of his film. Regardless, "My Funny Valentine" is an especially appropriate choice for Minghella's version of *The Talented Mr. Ripley,* if only because the lyrics are by Lorenz "Larry" Hart, a gay man who is clearly suggesting that heterosexual romance is a joke. When Tom/Damon uses his prodigious abilities as a mimic and sings "Funny Valentine" in a Bakeresque voice ("You can't tell if it's a man or a woman") while Dickie and a group of male musicians accompany him, he enjoys the homoerotic thrill of sharing an intense moment with Dickie.

Although Tom reaches a pinnacle when Dickie's saxophone embroiders his appropriately androgynous performance of "Valentine," Miles Davis helps provide an even more significant jazz moment in the sexual tension between the two men. In a deeply homoerotic scene, full of tight close-ups and pregnant pauses, Tom and Dickie play chess while Dickie sits nude in the bathtub. The music is "Nature Boy," recorded by Charles Mingus in 1955 for his own Debut label and featuring the trumpet of Miles Davis. Still in his shirt and trousers, Tom runs his fingers through the warm bath water and says, "I'm cold, can I get in?" Slightly uncertain but not afraid to let a note of teasing into his response, Dickie says no. He then leaves the tub, exposing his nude body to Tom as he walks away to pick up a towel. He looks over his shoulder to see that Tom is watching him in the mirror. Tom quickly turns away.

This is the turning point in Tom's erotic fortunes. For Dickie, Tom has become a burden, as much because of his emotional vulnerability as because of his need to keep Dickie on his own timetable. Moments after the scene in the bathtub with "Nature Boy," Tom is literally shut out of Dickie's life when Freddie Miles arrives and almost completely steals Dickie's attentions. When Freddie pulls up at the outdoor café in Rome where Dickie sits chatting with Tom, the music of a jazz saxophone seems to be coming out of his car radio. The music, however, continues uninterrupted into the next scene at a record store where Freddie literally seals himself into a listening booth with Dickie so that they can share a set of headphones. Tom is on the outside looking in, devastated that Dickie is much more in his element with Freddie. Freddie adopts an almost ghoulish posture as he slowly gyrates to the music and fixes his gaze on Tom, clearly aware that he is looking at a parvenu upstart. At this point, Dickie wants only to lose himself in the music and cares little about his schedule for the rest of the day. Nevertheless, Tom taps on the window of the listening booth to announce the departure time of the train they had planned to take back to Mongibello, clearly hoping that Dickie will join him. Freddie shakes his head and snorts with derisive laughter at Tom's joyless, compulsive behavior.

In spite of his low tolerance for jazz, and in spite of the later scene in which Tom sheds tears at a performance of Tchaikovsky's opera *Eugene Onegin* after he has killed Dickie, the recording of "Nature Boy" seems to be entirely consistent with Tom's emotional yearnings. And yet the film never acknowledges the extent to which it allows music by Davis and other African American artists to work its magic on the characters. Even with all their passion for jazz, Dickie and Freddie have only the most superficial interactions with black people, a truth about two bohemian rich kids that the film also neglects to acknowledge.

Right Notes, Wrong Cause

An even more perversely color-blind use of Davis's music is in Gary Ross's *Pleasantville* (1998). The film has absolutely no African American actors, and yet the white inhabitants of a 1950s TV sitcom are allowed to have a civil rights revolution of sorts. The premise of *Pleasantville* is that two teenage siblings from the present (Tobey Maguire and Reese Witherspoon) are magically transported into the black-and-white world of an old sitcom, "Pleasantville," clearly based on "Father Knows Best," which had successful runs on three different television networks between 1954 and 1963. David (Maguire) is a serious fan of the program, even indulging in trivia games that reveal his complete knowledge of the characters' lives. Unlike the nerdy David, who is out of place among his peers, Jennifer (Witherspoon) leads a group of postmodern teenage girls and has no trouble attracting boys. Jennifer is appalled to be "stuck in Nerdville" when she and her brother are transported. But when she sees the blandly attractive Skip (Paul Walker) drive by in his car, she quickly finds Pleasantville more interesting. To David's horror, she starts bringing color to the lives of the black-and-white people, at first by introducing them to sex.

According to the logic of Ross's film, the people in Pleasantville know only as much about life as was shown on TV in the 1950s. They do not have sex, for example, nor have they ever seen a double bed. And because no one ever reads a novel in the TV show, the books in the library have blank pages, and so on. As Ross is at pains to point out in his commentary on the DVD release of the film, the residents of Pleasantville turn colorful whenever they have some kind of transformative experience. Young people are most open to change, it seems, and because sexuality makes for fast and fundamental transformations, the town's teenagers are the first to earn their colors. Later on, characters change color because they have become angry or highly emotional. After Jennifer hustles Skip off to Lover's Lane for his first sexual encounter, he sees a vivid red rose on a bush as he drives home. As Jennifer the sexual adventuress begins to influence behavior throughout the high school, color suddenly appears as a pink bubble of gum emerging from a girl's mouth and as a red taillight on a car from which hang the suggestively swaying limbs of young lovers. Everything else in these early scenes remains in black and white.

As it works its way to the most profound transformative moment, the film sets up a musical hierarchy. When Jennifer first begins seducing Skip exclusively in black and white, the audience hears the wholesome voice of the white Pat Boone singing the pop ballad "Mr. Blue." When the first traces of color begin to appear, audiences hear Gene Vincent, who might be called a "white black singer," hiccuping his way through "Be-Bop-a-Lula." As more people turn colorful, we hear the African American Lloyd Price shouting a grittier example of rock 'n' roll, "Lawdy Miss Clawdy." Later on, as the young people in Pleasantville begin to realize that David knows much more about life than they do, they congregate in the soda shop where he works. Previously a brightly lit diner where teens listened to a jukebox and consumed ice cream sodas, the shop has become darker with light filtered through venetian blinds, giving the scene a film noir effect. As Ross points out, the place has been made to resemble a coffee shop where beatniks would have assembled back when the sitcom was first shown on television. Consistent with the soda shop's modernist ambience, the audience hears the Dave Brubeck Quartet playing "Take Five" as David arrives for work.

As Brubeck's quirky anthem of white hipness continues to play in the background, the young people in the shop ask David questions about what lies outside Pleasantville. Whereas the pop rock of Gene Vincent and Lloyd Price played behind scenes of sexual discovery, the film now associates the modern jazz of the 1950s with thinking rather than feeling. David soon discovers that one of the teens in the shop has been reading *Huckleberry Finn,* thanks to a halting attempt by Jennifer to tell the boy what ought to be inside a book with blank pages. Because she read only as far as "the part about the raft," only the first pages of the novel have, according to the film's logic, filled themselves in. David, however, has been more conscientious about his homework. The wide-eyed congregation of teenagers is suddenly obsessed with what happens to Huck and Jim.

The camera closes in on the face of the perky blonde cheerleader Margaret (Marley Shelton) as she asks David to tell them what happens in the novel. As David begins to talk about Huck Finn and watches while *all* the pages in the book are dutifully filled in, Brubeck's music gives way to a new recording. We then hear what is surely the most elegant music in the film and unquestionably one of the most important recordings in the history of modern American music, the Miles Davis Sextet's 1959 rendering of "So What." Davis's solo occupies almost a full minute of *Pleasantville*'s soundtrack while a great deal happens on the screen. The elegant but vernacular sounds of Davis's trumpet accompany the discovery among the town's young people of a literature that is about as radical as the timid liberalism of the film is prepared to endorse. Even though David's interpretation of *Huckleberry Finn* is basically a conservative one, the film uses Davis's music to impart a sense of wonder and experimentation as David tells the town's teenagers about Huck.

In laying out the plot of the novel, David refers to Nigger Jim simply as "the slave." As the innocents sitting in the soda shop listen in wide-eyed anticipation, David explains that as Huck and Jim try "to get free, they see that they're free already." The film suggests that freedom is internal and not about the daily conditions in which people actually live their lives. In his commentary, Ross says that *Huckleberry Finn* is a "picaresque adventure" about getting knowledge, an important theme he claims for his film. He also mentions the many times that the book has been banned, but he neglects to mention that the book is banned not because of politics or scatology but because of its repeated use of the word "nigger." In the 1950s there were no national movements to ban the book. Only after black students began making demands in the 1960s did the book begin to disappear from libraries and reading lists. The other book that David introduces to the curious young people, *Catcher in the Rye,* was in fact banned from school libraries in the 1950s, specifically for the explicit language used by the teenaged narrator. For Ross, however, the two controversial books are an appropriate pair to drive home his theme that knowledge—especially knowledge that is controversial or threatening—has the power to change people. It's a valid point, I suppose, but Ross misses much larger points about what the books are actually saying as well as what his film is implying.

As the youthful residents of Pleasantville rapidly acquire color and line up at the library, the black-and-white city fathers attempt to control the transformations, even putting a "No Colored" sign in a shop window. Ultimately, David is arrested and put on trial in a courtroom scene that is clearly designed to recall a moment in *To Kill a Mockingbird* (1962) when the townspeople are strictly segregated: "colored" people sit in the courthouse balcony while white people—or in the case of *Pleasantville,* black-and-white people—sit on the ground floor. Taking the stand, David successfully provokes all the black-and-white characters into experiencing some strong emotion, thus turning all of them colored.

When David brings color to the town's more conservative citizens, he says, "It's in you and you can't stop something that's inside you." Just as David suggested that the freedom sought by Nigger Jim was always already inside him, he now reveals that there was always already a colorful person inside each and every person in Pleasantville. All strife ends when everyone discovers this truth. But *Pleasantville* disingenuously sidesteps any substantive issues by presenting everyone as *also* the same on the outside. Thanks to the magic of the movies, we're all colored. The allusions to civil rights, an unstated part of the film's dynamic from the outset, no longer matter. *Pleasantville* suggests the civil rights revolution of the 1950s and 1960s has become so much a part of the American story that it belongs to all of us and can be just as valid when everyone is white. And so long as Miles Davis and his side-people remain invisible throughout the film, audience members can respond to their own feelings about the music rather than to the music itself.

The disappearance of master texts and the free-flowing, non-hierarchical exchange of diverse elements is often called postmodernist, certainly in the forms identified by Fredric Jameson. In one sense, *Pleasantville*'s use of Miles Davis's music to support the sexual and intellectual awakening of naive white teenagers is consistent with the corporate strategy of using Louis Armstrong's image to sell Coke. Great modernist achievements are thus commodified. On the one hand, we can celebrate *Pleasantville*'s bland embrace of Miles Davis and the civil rights revolutions of the 1950s and 1960s as a sign of racial progress in the United States. On the other hand, so long as the race of Davis and his sidepersons is invisible, and so long as a civil rights revolution is played out entirely among Anglo-Americans, the celebration must be brief.

There are several ways of thinking about these films as a group. With *Elevator to the Gallows, Street Smart,* and *The Hot Spot,* we could recapitulate the familiar narrative of Davis's decline: he takes great pains making the music for *Elevator to the Gallows,* but thirty years later he is simply providing generic doodling for films like *Street Smart* and *The Hot Spot.* I'd rather not buy into that narrative completely. Although jazz purists will tell you that Davis sold out in the late 1960s and continued to record conventional, throwaway pop music for the rest of his career, there are many other ways of responding to the music he made in those final decades. For one thing, Davis did not wish to repeat himself. He makes the definitive jazz soundtrack for a film in 1957, and then moves on. Been there, done that. Later he tries other approaches to the art form, for example, taking the unique opportunity to record with folk blues musicians like John Lee Hooker and Taj

Mahal in *The Hot Spot*. We could even argue that Davis's flamboyant concert appearances of the 1970s and 1980s were his own dramas with music and that he was less interested in Hollywood's dramas with music. By playing with blues musicians for a film score, or in concert with musicians from India, Africa, and Latin America, Davis was continuing what Gary Tomlinson (1991) has called his "cultural dialogics." These supremely modernist dialogues with people from other cultures first became vital when he worked with French filmmakers and French musicians in creating music for *Elevator to the Gallows*.

We can also make different cases about the role that Davis's music plays in the white Hollywood cinema of today. Films such as *Runaway Bride, The Talented Mr. Ripley,* and *Pleasantville* deny personhood to African Americans and keep them offscreen at the same time that they use black music to give depth and romance to their white characters. Like many white modernists in the twentieth century, filmmakers such as Gary Marshall, Anthony Minghella, and Gary Ross have claimed the great achievements of black Americans—including jazz and the civil rights movement—for their white characters without acknowledging any obligation to African American people. In the case of Miles Davis, however, we have a music that long ago transcended its historical and personal moment and has provided a universe of compelling musical signification for filmmakers as well as for the rest of us.

EXPERIMENT IN TERROR
DYSTOPIAN MODERNISM,
THE POLICE PROCEDURAL,
AND THE SPACE OF ANXIETY
William Luhr and Peter Lehman

Modernism, in its aggressive rejection of the nineteenth-century past, embraced and constructed new technologies, spatial structures, modes of human interaction, modes of representation, and sexualities. The movement has traditionally been associated with the modern urban landscape. In the postwar cinema, film noir, with its central trope of urban decay, of the failed utopian urban dream, became a premier site for dystopian modernism. Film noir maps out the modernist impulse gone bad on a landscape whose denizens are alienated not only from continuity with nineteenth-century traditions but also from utopian modernist aspirations. It presents modern experience and individual identity as fragmented, disjointed, and often incoherent (see Karl 1985).

Postwar anxieties about the fragmentation of identity often evoked the relationship of the individual to the modern state. Wartime fascist governments had been categorized as destructive of individual freedoms, and the defeat of those governments had been perceived as a pathway to a liberated world. For many people, however, that liberation never came; instead, they saw new modes of social oppression emerging in the postwar world, whether the totalitarian regimes in Soviet Russia and the Eastern bloc countries, the national security state in the United States, or a generalized anxiety about governmental intrusions upon individual freedoms, even identity. The 1940s produced both the alienated contemporary urban landscapes of film noir, reflective of contemporary experience, and George Orwell's *1984,* a novel that projected the anxieties of the era onto the future. Orwell's futuristic novel introduced to the popular consciousness the notion of an after-modern, technologically advanced society that has degenerated into a dystopia. A central emblem of the society's advanced technology as well as its dehumanization lies in its controlling, state-sponsored surveillance—"Big Brother is watching you!" That omnipresent surveillance erodes the freedoms and compromises the very identities of those subject to it. Its purpose is to ensure that everyone rigidly conforms to state policy; that very compulsion to conformity drains individual identity and leads to human interchangeability.

The late 1940s presented state-sponsored surveillance in a radically different light in the police procedural film, a subgenre to film noir. Police procedurals (the procedural also appeared at this time in radio and television shows, like "Dragnet" and "The Line-Up," and in fiction) dealt with the world of crime as film noir did but concentrated less on individual criminals (as in *Double Indemnity* [1944] or *The Postman Always Rings Twice* [1946]) or on private investigators (as in *The Big Sleep* [1946]) and more on the procedures by which governmental agents (whether members of municipal police forces or national organizations like the FBI or the Treasury Department) went about the business of solving crime. Many of these films place special emphasis upon technologically advanced surveillance techniques as a major tool in criminal investigation. Procedurals of this era implied an alternative to dystopian works like *1984* because they posited a benign and not a malignant state. Although the detectives or agents in such films are functionaries of the state, their role is to ensure and not repress individual liberty. So it is that the narrative often places us behind their shoulders, letting us watch approvingly as they work.

Procedurals were often curious combinations of both utopian and dystopian modernist strains, utopian in that they showed benign state organizations using advanced technology to root out criminals, but dystopian in their emphasis upon the pervasive, ongoing, and expanding world of contemporary crime. This odd and at times contradictory mixture often extended to the stylistics of the films. *T-Men* (1947) provides a useful example. It concerns the efforts of the U.S. Treasury Department to uncover a murderous national gang of counterfeiters. The film's frame story resembles a utopian documentary. A "Voice of God" narrator describes the duties and advanced technology of Treasury agents; we see well-lit documentary footage of the monumental Treasury Building in Washington, DC, an interview with a former director of the department, and work being done in its sophisticated laboratories. The film employs an entirely different style to portray the world of the counterfeiting gang. Images of their world, in severe contrast to those of the Treasury Department, conform to those associated with classical film noir: darkly lit rooms and corridors, and sinister exteriors, including nighttime shipyards. The film presents the furtive and sleazy environments of underworld activity—pool halls, steam baths, back-room gambling emporiums, filthy boarding houses—in direct contrast to the well-lit, out-in-the-open world of governmental law enforcement. The Treasury Department images imply a bright world moving toward a better future; the underworld images imply a dark vortex of exploitation and doom.

In the post-1960s film noir revival, an important subcategory of neo-noir films links noir's trope of the decline of the modern with dystopian fiction's and science fiction's trope of the degeneration of the future. Films like *Blade Runner* (1982) and *Minority Report* (2002) conflate film noir and science fiction within a nexus of dystopian modernism and are centrally concerned with abuses of state power that lead to erosions and fragmentations of individual identity. In this, they place themselves within the Orwellian tradition. Both films mentioned above are also procedurals because they concern agents of the state dealing with crime.

Blake Edwards's *Experiment in Terror* (1962) appeared precisely between those two eras of noir—after the canonical era had ended in the late 1950s and before the "neo" revival began—but is significant to both. Edwards already had experience with the police procedural early in his career as a writer for "The Line-Up" radio series. *Experiment in Terror* is a procedural that follows the activities of the FBI in catching a perverse kidnapper, and it is particularly concerned with the implications of surveillance. This essay will focus on *Experiment in Terror* with reference to three concepts significant to modernism and the film noir subgenre of the police procedural that circulate around disjunction and alienation: the chronotope, the free-floating anxiety associated with the genre, and the new and perverse sexualities produced by modern technologies and spatial reorientations.

Vivian Sobchack introduced the notion of the chronotope into studies of film noir, referring to temporally specific places infused with the atmospherics of the genre and around which representative events of the genre commonly occur, for example, nightclubs, automobiles, desolate urban streets, luxury apartments with modernist architecture and artwork, and "hard-boiled" detectives' offices (see Sobchack 1998). These spaces can trigger the spectatorial anxiety associated with film noir, an anxiety that exists on a different plane from that of responses to disturbing places, characters, and activities in individual films because it is associated with the genre itself. Film noir is rich in subtextual insinuation, unsettling cues that something is very wrong. That menacing "something" is part of the generic atmosphere and is often left unspecified. It can be evoked by visual strategies that incorporate mysterious shadows, depths of darkness, and off-center framing; by dialogue that hints at dark deeds or motives that are never or only partially specified; by performances that seem to incorporate barely controlled and only partially motivated rage or terror. Contemporary audiences often understood such subtextual insinuation to refer to dark aspects of modern experience that censorship would not allow to be represented. Thus, while utopian modernism was intensely optimistic, promising the casting off of a dysfunctional Victorian past and the building of a brave new world in art, architecture, technology, culture, social organization, and human relations, the opposed dystopian strain saw such aspirations of the modern age as having failed and fallen apart. Life under such circumstances was dysfunctional, filled not with optimism but rather with anxiety and fear of further failure to come.

One of the most resonant of these anxieties is that of the destabilization and/or isolation of the individual.[1] A widespread postwar anxiety emerged in people who feared that changing social structures were causing them to lose their individuality, to become "organization men," "numbers," or "men in gray flannel suits." Many also felt that individual identity was menaced by foreign powers or ideologies such as communism. In Europe, one manifestation of this anxiety appeared with the new existentialist philosophy, which focused upon the profound isolation of the individual.

This free-floating anxiety associated with film noir relates to representational strategies, destabilizing techniques, and even reception contexts, particularly the evocation of presences not seen or barely seen, things hinted at beyond the frame lines. Such presences are of two kinds: those things within the film's story that lurk in or beyond the shadows, and those things that films of the era were not permitted to represent at all. Concerning the first, some films noirs employ chiaroscuro lighting in certain scenes where much in the frame is obscured in shadows, in the style of the horror films produced at Universal in the 1930s. Examples include *Murder, My Sweet* (1944), *Mildred Pierce* (1945), *Scarlet Street* (1945), and *The Killers* (1947). Such a strategy courts anxiety about what is "out there" (as well as what danger or perversity lies hidden within the character, as in *Scarlet Street* or *The Secret Beyond the Door* [1948]). The more indeterminate the obscured presence is, the more space opens up in the spectator's mind for a wide range of unspeakable horrors.

This indefinability relates to the second level, the unrepresentable. Much of film noir dealt with content contemporaneously considered transgressive and potentially censorable (whether fictional sources like *The Postman Always Rings Twice* that had earlier been deemed too racy to adapt for film, or themes like degrading sexual obsession), and contemporary audiences were aware of this, so the unspecified carried strong implications of an unspeakable transgression. The fact that it was not explicitly represented did not mean that it was not "there" or to be feared. This aura of a foray into the forbidden lent the films part of their contemporary appeal.

Experiment in Terror concerns a perverse killer, "Red" Lynch (Ross Martin), who terrorizes Kelly Sherwood (Lee Remick), a bank clerk, and kidnaps her sister Toby (Stephanie Powers) in order to get Kelly to steal $100,000 for him. FBI Agent John Ripley (Glenn Ford) is brought in and eventually kills Lynch. There is nothing particularly modernist or new in this storyline, but a great deal lies in its representational strategies and cultural implications.

The film is centrally concerned with surveillance, the fragmentation of modern experience and the body, and new structures of voyeurism and perverse sexualities. It begins when Kelly enters her dark garage and is seized by Lynch from behind. We see the terrified Kelly in close-up while Lynch's hand covers her mouth; neither we nor Kelly can see Lynch, whose face is concealed by shadows throughout the scene; his face is not revealed until later in the film. As he speaks in a creepy asthmatic voice, he gropes her body in offscreen space below the frame line. Beginning with premodern criminal intrusions, such as molestation and menace, the film proceeds to invoke intrusive strategies accessible only to the modern era.

Lynch makes explicitly clear that much of what he knows about Kelly, ranging from her body measurements, to her home life with her sister, to her bank job, to her daily routines, he has learned from sustained surveillance of which she has been unaware. As he obscenely utters her physical measurements, we suspect that he is not guessing them as he gropes her but, rather, stating what he already knows from his invasion of her privacy. He is terrifying her with his intimate knowledge of her. With its emphasis on menace, hidden surveillance, and violation of privacy, this aspect of the scene is modernist and characteristic of film noir. The scene also characteristically links the criminal to sexual perversity, not only through Lynch's obsession with Kelly's measurements but also through his heavy breathing and wheezing which further connote sexual perversion (as in the common expression of calling obscene phone-callers "breathers").

Kelly is terrorized in a particularly modern way by a man who, for most of the remainder of the film, is not present in her physical space. We never again see him touch her in a sexual way, although he repeatedly derives sexual pleasure from his control over her. After this initial intrusion into her physical space, Lynch terrorizes her primarily by telephone. She has no idea who or where he is when he calls. He could be in the next room or in another state, and the sexual pleasure he derives from her terror results in part from this modern, technological form of intrusion. This aspect of his menace renders her mounting anxiety free-floating. She cannot physically identify the person who is menacing her because she knows him only as a disembodied voice. At work, she stares anxiously into the faces of customers—Lynch could be any one of them—and she is afraid of everyone. When Lynch tells her to meet him at a singles bar, her situation renders her vulnerable to sexual debasement. She mistakes a man for Lynch and the man mistakes her glances, movements, and opening conversational remarks for a come-on. Believing the man to be Lynch, she allows the predatory seducer to lure her into his car and drive off. When she discovers her error, she risks her life by opening the door of the moving car and tumbling to the street. Later, when Lynch learns of her humiliation, he smiles sadistically.

Experiment in Terror creates a new, particularly modern space that goes beyond traditional chronotopes. Danger is no longer confined to "bad" places of a specific era, like dark alleys or back-street saloons; it can erupt anywhere. Indeed, one of Kelly's most terrifying experiences occurs in a restaurant at lunchtime in broad daylight. She has gone there with a co-worker whom she dates. Several undercover FBI agents are there eating lunch, watching everything carefully. What could be safer than lunch in a well-populated restaurant in broad daylight in the presence of a boyfriend and under the watchful eye of the FBI? Yet, moments after Kelly goes to the restroom, an elderly lady enters and shockingly reveals "herself" to be Red Lynch in disguise. After changing his guise and terrorizing her as a threatening man, he eerily and instantaneously reassumes the appearance of a frail old lady and leaves the restroom and the restaurant undetected.

The scene works on several levels. Ironically, in this general environment of pervasive surveillance and counter-surveillance, no one is sure of anyone, not even whom they are looking for or whether or not someone is a man or a woman. Of course, Lynch's transvestite disguise further connotes his sexual perversity, as does his intrusion into the women's restroom. But the scene also bears relation to an odd subplot in the film. A woman claiming to fear for a friend's life comes to Agent Ripley's office, where he interrogates her. Ripley quickly sees through her pretense: she fears for her own safety. When she returns home and hears a noise in her apartment, she calls Ripley, urging him to hurry and adding that he should not be shocked when he enters the apartment because she has an unusual profession. We soon learn that her profession is making mannequins. She lives surrounded by her work, with countless naked mannequins and body parts standing, lying, and hanging everywhere. Her bedroom is adjacent to her studio, and, in a particularly effective shot, we see the camera track down a row of mannequins as the woman returns to her bedroom, visible in the upper right rear of the frame. Suddenly, one of the mannequins turns its neck, and we realize it is Lynch, this time disguised as a mannequin! A mannequin, of course, is a copy of a living body, and here Lynch is imitating an inanimate body that imitates a living body. The image resonates on several levels, including, once again, that of sexual perversion both in how he stands among naked and fragmented bodies and in how he leers at the disrobing woman as she enters the intimate space of her bedroom. Soon after, Ripley will find her nude body hanging from the ceiling, reduced to the pure object status of the surrounding mannequins.

It would be difficult to find images more consonant with anxieties about the modern world's objectification and fragmentation of the body than those in this scene. This is a film in which the modern age allows Red Lynch mobility without motion (he can call and menace Kelly at work, at home, anywhere, without leaving his apartment), control without presence, and sexual pleasure without bodily contact—a film that constructs a profoundly disturbing, alienated, and alienating modern space. And the space is no longer linked to the landscape, but is something else entirely. The dystopian modern world need no longer manifest itself in a dark alley or in desolate nocturnal office buildings; it can emerge anywhere. Its very disjunction of body from experience produces new and perverse sexualities.

This disjunction is manifested in a pattern of human interchangeability that pervades the film, an interchangeability that erodes traditional presumptions about the unique identity of individuals. The woman who makes mannequins creates what at times appear to be disturbingly accurate bodies or body parts. We not only mistake Red Lynch for a mannequin but the woman herself is hung upside down like one of her mannequins after Lynch murders her. At one moment she appears in an erotic light, disrobing while—without her knowledge—Lynch watches, but shortly thereafter she is briefly mistaken for one of her own mannequins and is as lifeless as one.

For much of the film, Lynch himself appears to have an unstable, free-floating identity. He is able to disguise himself in plain sight as an old woman, as everyone, and as no one. At her bank and in the singles bar, Kelly looks suspiciously at everyone because anyone could be Lynch. This is a world in which a woman can pass for a mannequin and vice versa, one in which an old woman or a mannequin, or anyone at all, can be a male kidnapper. Identity is unstable and malleable, no longer fixed, unique, and obvious.

This changeability also extends to the FBI. A major difference between detectives in the police procedural and those in either the British detective tale as typified by Sherlock Holmes or the American hard-boiled detective tales of Dashiell Hammett and Raymond Chandler lies in the procedural's implicit rejection of individual agency. Detectives in the earlier traditions often single-handedly solved crimes that the police had failed to solve. The private detectives often worked in isolation, relying on intelligence, intuition, and sheer nerve; without their intervention, the cases might never have been solved at all. Detective figures in procedurals tend, to the contrary, to be team players and, as such, interchangeable. Agents like Ripley have no apparent private life whatsoever, and the film indicates that he is interchangeable with other agents in his local office or, for that matter, in the national bureau. If Ripley had not picked up the telephone when Kelly called, presumably another agent would have handled the case as effectively. It is true that Kelly meets him and derives comfort from the knowledge that he is on the case, but she also gains some feeling of security from an agent monitoring her telephone, whom she never meets. When she goes off to meet Lynch, she knows that agents are watching her, but she has no idea who they are or what they look like. The implication is that it does not really matter whether or not Ripley is *personally* on the scene; the FBI agents who are there will do the job.

In the postwar era, the FBI, drawing upon heroic images of the World War II military, presented itself in the image of a peacetime army. All agents were regimented and served the greater good. Individualistic lone "cowboys" were frowned upon as subverting this group dynamic (see, as well, Robertson 2000). Technological expertise and the application of scientific methods to crime solving were part of this image, and the FBI laboratories became internationally famous. Everyone worked as part of a team there. The flip side of this arrangement, of course, lay in the erosion of individuality implied by this ideology, corresponding with a major postwar anxiety. If everyone was an interchangeable part of a team, where was the space for individuality? A fascinating gloss on this quandary appeared in the popular television series, "I Led Three Lives" (1953–1956). The main character was an undercover FBI agent, Herbert A. Philbrick (Richard Carlson), who posed to the public as an insurance agent. His "third" life was as a spy who had infiltrated the Communist Party. He did not disguise himself for his different roles—he looked exactly the same in all three. And all three roles could have been taken by anyone else in any of the three groups—insurance agents, FBI agents, Communists. Implicitly, in defending the United States against identity-eroding Communists, Philbrick was becoming exactly like them. The opposing political forces competing for the modern world shared a common element—devotion to corporate ideology.[2]

The most popular film star of the postwar era was John Wayne, whose star image fascinatingly engaged and countered postwar anxieties about erosions of individuality. His star image was primarily constructed upon two oppositional types of roles: a member of the World War II military and a cowboy of the old West. Portraying a military man in films like *Sands of Iwo Jima* (1949), *Back to Bataan* (1945), and *They Were Expendable* (1945), Wayne appeared as a hero in uniform. Although his characters lived lives of rigid conformity and discipline—they wore the same uniform as others and followed orders from superiors—they nevertheless implied that individual heroism and conformity were not incompatible. At the same time, however, Wayne became identified with his roles as an old-West cowboy, an entirely independent, self-determining individual. Both roles spoke resonantly to postwar anxieties, the first in asserting that a man could retain his individuality in an environment of conformity and submission to authority, and the second in recalling an image of heroic self-determination from the national past.[3]

Police procedurals of the late 1940s and 1950s represented police or federal agents serving benign institutions committed to the public good. The films seldom questioned the motives of the agencies or of the individual agents. That would change in the era of the Vietnam war and Watergate in the late 1960s and 1970s, when critiques of the motives and the integrity of governmental agencies became widespread. Below, we will discuss *Dirty Harry* (1971) in this light. Although *Experiment in Terror* does not make such an overt critique, it does present the FBI in a dark, at times inhuman light. The agents are not the oppressive governmental police of *1984*, but neither are they the benign family-oriented men of films like *The FBI Story* (1959);

rather, they contain elements of both. For viewers familiar with the genre, *Experiment in Terror* gives the sense that something has changed in the world between the late 1940s and the early 1960s, and not for the better.

The film constantly reconfigures and questions spatial significance. It opens with ambiguous moving shots of a car crossing a bridge—the shots themselves are literally free-floating, because the camera moves through the sky unattached to anyone's point of view. During these opening shots we have no notion of who is going where or why. We simply experience disoriented movement through a nighttime urban landscape. In such a modern environment a telephone can instantly transform or create an intimate, a perverse, a helpful, and a totally anonymous aural space. Edwards also emphasizes that the same technology that causes terror can also ease it, because the police use the same surveillance on Kelly Sherwood that Lynch presumably used when he initially cased her. In a remarkable sequence we see Kelly in bed, a phone with an open line to the FBI clutched to her breast. As she lies alone, she nervously lifts the phone to her face and asks if anyone is there. She is comforted to learn that the officer on duty is at his station. Creating a startling contrast, Edwards intercuts shots of Kelly lying in bed with shots of the male officer wearing headphones and sitting at his high-tech station.

Although Lynch is subject to FBI surveillance, the film focuses more upon the power he wields and the pleasure he derives from his own surveillance and intimidation of Kelly. And Agent Ripley, far from supplying a traditional heroic figure of comfort and identification, is disturbingly distant, a nearly inhuman automaton, himself part of this alienating, anxiety-producing, modern urban landscape. When the troubled mannequin maker visits him, she is clearly distressed and at several points seeks a gesture of human response from Ripley that would give her hope or encouragement. Showing no emotion, he simply recites the cold facts of the law.

In a related manner, Ripley shows no romantic interest in Kelly, even though she is a single, young, attractive woman; she in turn shows no romantic interest in him. Casting such appealing stars as Glenn Ford and Lee Remick intensifies audience expectations of romance, but, since none occurs, the conventional romantic coupling between the victimized woman and the male savior embodying the

Law, a common resolution in the Hollywood cinema, is absent here. Indeed, after Toby is rescued, we never even see Ripley and Kelly together again in the film! In place of the traditional heterosexual embrace, we see the two sisters run into each other's arms as Ripley continues his pursuit of Lynch. In stark contrast to Kelly, whose home and family life are central to her characterization, the film gives Ripley no life outside of his job as an FBI agent—no home life, family, friends, romantic attachments, interests, or hobbies—no humanizing attributes at all. He is his job and nothing else. Nothing and no one is comforting and reassuring in this dark world.

Ripley's near inhuman coldness becomes even more complex within the context of Lynch's unexpected humanity. Here again the film demonstrates a profoundly modernist notion of character as not unified and harmonious but instead contradictory and complexly unstable. Modernist culture from the beginning showed an interest in fragmenting traditional notions of character and personality. We can see this tendency in late Victorian novels, such as Robert Louis Stevenson's *The Strange Case of Dr. Jekyll and Mr. Hyde* and Oscar Wilde's *The Picture of Dorian Gray,* which are constructed around characters whose apparent identities are chimeras. Outward projections have little to do with what lies inside those characters, characters that embody grossly contradictory personalities and traits. Freud's writings and the new field of psychology that emerged at the same time as modernism have parallels with this notion of character. Freud described personality as not a single unified entity, as in traditional notions of the soul, but rather as the result of bundles of often oppositional traits being in tension with one another. Modernist artistic movements like Cubism, which literally fragmented the traditionally unified human image, also made this understanding apparent. A theme of modernist films like *Citizen Kane* (1941) is that character is not fixed and unified but complex, unstable, and almost impossible to define.

Within the conventions of Hollywood cinema, little could be more fixed than presumptions that a sexual pervert who is also a kidnapper is entirely evil. Indeed, the belief that someone capable of such crimes is incapable of doing any good carries a certain comfort and security, yet *Experiment in Terror* erodes such notions. Much as Ripley becomes involved in a subplot with the mannequin maker, Lynch becomes involved with Lisa Soong (Anita Loo), a Chinese woman who is a single mother with a sick child, Joey (Warren Hsieh). The contrast is extreme. Whereas Ripley treats the terrified woman without a trace of emotion or sympathy, Lynch has apparently taken a genuine interest in both mother and child. They become a family of sorts with "Uncle Red" bringing gifts to Joey in the hospital.

Indeed, it is Ripley who appears menacing to Lisa and coldly manipulative of Joey when he shows up at their apartment and the hospital to investigate them. The mother wants nothing to do with him and cooperates with the investigation only on the advice of her lawyer. In fact, she repeatedly defends the kindness and generosity that Lynch has shown to her and her son. Ripley turns a deaf ear, and, when he is not making Lisa uncomfortable with his probing questions, he feigns an interest in the sick boy as a way to gain his sympathy and question him about Uncle Red. Joey clearly loves Lynch with the same genuine emotion that his mother shows.

This subplot is further complicated, of course, by the fact that Ripley happens to be right and Lynch is a dangerous criminal. But the film does not define him exclusively in that capacity, and it is here that *Experiment in Terror* becomes quite complexly modernist. Lynch is not, for example, planning to kill Lisa or to kidnap Joey; the relationship he has with them is genuine and he *is* capable of doing some good. In this regard, Lynch resembles certain highly publicized media examples in 2004 of seemingly good husbands and fathers-to-be who have been accused of murdering their pregnant wives; only during the investigation was it revealed that they had been leading double lives. The public fascination with such figures goes well beyond simple questions of guilt or innocence and focuses on the sordid hidden aspects of the husbands' lives. One man may be a compulsive liar who had many extramarital affairs, and a second may have built a life of deception concerning his education and career. A strong sense of the convincing veneer of resolute decency that people have been able to maintain for years frequently emerges as part of the television narrative of such cases. Indeed, in two contemporary cases even the mothers-in-law and fathers-in-law initially stood strongly behind their sons-in-law in much the same manner that Lisa stands behind Lynch, citing firsthand evidence of their goodness and kindness. A psychologist commenting on one case on cable television reminded viewers that it was indeed quite possible that the accused husband had done much good in his life, that people who do evil things are seldom entirely evil. *Experiment in Terror* shares this disturbing, modern psychological notion, which is strongly underscored in two scenes: one with Lynch and his teenage victim and the other in the film's final scene.

After having kidnapped Toby, Lynch prepares to rape her. She hysterically screams and pleads with him and, abruptly, he relents, for no apparent reason other than that he does not have the heart for it. Her genuine distress has extinguished his sexual desire. Later, as Lynch lies dying in the film's final scene, a close-up of the anguished expression on his face creates another strong moment of sympathy for him. The labored asthmatic breathing we now hear does not connote sexual perversion so much as horrible, genuine suffering, a sound that stands in for the film's absolute refusal to tell us anything about what motivates Red Lynch; he is human, he has suffered in his life and, for a fleeting moment, we feel for him.

The final scene of *Experiment in Terror* not only links the film to classic film noir but also looks forward to films that would follow in this tradition, such as *Dirty Harry*. *Experiment in Terror* ends in (the then three-year-old) Candlestick Park, representing the stadium in two drastically opposing ways. We first see it packed with tens of thousands of people sharing this communal, celebratory space while they enjoy a baseball game. Moments later, however, it becomes an empty and menacing shell. Lynch, who was anonymous among the throngs of spectators leaving the stadium is, once again through the use of modern technology and communication, identified and singled out from the crowd. Pursued by Ripley, he flees onto the dimly lit playing field that is now surrounded by empty seats. Suddenly, bright lights from a helicopter illuminate Lynch. He is shot by Ripley and collapses on the pitcher's mound. Ripley approaches the dying man and the final shots of the film are dissolved into one another as the camera rises nearly straight up in the dark night sky. The victorious FBI agent and his men form a closing circle around the dead criminal as they all become smaller and smaller figures in the frame.

Dirty Harry, directed by Don Siegel and made almost a decade later, includes a strikingly similar scene. This time, in place of Ripley's cold FBI agent, Harry Callahan (Clint Eastwood), an angry and vengeful San Francisco police detective, chases a suspect onto the playing field of Kezar Stadium. Like Lynch in *Experiment in Terror*, the suspect is a sexual pervert who has kidnapped a girl. He falls to the ground and Callahan stands over him much as Ripley stood over Lynch. Once again, a helicopter shot shows the men as the camera rises high into the night sky.

The character, narrative, and stylistic features of these two scenes are so strikingly similar that it appears that Siegel is paying homage to Edwards, although we have no extratextual evidence that he intended to do so or even was aware of the earlier film. Either way, the image of a law officer standing over the prone body of a sexually perverted kidnapper of teenage girls in an empty, well-lit stadium at night while the camera rises high into the sky above becomes itself almost a new chronotope of the modern crime film. We have seemingly become a society in which perverse crime is a spectacle, not for living, breathing fans sitting joyfully in their seats, but rather for some unknown, alienated spectator as the camera moves high into the dark night sky. From the opening ominous helicopter shots of cars crossing a bridge, coming from we know not where and going to we know not where in the dark of night, to the closing helicopter shots in the empty stadium, *Experiment in Terror* creates a world where anonymity, darkness, perversity, and technology are intermingled everywhere. The image of that cold agent standing over the dead body offers little comfort in an environment that seems to harbor and breed such terror.

It is perhaps within this context that we can best understand a curious minor character in the film: a police informant nicknamed Popcorn (Ned Glass) who is always carrying and eating from a bag of popcorn, a habit that associates him with movie theaters. What is unusual about Popcorn, however, is that when we see him sitting in a movie theater, enjoying a movie and eating popcorn, he is watching a silent slapstick comedy. In 1962, when color and widescreen were becoming the norm, as sound had been the norm since 1928, silent cinema was commonly perceived as a crude remnant from the ancient past. Popcorn's nostalgia for such cinema (which Edwards himself shares) marks him as longing for the premodern past or, more precisely, that moment when the premodern was giving way to the modern. Indeed, Popcorn's method of gathering information is old-fashioned eavesdropping and contact with sources as opposed to the sophisticated surveillance technology employed by the FBI, and his status as "old-fashioned" marks him as unfit for survival in this new high-tech world. He is murdered, interestingly enough, as he uses the telephone.

Cinema has a long-standing tradition of staging scenes of horror and terror in front of a crowd of spectators who have gathered for purposes of entertainment, sports, or politics. In Alfred Hitchcock's *Murder!* (1930), a circus trapeze artist commits suicide by hanging himself in front of a crowd gathered to enjoy a circus performance. Something similar could easily have been contrived in *Experiment in Terror,* with Ripley chasing Lynch onto the baseball diamond in the midst of the game and killing him as horrified fans and players looked on. Instead, Edwards imagines modern horror as occurring in the tangible absence of such a crowd. He experimented with a related idea in *Breakfast at Tiffany's* (1961), the film he made the year before *Experiment in Terror.* In one scene, Paul Varjack (George Peppard), who is in love with Holly Golightly (Audrey Hepburn), follows a suspicious man into Central Park. The scene builds with ominous suspense, all the more noticeable in tone because it contrasts with much of the light, romantic, comic tone of much of the rest of the film. The two men finally confront one another, the only people in the seating area before an empty band shell, and Varjack is surprised to learn that the man is Holly Golightly's husband. This intensely personal and private drama unfolds in the empty performance space, and much of the scene's effect comes from the contrast inherent in this intimate drama playing out in a space created for crowds to watch a public performance.[4]

Elias Canetti's influential *Crowds and Power* (which appeared in German in 1960 and in English in 1962) analyses the social/psychological/historical significance of crowd dynamics, including the shift from individual psychological characteristics into crowd psychology. Canetti describes one of the central elements of a crowd as the desire to expand, often with frenzied desperation. The flip side of this desire, of course, is a crowd's fear of dispersal, of ceasing to exist. Canetti speaks of sports stadiums as places where the frenzy of the crowd, while still potent, can be socially contained (Canetti 1984). But *Experiment in Terror* presents a stadium emptied of the crowd we have just seen. Implicitly, the very reason for the stadium's existence is gone; hence, that setting has a haunting atmosphere of desolation, absence, ghostliness.

In these films from the early 1960s, Edwards shows that the absence of crowds in public spaces has become an important characteristic of modern urban life. *Breakfast at Tiffany's* is set in New York and *Experiment in Terror* in San Francisco. In the former, the collapse of the traditional nuclear family and the rise of alternative, new sexualities that the older husband from the rural South cannot begin to understand become linked to a New York landmark, the band shell in Central Park; in the latter, Candlestick Park, with no spectators to witness the taking of a human life, itself becomes a terrifying landmark. Nor is there much comfort in knowing that cold automatons or vengeful, renegade cops are out there unobserved enforcing the law in what should be a space of communal activity and social cohesion.

Images of huge crowds in a single space emotionally united with a single purpose have served a wide range of twentieth-century utopian ideological agendas, from the proletarian solidarity in Soviet films of the 1920s, such as *Potemkin* (*Bronenosets Potyomkin* [1925]) and *October* (*Oktyabr* [1927]), to Nazi films of the 1930s like *Triumph of the Will* (*Triumph des Willens* [1934]) and *Olympia* (1938), to socially conservative films of the 1970s like *Star Wars* (1977). Stadiums provide ideal locations for such motivated mass gatherings. Filmmakers have also been drawn to the terrifying possibilities inherent in such mass gatherings in the modern world. In *Black Sunday* (1977), directed by John Frankenheimer—who was already famous for the political assassination in a public space in *The Manchurian Candidate* (released the same year as *Experiment in Terror*)—terrorists attempt to blow up a Goodyear blimp over the Super Bowl stadium packed with 80,000 spectators, including the president of the United States. The plot is ultimately foiled in front of a stadium full of terrified spectators. Similarly, in *The Sum of All Fears* (2002), the Russians plan to detonate a nuclear device during the Super Bowl.[5] *Snake Eyes* (1998) begins with a murder that takes place during a heavyweight boxing championship match in an indoor Atlantic City arena packed with 14,000 fight fans who witness it; the entire film takes place within the enclosed space of the arena.

An interesting variation on the stadium motif used in *Experiment in Terror* and *Dirty Harry* appears in *Twisted* (2004), a serial killer murder mystery directed by Philip Kaufman and once again set in San Francisco. The scene that introduces the first murder victim takes place at night against the backdrop of a San Francisco Giants baseball game with a brightly lit stadium full of cheering fans. The contrast, at times conveyed within single shots, between the detectives investigating the crime scene in pitch darkness and the brightly lit, noisy stadium full of communal joy comes close to containing the central dichotomy of the entire Candlestick Park sequence in *Experiment in Terror* compactly in one scene. Kaufman says on the DVD commentary track that he always wanted to make a film noir in San Francisco, but the closest he came was his remake of *Invasion of the Body Snatchers* (1978). He was attracted to this script precisely because it gave him this long-awaited opportunity. About the scene just described, he comments that it was shot on location during an actual Giants game, implying that he wanted the contrast between the cheering crowds in the stadium and the act of murder, of which the spectators are totally unaware.

The films that play out a fascination with the potential horrors of something going dreadfully wrong at large sports gatherings relate to the deeds that take place in the empty stadiums in *Experiment in Terror* and *Dirty Harry* or in close proximity to the crowded stadium in *Twisted*. Deserted stadiums invoke an even more extreme, dystopian dark side than the ones in which crowds witness horrific events. Abandoned stadiums testify to the dispersed hopes of mass unity, the corpse of celebration (in Kaufman's variation, a corpse literally lies in the darkness outside the ongoing celebration within the stadium). The empty seats evoke the ghosts of enthusiastic spectators no longer there, and embody a particularly modern indifference to whatever human drama occurs before them. One could hardly conjure an environment more unsettlingly appropriate to dystopian modernism's landscape of despair than the immanent presence of those empty stadium seats in *Experiment in Terror,* engulfed by the vast darkness of the night sky.

Notes

We wish to thank Elliot Rubinstein for his perceptive observations about modernism, camera positioning, and point of view in the opening credit sequence of *Experiment in Terror* in a paper delivered at the Society for Cinema Studies Conference years ago. That paper has resonated with us for many years and sparked the interest in modernism and *Experiment in Terror* that inspired this essay.

1. A good deal of recent work has been done on anxiety in film noir, including Oliver and Trigo (2002). E. Ann Kaplan's work (2004) on trauma also contributes to an understanding of the issue.

2. Some of the material on film noir and the postwar era in this essay is drawn from William Luhr's forthcoming book, *Film Noir,* which in turn draws on numerous sources, including May (2002), Naremore (1998), and Polan (1986).

3. For greater detail on the relationship between John Wayne's star image and post-war culture, see Luhr (2004).

4. For a quite different discussion of *Breakfast at Tiffany's* within the context of Blake Edwards's oeuvre, see Lehman and Luhr (1977, 60–66). The same work (1977, 66–70) discusses *Experiment in Terror.*

5. Related films that involve attempted public assassinations at crowded political rallies include *The Parallax View* (1974) and *Nick of Time* (1995).

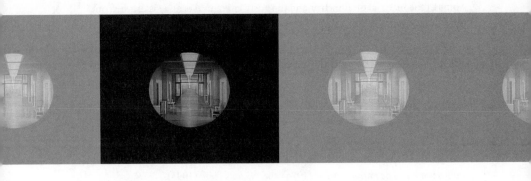

FULLER, FOUCAULT, AND FORGETTING
THE EYE OF POWER IN *SHOCK CORRIDOR*
David Sterritt

[T]he eye, a small white globe that encloses its darkness, traces a limiting circle that only sight can cross. And the darkness within, the somber core of the eye, pours out into the world like a fountain which sees, that is, which lights up the world; but the eye also gathers up all the light of the world in the iris, that small black spot, where it is transformed into the bright night of an image. The eye is mirror and lamp . . .

But perhaps the eye accomplishes the most essential aspect of its play when, forced from its ordinary position, it is made to turn upwards in a movement that leads it back to the nocturnal and starred interior of the skull . . . and the circular night of the iris is made to address the central absence which it illuminates with a flash, revealing it as night.

MICHEL FOUCAULT, "A PREFACE TO TRANSGRESSION"

Shock Corridor, a melodrama written, directed, and produced by Samuel Fuller in 1963, centers on Johnny Barrett (Peter Breck), a newspaper reporter whose obsession with winning a Pulitzer Prize leads him to feign psychiatric illness. Persuading his reluctant lover Cathy (Constance Towers) to pose as his sister and charge him with incest, he enters the hospital in hopes of solving a murder that was committed there and seeks clues by talking to patients who witnessed the crime. Johnny himself goes insane in the end, exposing the mur-

194

derer but losing his own ability to speak or move. Fuller uses this story to conduct his own investigation of the 1950s era. Each of the three persons who witnessed the murder—a former soldier, a black activist, and a scientist—is obsessed with a prime paranoia of the postwar years: for the soldier, communism; for the activist, racial bigotry; and for the scientist, nuclear destruction.

The film begins with the camera gazing down what appears to be the corridor of the title. Most of the visual field is masked off, leaving a small circular image in the center of the screen, which gradually swells to reveal the entire space of the hallway. This process—irising—has been around since silent-movie days, but Fuller's use of it here suggests that vision and the eye are possible subjects or subtexts of this film. In any case, his gradual revelation of the image associates seeing with not seeing, and links the act of seeing with the act of controlling what is to be seen.

Meanwhile, a voiceover narration gives introductory plot information in a way that similarly combines accessible material—audible, coherent words—with signs that arbitrary limitations are at work. We do not see the speaker, and as a narrator he's as unreliable as they come: "This is my story," he tantalizingly tells us, *as far as it went.*" All of which indicates that our perception of the story will be controlled by forces outside our sensory grasp, and perhaps beyond our epistemological powers as well.

Every film has this quality to one degree or another, but rarely is it inscribed so emphatically within the movie itself, much less in the very first moments. Fuller underscores the presence of his control, and, going a step farther, he associates it with an ominous epigram from Euripides that fills the screen just before the corridor's first appearance: "*Whom God wishes to destroy He first makes mad.*" Coupled with signs of an invisible (godlike) power manipulating the film itself, this statement raises unsettling questions as to who "God" may be, whom this "God" may "wish to destroy," and what forms the "making mad" might take.[1] Will the answers be worked out within the narrative? Might we ourselves be subjects of the power games to follow? Thus does Fuller force consideration of issues that Michel Foucault has formulated in phrases such as these: "The question of power remains a total enigma. Who exercises power? And in what sphere?" (1977a, 213)

In his writings on power and modernity, Foucault explores various areas that have attracted Fuller's attention as well, including the nature of power relations; the interplay of power, knowledge, and discourse; the development and operation of social norms; and the relationship of such norms to mental illness and other forms of allegedly aberrant behavior. All are key concerns of *Shock Corridor,* which probes them through a combination of Fuller's own boisterous, quintessentially modern sensibility and a concatenation of B-movie devices creatively used.

In this essay I intend to look at *Shock Corridor* through a Foucauldian lens. I do not mean to suggest that Fuller had firsthand familiarity with Foucault, or that the discursive practices of the two men have a great deal in common. I do think, however, that Fuller's modernist melodramatics reveal a surprisingly cogent grasp of the kinds of power relations that are among Foucault's most abiding preoccupations.

Underlying much of Foucault's work is a concern with the cluster of epistemological paradigms—the *episteme*—containing and guiding the thoughts and practices of a given epoch. These are often manifested through operations of causing, allowing, or imposing visibility. In his key work, *Discipline and Punish* (1979), for instance, Foucault contrasts a historical instance of sadistic criminal-justice chastisement with a meticulous "timetable of observed activities," illustrating how "spectacle" and "surveillance" constitute "two ways crime was made visible in the body" for purposes of edifying (and deterring) the multitude who watched. Similarly, in *The Birth of the Clinic* (1975) he juxtaposes a physician's examination of a brain with a medicinal "bathing cure," two ways of organizing "the space in which bodies and eyes meet" (Rajchman 1988, 91).[2]

Many of the words in the phrases just quoted—visible, spectacle, surveillance, space, eyes, bodies—suggest how intensely visual Foucault's thinking often is. And he sees all kinds of knowledge, including visual kinds, in the context of power. Power relations are "changeable, reversible and unstable" (1987, 123), he tells us, constituting a sort of dispersed force field rather than a type of private property or individual domain. Truth is also fluid and mutable, articulated by people "who arrive at . . . agreement" within particular "practices of power and constraining institutions" (1987, 128). In visual terms, the notion of socially constructed "truth" provides a passageway between what can be seen or shown, on one hand, and power relations, on the other.[3]

Shock Corridor takes place in a mental hospital that combines features of the clinic and the prison, institutions that Foucault exhaustively studied. Johnny goes there to get a story. In other words, he wants to produce what Foucault calls "true discourse," always based on "an ensemble of rules" and "procedures which lead to a certain result," ratified in advance by (unstated) cultural consensus (1987, 127). The hospital also wants to generate "true discourse" from power-based rules and procedures; but, diverging from journalism, it draws its most potent varieties of power from "the form of scientific discourse and the institutions which produce it" (1980c, 131).[4] Part of the film's drama comes from conflict between journalistic and medical discourse, each meant to induce "regular effects of power" but quite different in their goals. Johnny's aims are historical discovery, public communication, and professional acclaim; the hospital's aims are to objectify, categorize, and normalize its inmates according to medical and psychiatric models. Johnny, of course, is one of those inmates.

Blind Word/Mute Vision

Film theorist Christian Metz has called cinema a "language" with (perhaps paradoxically) no underpinning "language system" to provide a consistent foundation for how it is used (see Metz 1974). Cinema thus represents, in Metz's view, a virtually infinite field of expressive possibilities. In this context it is interesting to recall Foucault's paraphrase of remarks made by physician Philippe Pinel around 1815 with regard to the clinic in the early nineteenth century: "If the clinical domain is open only to the tasks of language or to the demands of the gaze, it will have no limits and, therefore, no organization. There is boundary, form, and meaning only if interrogation and examination are connected with each other" (1975, 111). One can rework this observation by replacing clinical terms with filmic ones: "If the *cinematic* domain is open only to the tasks of *narrative* or the demands of *sensory impact*, it will have no limits and, therefore, no organization. There is boundary, form, and meaning only if *literary* and *audiovisual* functions are connected with each other."

In hospitals, the desire to link interrogation and examination—the spoken and the seen—led to what Foucault calls a historical passage "from the *totality of the visible* to the *over-all structure of the expressible*" (1975, 114; emphasis in original). In cinema, the impulse toward transparency and coherence has led to a comparable movement from emphasis on the purely visible—think of *actualités* by the Lumière brothers and spectacles by Georges Méliès—to a reliance on formal conventions that subordinate *sensory* priorities to *narrative* and "*poetic*" functions.

History never takes a consistent course, however, as Foucault frequently reminds us. Not all filmmakers are content with classical cinematic forms, and Fuller stands with the ornery ones. His best movies combine narrative and poetic functions with a sensory impact so direct that critics often use the term "primitive" to describe it.[5] His wish to tell stories through hard-hitting images and sounds recalls Foucault's description of an epistemological "myth" nurtured by nineteenth-century physicians: the ideal of scientific investigation as "a pure Gaze that [is also] pure Language: a speaking eye." This eye "would scan the entire hospital field . . . and as it saw [ever more] clearly, it would be turned into speech that states and teaches. . . . This speaking eye would be the servant of things and the master of truth" (1975, 114–15).

Fuller's project, like those of Foucault's clinician and Fuller's own Johnny Barrett, is to mobilize a "hearing gaze and a speaking gaze" representing what Foucault calls "a moment of balance between speech and spectacle." This balance is "precarious," however, because it rests on a far-reaching assumption: "that all that is *visible* is *expressible,* and that it is *wholly visible* because it is *wholly expressible.*" Foucault shows how this assumption failed in medicine, dooming science's dream of unifying "the visible and the describable" (1975, 115–16). The equivalent assumption has also failed in cinema, where spectacle and language may take parallel paths but cannot be interlocked components of one another. Gilles Deleuze illuminates this dilemma further in his writing about the disjunction between seeing and speaking in cinema. "As long as we stick to things and words we can believe that we are speaking of what we see, that we see what we are speaking of, and that the two are linked: in this way we remain on the level of an empirical exercise," he suggests.

But as soon as we open up words and things, as soon as we discover statements and visibilities, words and sight are raised to a higher exercise that is *a priori,* so that each reaches its own unique limit which separates it from the other, a visible element that can only be seen, an articulable element that can only be spoken. And yet the unique limit that separates each one is also the common limit that links one to the other, a limit with two irregular faces, a blind word and a mute vision. (1988, 65)

From the desire for "a hearing gaze and a speaking gaze," then, our journey has taken us to "a blind word and a mute vision." Yet we are not at an impasse. The visible and the articulable, Deleuze continues, "comprise a condition and a conditioned element, light and visibilities, language and statements," whereby "the condition does not 'contain' the conditioned element but offers it in a space of dissemination, and offers up itself as a form of exteriority." Although we cannot really speak of what we see, or see what we speak of, we can approximate meaning by "[s]peaking and *seeing at the same time,*" argues Deleuze. He posits that "[I]t is between the visible and its conditions that statements glide" (1988, 66, 67; emphasis in original).

This is a basic principle of modern cinema, and some filmmakers—including Fuller—like to foreground their jurisdiction over it. The director does this in the opening moments of *Shock Corridor* by presenting three interwoven elements: the sight of the corridor, the sound of Johnny's narration, and the punctuation of the irising device. Fuller's control of the camera lens connects him with the protagonist whose voice we hear. Each will try to formulate "a hearing gaze and a speaking gaze," that is, to gather knowledge and power through combined interrogation and examination—Johnny by snooping and interviewing for his newspaper story, Fuller by drawing images and narrative into cinematic alliance. Significantly, neither will succeed. Johnny's ability to speak will be destabilized by the sights and sounds he encounters, and submerged by the inscription on his body of psychiatric discourse carried to its reified extreme. Fuller will (re)discover the impossibility of merging narrative and sensation in such a way that each is able to keep its own identity and impact. The mythical "speaking eye" proves unreachable once more. What *can* be evoked is a semiotic boundary line that fuses the "blind word and mute vision" even as it marks the border between them, drawing "visibilities [and] statements" into a persuasive if illusory coalition.

"Incorrect" Cinema

The wish to conjure up this ephemeral alliance is a driving force behind Fuller's "primitive" disregard for Hollywood norms, his affinity for marginalized tropes and techniques, and his eagerness to cross borders that ordinarily separate the "correct" from the "incorrect" in cinema. A desire to test and explore boundary relations, including the intersection of "blind word and mute vision," often lies at the heart of his work. *Shock Corridor* provides numerous instances. On a technical level, one observes the interactions of color and black-and-white cinematography, of kinetic montage and long-take dialogue scenes, of static and moving camera work, and even of "professional" and "amateur" filmmaking.[6] On a thematic level, one observes the interactions of sanity and insanity, of normality and transgression, of therapeutic and punitive interventions, and of power and knowledge themselves.

Conceptualizing human consciousness not as a firmly delineated structure but as a "mobile margin, passing from knowledge to knowledge," some gestalt theorists see the subject as an entity that, in Donald Morton's words, "continually problematizes and politicizes [itself] rather than delivering [itself] up to a comfortable and stabilized identity" (1990, 230).[7] Fuller evokes this unbounded, ever-tentative condition by mobilizing the cinematic margin in two ways. For one, he ceaselessly probes and teases accepted standards of mainstream-film construction; for the other, he embodies his drastic aesthetic ideas in cheaply made B pictures populated largely by characters from the fringes of "polite" society. These pictures often problematize the coherence and accessibility of his movies for average consumers (and politicize them, in ways that are *themselves* problematic) rather than serving and stabilizing cinematic conventions. Such a work as *Shock Corridor* is therefore not a straightforward Saturday-night entertainment but rather a complicated, closely woven skein of rowdily clashing elements—for example, the sanity and insanity that collide within Johnny, a "sane" person who undertakes an "insane" mission and subsequently loses his "sanity" to therapies aimed at managing "insanity"!

Thus does Fuller construct a visual/sensory and narrative/poetic realm wherein both cinema and subjectivity have been "reunderstood in terms of displaced persons, of subjects dispersed across a set of contradictory discourses, and of knowledge-dissemination as knowledge-displacement," to quote Morton once more (1990, 239).[8] Such displacements, dispersions, and contradictions are Fuller's stock in trade, rooted in his habitual fascination with the movement of meaning along boundaries and with the productive displacement, dispersion, and contradiction necessitated (and facilitated) by cinema's own impracticable urge to fuse "blind word and mute vision" into a utopian "hearing and speaking gaze."

The primary narrative settings of *Shock Corridor* are themselves riddled with borders; but in keeping with the film's pessimistic outlook, these are depicted as boundaries that *limit* rather than interfaces that *fuse*. The hospital in which Johnny attempts to mobilize the "speaking eye" of his investigation is a conspicuously bounded place, with a multitude of rooms branching off the confining corridor that dominates the institution and the lives of the patients within it. It is a tragic location that fails to cure its ailing inhabitants, harbors sexual aggression and murder, and attacks the mind and body of a putative hero who aims to expose its most deeply hidden secret—and all of these sinister traits are perceptually inscribed in the sterile symmetries and rigid demarcations that prevent statements and visibilities from meaningful passage along and among the place's various borders. Even the "corridor" of Cathy's dressing room is a more fertile and productive space than its counterpart in the hospital, because it allows some small measure of security and solidarity for its occupants.

In addition, Fuller ironically echoes the symmetries and rhymes of the film's social/political/architectural discourse with symmetries and rhymes in the film's own self-reflexive structure. Compare, for example, the manner in which the three witness-characters symmetrically invert varieties of 1950s-era paranoia; and note such extravagant visual rhymes as the correspondence between Cathy's headpiece in the striptease scene and African headdresses in the activist's hallucination scene.[9]

The hospital's most threatening spaces are among its most strictly segregated: the "nympho" ward, with its hysterical sexuality; the "hydro" room, where body and mind are visually severed (as isolated heads hover over concealed trunks and limbs) and where the murderer is ultimately found; and the kitchen, where the killing took place and the climactic struggle is most ferociously waged. Still, every area of the institution falls under the conceptualizing gaze of the hospital staff, which is ineffective at solving power/knowledge dilemmas that might interest the world at large—the murderer has committed his crime, the clinicians have no idea how to solve it, and mental dysfunction is warehoused rather than cured under their care—but seems quite puissant with regard to its own small concerns in its own limited domain. Like the late-eighteenth-century hospital and prison authorities whom Foucault discusses, the staff here seeks to "eliminate the shadowy areas of society" by keeping potentially aberrant members under close and continual control, employing formulas of "power through transparency" and subjection by "illumination" (1980a, 153–54), and thus mimicking the project implicit in Jeremy Bentham's unrealized "panopticon" design, which Foucault describes as a hypothetical "space of exact legibility" that aims to make "the areas of darkness in man . . . disappear" (1980a, 154).[10]

Deterring Eyes

The hospital is not panoptical in a literal sense, of course. The fundamental point of the panopticon is to make inmates internalize the "policing" process, on the assumption that an ever-present *possibility* of observation is a never-ceasing deterrent to deviancy. In the hospital of *Shock Corridor,* the threat and practice of scrutiny-by-gaze are intermittent rather than constant; nobody seems to notice, for instance, when Cathy moves to kiss her "brother" passionately in the visiting room, and she does not seem surprised at this. Internalized regulation and self-discipline are emphatically supplemented here by the external "policing" of the hospital staff, especially in the "public" corridor, where social activity takes place under plainly visible surveillance. The obviousness of such surveillance does not dilute its potency, and the institution's putative purpose as a place for healing (or at least ameliorating) illness seems secondary to its more essential purpose as a place where the abnormal is normalized (or at least constrained) through practices of observation and control by a staff that has ready access to therapies (and restraints) that everyone acknowledges to be punitive.

For instance, Johnny admits he has "learned [his] lesson" after an electroshock session, whereupon the attending physician chuckles with delight, a reaction that Johnny accepts as a matter of course—just as a patient of Pinel might have accepted a "frankly juridical" administration of the disciplinary shower, which Foucault calls "the habitual punishment of the police tribunal that sat permanently at the asylum" (1973, 266).

The key point here is that the hospital and the prison become indistinguishable in *Shock Corridor,* because no one questions the equation of *abnormal* behavior (that is, actions not sufficiently normalized) with *criminal* behavior. The acceptance of this equation by the victims as well as the wielders of power is the *functional* equivalent of panoptic "internalization" that keeps the subject under the psychological as well as physical domination of constraints (actual and imaginary, visible and invisible) imposed from outside and above. Foucault gives the term "subject" a dual definition: the condition of being "subject to someone else by control and dependence" and also that of being "tied to [one's] own identity by a conscience or self-knowledge." Each of these meanings, he argues, suggests "a form of power which subjugates and makes subject to" (1984, 21). Johnny begins his odyssey with a seemingly secure sense of self-knowledge, but forfeits it to the institutional aggression (interrogations, examinations, "all kinds of tests") that the hospital inflicts on him at his own invitation. Fuller thus demonstrates the inability of self-knowledge to forestall the most self-destructive and insidious of sociocultural power/knowledge ploys.

We must remember, too, that Fuller's protagonist is under the controlling gaze not only of the clinicians in the narrative but also of Fuller himself, who inaugurated the film by artificially and arbitrarily inscribing his own circular "eye of power" (Foucault 1980a, 146–65) over its initial image. The decisive stages in Johnny's subjectification therefore take place under two kinds of close scrutiny: narrative gazes *within* the story and a cinematic-technological gaze *upon* the story. Both are inevitably complicit with what Foucault calls "bio-power," the complex of social-psychological disciplines that in modern times have "brought life and its mechanisms into the realm of explicit calculations and made knowledge-power an agent of transformation of human life" (1980b, 143).

To state this thesis in psychoanalytic terms: Johnny is the protagonist of a film in which he is inscribed in two specifically *scopic* regimes—that of the narrative and that of the filmmaker. Within the scopic field, the subject of representation is inevitably "a picture," according to psychoanalytic theorist Jacques Lacan, and it is the *being-looked-at* function of this picture that resides "at the heart of the institution of the subject in the visible." What determines the subject, Lacan asserts, "at the most profound level, in the visible, is the gaze that is outside. It is through the gaze that I enter light and it is from the gaze that I receive its effects. Hence it comes about that the gaze is the instrument through which . . . I am *photo-graphed*" (1978, 106; emphasis in original).

Lacan is not speaking here of "the philosophical problem of representation" or of politicized technologies of the body, both of which Foucault discusses in various works; rather, he is exploring the issue of *self-knowledge* and by extension the *subjectification* that is also at the core of Foucault's ideas (and, incidentally, at the core of Johnny's destiny). Lacan takes as a given "the fact that there is something that establishes a fracture, a bi-partition, a splitting of the being to which the being accommodates itself, even in the natural world." (One thinks again of the split between visibility and expressibility that shatters the "speaking eye" in Foucault's view.) In extreme situations, such as sex and death, Lacan continues, "the being breaks up, in an extraordinary way, between its being and its semblance" and "gives of himself, or receives from the other, something that is like a mask, a double, an envelope. . . . It is through this separated form of himself that the being comes into play in his effects of life and death." In the human world (as opposed to the deracinated "natural" world) the human being— "the subject of the desire that is the essence of man"—is not "entirely caught up in this imaginary capture" but rather "maps himself in it." This mapping is effective to the extent that the subject "isolates the function of the screen [that is, the plane of intersection of the gaze and the subject of representation] and plays with it. Man, in effect, knows how to play with the mask as that beyond which there is the gaze. The screen is here the locus of mediation" (Lacan 1978, 106–7).

Johnny has lost control of the "mapping" and "playing" functions that separate the "mask" from the "gaze" and allow the subject to escape engulfment in the imaginary. Or rather, he has never had this control, which has always already belonged to dominant power figures both inside and outside the narrative. Johnny's deliberately assumed mask fails to shield him from the machinations of power that assault him within the institution that he has penetrated and within the narrative that, one might say, has penetrated him. Regimes of controlling bio-power ("all kinds of tests") blind his vision as well as his word, mute his word as well as his vision, and instigate his fall from the symbolic order of language even as his movement along the corridor's axis comes to a paralytic halt and both of his voices (embodied and disembodied, dialogue and narration) drop irretrievably from the film. Thus does the "hearing and speaking gaze" manifest its own impossibility: through Johnny's entry into senseless and sense-less catatonia; through the hospital's failure on every level except that of its own brute self-sustenance; and through Fuller's recourse to a visual closure that resists narrative resolution, reimposing his omnipotent blockage of the visible field (via the return of the Euripides inscription) while his surrogate within the story (Johnny) presides sightlessly and silently over the corridor's reception of a new victim.

Liberation

We have noted that notions of socially constructed "truth" can provide a discursive hinge or passageway between power and vision. Truth is never "outside power, or lacking in power," Foucault insists:

> Truth is a thing of this world: it is produced only by virtue of multiple forms of constraint. . . . Each society has its regime of truth, its "general politics" of truth: that is, the types of discourse which it accepts and makes function as true; the mechanisms and instances which enable one to distinguish true and false statements, the means by which each is sanctioned; the techniques and procedures accorded value in the acquisition of truth; the status of those who are charged with saying what counts as true. (1980c, 131)

Truth is therefore profoundly social, profoundly political, and profoundly intertwined with both power and visibility, which is itself "a matter of a positive, material, anonymous body of practice" that determines what is allowed to, and indeed what is able to, be seen and shown. Because of these "constraints of thought," Foucault argues, we are not free in what we see. At the same time, though, "we are much *more* free than we think," because the sheer existence of visibility as a sociocultural phenomenon opens seeing to the possibility of "historical change or transformation" (Rajchman 1988, 93).

In a surprisingly Foucauldian spirit, Fuller opens vision to change precisely by revealing how thought determines what we are able to see, and how different our ideas might be if "truth" resided not only in the power centers that claim it—such as journalism, psychiatry, and the commonsensical prejudices of mainstream cinema—but also in a realm of liberated creativity that played at constructing "a hearing gaze and a speaking gaze" for the sheer audacity of the exercise, regardless of the chance for success. In the process he transgresses filmmaking norms that favor narrative clarity over sensual immediacy. To the Foucauldian question of who exercises power and in what sphere, *Shock Corridor* replies that the answer must remain an enigma, because knowledge, discourse, and vision are—like God—everywhere, nowhere, and ineffable. To the equally Foucauldian question, "What difference does it make who is speaking?" the movie answers: All the difference and no difference at all, because the person whom God wishes to destroy, He first makes mad, which in the case of Johnny Barrett means traumatized, paralyzed, and mute.

It is essential to observe, however, that Johnny's ultimate silence and immobility do not in themselves signify the "destruction" mentioned by the epigraph. According to Euripides, the person singled out is *first* made mad. Thus, Johnny has been only *prepared* for destruction; one need not assume that his condition at the end of the story is worse than at the beginning, when he was obsessed with career advancement and public approval, or in the middle, when he struggled with the hospital's punishments and threats. In the final analysis, Johnny's catatonic trance may be a blessing, as the movie hints with one of its recurring motifs. At one point in the story we see a picture of the Statue of Liberty on an office wall; much later, a patient's arm rises upward mimicking its pose; and Johnny's outstretched arm recalls this gesture just before the end.[11] He may have achieved "liberty" at this point, even if some God-sent "destruction" still awaits him—liberty not only from the oppressive clinic/prison but also from the drives that impelled him there in the first place and from the force of Fuller's cinematic gaze, which has hitherto allowed him no rest.

Forgetting

Foucault follows Friedrich Nietzsche when he argues that putative "truth" is ultimately an egregious form of error. Nietzsche found thought itself "an arbitrary fiction," because, in Allen S. Weiss's words, it deceptively abstracts "a few elements from an infinitely complex set of events," serving only the "will to power" or the body that manifests that will (1989, 27). Johnny's fall from language and meaning may therefore represent not destruction-by-god or "the zero-degree noiselessness of death," but rather his escape from socially constructed thought into what Weiss calls "that moment where sovereignty is elliptically expressed as incommunicable inner experience" (1989, 27–28).[12]

As noted earlier, Johnny begins the story in a state of obsessive involvement with examination and interrogation. To pursue these activities, he sublimates his libidinal energy—note his bogus incest fantasy and lack of a normal sex life—into what he considers praiseworthy professional work. But his desire to find sociocultural "truth" is frustrated by the "insane" discourses he encounters in the hospital, thrusting him away from his intended historical track and toward the contrasting realm of what Nietzsche and Foucault call genealogy. To quote Weiss once more, genealogy reverses the sublimation process associated with cultural meaning, instead revealing "the multiplicity of the body which is concealed and repressed by the ego" and the contingencies from which "the fiction of the self is formed." This process involves what Foucault calls counter-memory, "an active forgetting which is a movement towards unknowing, where the silent but excessive articulations of the body with other bodies are effected," reinstating the "possibilities of joyful expenditure, of laughter . . . or silence" (Weiss 1989, 28; ellipsis in original).

Johnny's forgetting begins abruptly and builds rapidly toward stillness and muteness. This process may be seen as destruction-by-god, but we might also view it as the bodily graphesis of liberation and joy. It leads not only to Johnny's lack of speech and movement, but also to his independence from culturally produced meanings, and—not incidentally—it reasserts Fuller's freedom from the norms of conventional cinema. Note how the heroine desperately tries to achieve Hollywood's customary "lovers' clinch" in the last scene, only to meet utter intransigence from her immobile partner. "What a tragedy," grumbles the newspaper editor who shares the scene with them. Yet this tragedy may be a triumph. If counter-memory calls for a sort of aggressive, proactive amnesia, Johnny must now be the busiest as well as the most liberated of the film's major characters, with forgetting as his project and phantasms as his new and intimate companions. These "phantasms" are the incommunicable *topoi* conjured up by Foucault in his "Theatrum Philosophicum," where he uses the term to signify elusive impulses "created by fear or desire." They "topologize the materiality of the body" while crying out to "be freed from the restrictions we impose upon them, freed from the dilemmas of truth and falsehood and of being and non-being." Because the "metaphysics of the phantasm revolves around atheism and transgression" (Foucault 1977c, 169, 170, 171), we may conclude that Johnny is now freed by the former (atheism) from the god that threatened to destroy him, and by the latter (transgression) from the oppressive limits of what Foucault calls "that zone which our culture affords for our gestures and speech" (1977b, 30).

Foucault writes that the relationship between transgression and constraint may be like "a flash of lightning in the night which . . . gives a dense and black intensity to the night it denies . . . and yet owes to the dark the stark clarity of its manifestation, its harrowing and poised singularity; the flash loses itself in this space it marks with its sovereignty and becomes silent now that it has given a name to obscurity" (1977b 35). The lightning bolt conjured up by Fuller during the climax of *Shock Corridor* flashes along the invisible boundaries of normalizing discourse, marking Johnny's silence not only as a fall from the symbolic order of language and sociality but, more important, as an accession to the body and an entry into the "rigorous language" that "arises from sexuality," as did the film's own narrative. This language may, in Foucault's words, lift Johnny "into the night where God is absent, and where all . . . actions are addressed to this absence in a profanation which at once identifies it, dissipates it, exhausts itself in it, and restores it to the empty purity of its transgression" (1977b, 30–31).

This seems a brave new corridor for Johnny to explore, and if Fuller does not follow him into it, the reason may be only that the epistemo-logical paradigms of modern cinematic discourse have not yet found ways to render visible what might transpire there.

Notes

An earlier version of this essay was presented in a panel organized by Christopher Sharrett at the Conference on Literature and Film held by Florida State University at Tallahassee in January 2002. Thanks to Robert Sklar and Allen S. Weiss for ideas and inspiration.

1. The ambiguity is marked still more by the appearance of the epigram (dated 425 B.C.) entirely in upper-case letters, eliding the distinctions between God/god and He/he. Because the usage is singular (not plural: "the gods"), one may assume that the monotheistic God is intended; but the point remains uncertain in view of the polytheistic culture in which Euripides wrote. No translator is identified.

2. Foucault is so fascinated by the twin notions of sadistic chastisement, on one hand, and carefully constructed schedules, on the other, that the first chapter of *Discipline and Punish*, called "The Body of the Condemned," begins with (a) an account of an eighteenth-century regicide in 1757 being ripped apart with red-hot pincers, then burned with sulphur, then doused with various molten, boiling, and burning substances, then drawn and quartered, then immolated; and (b) the timetable for a typical day in a nineteenth-century Paris prison, from rising at 6 a.m. through hand washing at 4 p.m. and undressing for bed in early evening. Between them, Foucault notes, these episodes "each define a certain penal style" fashionable less than one hundred years apart (1979, 1–7).

3. Although the phrase "socially constructed" is appropriate here, I do not want to commit the common error of suggesting that Foucault is as extreme a "social constructionist" as some poststructuralists and postmodernists have made him out to be. "That depends," he says, when asked whether truth is a construct. He adds by way of example that an "anthropological description" may be counted in some degree a "description" rather than a "construct," and says he does not mean to imply "that there is nothing there and that everything comes out of some-body's head." See Foucault (1987, 128).

4. This phrase delineates one of five "traits" that Foucault sees as characterizing "the 'political economy' of truth" in "societies like ours."

5. For examples, see Sarris (1968, 93–94) and Moullet (1985, 149). Recognition of the interplay between narrative/poetic functions and sensory/visual impact has

played a strong role in critical commentary on Fuller's work. "One of the great qualities of the movies is their heterogeneous inclusive nature," writes one critic who turns to film history in Fuller's defense, "the fact that they explore in valid ways the whole range from the most extreme artifice . . . to the extremes of documentary realism. . . . Just as the essence of Fuller's themes is conflict and contradiction, so too is the essence of his style [which] conveys not grace but energy. His movies are as brutal and harsh to look at and to hear as the world they depict" (Garnham 1972, 25–26). Another critic counts among Fuller's virtues "unencumbered sensation" and "moral idealism," as well as other narrative/poetic traits (Millar 1980, 403). Other critics could readily be cited.

6. In hallucination sequences, Fuller uses footage that he shot informally while scouting for locations.

7. Morton is discussing Paul Goodman's version of gestalt therapy.

8. The phrase is from Morton's description of a community in one of Goodman's fictional works.

9. A less obvious rhyme is that between Johnny's injured appearance during his interview with the soldier (caused by his violent encounter with "nymphos" slightly earlier) and the placement of the soldier's hallucinatory vision in Kamakura, Japan, a location known not only for its thirty-seven-foot-high sculpture of the Buddha but also for the fact that Japanese women who have undergone abortions traditionally place sacred memorial statuettes near this sculpture.

10. The words are Jean-Pierre Barou's. Bentham conceived the panopticon as an innovative penal complex where a central guard tower would be perpetually in view of prisoners inhabiting a circular structure around it; because no inmate could know whether a guard was watching or not at any given moment, every inmate would have to internalize the observation process, behaving *as if* the "eye of power" were operative all the time.

11. The allusion to the Statue of Liberty also evokes the image of the Buddha of Kamakura, projecting its monumental serenity (and overlooking a multitude of unborn souls) during the soldier's hallucination.

12. The term "sovereignty" is used here in the sense of an internalizing "doctrine of *formations of sovereignty*" that Nietzsche proposes "[i]n the place of a [falsely scientific] 'sociology'" (qtd. in Weiss 1989, 27).

NOTHING SACRED
MODERNITY AND PERFORMANCE
IN *CATCH ME IF YOU CAN*
Murray Pomerance

Dat *wuz* de smartes' dodge!

MARK TWAIN, *HUCKLEBERRY FINN*

A History of the Modern Moment

Akira Mizuta Lippit writes, "The effort to define the human being has usually required a preliminary gesture of exclusion: a rhetorical animal sacrifice. *The presence of the animal must first be extinguished for the human being to appear*" (2000, 8; my emphasis). Here, conflated, we have two ideas: that in some systematic way (accessible to our rational calculation and discernment) the human world represents an apotheosis of the animal one, even a distinct and superior transcendence; and that the "natural" function of humanity—read civilization—is to replace the animal spirit with something erected upon it but qualitatively and ontologically remote, something "better," a post-animality. This idea of progressive development has appealed broadly to theorists (Nazi and otherwise), from Ernst Haeckel's suggestion that "ontogeny recapitulates phylogeny" through Charles Darwin's hierarchy of species and Herbert Spencer's "survival of the fittest" to Nietzsche's superman. In all of these formulations, the early origins of present success have been characterized retrospectively as primitive, undeveloped, and low.[1] Like Haeckel's ontogeny, but perhaps more visibly, social structure may recapitulate phylogeny; if for Haeckel the individual's growth itself mirrored—through successive and progressive stages—the historical development of species, then societies, as Spencer suggested, might themselves be thought to "grow" and "outperform" each other, to "develop" and become "superior." I would like to twist this idea in the light of play.

As an idea, the extinguishing of one form and its replacement by another may suggest the transition from a feudal to a capitalist social order, a transition that involves the formation of the modern, from the premodern, man.[2] In Marshall Berman's "Machinery and Modern Industry" we read that this modern type comes to replace a very specific formation—the individual who is capable of only limited production—and must therefore be embodied by a person "fit for a variety of labors, ready to face any change in production, for whom the different social functions he performs are only so many modes of giving free scope to his own natural and acquired powers" (Berman 1988, 355n8). This modern man, accustomed to a continual movement from function to function and as such an adept at social circulation, masquerade, urban gregariousness, and the accommodation of strangers (not to mention easy adjustment to the displacement of his saleable labor from his perduring self), is what David Riesman (1950) calls "other-directed" and what Kenneth Keniston, a generation later, deems intensely "moral" (1965). Morality and other-direction are modern emphases. Warren Bennis and Philip Slater describe the world in which such a person stands ready to "face any change in production" as a "temporary society" (1968), and imply a relation between temporariness and modernity. Further, as Marshall McLuhan and others have pointed out, the actual situation of the "temporary society" is surely in rationally calculated action, not geography, and can as likely be topologically global as communal, as likely electronic as spiritual. Its social organization is more aptly described by Max Weber's rational-legal (bureaucratic) type of authority than by either the "charismatic" or "traditional" type. The person who adapts easily to rational-legal authority, who is comfortable in the "temporary society," is the true citizen of the modern age.

The time of which temporariness is a function exists, as Anthony Giddens puts it, "emptied out" of space (1991, 17). Modern, temporary social relations are, for him, "disembedded," arranged to produce a set of economic relations dependent upon movement, scheduling, and the mapping together of vectors disconnected from place and community. That apparently nameless "Girl" (Maria Schneider) in Michelangelo Antonioni's *The Passenger* (1975), who says, "People disappear all the time (whenever they leave the room)," is pointing to nothing less than the modern condition, its circulatory function, and also to time, which also disappears as an existential fullness when it is disembedded from place. For Giddens, disembeddedness reflects modernity's formation of, and dependence upon, social structures in which the local and the familiar—what Talcott Parsons (1951) called the "particular" and the "specific"—are suddenly supplanted by relatively more globalized conditions in which numerous previously isolated experiences, extremely disparate in temporal and spatial setting, are interrelated and unified through elaborate systems of navigation and communication that bring about a social order founded upon what Parsons called the "universal" and the "diffuse."

One notable fictional adept of such modern conditions is the criminal protagonist in Fritz Lang's *Dr. Mabuse, der Spieler* (1922). In his striking analysis of this film, Tom Gunning (2000b) shows how Lang kenningly links the elaboration of railway timetables (see Schivelbusch [1986, 188–97]) with the calculable fluctuations of the stock market. In both cases, what had been local and fixed—the sense of personal movement through space and one's appreciation of value—came under the dominion of broad technologically based social systems, here the railway timetable and the operations of the market. As both movement and money were detached from local terrain and community and reconnected to what Gunning refers to as the broad system of circulation, there developed the everyday experience of modernity, a new relation of the self to a vastly interconnected, and yet unpersonal, world organization.[3] For Gunning, Dr. Mabuse's criminal masterwork, the center of the film, is precisely an example of a man's cunningly choreographic utilization of a number of factors—knowledge of the train schedule, control of workers at a distance through telecommunication (and, ultimately, telekinesis), sophisticated awareness of the workings of the market—in order to bring about a state of terror, disorganization, and criminal autocracy.

As a central organizational feature of such a complex social arrangement, Wolfgang Schivelbusch (in his discussion of the department store) suggests a special form of perception, a mode of attention in which objects are, precisely, "attractive in their state of dispersal": "In the transition from the traditional retail shop to the department store, the customer's perception of the goods changed in a manner analogous to the traveler's perception during the transition from coach to train, and to the Parisian's perception during the process of his city's Haussmannization. . . . The landscape that was seen in this way was no longer experienced intensively, discretely . . . but evanescently, impressionistically" (1986, 189). "Panoramic" perception, as Schivelbusch terms it, implies constant motion. Any one particular location is thus only the pretext for movement toward it, through it, and out of it, the stage upon which actors engaged in temporary relations make entrances, effect interconnections, and take exits, using a system of synchronization that turns all local preparations, events, and resolutions outward toward an otherness that controls without participating (like Lang's Mabuse on the telephone in his study or gazing at a potential victim across a gaming table before stunning his mind), that is distant and discrete yet empowered by virtue of the rationality of the system in which it works.

Lippit's "animal," which must be "extinguished" to make a modernity like this, can be taken broadly to include all aspects of what precedes—both historically and personally—this condition we like to think of as full and rational humanity. One must here include open performance, that playful mock-up and rehearsal of (and, therefore, overture to) the intelligibly ordered, vitally functioning, serious adult social situation (focused at some moment in time and some point in space as the *trope* [Schivelbusch 2003, 6]). Play must be seen as "not yet developed," "not yet everything we can do," "not yet the epitome of action." Modernity eclipses it. However articulate, informed, and deft a performance might be, it would seem always to be, *as long as it is* a performance, socially insufficient, a partial adjustment to circumstance merely or a childish and only tentative playing out and playing with the conventions of rigorous, committed activity. Mabuse's tendency to play, for example (although he commands the scene modernistically by using the system of circulation, still he dominates his victims and controls his underlings through the agency of playful disguise and characterization), is terminated abruptly as he is finally caught: caught at a point when he has let all his characterizations dissipate and trapped himself, as it were, backstage; and caught by a hunter who has all the techniques and technologies of modernity at his ready disposal, and who never plays.

In complete modernity, if there can be such a state, performance is everywhere and yet everywhere treated as unperformed. If we consider Mabuse as omnipotent criminal mentality, and take note that his actions depend upon his ability to masquerade as a number of different characters, we may reflect that his success also depends literally on our forgetting that his characters are laid on; as soon as we begin to see him acting, he begins to fade and fail. Mabuse's acting itself—I mean his acting as the gambler, the old man at the séance, and so on, and not Rudolf Klein-Rogge's acting as Mabuse doing all this acting—is not exactly so fulsome as to be invisible, such as is, for example, the acting of Bernhard Goetzke as the detective Von Wenck. What adds to the credibility of Mabuse's characters is the fact that we see them almost exclusively in medium and long shots, so that they are readable mostly through gesture and stance. Therefore, for us, seen situationally, Mabuse's acting is not performance but being. For the "animal" to be "extinguished," however, for the almost modern to become wholly modern, the apparent performance must be renovated so that it becomes pure action; the acting must be hidden and in fact transcended, even, and especially, when seen up close. (Mabuse must be transformed into Von Wenck.) Even though people go through their lives in masquerades, they must choose not to reveal the acts of masking or unmasking that produce masquerade and thus display it openly as such.

Catch as Catch Can: Performance as Malfeasance

In Steven Spielberg's *Catch Me If You Can* (2003), deprecation of performance is exactly the view taken of the behavior of Frank Abagnale Jr. (Leonardo DiCaprio) by John Hanratty (Tom Hanks), an FBI special agent dedicated to and properly fixated upon the presumably more stable and resolved—certainly the more grown-up—activities of surveillance, circumspection, and scrutiny. In this film, it is unresolved lowness (desperation), subjugation (although suitably

extended and developed, yet persistent and elemental) to forces of social control, and avowed failure to feel the world's gravity (a witty
mien) that lend performance—Frank's way of being—its "animal,"
prehuman aspect. We may think of Frank's systematic and repetitive
playing-out—he transforms himself into a pilot, a doctor, a lawyer—
as "monkeying around," of his sustained performance as "monkey
business." As Frank acts through the instrument of DiCaprio's body,
he seems wild, uncurtailable, extralinguistic, cannily immediate.

Spielberg's twenty-first film, *Catch Me If You Can* relates the biography of a working-class boy who, bent on pleasing his disconnected, alcoholic father (Christopher Walken), ends up as one of the great im-
postors of the twentieth century. When his parents separate while he is
in his teens, he sets out to make a life for himself by passing fake
checks, an endeavor to which he devotes his keen attention and sharp
perception to the point of obsession. He becomes very accomplished,
so much so in the case of constructing false identification and procur-
ing for himself the credentials and uniform of a commercial pilot that
he soon has the ability to get into the cockpit of virtually any aircraft
flying and gains the sobriquet in the trade press of the "James Bond of
the skies." Like any astute actor, Frank Abagnale Jr. has learned to attend to the operative, salient features of a performance, the nuances
that immediately catch people's eye and purchase their acknowledgment and assent (airline pilots are handsome, speak with a drawl, and
show beneficence to admiring little girls). As he discovers (in our
view) early on, in most circumstances people tend to eschew method-
ical inspection in favor of the quick, approving glance.[4] Soon enough
he is running an emergency unit in a hospital and then practicing at
the Louisiana bar.

Dogging his tail throughout this extended escapade is the FBI in the
person of Hanratty, a systematic and tenacious hunter (in the Spiel-
bergian tradition) who has made Frank his own private great white
shark. In the end, he catches the charming young forger on Christmas
Eve—in the small French village of Montrichard, to be precise, in an
imprimerie where Frank is engaged in counterfeiting bills. Hanratty
extradites him to the United States and sends him to jail, from which
ignominy the detective returns to rescue our hero soon enough, real-
izing that there is no one alive better equipped to help the agency in its
neverending hunt in the forests of criminality. The film concludes

with Frank swept up in the daily paperwork of the FBI, now a thoroughly modern man who can "perform" his duties on the job with such aplomb that it looks to any eye as if (sadly) he is real.

At the end of *Der Spieler,* Mabuse, too, is captured in a counterfeiting plant. The inhospitable secret bastion of one of his flunkies, it is his last hiding place, one in which he finds himself trapped as the police come to tear him away: the counterfeiter who has been working for him there took pains to install (to his boss's delight) in the trap door that is the emergency escape a locking mechanism that the police would never be able to pry open from above. Now, fortune has placed Mabuse himself above that door, and he cannot pry it open. We see him groveling on the floor and, in an insert shot (a technical illustration), a close-up of the trap door mechanism sliding into locked position.[5] Mabuse tries chipping away at it with his pocket knife, to no avail. His look is wild-eyed, lost. How is it significant that Spielberg's Frank Abagnale is modeled on this Mabuse?

Beyond the parallelism between Hanratty opening the sequence by striking the red button that turns off the printing machines (thus causing newly printed bills to flutter through the air in all directions) and Mabuse, having fallen into a delirium of desperation, imagining the stilled machinery of his counterfeiting operation to *start up,* taking on human form as it pulses and writhes hopelessly, there is the dilapidated, reduced state of both Frank and Mabuse in their counterfeit traps, the first in a grease-stained undershirt and shining with sweat, as he struggles to accommodate himself to Hanratty's presence, and the other with his clothes torn, his powerful gaze gone awry, his malevolent rationality turned to an insane and unfocused panic. Both Mabuse and Abagnale are criminal masterminds, the latter a butt of comedy only because in his brilliance he is so young (and in many ways innocent). Both, indeed, are prodigies of criminality and modernity, sharing an obsession with circulation through disguise and counterfeit identity, a passion for eluding the police, a tendency toward manipulative romantic involvement—Mabuse with the exotic dancer Cara Carozza (Aud Egede Nissen) and the socialite Graefin Told (Gertrude Welcker), and Abagnale with Brenda Strong (Amy Adams) and the prostitute, Cheryl Ann (Jennifer Garner)—and a facility in using either technologies of communication (Mabuse) or the ambiguities of language and situational speech (Abagnale) to make gain. Both succeed by forging personalities through theatrical performance, Mabuse in an earlier time, when impersonation could be accomplished more easily than in America of the 1950s, to be sure, but also in a style revealed to us at a mature state of development. Abagnale, by contrast, is shown from his earliest moments of masquerade, learning its power and mastering the techniques for eluding the "grasp" of the detective-citizens who surround him on all sides. If—at least at the beginning of *Der Spieler*—Mabuse operates with a gang of confederates, each an expert under his direct and precise control, Abagnale, for his part, uses the people around him, in their everyday personifications as workers, friends, and professionals, to lever his performance successfully. His technique is even more elaborate and sophisticated than Mabuse's, his rational control of the situation of his crimes even more penetrating and precise.

The "trap" in the Montrichard sequence of *Catch Me* is a verbal construction, one that works quite as efficiently as the locked trap door in *Der Spieler* to bind the desperate criminal into a position from which he can conveniently be seized. Hanratty has convinced Frank that, although he is himself unarmed, a battalion of gendarmes is waiting outside. If Frank attempts to walk out the door they will most certainly kill him. "Is that the truth, John?" asks Frank. "Is that the truth?" He is now pinned in precisely the kind of verbal construction that he has spent his young criminal life perfecting, telling others what they should see, in effect (as he accuses Hanratty of doing to him), and thus directing the state and development of their belief in a reality he had managed to his own benefit. In a similar way, Mabuse had once used his preternatural powers of the gaze to pinion and imprison hapless victims, to force underlings to do his bidding, to lock people into his system of control; and finally, he is locked in himself.

Frank's inability to determine whether Hanratty is deceiving him is no marker of his personal weakness; nor, although he repeatedly congratulates Hanratty on the good "performance," is it a reflection of the detective's brilliant acting. Implicit in Frank's vulnerability to Hanratty's insinuations is the vulnerability of all of his victims to the stories he spun, which is to say, anyone's vulnerability in a world where movement, presentation, artifice, impression, and surface take precedence over deep-rooted knowledge and experience.[6] In modernity, the precise sort of criminality produced by Frank Abagnale ascends to prominence when produced with sufficient skill, and precisely the type of detection undertaken by John Hanratty is called into play. Similarly, in *Dr. Mabuse, der Spieler,* the criminality of Mabuse, with its staged performance and reliance on predictably scheduled events and behaviors, his "comfortable fit within the systems of modernity" (Gunning 2000b, 104), becomes culturally prominent and a specific challenge to the powers of a detective like Von Wenck. To catch Mabuse, he must learn to recognize a criminal who masters "the effacement and control of identity," to understand how modern man "assumes an identity that is proper for the situation he puts himself into" (Gunning 2000b, 101).

Lang's film both exemplifies and routinizes its subject. The action is spelled out—as Gunning brilliantly reveals—in the context of the "'empty' forms of modernity: the disembedded co-ordination of space and time; the fluctuations of the money economy; and the gamblers' surrender to the mechanics of desire" (2000b, 112). Mabuse and his cohorts are operating the modern world. "Mabuse's fictional identities do not so much attack the system as exploit its structure for his own ends" (Gunning 2000b, 101). In relation to the playing out—the *spieling*—of the theatrical performances he contrives, Mabuse's actual guising and preparation are given extremely short shrift here, it being taken for granted by Lang that the imbrication of performance and modern life are so intensive and so complete that we may easily take the actual construction of the roles as read, and, indeed, take as read that other social performers in the scenes may also be constructing their public selves, here in such a way that Mabuse can predict absolutely what they will have been trying to accomplish and gear his own performances to artfully (invisibly) interfere with theirs.

For Spielberg, however, two contradictory impulses would seem to operate at once. He is romantic (premodern) enough in sensibility to find the thought of performance exciting and worth dramatizing in its own right. And, as a veteran of considerable moviemaking in the Hollywood system, he is sufficiently attuned to the modern sensibility to know that interrelated performances are everywhere, on all sides. Because performance, for him, is so omnipresent, it is invisible and has, perhaps, been forgotten; thus he finds it a worthwhile exercise to bring the mechanics of performance back into frame, and his construction of Abagnale's character and exploits is specifically managed with a view to showing the backstage in detail. In this way, Frank seems to be "monkeying around," trying out adult humanity. A further impetus is given by Spielberg's long-standing sensitivity to the experience of adolescence, that time of life when adult roles are being tried on and experimented with, but usually by people with less talent at performance and less rational control of the complex social scene than Frank possesses. He is a criminal whose stagings can and must be brought to light; but at the same time he is a kid who must stage in order to learn how to grow up. In *Catch Me If You Can,* the impulses played out in *Empire of the Sun* (1987) meet the social vision played out in *Dr. Mabuse, der Spieler.*

In *Catch Me If You Can,* we are regaled with the story of a young confidence trickster of unsurpassed talents. His performance is therefore neither impulsive nor precisely natural, although it appears to spring from him spontaneously; it is witting and deeply calculating, a betrayal of an astute deconstruction of social arrangements on his part. The play-acting here, then, far more than an attribute of character and a feature of situational décor, constitutes both the singular professional devotion and piety of the central character of the film and the theme of the character's story. *Catch Me* is not merely action acted; it is *acted* action acted. Nor is Frank's "monkey business" in *Catch Me* a new theme for Spielberg. It informed the ignorant bravado of Matt Hooper (Richard Dreyfuss) in *Jaws* (1975), the precocious aestheticism of Roy Neary (Dreyfuss) in *Close Encounters of the Third Kind* (1977), Professor Indiana Jones's (Harrison Ford) adventurous masquerade with bullwhip and fedora (1981), E.T.'s camouflage as a stuffed doll (1982), young Jamie's play piloting in *Empire of the Sun,* Peter Pan's playing around as the stock broker Peter Banning (Robin Williams) in *Hook* (1991), the "human intelligence" of the velociraptors in *Jurassic Park* (1993), and the verisimilitudinous mechas of *Artificial Intelligence: AI* (2001). In the last of these films, it is Gigolo Joe (Jude Law) whom we find "onstage," rather than young David (Haley Joel Osment), who, though clearly innocent and gracile, is the least playful mecha around. At any rate, Spielberg has consistently been interested in showing growing up as a performative—and thus incomplete—engagement with adult status, responsibility, and obligation. Even the puissant, eponymous Schindler (Liam Neeson) displays an early tendency to play at being charitable and humane, to experiment with the feelingful self-esteem that must accrue to a hero, before actually acceding to the role of Salvific Presence and losing his sense of self in the maelstrom of his struggle to save Jews by assembling his list.

Show Business

To be sure, Frank Abagnale is not always seen in the full flush of staged pretense. He is sometimes mobilizing preparations for pretenses to come, both with apparent genuineness, as when one night by lamplight in a tenement he deftly reinscribes his driver's license to add ten years to his life, and in what might be called a "ritual of anticipation," where he must act his way into costumes, props, and settings to set up a later performance. To get a pilot's uniform, for example, he picks up a Southern twang by listening to pilots checking into a hotel; then uses it while telephoning the purchasing department of Pan American Airways to beg for help with a "lost uniform." More vocal than Mabuse, he is no less hypnotic. To the old tailor who is fitting him and wondering why he is so nervous, Frank says demurely, "How would you feel if you lost your uniform in the first week on a job?" Because we can see the preparation for Frank's performance and aspects of its construction, albeit not always with knowledge of what we are watching when we are watching it, the ensuing masquerade is ultimately perceivable as such and provides a double pleasure: it is occupational achievement by an untrained or scantily trained amateur with professional panache—easy virtue; and also labor apotheosized, the completion of an arduous project to whose early stages we have borne witness. All these details are necessary for Spielberg, whose theme is the role of performance in capitalism. We must see and admire Frank's monkeyshines for their performative qualities and for the precise labor involved in producing them, not simply be taken in (as is, for example, Frank's utterly credulous mother [Nathalie Baye]). What makes performance actually look like performance is our view of its backstage. As Erving Goffman puts it, "A glimpse behind the scenes can be a device for inducing the belief that you are seeing the backstage of *something*" (1974, 475), this *something,* I might add, being itself a pretense of something untransformed that typically does not occupy a stage. That we may find it appealing does not make Frank's role-playing a construction that we throw ourselves into taking seriously, a proposition we believe. What is impressive about it is that the show has focused the attention of the august FBI. In taking delight at Frank's monkeyshines we can be insiders to a scam that is gulling an audience of professional critics.

Obversely, that a construction might not have its backstage visible need not lead us to take it seriously at face value, yet we do this, too. Hanratty seems to be real in another sort of way (as prison cells and bank notes are real) and not a con man only acting as an agent, this exactly because the camera does not reveal his rehearsals as it does Frank's. In every instance of explicit dress-up the performer is taken to be not quite the social being he is pretending to be; thus, we may read him as being marginally less than fully and maturely human, the "animal that must be extinguished for the human being to appear." The ostensible performance seems less a flowering of humanity present than a preparation for a humanity to follow. Performance must be terminated, and the fictive role evaporate, before we take ourselves to be in the presence of a "real" person (one such as Hanratty). And as "real persons," of course, Mabuse and Abagnale must face up to the truth of their histories and submit to the law. This is the bond that ties them most firmly.

Naked Interest

But such a depreciation of theatricality is merely a throwback to feudal perceptions and social arrangements. Marshall Berman suggests that Marx's theory of modernization implies a quite different perspective, if not specifically on what I am calling performance, then on the social circumstances that subtend a transitory, situational, provisional adaptation of personality and identity—circumstances that performance epitomizes. "The pathos of all bourgeois monuments," writes Berman—and we must remember that stable and unwavering personality and identity, feudal personality and identity, constitute a monument—"is that their material strength and solidity actually count for nothing and carry no weight at all, that they are blown away like frail reeds by the very forces of capitalist development that they celebrate" (1988, 99). He goes on to quote Marx:

> The bourgeoisie has torn apart the many feudal ties that bound men to the "natural superiors," and left no other bond between man and man than naked interest, than callous cash payment. . . . The bourgeoisie has stripped of its halo every occupation hitherto honored and looked up to with reverent awe. . . . In place of exploitation veiled by religious and political illusions, it has put open, shameless, direct, naked exploitation. (1988, 106)

What this suggests to Berman is a social order in flux, a bourgeois drive that renders social forms, institutions, and relationships disposable, "capitalized for fast depreciation and planned to be obsolete, closer in their social functions to tents and encampments than to 'Egyptian pyramids, Roman aqueducts, Gothic cathedrals'" (1988, 99). Continually shifting social relations under bourgeois capitalism require more fluid and transformable occupational commitments than did the rigid relations in feudal society. To understand advanced capitalism, therefore, one must invert the feudal order and the style of behavior that maintained it. In advanced capitalism, the fully human and committed citizen is precisely the one who enters and then leaves an occupation, in essence "performing" it, playing at it, or "monkeying around." Here it is hardly that the animal must be extinguished to make way for the human. Now the relatively fixed and stable human of the feudal age is extinguished by commodity capitalism to make way for the animated performer, the man of surfaces.

To handle this new contemporary man, John Hanratty is at a loss, being as he is an atavism who finds himself—in the chase that is Spielberg's structure in this film, and perhaps (given Spielberg's psychological realism) more generally as well—a giant leap behind. If he is continually unable to grasp Frank's fleeting, disappearing form in the vast social circulation his surveillance technology so intensively plumbs (thus substantiating a reading of the film's title as a charming thumbing of the nose by Frank), he is unable, too, to catch Frank's drift, to comprehend why Frank would devote himself to a life of performance, chicanery, and fraud when he clearly has the intelligence and talent to "really become someone." Hanratty is not out of breath as he races behind his prey; he is out of theories, out of touch with the modern world in which Frank moves with such brilliant agility. Hanratty cannot fathom the full range of Frank's techniques, social and mechanical—nor can the audience, positioned by Spielberg at Hanratty's innocent perspective and thus continually shocked at the ingenuity Frank puts on display, as when he fleeces Cheryl Ann for four hundred dollars cash by "innocently" allowing her to insist that he endorse over a New York Savings and Loan "check" for fourteen hundred dollars in payment for a thousand-dollar evening and accepting the change she produces from her bra.

Most significantly, however, Hanratty underestimates Frank's thoroughgoing professionalism as a performer (exactly, I suspect, as most viewers of this film underestimated the professionalism of Leonardo DiCaprio "monkeying around" as Frank "monkeying around"), a professionalism that leads him to the greatest creative freedom and sensitivity in his use of materials, attitudes, approaches, and styles. At one point, for example, Frank ingratiates himself in the home of a celebrated prosecutor (Martin Sheen) by pretending to be a fledgling lawyer in search of a mentor. To keep up this act, he must contrive to pass the Louisiana bar exam. For the remainder of the film, a flabbergasted Hanratty obsessively peppers him on the telephone about it: "How did you cheat on the bar exam in Louisiana?" Hanratty's self-serving commitment to the idea that the law is a respectable and durable social institution, impervious to corruption or manipulation and thus on a fundamental level "authentic," blocks him from imagining any way Frank could have faked earning that diploma in so short a time. But the joke is on Hanratty, and on those of us who have been taking his precapitalist view of Frank seriously. In such a view, Frank's identity as a mountebank, his tendency always, everywhere, and by any means to scoff at conventionality and legality, has a solidity and permanence, a supreme value, whereas Frank himself is committed only to situational naked interest, as we must wait until the end of the film to learn. There he confesses, "I didn't cheat. I studied for two weeks and I passed." Even diligent hard work may be part of a performance, and Frank, the consummate actor for whom performance is piety, is not above doing whatever will make performance possible. For Hanratty, however, intensive study is sincerity, a denial of performance; so, ironically, he thinks Frank is beneath it. "Is that the truth, Frank?" he pushes. "Is that the truth?" To his credit, Frank changes the subject.

Defrocking Priests

Given his commitment in this film to revealing the bourgeois trans-formation of social life, it is not surprising that Spielberg's concentra-tion on Frank's imposturing is fixed in precisely those occupations "hitherto honored and looked up to with reverent awe," which Marx thought the bourgeoisie had "stripped of [their] halo" (Berman 1988, 115), namely, "the doctor, the lawyer, . . . the man of science," who "think they have the power to live on a higher plane than ordinary humanity" (Berman 1988, 116). (In Spielberg's case, the "man of sci-ence" is an airline pilot who really does live *in* a higher plane!) Frank is configured as an ultimate agent of capitalism, that force which, in Berman's words, destroys the "aura of holy dread and radiance" (1988, 115) around those who perform certain "honored" occupations. "Nothing is sacred, no one is untouchable, life becomes thoroughly desanctified" (Berman 1988, 115). As a "doctor," for example, Frank not only poses inauthentically but even manages to make a healthy liv-ing, exchanging his ersatz persona as commodity in a shifting and fluid market that is ill-equipped to verify his status. His crime of im-posture is thus drawn as both a profanity against honor and an abuse of the economy.

Profanity and abuse call up moral forces, those whose commitment is to superintend the workings of the social order. But in the modern world, the state's capacity to utilize and sanction orderly force—polic-ing—must meet the rigorous demands imposed by the dissolution of a fixed and solid world and its replacement by a diffuse pattern of movement, masquerade, and secrecy. In its focus on crime, *Catch Me If You Can* is a detective story, a narrative form that, according to Tom Gunning,

depends explicitly upon the modern experience of circulation. While circulation relies on an evolving process of rationalization of time and space, the very intricacy and speed of these routes of transfer and exchange create a counterthrust in which stability and predictability can be threatened. The detective story maps out two positions in this dialectical drama of modernity: the criminal, who preys on the very complexity of the system of circulation; and the detective, whose intelligence, knowledge, and perspicacity allow him to discover the dark corners of the circulatory system, uncover crime, and restore order. (Gunning 1995a, 20)

But for both Frank, the "criminal," and Hanratty, the "detective" who "restores order," the finale of *Catch Me If You Can* dramatizes a crisis of identity. In commodity capitalism, the "order" that is restored may have considerably more to do with the "counterthrust in which stability and predictability can be threatened" than with a stable hierarchy of positions and perceptions, even if surface appearances to the contrary are given through Hanratty's bureaucratic dominance.

The set-up is a scene late on a Friday afternoon in Hanratty's cubicle at the FBI, where Frank—freed after his jail sentence on the condition that he work with the bureau to assist in apprehending forgers and impersonators such as himself—rather sweetly asks Hanratty if he can come to work with him tomorrow morning. It is the bonding of youth to experience, an open and unguarded affiliation. Tomorrow there's no work, explains Hanratty a little gruffly; it's Saturday. "Well," says Frank, with a desperate vulnerability we have never seen before, "what should I do?" This is a deliciously revealing moment. In Frank's discomfiture with the bureaucratic world we see that his devotion until now, from Hanratty's perspective, has been only "work," utterly conventional and routinized in form, intention, and temporal organization, only a nine-to-five put-on to pay for a life of shabby gentility.[7] But Frank, a consummate performer not only by profession but also by religion, has no stable essence underneath his role, no mundane dressing-room self. His self is his character; his only a naked interest. Yet now he requires the resources of the FBI offices for engaging himself as an expert, and if the offices are shut, there is no confidential dossier in which that interest can be clothed, no bad checks to scan with his expertise. Frank lacks a script, but in modern capitalist society, with stable and perduring occupation replaced by temporary, dissolvable employment—situated performance—scripts, even improvised scripts, are everything.[8] He goes to his own cubicle and slyly cuts a photograph of himself from the FBI logbook, filling time in the only way he knows.

Next we see Frank strolling down a long corridor at an airport, costumed nattily as a pilot once again. His step is confident, animal. The light on him is ethereal, unreal, the queer place—in shape it is something of a birth canal, but it is lit like a surgery—silent as a temple. Hanratty slyly appears on his tail. "We'll send you back to Atlanta . . . for fifty years," says he, and Frank, continuing in his stride without looking around, as the camera tracks backward ahead of him, answers, "I know that." Hanratty presses: "I had to convince my bosses at the FBI and the Attorney General of the United States that you wouldn't run." And then, catching up, he softens: "I'm gonna let you fly tonight, Frank. I'm not even gonna try to stop you. 'Cause I know you'll be back on Monday." Frank turns to face him. "How do you know I'll come back?" They are standing under a "LOBBY & BAGGAGE CLAIM" sign, appropriate because they are "claiming" and trading off the "baggage" of their identities at this moment. Hanratty points back down the long corridor. "Look . . . nobody's chasing you." Indeed, the corridor could not be emptier, colder, more hermetic. Hanratty turns on his heels and walks away. On Monday morning, albeit a little late, Frank does appear for work, ready now to help be a "catcher" of other performers in continuous circulation (flight).

A superficial reading of this scene, undertaken from Hanratty's point of view, suggests the stasis of the "secure" office job as the sober antithesis of the check and identity forger's "anxious" circulation. To cap this interpretation, the camera pulls back from the office in the final shot of the film to reveal Frank swallowed in a sea of "secure" white-shirted bureaucrats swiveling at their desks and pacing in whispered discussions with "important" paperwork in their hands.[9] Frank's reprise performance as a pilot is thus definable as an obscenity, a contradiction of this busy, yet stable scene. If Hanratty holds the power to halt Frank's circulation, it is, after all, a legitimate power, rooted in the relatively serious and predictable stability of social institutions. Hanratty occupies his position as investigator in an envelope of perduring commitment to authenticity in economic exchange (exactly the authenticity committed to by the dupes whom Dr. Mabuse fleeces, indeed). Hanratty is not playing at being an agent; he "really is" one (like the very serious, even witless Von Wenck), just as all the law-abiding adults in his world are "real" in what they do. His mission is to socialize the wayward youth toward exactly such a stability and a locus as are his present securities. It follows that Frank should be read in the end as having shed his "useless" obsession with acting and come to a resolve that he "really belongs" in the FBI office and in this feverishly organized, read "comprehensive," way of life. He who had once been a catch is a catcher at last.

But this reading is undermined, I think, by the way Spielberg actually films these moments and by the implicit meaning of the film to this point. The casting of, and the performances by, Hanks and DiCaprio are clearly meant to suggest that Hanratty is tedious and oldfashioned and that Frank is utterly engaging and hip to quick-scan consumerist perception. By emphasizing Frank's helplessness outside of the circulation of performance, the scene in Hanratty's cubicle raises a chilling specter of loneliness, isolation, and vacuity as he tries to imagine what to do for a whole weekend when, paragon of roleplaying, he has *no role to play.* In the long corridor at the airport, the camera position favors not the diligent pursuer but the masquerading Frank, his ease of manner and confidence evident in every syllable and gesture. When Hanratty says that he will let Frank fly, he does so with the sincerity of a loyal friend; and so Frank has the escape valve if he needs to escape from this escapade, yet he does not, but walks forward to his plane. For him, flight is nobility, not reaction. And more: the dexterity and swiftness with which he clips that image of himself in the office suggest that his term in prison and the exhaustion of his yearslong dash away from Hanratty's longer arms have not in fact vitiated Frank's energies as a performer. He has plenty of tricks in reserve, and the same witty navigational skill as ever. What the film really leaves us to imagine is that Frank will keep his day job at the FBI and take acting gigs on the weekend. And more: that his role as adviser to the FBI will extend him in the particular sense that, demanding little of his many talents and requiring him to reveal no secrets he is not prepared to share, it will offer a modest but decent paycheck and a base of operations with access to photographs and information. Frank is still on the move at the end of the film, and is accelerating.

The holders of the high occupations that bourgeois capitalism tears down and that Frank in this film mocks and imitates, writes Berman, "turn out to be just about the only moderns who really believe that they are called to their vocations and that their work is holy" (1988, 116). Frank, in this light, is in the business of defrocking priests. And may we not add to this sanctified list, at the beginning of the twenty-first century, movie actors, some of whom believe, surely as much as doctors and lawyers—and also claim on "Inside the Actors Studio" and elsewhere—that they are called to their professions, and some of whom surely occasionally act as if they are holy? Are actors and film-makers deeply (feudally) what they seem to be, or are DiCaprio's and Hanks's appearances and displays in front of our eyes provisional and situational—therefore, in capitalism, central performative construc-tions? Is DiCaprio not acting as an actor when he acts Frank acting as a doctor for us? After all, like any other workers in contemporary life, those in "high" occupations—and certainly actors—must "'sell themselves piecemeal' to an employer willing to exploit their brains for profit. They must scheme and hustle to present themselves in a maximally profitable light" (Berman 1988, 117). Believing one *really is* an actor (or a doctor, or a lawyer) is hardly enough. One must al-ways seem.

Like Mabuse, Frank knows this. His knowledge, its antecedents, and its implications constitute the subject of Spielberg's film. Frank knows, for instance, that a sophisticated professional's need to present himself in "maximally profitable light" can be jeopardized by display-ing the kind of specific expertise to gain which a long, arduous, expen-sive, and committed training (which he does not have) is necessary; he knows that august professionals do not successfully market themselves by showing off what they can do (and he cannot). So once in a while *not performing* is the ultimate performance. A charmer if ever there was one, Frank is in the know about his real existential position in an economy of circulation, and appropriately wise about the real avenues through which work in high occupations can be obtained and retained under bourgeois competition. He knows how to assume a virtue if you have it not. Spielberg has often been castigated for a similar, appar-ently superficial, charm, as though it is not a form of kenning.

But what logic could suggest that Hanratty himself—or any one of us—is not an imitator circulating through performance, even though, like us, he boasts his own bona fides? Notwithstanding the fact that the characters we see are being put on by actors and, in the case of DiCaprio, who is a matinee idol and international celebrity, that even the actor is being put on by someone else, where are the limits to performance in this film? As I have suggested, the perception that Hanratty throughout the film seems to have a "real" occupation, while Frank seems not to, is an effect of his not apparently being scrutinized, Spielberg's camera continuing to focus on Frank as the performer and leaving Hanratty to seem "genuine" and "stable." But further: what logic might lead us to expect that even if he is not performing, even if he is as genuine as he claims to be, Hanratty and his sort will endure? Perhaps that final shot of the busy, busy, busy FBI agents swirling around Frank so sententiously is Spielberg's last, mocking gesture. For it is Frank, not Hanratty, who is Spielberg's alter ego. In advanced capitalism, genuineness and stability are gone with the wind. Social life is perduringly provisional, fleeting, a prospectus to be invested in for interest. In such an age, if he really is stable and only that, if he really does look down on Frank's fleeting accomplishments, it is Hanratty who will face extinction, while Frank dances forward in the deliriously temporary precincts of the bourgeois economy.

Notes

1. Ernst Haeckel (1834–1919) is described by Steven Jay Gould as "Germany's leading evolutionist in Darwin's day." On his tree of human evolution, *Homo sapiens* reached back to a creature called *Homo stupidus*, "a hypothetical cretin itself descended from the true missing link joining apes and humans." See Gould (1985, 438–39).

2. Both Haeckel and Spencer were exceptionally useful to the National Socialists in the 1930s. Adapting their philosophies, the Third Reich was able to posit its paragons as Ultimate Men—*Ubermenschen,* superiors in a chain of progressive creation—and Nazi ideology gained a cachet of modernism.

3. This everyday experience is related to the linkage, in very early modernism of the sixteenth century, between social derangement (such as was instigated by Martin Luther) and the birth of the printing press, which produced a similarly "disembedded" experience of meaning. A simultaneous amplification and diminishment of the situated meaning that local speech had carried as expression was now conveyed to a wide (and dislocated) audience of readers. I am grateful to Ariel Pomerance.

4. In the modern world we are all like Walter Benjamin's detective, who "develops forms of reaction that are in keeping with the pace of a big city. He catches things

in flight; this enables him to dream that he is like an artist. Everyone praises the swift crayon of the graphic artist. Balzac claims that artistry as such is tied to a quick grasp" (Benjamin 1997, 41).

5. "What is crucial," writes Thomas Elsaesser (2003, 27), "is that the close-up in Lang's *mise-en-scène* does not simply regulate or conflate distance and proximity: it introduces a 'beyond distance and proximity.'"

6. I discuss vulnerability to stories in my essay on *Vertigo* in *An Eye for Hitchcock* (2004).

7. For more on the routine and mundane aspects of criminal work, and its situational legitimacy in the career of the thief, see McIntosh 1971.

8. Indeed, the script has been the prime element in the motion picture business since the early days of the studio system. See Bordwell, Staiger, and Thompson (1985, 136–38).

9. This shot is something of an homage to the ending shot of François Truffaut's *Fahrenheit 451* (1966).

ON THE MOVE

LEGACIES OF WEIMAR CINEMA
Patrice Petro

I would like to reflect on the title of this essay—"Legacies of Weimar Cinema"—by focusing on the circulation of images, performers, genres, and personnel between Hollywood and Berlin in the 1920s and beyond. Three concepts guide my analysis. First, the notion of impermanence. I contend that Weimar cinema inaugurated an exploration of modernity defined by states and conditions of impermanence. In this regard, I refer not only to long-standing modernist notions, such as the loss of fixed values in the wake of industrial expansion and capitalist exchange, but also to the impermanence of gendered categories and sexual identities in the face of an increasing visibility and mobility of classes, races, sexes, and nations within an urban context.

This understanding brings me to my second concept, that of the international or global. The exploration of impermanence was not confined to Weimar Berlin or to Germany in the interwar years but was in fact part of what created and helped to sustain an international urban culture. This urban culture was exported and circulated worldwide, from Berlin to Paris, Los Angeles, Chicago, New York, and Moscow, through the work of immigrants and exiles in all realms of the film industry and, still more broadly, via the flow of ideas, images, and peoples around the globe.

Finally, I want to say something about Weimar cinema in relation to its afterlife in Hollywood and beyond. In its smart, skeptical, and sophisticated reflection on states of impermanence, Weimar cinema remains a compelling site for thinking about modernity and how we live in the modern age. As Edward Said has written, "Texts that are inertly of their time stay there; those which brush up unstintingly against historical constraints are the ones we keep with us, generation after generation" (2003, 26–27). In what follows, I hope to suggest why we should endeavor to recall Weimar cinema today.

This project has become especially important, given the way some of the best work in film history is now being written and conceived. Recent years have seen the growth of a specifically feminist film history, focused largely on "early cinema." Early cinema is usually said to begin with the introduction of film in 1895 and to end, depending on the criteria for what constitutes "early" (as opposed to "classical") cinema, variously in 1907 or 1914 or sometimes as late as 1917. Scholars of early cinema are aware that this chronology provides nothing like a neutral temporal frame. It has everything to do with an understanding of a shift from a cinema ruled by spectacle and attractions to one predominately narrative in design (see in this regard Gunning 1990). As one feminist historian has written, "The focus of interest remains insistently on the turn of the century, where the hype over attractions has accentuated a film form potentially dominated by exhibitionism rather than voyeurism, by surprise rather than suspense, and by spectacle rather than story. The concept of attractions is, admittedly, seductive for feminists, especially insofar as it removes the cinema from the totalizing terms of a controlling and gendered gaze" (Bean 2002, 6).

I find this argument at once compelling and troublesome. Compelling, because it speaks to the desire to locate cinematic traditions outside of oppressive formal structures and institutionalized constraints. And troubling, because it begs the question of whether we need the terms and historical division separating "early" and "late" in order to remove the cinema from the "totalizing terms of a controlling and gendered gaze." Would we not do better to rethink those very conceptual categories that limit our understanding of film history as well as film form? As a historian who has focused on cinema in the

1920s and 1930s, I am bothered by the way in which the new feminist film history leaves little space for thinking about this, and other, in-between periods in film history. As a case in point, the Weimar period, between world wars, encompassed silent and sound film and witnessed the institutionalization of cinema and the enormous growth of a specifically female audience, which in itself posed a challenge to traditional class barriers as well as to racial and sexual taboos.

To be sure, implicit in the new film history is the notion that early cinema—that is, cinema before 1917—is much closer to our own time than the so-called classical cinema, which developed formally and institutionally alongside an extended period of economic expansion, led by the United States, that lasted well into the 1950s. Those who argue that early cinema is prescient of our own modernity claim that it emerged and drew inspiration from various visual entertainment forms; thus, its identity was fundamentally chaotic, protean, and inter-medial. In this view, cinema's current chaotic present—its lack of a secure identity, the result of competition from new image technologies and changing conditions of production, distribution, and reception—is more accurately reflected in the projected images and experimentation of the turn of the twentieth century.

But is an analysis of the complex relationships among art and entertainment forms made difficult by the cinema itself, or by our theories and histories of it? What is gained, and what is lost, in constructing film history according to the terms "early" (roughly 1895–1917 or thereabouts) and "late" (after 1960)—terms that bracket off the greater part of the twentieth century? Here, the example of Weimar cinema is instructive. For example, Weimar cinema can be construed as "late" early cinema or as "early" late cinema, depending on the argument or point of view. It is taken as either the last gasp of a modernist experimentation in the popular cinema—an instance of what is often now called "vernacular modernism" (see Hansen 2000)—or an early example of classical narrative style. In fact, it is both. Needless to say, the Weimar cinema was a continuation of so-called early cinema, not only in its experimental narrative forms but also in its expansive, unforeseen, and dizzyingly complex circulations within an international urban flow.

Diasporic Weimar

To take just one example, we may consider Josef von Sternberg's *Blonde Venus* (1932). Although often considered a conventional Hollywood narrative film, it is as much a trace of an international urban culture as it is an example of classical narrative codes and conventions. Marlene Dietrich is a key figure here, particularly insofar as the film acknowledged her as an icon equally of Berlin and Hollywood. Indeed, *Blonde Venus* self-consciously comments on Dietrich's move from Berlin to Hollywood. Like the character she plays, Helen Farraday, Dietrich is explicitly German. Much of the dialogue is in German in the opening sequences of the film, which establish how Helen meets her future American scientist husband in the Black Forest (as she swims naked with a group of other female performers, who are taking a break from their next appearance on stage). *Blonde Venus* is thus literally about bringing Farraday/Dietrich from Germany to the United States, where she conquers its capital (in this film, of course, America's cultural capital, New York) as well as the cultural capital of Europe (Paris).

Significantly, Dietrich's persona in this film, particularly her identity as the "Blonde Venus," was drawn from many sources, among the most important of which is Josephine Baker, whose all-black revue was a sensation in Europe of the 1920s. Baker was different from Dietrich in many ways, not least of all in her reputation for comic as well as sexual excess and in the source of her performance style in African American traditions. But Baker aspired to perform with the same kind of elegance and sexual sophistication that we now associate with Dietrich, and Dietrich clearly drew upon Baker's performances of sexual knowledge and sensual abandon, without, of course, taking her own to the same extremes. (At times Baker performed completely naked, other times wearing only a banana skirt, and still other times in full male formal dress.) Historian Nancy Nenno points out that, for the German public, Josephine Baker was not merely "the primitive but also the elegant, well-dressed, modern American woman who conquered its capital. Baker's persona and her performances coincided with Berlin's own image as both highly elegant and exceedingly decadent, as combining both American and European elements. During the 1920s, Berlin was fascinated with America and actively sought to model itself as the most 'American' of European cities" (Nenno 1997, 155).

In light of Nenno's remarks, the ironies abound when we consider how the German Dietrich copied the African American Baker, quoting from her performances and career trajectory (from the stages of Harlem to the nightclubs of Paris) in her role as the "Blonde Venus." The now infamous "Hot Voodoo" number in *Blonde Venus* can indeed be read as a direct quotation from Baker's routines; such a reading certainly erases the source of that quotation in an explicit, yet no less outrageous, play with sexual and racial identities. It is interesting to compare the "Hot Voodoo" number from this 1932 Hollywood film with Dietrich's earlier cabaret performance in the 1930 German film that launched her international career, *The Blue Angel* (*Der Blaue Engel*). There, Dietrich performs in a provincial German cabaret to a racially mixed audience that prominently features black members. In *Venus*, however, transported to New York, she performs for an ethnically diverse but still white audience in Harlem, in which African Americans are visible only as the hired help or supporting cast for the racially charged Blonde Venus. Dietrich's German "New Woman" in America was but a copy of an imaginary African American styled by Josephine Baker for European audiences, thus an ultramodern primitivism, which evoked racial distinctions and oppositions only to push them to an uncomfortable and volatile extreme.

To put this another way: at her most "American" (*Blonde Venus* is Dietrich's only film with von Sternberg in which she plays a German American housewife, rather than, say, a Russian empress), Dietrich is still portrayed as "foreign" and fundamentally "German." And at her most "German," she imitates the performance style of an African American artist—after all, what is this German housewife doing performing in a Harlem nightclub?—whose own career flourished in Europe but foundered against the deeply embedded and institutionalized racism in the United States. Indeed, when Baker returned to America, searching for the success she had found in both Paris and Berlin, she was told that American audiences were not ready for a black woman who embodied both sexuality and sophistication. By that time, Dietrich was finishing her seventh and final film with von Sternberg, and had been firmly established in Hollywood as both legend and star.

This comparison brings us back to an essential component of German cinema in the 1920s, namely, its irrefutably international and diasporic character. To be sure, as many scholars have noted, the rise of National Socialism ensured that Weimar culture, and not just its cinema, would be dispersed "to the furthest parts of the world: to Brazil, where, after writing a beautiful, if nostalgic memoir of *The World of Yesterday,* Stefan Zweig committed suicide; to Mexico, where Anna Seghers wrote her extraordinary memory of childhood, 'The Excursion of the Dead Girls;' to Palestine, where Arnold Zweig lived and wrote in misery; and to the United States, where Thomas Mann and Bertolt Brecht created some of the masterpieces of twentieth-century German prose and drama" (Kniesche and Brockmann 1994, 4). In the 1920s and early 1930s, however, Hollywood and Berlin were also equally part of a vital, and highly competitive, international film culture, which involved trade wars and quotas as well as the welcome and calculated exchange of personnel (including German directors like F. W. Murnau and actors like Emil Jannings, as well as American actresses like Louise Brooks and directors like von Sternberg). Needless to say, *Blonde Venus* was very much a part of this international film culture, even if now, by virtue of our theoretical and historical categories, it is typically considered a classical Hollywood film, part of the Dietrich/von Sternberg cycle or an early example of the "fallen woman" or "maternal melodrama" genres in American cinema.

The point I want to make is that Berlin during the Weimar years was a node within a network of global cities that included London and Paris, Moscow, Mexico City, Los Angeles, and New York. Via this network, images, performers, and personnel traveled across temporal and cultural boundaries to emerge as part of a new ensemble. But this position raises another question: What, if anything, was specific to Weimar cinema and culture? The editors of a volume on Weimar culture put it this way: "The true home of Weimar culture was Germany, and that culture could never be the same anywhere else. Ultimately, the story of Weimar culture is the story of irrecoverable loss and unfulfilled promise. The ghosts of that loss and that promise continue to haunt us on both sides of the Atlantic" (Kniesche and Brockmann 1994, 18).

Cynical Weimar

How can we account for the specificity of Weimar culture without discounting its internationalism or diminishing the impact of its global circulation? How do we assess its contributions and account for its most distinctive qualities and enduring styles? Many scholars have argued that the cinema and the arts in Weimar Germany were permeated by a mood at once pessimistic, critical, and melancholy (see Sloterdijk 1987; Kniesche and Brockmann 1994; and Widdig 2001). These qualities imbued a particular mise-en-scène that was antipsychological and antinaturalist, focused on qualities of abstraction and design. Weimar culture has been described as erotic and coldly calculating, thoroughly artificial and undramatic, preoccupied with the deceptive play of acerbic and often morbidly ironic appearances. Most famously, critical theorist Peter Sloterdijk locates in Weimar culture the founding period of a new cynical consciousness that is still very much with us today. "For reasons that can be enumerated," Sloterdijk writes, "Weimar culture was cynically disposed like scarcely any previous culture; it gave birth to an abundance of brilliantly articulated cynicisms, which read like textbook examples. It experienced the pain of modernization more violently and expressed its disillusionment more coldly and more sharply than the present could ever do" (1987, 389). Although Sloterdijk does not mention or explore it, the various cynicisms he describes are inseparable from the changing status of women in modern societies. Indeed, the apprehension, particularly by women, of the malleable, impermanent contours of gender and sexuality had as much to do with Weimar's cynical and ironic dispositions as with the erosion of religious and metaphysical beliefs.

In his book on Weimar culture, historian Bernd Widdig begins to capture something of this gendered experience of impermanence. In a wide-reaching analysis of symbolic, philosophical, and visual representations of hyperinflation and equally rapid currency devaluation, Widdig shows how Weimar modernity was coded as feminine and accompanied by an iconography that often depicted women and the city as demonic, irrational, amoral forces. In his analysis of a contemporary monograph entitled *Moral History of the Inflation Period,* written by Hans Ostwald and published in 1931, Widdig explains how the decade of the 1920s in Germany was experienced as a time of ceaseless erosion, and definitive overturning, of nineteenth-century (read, masculine) values. Widdig offers a collection of historical anecdotes and vignettes of everyday life in the early 1920s by way of a long list from Ostwald:

> Looking back at the years of inflation the crazy image of a hellish carnival comes to mind: Plunderings and riots, . . . painful hunger and wild gluttony, rapid pauperization and sudden enrichment, excessive dancing and horrible misery of children, nude dancing, currency conjurers, hoarding of material assets, . . . occultism and psychics—gambling passion, speculation, a divorce epidemic, emancipation of women, early maturity of youth, Quaker-food kitchen, . . . police raids and racketeering, jazz and drugs. (2001, 7)

Widdig explains that for Ostwald, "the period of inflation marks the time of a radical transvaluation that affected all spheres of society and culture." Again, he directly quotes Ostwald describing his experience of the inflation: "Someone who once was rich and could afford all luxuries suddenly had to be happy if caring people gave him a bowl of soup. Little apprentices in banks turned overnight into 'bank directors' with endless supplies of money. Poor foreign pensioners could come to Germany and live on their *valuta* like princes." Widdig comments: "Everything suddenly had turned around, and for Ostwald, whose social codes were rooted in imperial Germany, the sudden transgressions of established gender roles were particularly threatening. He saw family structures falling apart, 'an erotic ecstasy jumbling up the world,' and women becoming more demanding, especially in erotic matters." Again, Widdig quotes Ostwald: "We experienced a particular rejuvenation in women. Grandma with bobbed hair danced in a short skirt with young men in the foyer, in a coffee-house: wherever she found an opportunity. Mama danced with friends. The nanny took the opportunity and danced as well—and the children at home were all alone" (2001, 7–8).

According to Widdig, runaway inflation marked a radical turning point not only for Weimar Germany but also for the modernizing world. It signaled the final breakdown of nineteenth-century values in a rapid process of modernization, including the expansion of mass culture directed at a cross-class, cross-generational, largely female, but increasingly diverse public that was oriented toward leisure and consumption. Widdig explores the conceptual link between gender, inflation, and the perception of "modernity out of bounds" in a range of texts and images that gave expression to various male fantasies and anxieties, as suggested, for example, by the Ostwald text he quotes. But what of impermanence figured not simply *as* feminine but also *by* and *for* women in the images and films of the era?

There are, in fact, several notable films and works of art that attest to an experience of impermanence that was at once variable and gender-specific. Marlene Dietrich is once again a key figure, particularly in her performance as Lola Lola in *The Blue Angel*. At once maternal and openly sexual, Dietrich as Lola also projected an image of bisexuality and a liberating sense of detachment and self-irony. As I have described elsewhere (Petro 2002, 95–123), hers was not a self-reflexive cynicism or coldness born of unease and foreboding (what Sloterdijk, for instance, describes as Weimar cynical reasoning). It was rather an embrace of the ambivalence of appearances and thus an acknowledgment of what had been gained as well as lost in the wake of cultural dislocation and the experience of impermanence.

Theorists have often invoked critic Kenneth Tynan's words to capture the qualities that were the very signature of Dietrich's—yet not only Dietrich's—Weimar style. Tynan famously wrote that Dietrich "has sex but no positive gender. Her masculinity appeals to women and her sexuality to men. She lives in a sexual no man's land—and in no woman's either. She dedicates herself to looking, rather than to being, sexy. The art is in the seeming" (Tynan qtd. in Garber 1993, 16–17). Rather than linger over oppositions between masculinity and sexuality, appeals to women versus those to men, we should understand the key term here to be "appearance" rather than "essence," the difference between seeming and being. These terms can be extended to include a range of Weimar films and images, spanning Fritz Lang's exploration of the duplicity of vision or Ernst Lubitsch's play with the rituals of desire or Hannah Hoch's fascination with the construction of sexuality and race through fragments, masks, and disguises. Indeed, it is fair to say that Weimar culture sustained an exploration of various forms of open duplicity—sometimes cynical, often ironic, and other times indifferently engaged—cataloging a range of Weimar locales and types familiar from the illustrated press and the drawings of artists like Otto Dix, Christian Schad, and Georg Grosz: gambling dens and street corners, transvestites and mannish women, pimps and prostitutes, new urban subcultures and vigilante groups.

What is remarkable to me is the way in which the narrative of Weimar modernity—and Weimar urbanism—has been weighted toward a violent, frankly erotic and unemotional, cynically misogynist view of modern life, which has now become the sign of Weimar authenticity. Lost and devalued in this account is another lineage and Weimar legacy, involving women and gender and sexual improvisation, that had perhaps the greatest impact on Hollywood cinema and beyond. This legacy has important ramifications for thinking about women and cities and the flow of images, ideas, and people, a subject to which I would like to turn now, in some final thoughts about states of impermanence as they were circulated in the work of German immigrants and exiles after Weimar culture in Germany virtually ceased to be.

Germany in Hollywood

The German (and Austrian) community in Hollywood in the early part of the twentieth century included directors (F. W. Murnau, Ernst Lubitsch, Fritz Lang, Paul Leni, E. A. Dupont), producers (Erich Pommer), writers (Thomas Mann, Bertolt Brecht, Billy Wilder), composers (Arnold Schoenberg, Ernst Toch, Ernst Krenek, Erich Wolfgang Korngold), and performers (Emil Jannings, Pola Negri, Lya de Putti, Conrad Veidt, Marlene Dietrich, Peter Lorre). They did not all arrive at the same time or for the same reasons, and not all chose to remain in the United States. As film theorist Thomas Elsaesser has pointed out, "There are problems in writing about the German émigrés as a group, and of their films as a body of work. . . . Each director, each technician and each film participates in several histories at once. The individuals have their own history, and exile is always a personal tragedy that finds little consolation in numbers" (1984, 279). Despite these caveats, historians have generally referred to "two waves" of German migration to Hollywood. The first wave is said to have begun in the early 1920s. The artistic prestige and technical innovations of Weimar cinema in the 1920s made German directors, actors, and technical people attractive to the film industries elsewhere. As one historian describes it, with "their strong orientation toward foreign markets, Hollywood studios hoped that the employment of top personnel from Germany might weaken the Weimar film industry, while the cultural sensibilities of this personnel might in turn make their Hollywood films more accessible to Central and Eastern European audiences, especially in Germany itself" (Kramer 2002, 231). Thus the first wave of German migration brought actresses like Dietrich and directors like Lubitsch and Murnau to America because Hollywood was buying talent to enhance its own industry while simultaneously neutralizing competition abroad. Elsaesser has shown that what made the Germans a prominent force in Hollywood was their professionalism, technical expertise, and experience in a mature, developed industry, "which is why," he points out, "they could adapt themselves so well to Hollywood, and could leave their mark on so many different genres, cycles, and modes" (Elsaesser 1996, 138). The first wave of German migration to Hollywood must be seen within this international context, where the film industries of France, Germany, and Hollywood alike competed for shares in U.S. and European markets. There was considerable movement and flow among these various national industries, Elsaesser notes, as evidenced by the production of films in multiple language versions and the leasing and hiring of one another's assets, whether stars, production facilities, patents, or distribution rights.

If the first wave of German immigration was primarily economic in nature, the second wave, though clearly economic as well, was also motivated by political developments. The Nazi takeover of the German film industry in 1933 and the rescinding of the contracts of Jewish personnel brought about mass emigrations and an exodus of talent. Between 1933 and 1952, more than fifteen hundred German and Austrian émigrés and exiles worked in the Hollywood studios. Many returned to Europe in the 1950s, but many more remained in Los Angeles, where they left a profound mark on what some now assume is a classically American style.

Most historians claim that the Germans excelled at two particular Hollywood genres: film noir and film comedy. Interestingly, these genres derive from urban experience and an urban milieu. Film noir's dark, critical, and self-reflexive vision was clearly urban, whereas the comedies were infused with references to sexual liberation, modern entertainment, and mass consumption that marked them as both urban and urbane. To be sure, film noir has garnered more critical attention than film comedy in discussions of the German influence in Hollywood. Indeed, film noir is typically seen as indebted to Weimar film and art traditions. Noir's stylized projections of inner states, for example, are linked to expressionism. Its dark cityscapes and high-contrast lighting projected a mood of fatalism, disillusionment, and cynicism, providing a filmic equivalent to Sloterdijk's cynical consciousness. Finally, the generic influence of the Weimar "street film" and its conventionalized character types—psychopathic males, sexual murderers, and prostitutes—are seen as formative to noir generic conventions, as is the fact that many noir directors were of German, Austrian, or other European descent: Fritz Lang, Robert Siodmak, Otto Preminger, Billy Wilder, Curtis Bernhardt, Anatole Litvak, Edgar Ulmer, Max Ophüls, Douglas Sirk.

Yet, however compelling these influences might seem, it is important to underscore that most film historians and theorists today take issue with this understanding of the "German roots" of film noir. For instance, they have pointed out that American directors used expressionist lighting codes as early as 1915 and that few of the most prominent noir directors actually made urban crime films in Germany. Most tellingly, they argue that film noir is itself an unstable generic category that exists entirely in criticism, having been invented by two generations of Parisian intellectuals, most of whom declared the form extinct soon after they named it. Film critic James Naremore points out that "noir is not merely a descriptive term, but a name for a critical tendency within popular cinema—an antigenre that reveals the dark side of savage capitalism." He adds that "if we could ask the original French commentators what American noir represented, they might argue that it was a kind of modernism in the popular cinema" (1998, 38). Though there can be no doubt that the appropriation of talents and ideas from Europe had an enormous impact in the United States, the notion that film noir is fundamentally "German" misses what I have described as the international dimension of Weimar culture and the fact that, as a critical category, film noir is an idea "constructed ex post facto by critics"[1] and embraces a variety of styles, themes, and conventions.

But is it only film noir that reveals the dark side of capitalism or captures a kind of modernism in the popular cinema? To be sure, the critical fascination with noir has established the view of overwhelming "German influence" in Hollywood as well as counter-claims for noir's status as largely discursive. It has also had the unintended effect of deflecting attention from exile cinema's most enduring popular genre, film comedy, which was received to great acclaim in America just as it had been in Weimar Germany.

Clearly, film noir and film comedy in the German exile tradition are two sides of a coin. Both shared a concern with modernity, urbanism, and the emancipation of women, and both brought new subjectivities into being. But whereas noir and crime films were by turns stylish, cynical, and misogynist—emphasizing nostalgia, loss, and lack—the comedies were stylish in their own way, revolving around themes of impersonation, role reversal, and cross-dressing, all aimed at exploring the rituals of seduction with deep skepticism and humor. I will return to the question of German émigré film comedies in a moment, in an analysis of Billy Wilder's 1959 film *Some Like It Hot*. Here, however, I want to say more about the context for German émigré films, because they were viewed by contemporary audiences against a backdrop of dramatic social change that has direct bearing on the circulation of images between Hollywood and Berlin.

In an excellent study of urban entertainment in 1920s New York, historian Marybeth Hamilton explores the emergence of a new generation of film- and theatergoers who were in revolt against the codes of sexual restraint prized by the nineteenth-century middle class. Hamilton explains that the rebellion was spearheaded by middle-class women, "who decked themselves out in lipstick and silk stockings and became ardent patrons of movies, nightclubs, and dance halls. In New York, they forged a new craze for slumming, for exploring cultures and styles beyond the respectable pale: the 'primitivism' of African Americans in Harlem, the flamboyance of the city's gay men, and the aggressive eroticism exhibited by prostitutes, who put sexuality on public display" (1997, 2).

This description of urban New York obviously resonates with many historical accounts of urban Berlin in the 1920s (and also resonates with the themes, settings, and atmosphere of Weimar cinema's most enduring films, such as *The Blue Angel*). But the crucial point is this: the early part of the twentieth century witnessed a remarkable generational shift in the consumption of popular culture. At the turn of the century, Hamilton notes, "saloons and burlesque halls offered under-world entertainment to underworld audiences, shows where per-former and audience shared membership in a world the respectable strictly avoided, and their patronage was very limited—working class men, a few slumming gentlemen, and virtually no women except prostitutes" (1997, 66). But all this changed in the 1920s, when middle-class patrons, mostly young women, flocked to the movies and theater, eager for racy tales of prostitution and exposure to the world of speakeasies, Harlem nightclubs, and drag balls hosted by an emerg-ing gay subculture. Thus were the 1920s a turning point for women in the cities—for their visibility, mobility, and economic clout within an urban culture not confined to New York or Berlin or Paris or London but interconnected through an entertainment network at once cosmo-politan and international.

Liking It Hot

Ernst Lubitsch is perhaps the best-known Weimar émigré director of German and Hollywood film comedies. Here, however, I want to focus on a film by a German exile rather than German émigré—someone who came to the United States in the second rather than the first wave of emigration to Hollywood, and whose work, especially *Some Like It Hot*, has direct bearing on the issues and themes I have raised.

Billy Wilder left Germany in 1933 and arrived in America in 1934, after less than a year's stopover in France. A scriptwriter by trade, he made the decision to leave Germany in view of Hitler's rise to power, but his final destination was never in doubt. As German studies scholar Gerd Gemunden explains, "there is a decidedly transcultural dimension to Billy Wilder's work, a status of being in-between nations, and drawing on very distinct cultural sensibilities. . . . Although Billy Wilder had his eye on America from the very beginning of his career, the European baggage he carried with him would always be present." Throughout his career, Wilder would draw on this German and cen-tral European background, "infusing his American material with gen-erous helpings of Jewish humor, fin-de-siècle decadence, or Weimar German modernism. If his early scripts at UFA attest to his fascination with things American—speed, gangsters, Hollywood stardom, and life in the modern metropolis—his American films revisit Germany and Europe from the perspective of a thoroughly Americanized artist and U.S. citizen, confronting the traditions of the Old World with the achievements of the New" (Gemunden, n.p.).

Some Like It Hot was released in 1959. Significantly, however, it is set in the 1920s and reflects on this era of filmmaking (not unlike an earlier Wilder film, *Sunset Blvd.* [1950], which also takes 1920s cinema as its referent). Filmed in black and white, *Some Like It Hot* is thoroughly self-conscious in its play with genre and with notions of performance and appearance. The film tells the story of two unemployed Chicago musicians, desperate for work, who accidentally witness the St. Valentine's Day massacre. They escape from the mob by dressing as women and joining an all-girl jazz band en route to Florida. The performances by Tony Curtis (Joe and Josephine) and Jack Lemmon (Jerry and Daphne) have often been described, and not without reason, as near-perfect in timing, inflection, and pace. But what is equally remarkable is the way in which the film simultaneously sustains two separate genre traditions: it is at once a kind of noir-inflected urban crime film and a comedy involving slapstick, gender-bending, and visual and verbal sexual innuendo. It is as if Wilder were attempting to fuse the twin strands of the German émigré legacy in one film.

Although the film begins in a gritty urban milieu, filled with gambling, gangsters, and speakeasies, it quickly moves from this noir setting (and darker version of the Weimar legacy) by shifting to a train headed to Florida and then to a seaside resort, where the focus turns from crime and poverty to entertainment, leisure, and gender performance. All of the characters are self-consciously performing their roles, whether it is Jack Lemmon as Daphne, or Marilyn Monroe as Sugar Kane Kowalczyk, or Tony Curtis as the saxophone-playing Josephine and, later, as the wealthy tycoon Junior, who spoofs Cary Grant's voice and demeanor and feigns impotence in a mock seduction scene with Sugar Kane aboard "his" yacht.

It is interesting to note that *Some Like It Hot* was actually based on a Weimar film script, which was sold to a French company by the scriptwriter, Robert Thoeren, in his first year of exile in Paris. The French film version, entitled *Fanfare d'amour* (*Fanfare of Love* [1935]), was remade in Germany in 1951 by Kurt Hoffmann and released at a time when the German studio system was just emerging from the rubble of the war and producing a cycle of postwar "rubble films"

(Horak 2002, 34). Interestingly, in this postwar German version the central male characters blacken their faces to play with black bands, masquerade as gypsies, and only later cross-dress to join an all-women's band. If this film references the Weimar legacy in troubling and obviously racially charged ways, the Wilder remake released eight years later also evokes legacies of Weimar cinema, here focusing not on race or ethnicity but on the complexity and fluidity of sexuality and gender roles.

Of course, the 1950s in the United States, like the Weimar years, were an in-between time in film history: a time when the studio system was weakening, the advent of television was threatening, and the influence of the Production Code and its censorship restrictions was declining. The closing scene of *Some Like It Hot* has long been considered a provocative challenge to the Production Code, featuring the greatest fade-out line in film history. Speeding off in a swank motorboat, Daphne (Lemmon) tells "her" rich suitor, Osgood (Joe E. Brown), that she cannot marry him and gives a list of reasons: her shape, her hair color, her smoking, her sinful living arrangements with a saxophone player, and her infertility. Osgood is unfazed, so Daphne rips off her wig and declares, "I'm a man!" to which Osgood replies, "Well . . . nobody's perfect."

As wonderful as this scene is, I believe another sequence best captures the film's sensibilities and recalls the exploration of modernity defined by states and conditions of impermanence that remain a lasting Weimar legacy. The scene involves Lemmon and Curtis performing as Daphne and Josephine and takes place after two parallel, cross-cut seduction scenes, the first featuring Curtis and Monroe, the second featuring Lemmon and Brown. After a night of tango dancing and sexual abandon, Josephine and Daphne are back in their hotel room. Daphne gleefully reports to Josephine that Osgood has proposed marriage. Euphoric, lying on the bed, and still in drag, Daphne/Lemmon articulates a comic logic whereby artifice and appearance seem not only reasonable but even desirable. Shaking a pair of maracas for emphasis after each outrageous line —

Daphne: "I'm engaged."
Joe: "Who's the lucky girl?"
Daphne: "I am!"

—Daphne is still absorbed in and thrilled by the previous evening. She visibly expresses bodily pleasure as she surrenders to the woman within. Earlier on, of course, when Lemmon first emerged in drag, all he could do was complain about his dress and how hard it was to walk in heels. By now, however, he is so comfortable in his role that he wears the shoes, dresses, makeup with ease and at one point even dons a bathing suit without a thought, which is not surprising, given that to be a man in this film means to be impotent or a killer or on the run from one or the other.

This marked shift in sensibility is as much visual as narrative, evidenced in a notable transformation of visual codes. In the earlier sequence, when Lemmon and Curtis first appear at the railway station in drag, they ogle Sugar Kane's legs and behind, and comment on her physical movement in a classically motivated male point-of-view shot: "Look at that," says Jerry/Daphne. "It's just like Jell-O on springs! I tell ya, it's a whole different sex." Near the end of the film, however, in the sequence that follows their night on the town, this male point-of-view shot is noticeably missing. Lemmon's euphoric performance as Daphne, lost in romantic fantasy and still visibly possessed by the tango, is decidedly exhibitionist—neither voyeuristic nor masculine nor understandable within the terms of an objective or controlling gaze.

Indeed, the film itself could be described more broadly as an elaborate and self-conscious escape from the world of men: an escape from the urban crime drama for the world of women and comedy, an object lesson in the need for men to abandon their sexual identities in order to survive. Although not entirely or exactly feminist, the film nonetheless forces its audience (and its central male characters) to experience the world differently, as women do—subject to unwanted sexual overtures, male voyeurism, and the constraints and pleasures of feminine culture. This is the source of much of its humor—for women as well as men.

But the film's enduring appeal, I would argue, lies in its suggestion that gender and sexuality are not fixed or permanent or essential qualities. They are instead fluid and impermanent—fluid in the physical space of performance and impermanent both onscreen and in the theater, just as they were in the 1920s in Berlin, New York, and beyond. Needless to say, this interpretation complicates assessments of

251

the so-called classical cinema and the dividing lines between films dominated by exhibitionism rather than voyeurism, surprise rather than suspense. Indeed, only a year after the release of *Some Like It Hot*, another director, also schooled in Weimar cinema, released the gender-bending, mixed horror/comedy film called *Psycho*, capitalizing on Wilder's success and stumbling upon yet another remarkable generational shift in the consumption of popular culture (in this case, the emergence of a middle-class youth market). Like Hitchcock's film, Wilder's *Some Like It Hot* draws upon the pleasurable performance of gender but also directly references an earlier international urban culture and its lasting, dare I say, permanent influence in impermanent times. In the process, it reveals how traces of Weimar urban culture travel across temporal and cultural boundaries, and how later history reopens and challenges what appears to have been definitively, irrevocably lost.

Note

1. This is Naremore's point, but it is also made by Thomas Elsaesser (1996).

GETTING LOST
ON THE WATERWAYS OF *L'ATALANTE*
Tom Conley

More than a few historians of cartography observe that "modernity" or the "modern age" begins with printed maps. Before the advent of print culture, maps were far and few between. Often a manuscript or an object of veneration in a sacred space, a *mappamundi* did not provide its users with information about their location or about the physical nature of the world. The map, often found in churches or manuscripts, was iconic rather than locational. An object for contemplation, the map tended not to tell the spectators who gazed upon it exactly where they were but to encourage reflection on the ordered immensity of the world within the watery surround of its *ecoumène*, or ocean sea (Schulz 1978; Mangani 1998). In the printed map that succeeded the manuscript, initially found in editions of Ptolemy's *Geographia*, was ingrained the idea of the world to be seen as a "theater." To Abraham Ortelius and Gerard Mercator are owed the first atlases in which the entirety of the world is represented within the confines of a book. In them we perceive a sense of totality and of region and regionalism. Readers begin to look for the places that identify them as the subjects they are. In their atlases are found the beginnings of "locational imagery," of administration and planning on national and global scales that exploit spatial reason for the ends of social control. The implementation of the atlas might thus be considered to be a first stage of modernity (Jacob 1992, 98–106 [on the atlas], 430–31 [on locational effects]).

In *The Mapmaker's Quest* (2003), David Buisseret notes that before the invention of "locational imaging," a name attributed to cartography in the age of global positioning systems, an individual's sense of "region" or of topographic identity becomes correlative with the emergence of maps in print culture. Now if, too, modernity involves a subject's perception of his or her subjectivity, some of its origins must indeed reach back to the dissemination and exploitation of cartography. Such also are the vital political inflections J. Brian Harley brings to the topic (2001). Other historians of cartography concur that the modern world "as we know it" becomes visible on national maps dating from the 1860s. For the first time, lines in colored ink, contrary to earlier projections that had been without national borders, trace and delineate political, religious, and geographical boundaries that identify those who live and move about them. The same maps are suddenly riddled, too, with cross-hatched, dotted, and ruptured lines depicting systems of paved and unpaved overland roads, networks of railways, and circuits of navigable waterways cutting across or running parallel to major rivers. Some of the routes are real and others, virtual, are drawn to project the hopes and desires of engineers of state wishing to impose on the land a vision of control. The same maps ramify into intricate webbings that often obscure the topographical features that earlier cartographers and their assistants had carefully drawn by hand and named in accord with existing gazetteers.

And still other groups of cultural geographers adduce the advent of the "modern spirit"—or what, at the time of World War I Guillaume Apollinaire called *l'esprit nouveau*—to the emergence of the paradox of cartographic control and liberation. Control, for the reason that new maps and mappings were used, like today's electronic registries, to account for the movement of sizable masses of people; the new maps were diagrams that predicted the ways that national policies could monitor the flow of populations and, as needed, keep them in check. And liberation, because the map user could fathom the possibility, as Apollinaire's master, Charles Baudelaire, had put it in English in his *Poèmes en prose,* of getting lost or, with eyes set on the map, of going "anywhere out of this world." In this way the map that aided industry and tourism in the "age of mechanical reproduction" had the doubly binding effect of offering an illusion of freedom while remaining a form of locational imaging. It told subjects where they were in real space and time while allowing them, like the new medium of cinema, to imagine escape and passage to places far from the scourge of social contradiction and conflict.

A Plan and *Un plan*

In this essay I shall hypothesize that what we think might be the modernity of cinema is tied to the way film's locational powers, like those of a map, are configured and even theorized within its own form. Viewers might believe that any number of shots in a film can carry a sense of location and precise social and geographical placement. Cartographic information tells us where the narrative or documentary is taking place. But it also cues the reaction on the part of the spectator that he or she is *not* there, and that the information about location yields the paradoxical effect of summoning the stability or veracity of the sites being shown. "You are here," says the film, to which the spectator responds, "No, I am not . . . but then again, where am I, and why am I here, in front of these very images? What has conduced me to suspend and then retrieve disbelief about the spatial images I am witnessing?" These questions come forward most frequently when we discern the presence of maps in movies. A map glimpsed in a narrative film often offers geographic verisimilitude enough to let its power of illusion take control. Yet the same map can also provoke an antithetical reaction, a nagging suspicion not only about the nature of the space given in the film but also about how and why the spectator relates to it (see the introduction to Conley 2005). In general, then, a map in a film can prompt us to ask how and why, in a greater psychogeographical way, we perceive the aesthetic, political, and historical relations we hold with cinema.

The project in the paragraphs that follow is to study the paradox of cartographic information through a classic film, Jean Vigo's *L'Atalante*

(1934), in which, for a brief but decisive moment, a map emerges and disappears. This film, as many critics have shown, is an essay on space that both dilates and contracts through alternate depictions of labor and illusion. The modernity of its geographic consciousness, however, has much to do with the way its map defines the space in which the film is made and its narrative seems to move.

To begin at the beginning, the title is an enigma. Does *L'Atalante*, a name Vigo applied to a vessel called *La Louis XVI*, refer to the myth of the eponymous goddess—described by Montaigne as "a girl of excellent beauty and wondrous disposition" (1950, 930)—who defied the thousands of men who wanted to marry her by beating them in footraces until Hippomenes dropped three golden apples along her way to divert her? Might it refer to what the producer of the film, Jean-Louis Nounez, said of Vigo after *Zéro de conduite* (1933) had been a commercial failure: "Yes, I've lost money with Vigo, but that's okay. Vigo has a lot of talent [*beaucoup de talent*], and I see what he needs. We have to give him a really anodyne scenario; then he can expend himself with all his genius, but censorship will not intervene" (qtd. in Lherminier 1967, 165). To Nounez's intuition of *talent* refracted in the title might be added a sense of mood. If by his name Vigo's father, Miguel "Almereyda," was affiliated with Spanish anarchists, in "L'Atalante" we hear the echo of *talante*, of a mood or atmosphere of the kind shown around the name of the boat seen in the very first shot of the film. Further, the presence of the sea beyond, of *l'Atlantique*, upon which the hero gazes when arriving at the "destination" of the film, cannot be discounted.

And the plot is disarmingly simple. Jean (Jean Dasté), the young captain of a *péniche* (barge) that transports goods to and from the coast and country of France, marries Juliette (Dita Parlo), a simple country woman who wishes, like every principal character in every major French novel of the nineteenth century, to go to Paris. The nuptial ceremony bears the aura of a funeral. Once the couple is on board and at work, little time passes before the strain of conjugal life is felt. Juliette yearns for the City of Light but meets and frolics with the captain's older mate, Le père Jules (Michel Simon), a trickster and an anarchist of sorts, who spurns every inherited value. The captain discovers them at play and becomes enraged. The boat docks at the Parisian suburb of Corbeil. After meeting a dream-peddlar (Gilles Margaritis) in an *estaminet* (tavern), Juliette slips ashore to explore the city before her jealous husband decides to weigh anchor and leave her behind. Soon depressed and traumatized by her absence, he loses his grip on life. After a petty boss (Maurice Gilles) in the company for which they work in Le Havre threatens to fire the crew, old Jules takes it upon himself to find the captain's wife.[1] He retrieves her in Paris, brings her back to the barge, and deposits her in the cabin where her husband had been awaiting her arrival. The film ends with an aerial shot of the barge that seems to aim upward as it cruises on waters that sparkle in bright sunshine, before the camera moves ahead and leaves the boat behind and below.

In the Foreman's Office

The map appears in the twenty-second chapter of the recently restored DVD version of *L'Atalante*.[2] At the end of the twenty-first, the captain, the first mate, and the cabin boy (Louis Lefebvre) have just arrived at the destination of Le Havre (literally, the "haven" or "heaven," the port that had earlier been named Le Havre de Grâce). Not knowing where to turn, Jean runs along a seawall at the shoreline of the city, descends to the beach, looks outward, sprints toward the water, stops, turns about, and looks blankly at the horizon. He is next seen walking back to the port where a crowd of onlookers follows. One person calls him "encore un marin saoul" (just another drunken sailor). Jules takes him under his wing and back to the vessel where they prepare to report to the foreman's office. The squat and robust foreman, sitting in squalid and hopelessly messy quarters, reprimands the first mate for no apparent cause other than to show the employee that he and everyone else in the ambient world amount to human trash. The stern words, which the mate lets pass into one ear and out the other, are accompanied by the sight of an immense wall map that appears to be a projection of the fluvial routes of France. Its western side is rent by a tear in the area of the northwestern coast that includes Le Havre, while the other waterways are made visible by lines connecting smudges and greasy fingerprints at the sites of cities. The map's flatness and posterlike style calls attention to the photographic style of the film and effectively locates the scenes shot along the waterways in the earlier sequences. It articulates, too, the ways that the narrative is tied to a new geographic sensibility inhering in the cinematic medium.

Prior to this scene, as they leave the madding crowd, Jules warns Jean that there will be hell to pay in the foreman's quarters. A long fade-out ends this capital sequence (chapter 21), which crowns the arrival in Le Havre. The break signals the beginning of the next sequence, composed of nine shots, which is framed by two establishing views taken from the deck of the boat. In the first, in the foreground, the deck of the boat cuts across the frame at a slight diagonal parallel to a brick road below; beyond, in the background, is an uninviting zone, a *terrain vague* site of industrial passage. Beyond the brick path is a swath of ground, dotted with bits of detritus, on which grow grass and weeds. On the other side is a long barrier of stones piled up to separate the waterway from what to our eyes looks like parallel lines of railroads and highways on which trains and vehicles speed across the upper quarter of the frame. Some modern buildings emerge through the polluted atmosphere while boxcars and flatcars roll smoothly from left to right on an almost endless array of rails.

Here and elsewhere the film signals a spatial affiliation with modernity. Apollinaire's *esprit nouveau* had begun in the "zone" or periphery of Paris, where laborers, migrant workers, and the homeless found shelter and dubious salvation. So also in this film: the outskirts of Paris are the site of living conditions where trash and rubbish seem to be the archaeological strata of residue accumulated since the Industrial Revolution. These *terrains vagues* qualify as the disconnected areas that Gilles Deleuze associates with neorealism, "the city in demolition or reconstruction," a sort of "urban cancer, a dedifferentiated fabric," in which what he calls the "sensori-motor linkages" that in the realm of realism had held the attention of the spectator to the image are now "worth nothing more than the turmoil that affects them" or "that mirrors or makes them distractive" (Deleuze 1985, 13; my translation). In these zones we witness situations where sight and sound become disconnected perceptions. No *habitus* or reassuring place allows either the personage or the spectator to be identified with them.

Vigo's shot is uncanny for its construction, particularly the way it seems to isolate the upper deck of the barge against the horizon of land. Set across the deck, with its point aimed directly at the industrial landscape, is the prow of a lifeboat on which the cabin boy idly reclines (as the sequence will reveal, his feet forward, his head below his hands). Jules, seated on the gunwale of the little boat and facing right, is dressed in black woolen togs, his head adorned with a sailor's cap and his feet in a pair of dark wooden clogs. The narrative begins when Jules barks, "Ah, vous auriez pu . . ." (At least you could have . . .), his words precipitating the captain's entrance into the shot from the lower right corner (marked by a shaft that intrudes into the foreground). Walking like a zombie, he approaches the mate. The next shot cuts directly to Jean in medium close-up, seen from a counter tilt, now isolated against the sky. Dressed in the same costume as his mate, he looks forward blankly as Jules's words continue to resound: ". . . pu vous raser. Pas convenable, ça, quand même" (. . . given yourself a shave. C'mon, it's not correct). After two seconds the camera cuts back to the site of the establishing shot. Jules stands up and moves while Jean continues to stare. The mate's movement reveals the whole body of the boy who remains dumbly and happily idle. In the span of almost five seconds he is shown wearing a pair of shorts that bare his legs below the knees; at the same time, the shoe of his right foot aims at the landscape, which, if the shot is read stratigraphically, is literally above.[3] As in the first shot, because Jules faces away from the camera, his voice, not located in the frame, is both *in* and *off*. Muttering to the boy, turning back before hobbling down onto the pavement, Jules leaves his parting shot, "Alors, reste là" (Now stay here), to which the child, talking over him, responds, "Ah oui, ça va" (Yeah, sure, okay). As the two men descend, Jean's body blending into the silhouette of Jules's prior to following him, in the background a locomotive chugs into the frame, also from the right, leaving a trail of steam in its path. Thus ends the shot framing one end of the sequence.

The transition to the interior of the office in the next shot could be taken to be a jump cut. All of a sudden, the setting is the office of the foreman. He is seen from the back, in three-quarter angle, seated in such a way that his head, in the center of the frame, occludes the shade of an electric lamp on which are pasted pieces of paper. It is placed between him and a man—the captain of another boat who is dressed in a woolen jacket—in the medium ground behind a pile of objects on the desk: papers under the foreman's forearm, rubber stamps, a sculpture of a nude on her knees, a pile of books, and the usual paraphernalia of bureaucracy. In the upper left corner of the frame, the lower right edge of a map hangs on the wall. To the right and adjacent to the foreman is a poster on a door (seen diagonally), on which is written in cursive letters, "Fermez la porte S.V.P." (Close the door, please). To the right are more piles of paper and a chair.

The scene is one of interrogation. The voice of the foreman resounds in the space, barking at the employee that he has not been doing his job. "Qu'est-ce que tu es ici?" (What are you here?). The underling responds: "Un rien du tout" (A nothing whatsoever). The foreman: "Un rien du tout?" The worker: "Oui, un rien du tout." The foreman raises his right arm to tell the mustached man to exit: "Un rien du tout. Alors, si tu es un rien du tout, passes à la caisse, fais-toi régler et fous-moi le camp" (A nothing whatsoever. So, if you're a nothing whatsoever, go to the cashier, get your pay, and get the hell out of here). After thirteen seconds the man defiantly turns toward the exit, uttering, "Je ne passerai pas à la caisse" (I'm not going to the cashier), adding (turning left and right) that he wants his *pognon* (dough).

The film cuts to a medium shot of the cashier's window protected by bars and wires.[4] Behind the window, under the sign "Caisse" (cashier), is a bespectacled subaltern, a *huissier* arched over his ledger with a pen in his right hand. The sailor, now seen from behind, addresses the cashier while another sailor in profile to the left sits idly and reads a paper, pausing to look at what is happening. The sailor asks for his money while the cashier rustles the pages of his ledger. The scene becomes the background for the entry of Jules and Jean in the foreground and from the left side of the frame, as the foreman, in voice-*off*, calls for the captain of the *Atalante*: "Ça ne va pas traîner longtemps avec lui" (He won't take much time). The camera records Jules and Jean en route to the doorway, as they occlude the scene in the background but briefly watch it from the same point of view as the spectator.

The grid bears analogy with the corner of the map seen in the previous shot, and so also does a calendar adjacent to the window and an official poster seen obliquely to the right. The shot dolly-tracks the two men, who approach the doorway of the office out of which the foreman's words, "Ah, vous voilà!" (So there you are!), are heard. As they approach the door, the camera pulls back slightly to show them from the back (in a three-quarter angle) readying to enter by the same door on which is posted "Fermez la porte S.V.P." The foreman asks to see the first mate and not the captain. When Jules pushes Jean aside and enters the room, the camera brings the map in the background into view. Jules has removed his hat, exposing his close-cropped pate as he pushes the distressed captain aside and enters the room himself. The camera further reframes the space, panning slightly left and right, as Jules grasps the doorknob when the foreman, doubling the words of the poster, shouts, "Fermes la porte! Je n'ai pas de temps à perdre" (Shut the door, I have no time to waste). The office beyond the door seems to be such a chaos of bric-a-brac and paper—a bureaucratic version of the first mate's quarters—that the foreman's head blends into the papers and pictures on display. Jules swings the door shut in such a way that the sign approaches the camera and insists for the third time that the "door is being shut," but now directly in the face of the spectator. The shot lasts twenty seconds.

The sixth shot, lasting eight seconds and taken with a slightly upward view, displays Jean immobile, lost in himself, seated in a chair to the right of the door that has just closed. The sign and the oval doorknob to the right are visible at the upper right quadrant of the frame. The molding that extends behind Jean's head enhances the diagonal aspect of the shot. His contemplation is interrupted when the sailor who was at the cashier's window enters from the left, leans over, and insists to the seated captain how true it is that "we're all nobodies" and warns that if Jean is waiting in line, he had better get to the window before it closes at six o'clock. The sailor leaves, and, for an instant, Jean is again shown in solitude.

The seventh shot, the commanding and longest one of the sequence, places the boss in profile, seated behind his cluttered desk and staring angrily at Jules, who stands in medium depth, to the left of the lamp where the sailor was seen just three shots earlier. Piles of dossiers and papers are stacked in the foreground; a typewriter sits on a thick volume to the left; the sculpture on the desk proves to be a squatting nude facing the foreman; behind him, on a bureau and next to a row of four empty wine bottles, more papers are piled helter-skelter. The map, seen obliquely in every one of the shots, is now fully visible. The vertical and horizontal creases of its folds imply that it is a route map that has been tacked onto the wall. A tear runs from an upper corner, down along the Bay of Biscay and into the western coast. The shard caused by the tear hangs over what would be the Bordelais. Smudges and holes, the result of dirty fingers continually touching the map, are found around Lyon, the southern Rhône, and Angers. Filth and grime are especially visible around Paris and the Île-de-France.

The details of the map come forward because of the duration of what is indeed a *plan-séquence* of more than one minute (one of the longer shots of the film), in which care is taken to show that nothing is happening. The foreman asks the mate if the captain is doing his work: "Alors, le patron de l'*Atalante,* est-ce qu'il fait son travail, oui ou non?" (Now, is the boss of the *Atalante* doing his work? Yes or no?); Jules hems and haws; the boss asks if the reports in the dossier are a bunch of jokes; Jules responds no, they are just rumors (*des racontards*); to which the foreman lashes back, "Tu soutiens que c'est lui qui commande l'*Atalante*" (You're telling me it's he who's the captain, etc.), pointing alternately at the dossier on the desk and at Jules, warning him that he had better watch out because he has pulled some fast ones both here and elsewhere. Jules grumbles, scratches his head, and bids for time: "Moi aussi, je saurais et qui aussi ne le saurait . . . mais je vais aussi vous raconter une bien bonne" (You'd know as well as I . . . so now I'll tell you a good one). Tapping the ashes of his cigarette in the ashtray and raising his right arm, the boss tells Jules to stop and asks once more the same (by now stupid) question, "Le patron, commande-t-il l'*Atalante,* oui ou non?" (Is the boss the captain of the ship? Yes or no?), to which Jules answers, gesticulating and huffing, that of course he is, and he doesn't just blow on its sails or push the barge from behind. Still playing for time, he filibusters: "Enfin, quand même, enfin, quoi, voyons, tout de même, enfin, quoi, c'est vrai, ça" (Sure, all the same, sure, now let's see, no matter what, sure, yeah, well, it's true). "C'est assez!" (That's enough!), snaps the boss, but not before Jules interrupts, "En mon opinion tout cela c'est chicané en effet" (If you ask me it's just a lot of palaver).

The camera dollies in toward the foreman, who tells Jules that he has a lot of other business and not just *L'Atalante.* He gets up, squashes his cigarette in the ashtray, and tells Jules to get out and arrange things with the boss. The camera draws in further and quickly pans over the lamp while it holds on the edge of the map behind the foreman's face at the upper right edge of the screen. In voice-*off,* Jules mutters, "On en parlera" (Yeah, we'll talk about it). The shot continues to catch Jules who puts his right hand on the door handle before it cuts to the room on the other side, where, to the right and almost staring at the camera, Jean sits dolefully. The door (the "Close the door, please" sign is to the left of Jean's head, at his eyeline) swings open, and Jules emerges from the space, continuing to mutter and then exiting right with Jean. The foreman, now seen through the doorway in the midst of his *paperasse* and dossiers, bellows that it's all unbelievable (*c'est inimaginable!*) before he picks up a stack of papers ("Who in hell are they taking me for with these dossiers!") and tosses it to the right, then comes forward and around the desk, demanding his next victims, the captains of *La Belle Amélie* and *L'Oiselet*. "Entrez! J'en ai assez à la fin!" (Come on, I've had enough of this crap!). He comes to the threshold and thus welcomes another captain, who raises his arm and wiggles his fingers to show that he could care less about all the invective. He enters, the foreman swings the door shut, and after twenty-three seconds the shot ends on the door with its sign—"Fermez la porte S.V.P."—in full view.

Underlining the closure of the door and the situation in which the sailors live and work, this shot sums up the spatial character of the entire sequence. In what follows, the camera returns to the barge and the point of view taken at the moment when Jules led his captain en route to the office. A slight difference is marked in the presence of a few coils of rope on the upper deck at the lower right edge of the frame, in front of the two men who walk in the same direction as they had when they departed (to the right) and with the same locomotive—so it seems—spewing steam and chugging in the background to the left. The only indication of any passage of time whatsoever from the beginning of the sequence until now is shown in the absence of the cabin boy in the lifeboat. The men climb upon the deck as the camera pans right, and the locomotive continues across the upper edge of the frame, leaving a trail of white fumes in its path. Other than the evidence of the boy's evacuation from the lifeboat, nothing has changed.

The omnipresent map would seem to ratify the realism effects of *L'Atalante*. It should indicate where the barges go and situate the itinerary of the boat, loaded with an unspecified cargo from inner France, by way perhaps of Parisian canals, to Le Havre. But it does not. The map, rather, tells us that we are in a series of places along industrial waterways that are "anywhere-whatsoever." Shown at the site of "arrival" ("nous sommes arrivés!"), the map marks the destination as a site of degraded exchange in which salvation for unrewarded labor and fatigue is a condition of unremitting labor and fatigue. The map suggests, too, that the former aesthetic world of art for art's sake, glimpsed here and there in the *tableaux vivants* in the film, is now one of labor for labor's sake. In this condition any single sense of place or location becomes coextensive with any other.

A Vignette

The sequence described above suggests that the bargemen live in a world where nothing moves or happens. Time does not flow as might a river. Or, if it does, it might follow the rhythm of Apollinaire's vision of the River Seine in "Le Pont Mirabeau," the poem of *Alcools* that registers the suicidal nature of modern life when the voice of the poem, suggesting that the author is staring at the water from a modern bridge not far from the Eiffel Tower, repeats in a refrain, "Les jours s'en vont je demeure" (Days go by, I remain). The shots taken inside the foreman's office attest to economic blockage and life lived in sempiternal constipation. The fat foreman sits in his mess; the nondescript cashier lives in the jail of his booth; the men who go from one door to the next, the ostensibly singular and collective heroes of the film, are "nobodies." The salvation of a month's pay comes at the price of living so precariously that no sign of a future can be gleaned anywhere in the world shown.

The map is a spatial marker complementing the sign on the door. As title cards or written signs inserted into the visual texture of the frame, both belong to the rhetoric of a silent film. "Fermez la porte S.V.P." reads as if it might be addressed to the sailors and the foreman at the same time. In the suggestion of its finality, it closes both the space of the office and the sequence, anticipating a change of shot yet also slamming the door on the spectator. In the second shot of the sequence in which the first captain answers the angry foreman's questions, the sign appears in the frame as a block of white space. Giving depth to the shot and emphasizing the huge pate of the foreman at his desk, it is set in visual counterpoint to the lower right-hand corner of the map. Along with a piece of paper tacked on the wall behind the captain's head (in frontal view to offer the illusion of a paper halo of sorts), the map, and the sheets hanging from the lampshade, the sign figures as a square or a white spot in an abstract field of tension, a depthless surface of contrasting shapes and textures. In the two minutes spent in and about the office the space loses the depth of field that would assure its mimetic value. The imperative on the door begs us to *read* the image and the virtual words and other signs pasted into the frame. The volume of the office gets flattened, and so also does the illusion of spatial play. It is as if the map were telling the viewer to "read" the space lexically, as a two-dimensional surface. The optical effect of a squashed space underscores what elsewhere the film is saying about the experience of modernity—that it is a hellish labyrinth in which we lose ourselves.

An Inner Geography

The tear on the map is more than a casual sign of the mess in the foreman's quarters. The shard of pendant paper covers the Bay of Biscay just as the upper edge of the frame keeps the Norman coast and the English Channel out of the field of the image. Implied is that no escape or passage to the sea is possible. The faint but distinctly drawn lines of the map suggest that it belongs to a genre that indeed emerged in the Second Empire with new cartographies of railways, roads, and routes of fluvial commerce. One of these was Girard and Barrère's "Carte des canaux de France et Belgique," drawn at a scale of 1:1,000,000, which especially highlighted the routes that led from France in the east and north to and from Belgium to the mouth of the Seine.[5] If, as is quite likely, the map in the film belongs to this genre, it alludes to various spaces that are shown in the outdoor sequences of *L'Atalante*. One, of course, is Le Havre, the port at the mouth of the Seine and the city in which the foreman's office is apparently located. Another is Corbeil, the town on the Seine to the north of the juncture of the rivers Loing (with a canal reaching to the Loire) and Yonne, where barges stopped en route to and from Burgundy and other areas of *La France profonde*. And the same map outlines a thick webbing of routes that run from Flanders and Belgium to and from the upper reaches of the English Channel down to Paris and points east and west. Encompassing much of the detail of the map and the smudges so visible in its upper parts, this network of waterways bears on the aesthetic origins of the film: on the ambience of the world that Vincent Van Gogh had depicted in his paintings of *estaminets,* northern cafés, locks of canals, ports on the channel, and life among the impoverished workers in and about his native soil.[6] Both the Dutch painter's world and the seemingly time-less, stolid, and even wooden character of inner France are mixed in the psychogeography inhering in what is seen on the wall.

Obvious on the map is the ironic allusion to Paris. Earlier in the film the allure of the city was tendered to Juliette through the mega-phone of a spring-driven Victrola (DVD chapter 4). Not long after (chapter 13), having stolen a megaphone from a bar, Jules returns to the barge at night, climbs a ladder, and finds Juliette squatting in soli-tude on deck. Through the mouthpiece that he aims at her ears he of-fers a gruff serenade of the city: "Paris, Paris, O ville infâme et mer-veilleuse . . . aux amoureux!" (Paris, O infamous and wondrous city . . . for lovers)—before his fall prompts a cut to Jean sleeping in his bunk. When the barge arrived in Paris (chapter 7), the touristic ele-ment of the film was limited to the sight of the boat going through the locks of the Canal Saint-Martin in the workers' quarter of the tenth *ar-rondissement.* In this sequence, Vigo takes care to show that when Juli-ette emerges from a hatch on the upper deck with clean laundry under her arm, she sees nothing of either the canal or the environing city. While the captain and the cabin boy fasten ropes and pull the boat into the lock, she wanders aimlessly below a blank sky. The men are shown from a low angle through the barriers of fences or railings, but she seems to see nothing before descending back into the cabin and, ultimately, the "real" Paris of Jules's cabin, in which she finds herself seduced amidst the sailor's memorabilia and bric-a-brac.

Paris becomes a distance point, a reminder of the whereabouts of the woman Jean left behind and whose image—it seemed when he descended the wall at the beach near the mouth of the Seine—was in-visible where the horizon of the sea met the air and fog of greater at-mosphere above. In the foreman's office and on the map on the wall, Paris, the most visible mark on the projection, is the site where no one can be located. The city "rhymes" with Le Havre at the point where the husband and wife are joined in their separation through the montage of the travails of their separate bedtime hours (chapter 22). In that se-quence the montage comes to an abrupt conclusion when Jules, standing on deck like a pylon in the midst of the cranes and bridges of the port in the background, cries, "On est arrivé!" (We're here!).

Where is *here*? Is it the wake-up call of the cut from the dream of fusion to the diurnal world of work? Or the wind that ruffles a flag in the background that seems to flutter from Père Jules's backside, emblematizing a sense of endless time that one novelist calls "flaps on the mast" (Woolf 1992, 69)? Nothing indicates that the space promises the new "heaven," "haven," or an inherent "*grâce*" of Le Havre.

The illogical distance between the cashier's office, the site of at least economic salvation in what is implied to be Le Havre, and Paris, the grimy hole in the map on the wall, is emphasized further in the shots that depict Jules in search of Juliette. In Le Havre, Jules takes his decision to hunt for Juliette, as if she were a needle in one of the Monet-like haystacks seen when the couple traveled from the country church to the *péniche* (chapter 1).[7] A straight cut is made from the inside of the boat to a street in Paris extending under a bridge (possibly by the Quai Valmy), on which a subway is passing. No mention is made about how Jules gets from Le Havre to Paris. A long establishing shot registers four cars of the train passing overhead and beneath an ample autumnal sky before, crossing the boulevard on which roll cars and a horse-drawn carriage, Jules emerges. He tosses a coat to the ground and weaves his way through the barren trees lining the avenue. The following shot, taken over a footbridge that might be the one that connects Belleville to the Quai Valmy, on the other side of the city, cuts to Jules selecting a vacant bench in a park where he can sit and find his bearings; further in the distance, a homeless soul sleeps in the cold on another bench. Seasoned viewers recall that in the following shots Jules finds a clue to the missing wife when he takes note of the Hôtel de l'Ancre (Anchor Hotel) in a popular district where scaffolding and work in the street have created yet another urban zone.

The convention of a happy end requires Jules to find Juliette. When he is first shown returning to the boat with her, an unusual framing effect places the couple at the vanishing point of converging perspectives drawn by the line of a *quai* going deep into the distance from the lower left corner of the frame. A trajectory thrown by the flat gunwale of the barge aims at the couple, and so also does the waterline of a broad width of the Seine. On the lower horizon, below a great sky that presses downward, are smokestacks jutting out of a mix of buildings and trees on the opposite shore. The boat is moored not in Paris proper, where Jules found Juliette, but, in greater likelihood, once again at Corbeil, the industrial site where it had been moored much earlier in the film. The effect of stasis is enhanced when the following shot, taken from the other side of the prow of the boat, registers the iron pylons and the *terrain vague* into which the heroine had first disappeared. When Jules puts her back into the boat, as if enclosing her in the cabin below with her hapless husband (who had not ventured on deck with the cabin boy to watch out for the couple's return), the camera records in the background an inhuman zone that could well be the site at the beginning of the sequence that led to the foreman's office. The reunion at the end of the film is betrayed in part by a spatial confusion. Where are they? They are docked in an indeterminate zone in a network of commercial waterways.

Waterways Modern and Postmodern

It is said that in making *L'Atalante,* Vigo refused to succumb to the desire on the part of his producer, Jean-Louis Nounez, to include, upon the arrival of the barge in Paris, panoramic shots of the city taken from the Eiffel Tower (Salles-Gomes 1998, 176). An icarian, transcending, even touristic view of the city would have run counter to the views of life seen from below, from the level of feet touching and treading upon cobblestones and asphalt. Paris, too, would have been seen outside of the context of the tension of the Depression and the rampant social contradiction that is everywhere in the film. Wherever a shot is taken from a high angle above, its subject is generally from the point of view of a character looking into the exiguous space of the cabin. When a shot is taken from a low angle and aimed upward, it records whatever the workers would see with their own eyes.[8] Especially noteworthy is the establishing shot of the gable of the *estaminet,* Aux 4 Nations (chapter 13), set against the skeletal branches of a tree in winter. In accord with the silent tradition that folds title cards into the narrative, the shot denotes the site of the episode that follows. The political and geographical implications are made clear when the bar and cabaret are implied to be a sorry analogue of a "League of Nations" that would legislate the end of social and political conflict. In a productive misreading, Warner (1993, 47, 49) calls the café Aux Quatre Saisons, possibly associating the name with the barren trees in winter or else, by removing the specificity of the time implied in the sequence, turning the political dimension into a more satisfying aesthetic direction.

In shooting the film, Vigo chose to use a northern network of canals that in most likelihood cut across the spaces that Impressionist painters had cultivated. He first sought, according to a letter written to Eugène Merle at the end of August 1933, counsel and connections (*quelques conseils, quelques tuyaux*) from Georges Simenon concerning "interesting areas (canals, locks)," "mariners' towns," and "photographic collections." Simenon replied with a choice of canals and waterways, some where the director might wish "an intense navigation in a rather sinister setting," and others where he might prefer "quiet decors, portraying the joy of life, casks of wine, people sleeping on the sloping shores, and a picturesque life of ease." And further, he wrote, "if you want crowded traffic with haulers, chains of barges, electric cranes, etc., you'll need to go toward Conflans, or then go up toward Lille or toward the Sambre" (qtd. in Lherminier 1967, 165). At the beginning of the second week of November the shooting indeed began at Conflans, a site near the juncture of the rivers Seine and Oise. The crew worked on the Saint Denis and Ourcq canals to the north and east of Paris, near Argenteuil and other sites that painters had earlier chosen for views mixing nature and industry.

If any decorousness is shown in these locations, it seems to be a function of plot points in the outdoor shots. Sites are chosen on the horizon where perspectival lines lead not to resolution but to polluted zones that bear uncanny beauty by the way they rhyme with our memory images of the paintings of Manet, Monet, and others. In chapter 13, en route to the Aux 4 Nations, the husband and wife run along the pavement of a seaway next to which a barge aims its prow toward smokestacks and loading docks. In chapter 18, after Jean has emerged from the water and climbed onto the vessel, Jules and the cabin boy set a Victrola on the deck in such a way that the perspective leads back to a chimney emitting a trail of black smoke in the sky. Renewing the heritage of the Impressionists who included traces of industry in their landscapes, these shots enhance the political dimension of the film. An escape in the illusion of movement and chromatic play in these works is countered in *L'Atalante,* where a promise of spatial egress is tendered and then withdrawn.

The canals and locks depicted on the map that we glimpse in the foreman's office, waterways that link the towns and cities of France to its coastline and to neighboring nations, had their roots in the ambitious project of "modernity" conceived by Henry IV, a monarch of keen visual and cartographic intuition, at the end of the sixteenth century. Under his inspiration and that of the Duc de Sully, his economic minister, the Atlantic Ocean was to "be joined to the Mediterranean by connecting the Rhône, the Loire, and the Seine" with ease and efficiency such that, according to the minister, "from Burgundy one would be able to travel to Venice in an ocean-going vessel on the Loire and Seine rivers in France, on the Rhine and Meuse" (Mariage 1999, 11).[9] The plan was monarchic in its aim to make Paris a hub of all the fluvial circulation and democratic in the virtual linkage of places of equal and sovereign value everywhere and anywhere in France. When we see Vigo's film in this context, it is clear that *L'Atalante* taps into the political and demographic history of the canals and even offers a searing critique of what might be their postmodern sequel.

A map current in 1993 and found in ensuing years in French travel agencies, "France tourisme fluvial" (Inland Waterway Tourism), depicts the very waterways that had been shown on the projection seen in the foreman's office.[10] On the borders of the map itself are shown barges of the style seen in Vigo's film, with the difference that they are now made for play instead of work. The canals and locks offer tourists gastronomical voyages from Paris to Dijon and a turn south to Lyon; they become literary and picturesque when paying customers can sail to the areas of Normandy that the Impressionists and Proust made famous. They also meld commerce and pleasure. "The waterway," the map announces, "is also a sure, economic, and ecological mode of transport. Did you know, for example, that a barge of 4,400 tons transports as much merchandise as 220 trucks or 110 boxcars?" By participating actively in the promotion of fluvial tourism, the French waterway authority (Voies Navigables de France) helps to assure the best possible service for pleasure travelers (*plaisanciers*). What had been an effect of locating the players and spectators of *L'Atalante* in an unremitting world of labor and unemployment is inverted into leisure and sightseeing. Labor was what caused the captain of the barge to lose his love, and labor is the only remedy to the depression of separation and loss. *L'Atalante* plots a geography of this state of being that can surely be called modern.

In an ironic coda, we might say that owners of today's barges could, in addition to their gastronomical and literary itineraries, add a cinematic component. Why not refurbish a *péniche* and take a group of tourists along the routes that Jean and Jules had followed—but with the stipulation that everyone stay on board and merely simulate the risks and travails that in Vigo's film the captain and his crew experienced? In place of Jules's museum of trash and bric-a-brac in the lower cabin, DVD projectors could be placed to show Vigo's film on rainy days or in the evenings. A cat with a fresh litter could be provided for bouncing entertainment. The project of turning the history of *L'Atalante* into fluvial tourism would be tantamount to transforming the modernity of the film into a condition of postmodernity.

Notes

1. Robin Wood provides a rich and prismatic summary: "The interest of the film lies in [Vigo's] engagement with material that was partly congenial in its unconventionality (life on a barge, with its freedom from the restrictions of established society, its alternative community of unsocialized eccentrics), and partly highly conventional (problems of the heterosexual couple, mutual adjustment to marriage, break-up and reunion" (1990, 61).

2. New Yorker Films Artwork (2003), based on a Gaumont (2001) restoration. In her treatment of the sequence, Marina Warner notes only that the "stress of the scene falls on the uncouthness of the white-collar employee and the gallantry of the worker, the old man, in protecting his younger captain" (1993, 62). For Warner, the admiration for the workers and their work runs counter to a general contempt for manual labor evinced in Renoir and other contemporary filmmakers.

3. Gilles Deleuze notes that films shot in industrial places are such that their images bring forward "the foundations of space, the settings, these mute powers that precede or follow speech, of a time before and after man. The visual image becomes *archeological, stratigraphic, tectonic.* Not that we are sent back to prehistory (there is an archeology of the present), but we move to the deserted layers of our time in which our own phantoms are buried, to the lacunary layers that are juxtaposed according to variable orientations and connections" (1985, 317; my translation). This quality, which Deleuze associates with modern cinema, surely has its origins in the placeless settings of *L'Atalante.*

4. It is one of four such shots in the film, attesting to the myriad barriers and frames that isolate or, in a strictly visual sense, dismember or cut across the players' bodies.

5. "Carte des canaux de France et Belgique," issued by Girard and Barrère in 1952 (Harvard University Map Collection 5830 1952.3), was modeled on the 1933 map and copied and reprinted without any changes in 1972 (5830 1972.1). The routes that it shows in solid black lines match those found on many similar thematic maps dating to the 1860s. Girard and Barrère's map seems to be the model for the one shown here.

6. In an article on Van Gogh (1983, 153–66) I tried to show that the sequence in *L'Atalante* of the first meal shared by the three protagonists in the boat is a *tableau vivant* of the painter's *Potato Eaters* and its variants. Actor Michel Simon is coiffed in the manner of the figure at the head of the table, and the lamp that illuminates the scene in the painting is doubled by the gaslight that hangs from the ceiling in the cabin. Vigo's allusion to Van Gogh is a sign of keen spiritual and political affinities with the work of the painter in his early years. The presence of Van Gogh further attests to a condition of bodily precariousness. Figured throughout the painter's work, as Georges Bataille elucidated in an early essay on him, are partial objects or fantasms of dismembered bodies, not unlike the pickled hands in the cupboard of Père Jules's quarters. The map in the sequence gives further spatial reason to the relation.

7. Monet, writes Guy Davenport, "begins with the sea on the channel coast, moves on to the lovely roads cut through forests, train stations . . . , boats, harbors, cathedrals. . . . And then his study began to go backward in time. European agriculture is a matter of draining marshes to get a meadow. Before he turned to the primal marsh for his final great study, Monet painted meadows, haystacks, country rivers, poppy-filled fields. And with him, Renoir, Pissarro, van Gogh" (1985, 165).

8. Shortly before his death, in an interview, published in *La Libre Belgique* (27 October 1933), Vigo noted his fondness for Mervin LeRoy's *I Am a Fugitive from a Chain Gang* (1932), implying that it avoided the usual fare of "pure political propaganda" (reprinted in Lherminier 1967, 93).

9. The development of canal projects in the seventeenth and eighteenth centuries is taken up in Konvitz (1987, 108, 111). See especially the 1811 plan for the Canal Saint-Martin (plate 4). As Konvitz describes it, "The new canal cut through buildings and streets, dividing the urban fabric along the city's eastern end from the Seine to the northern suburbs in much the same way as Georges-Eugène Haussmann's famous boulevards a half-century later."

10. Voies Navigables de France, "France tourisme fluvial."

FAST TALK
PRESTON STURGES AND THE SPEED OF LANGUAGE
Joe McElhaney

Interviewer: What about the rhythm of comedy writing?
Elaine May: What about it?

In a frequently quoted passage from her memoir *A Life on Film,* Mary Astor describes her difficulties in working for the director Preston Sturges on *The Palm Beach Story* (1942). According to Astor, Sturges was never entirely pleased with her performance: "I couldn't talk in a high, flutey voice and run my words together as he thought high-society women did, or at least *mad* high-society women who've had six husbands and six million dollars" (1967, 170). What Astor's account makes clear (if the films themselves did not already supply ample evidence) is the importance for Sturges's cinema of not only dialogue but also vocal intonation, texture, and, above all, *speed,* of getting the words out as quickly as possible.

Speed is, of course, one of the defining qualities of modernity: speed of physical and mechanical movement but also, via technology, speed of communication. It is a defining moment for Emma Newton (Patricia Collinge) in Alfred Hitchcock's *Shadow of a Doubt* (1943), when her relationship to a more genteel, premodern world is linked to her failure to fully comprehend the way in which the telephone carries speech from one person to another. Instead, she speaks loudly and slowly into the telephone, prompting her youngest daughter to deride her provincial mother, who "makes no allowance for science" but instead attempts to "cover the distance by sheer lung power." But modern speed of communication may also be tied to the very act of speaking itself, apart from any reliance upon technology. To talk fast is to be a type of modern character, someone whose brain—machine-like—quickly processes information, responds to the stimuli of the world, and then just as quickly turns the impulses back into spoken language. In Howard Hawks's *His Girl Friday* (1940), as Walter Burns (Cary Grant) tries to convince his ex-wife Hildy (Rosalind Russell) not to marry another man and thereby retire from journalism, he barrages her with a long, rapidly delivered tirade, whereupon Hildy mockingly adopts the lightning speed of the auctioneer in response. As Walter continues talking, the sounds she makes have no semantic meaning whatsoever but achieve their comic force through the incredibly rapid tempo by which she delivers them. She finally shuts Walter up before returning to the semantic domain by bursting out with, "Sold! American!"

Speed, in the playing of comedy, is at least as old as Aristophanes and at least as recent as *Monsoon Wedding* (Mira Nair, 2001). Its presence in films of the 1930s and 1940s like *His Girl Friday* or *The Palm Beach Story* is hardly, in and of itself, new or modern. What is important to determine, however, is the precise place of this conception of speed in the films of this period, particularly those of Sturges.

Beyond Babble

Although American cinema of the 1930s and 1940s cannot lay claim to full ownership of the territory of fast dialogue delivery (it is central to a number of Jean Renoir films of the 1930s, for example), it is arguably the national cinema and the culture that was most fascinated by the possibilities of its language being spoken as quickly as possible. The emergence of sound cinema in the late 1920s, occurring more or less simultaneously with the increased popularity of radio and recorded music, and in the midst of a culture that, more than any other, seemed to be fully embracing the speed and convenience of these new technologies, solidified and considerably extended a love of fast talk.

Sturges arrived as a screenwriter in Hollywood in 1932, during the same period in which a number of major writers from the New York stage also came to California to work in the movies, supplying American cinema with a new type of "smart" dialogue, or patter, laced with wisecracks and double entendres. By the end of 1932, developments in sound technology not only began to allow for increasingly sophisticated recording and mixing of sound (which would continue to develop over the decade) but also resulted in the speeded-up rhythm of many films, thanks to an increased mobility and freedom after the more static sound-on-disc and early sound-on-film recording methods of the late 1920s and early 1930s. Not all of American cinema was strongly affected by this change in speed. Strictly within the realm of comedy, directors like Leo McCarey and George Stevens showed little interest in it, while comic performers from the silent era like Stan Laurel and Oliver Hardy and W. C. Fields continued to perform in a slower, more deliberate style. But certainly, there is enough of an overall acceleration in tempo during this period to speak of an important stylistic change. Films like *Love Me Tonight* (Rouben Mamoulian, 1932), *Gold Diggers of 1933* (Mervyn LeRoy/Busby Berkeley, 1933), *Twentieth Century* (Hawks, 1934), *It Happened One Night* (Frank Capra, 1934), and *My Man Godfrey* (Gregory La Cava, 1936) are primary examples of this newly dynamic and accelerated Hollywood cinema, revolving around characters whose very being is determined by their manner of speaking—rapid, rhythmic, overlapping—characters who are rarely at a loss for words.

Even though he did not begin directing his own screenplays until 1940, Sturges is arguably the filmmaker of this period whose approach to dialogue is most closely bound up with its relationship to fast-paced cinema. Manny Farber and W. S. Poster make speed central to their 1954 essay on Sturges, written five years before his death from a heart attack at the age of sixty. Sturges is "a very modern artist" whose films are dominated by an "anarchic energy generated as they constantly shake themselves free of attitudes that threaten to slow them down" (1998, 91). The ways in which Farber and Poster make their case for the modernity of Sturges's cinema are key to any understanding of this filmmaker. In particular, they emphasize the mobile and panoptic nature of Sturges's films, in which action and narrative are fragmented, films forsaking plausibility and logic in their drive toward sensation and climax and in such a manner that they form a link with modernist experiments in literature, music, and the visual arts. In them, nevertheless, we may glimpse "the final decay of the bloated Victorian world" (1998, 101). Although Farber and Poster may exaggerate when they argue that the "emotional and intellectual structure of his work has so little in common with the work of other artists of our time" (1998, 104), they correctly point to the necessity of making certain distinctions between how Sturges handles the act of speaking in his films and how his contemporaries do.

Many of the classic comedies being turned out during this period in Hollywood were shaped by directors who began working during the silent period: Capra, Hawks, La Cava, McCarey, Raoul Walsh, William Wellman. Although spoken language is certainly central to their filmmaking during the sound era, the films themselves were often made in a relatively improvisatory manner: the script was sometimes little more than a loose springboard for the finished film. This method of filming was no doubt a holdover from the silent era, particularly in the approach to filming comedy. In effect, the film is created less through execution of the ideas contained within the predetermined pages of the scenario than through a continually evolving negotiation among scenario, director, and actors that takes place on the set. Later in his life, Hawks sometimes expressed an antipathy to the funny line as such. For Hawks, humor, at least in theory if not in practice, emerged out of behavior, gesture, and situation: "I don't use funny lines. They're not funny unless you see [the actors performing] them" (McBride 1982, 67), a sentiment that La Cava or McCarey might well have shared. This attitude is still apparent even in a director like George Cukor, who did not come to Hollywood until the sound era and whose origins were with the stage. Cukor created a cinema in which respect for the scenario, though greater than that of his silent-era predecessors, was shaped by a complex relationship between actor and text. Like the earlier directors, Cukor was still strongly invested in the sense of indexical immediacy and freshness in terms of the performances and the manner in which these performances were being caught by the camera at the precise moment of filming. Cukor's statement that the script is something that both frees and sustains him is revealing in this regard (Lambert 1972, 14).

The one major exception from this period in terms of this approach to film comedy is Ernst Lubitsch, whose background was within the more rigorous world of German cinema of the 1910s and early 1920s. His Hollywood comic films of the early 1930s engage in a much more precise form of editing, scripting, and shot construction, and the gestures and line readings of the actors likewise seem to be much more strongly controlled by the *auteur*.[1] The brilliant dinner sequence between Miriam Hopkins and Herbert Marshall at the beginning of *Trouble in Paradise* (1932) is structured as tightly as clockwork: every shot assumes an exact function; every movement, line reading, and gesture of the actors fulfills a predetermined conception. Lubitsch's cinema is a much more formalist one, structured upon ellipsis and repetition. The spectator's interpretation of the events through this structure becomes crucial for "completing" the film.

Sturges, on the other hand, although he wrote the scripts to several classics of the 1930s, more properly belongs to a development emerging during the following decade, that of the writer/director, and he is often credited as being the first of a particular breed that would come to include Billy Wilder and Joseph L. Mankiewicz. Like Wilder, Sturges began directing at Paramount; he ended his Hollywood career at Twentieth Century Fox in 1949, when Mankiewicz was three years into his own career as writer/director. Sturges's first film for Fox, *Unfaithfully Yours* (1948), sometimes suggests the world of Mankiewicz through the presence of actors associated with his films (Rex Harrison, Linda Darnell) and the high-flown and upper-class dialogue (for instance, of Harrison's Sir Alfred). The film also anticipates the tripartite forking narrative structure Mankiewicz would soon perfect in *A Letter to Three Wives* (1949) and *All About Eve* (1950). In the case of Sturges, this forking narrative would be framed entirely as the subjective, paranoid fantasy of one character, whereas in Mankiewicz's films it would assume the objective memories of three individual protagonists. Unlike Sturges, Wilder and Mankiewicz worked steadily throughout the 1950s and, after Sturges's death, continued to make films for decades to come (well into the 1980s, in the case of Wilder). In comparing the reputations of these writer/directors, it is important to note that Sturges's fame rests almost entirely upon his comedies, all but one of which were made between 1940 and 1949. Further, Sturges never collaborated with anyone on the scripts he directed; nor did he ever direct a film written by someone else, as Mankiewicz sometimes did.

Sturges's absolute control over his scripts led to a cinema in which dialogue assumes a function on a somewhat different order than in the films of his American predecessors in comedy. His cinema is not only verbal but also *dominated* by words, by the act of speaking as a powerful bearer of meaning in and of itself. It is a cinema of great wit and enormous verbal play, so rich in dialogue that it seems to be endlessly quotable. However, this quality of his films would not alone distinguish Sturges significantly from Wilder and Mankiewicz. All three directors greatly admired Lubitsch, and a certain rejection of the looser American approach to comedy in favor of a more disciplined and formalist European influence is evident in their films. For Farber and Poster, however, Sturges is the American filmmaker who also most closely inherited the tradition of the slapstick farce of the *silent* period—that is, its "*naïf* belief in speed"—while "combining its various methods, adding new perspectives and developing the whole in a form suitable to a talking picture" (1998, 93–94).

Indeed, slapstick moments abound in Sturges, from the comic chase early in *Sullivan's Travels* (1942) to Sir Alfred's fumbled attempts to record his own voice in *Unfaithfully Yours. The Sin of Harold Diddlebock* (1947) even stars a great comic star of the silent period, Harold Lloyd. Although Mankiewicz was the co-writer of one of the classic surreal crazy comedies of the previous decade, *Million Dollar Legs* (Edward F. Cline, 1932), such a comic sensibility has little place in his own work as director. His later approach to comedy is dominated by an expressive use of monologue, dialogue, and voiceover in which physical comedy is largely absent. The script for Wilder's first film as director, *The Major and the Minor* (1942), though rich in farcical possibilities, is handled in a more muted style; the actors are much less prone to fits of manic physical activity and outbursts in comparison with Sturges's characters. In Sturges, then, we find a cinema not only of talk but also of farce and, with this, the speed so necessary to farce—speed of physical movement but also speed of talk—as though the two systems of physical movement and speaking are engaged in reciprocity.

The notion that dialogue in film should not succumb to the temptation of merely recording the act of speaking—thereby making film an adjunct to theater—but should instead become a type of sound element engaged in a dialectical relationship with the image, was fundamental to much film theory and film practice of the early sound period, particularly in European cinema. It is unlikely that most American filmmakers working in Hollywood at this time were vitally concerned with such theoretical or utopian models of cinema, and a type of subordination of the image to that of language persists in various ways throughout the 1930s. The overlapping dialogue that is central to such fast-paced classics of this period as *My Man Godfrey*, *The Women* (Cukor, 1939), and *His Girl Friday* often becomes, through its rapidity, pure sound texture, generalized as gossip or chatter and devoid of clear semantic function. The gossiping women at the beauty salon in the opening sequence of *The Women* is a primary case in point. As the camera tracks, pans, and cranes around room after room of Sidney's Beauty Salon, the gossip of the women can initially be understood. (Woman One: "Oh, my dears, my dears, just think! That solid mountain of flesh is going to marry a jockey!" Woman Two: "Won't her husband fairly turn over in his grave?" Woman Three: "What's she got in common with a jockey?" Woman Four: "Horse feathers.") But as the rhythm of the gossip and the movements of the women from room to room accelerate, the gossip becomes unintelligible gibberish, like a phonograph record played at a too-high speed. In 1948, Eric Rohmer called for an end to the notion that dialogue's highest function in cinema is to exist as pure sound element: "The director's art is not to make us forget what characters say but, rather, to help us not to miss a word" (1989, 31).[2] For Rohmer, even Welles's *Citizen Kane* (1941) retains elements of this earlier language-as-sound approach, whereas in *The Magnificent Ambersons* (1942) Welles was able to break free and create a film in which "the smallest word is important" (1989, 31).

For all of Sturges's interest in speed, overlapping dialogue is virtually non-existent in his films. The same can be said of Wilder and Mankiewicz, but neither of these directors shared Sturges's general fascination with speed, at least not until Wilder revived the fast-talking tradition many years later (somewhat artificially) in *One, Two, Three* (1961). No matter how rapidly the dialogue is spoken in a Sturges film, every word is meant to be caught, the post–screening room sequence at the beginning of *Sullivan's Travels* being a classic case in point. Here, in a single take with three actors (Joel McCrea, Robert Warwick, Porter Hall) pacing—indeed circling—about the space of an office, we have dialogue fired off one line after another. As Librand (Warwick) and Hadrian (Hall) attempt to dissuade Sullivan (McCrea) from making his socially conscious film, the pace of their speech increases rapidly:

> Librand: That's the reason your pictures have been so light, so cheerful, so inspiring.
> Hadrian: They don't stink with messages.
> Librand: That's why I paid you 500 a week when you were 24.
> Hadrian: 750 when you were 25.
> Librand: A thousand when you were 26.
> Hadrian: When I was 26, I was getting 18.
> Librand: 2,000 at 27.
> Hadrian: I was getting 25 then.
> Librand: (I'd just opened my shooting gallery.) 3,000 after *Thanks for Yesterday*.
> Hadrian: 4,000 after *Ants in Your Pants*.
> Sullivan: I suppose you're trying to tell me I don't know what trouble is.
> Hadrian: Yes!
> Librand: In a nice way, Sully.

Regardless of the rapid-fire delivery, not a single word is lost. In this respect, the scene is quite different from the screening-room sequence in *Citizen Kane*, in which the dialogue of the reporters wavers between clearly articulated speech and overlapping babble that cannot be transcribed. What Sturges has done here is to combine two types of cinematic speech, as identified by Michel Chion: *theatrical speech*, in which every word is intelligible because it is expected to carry enormous psychological, dramatic, or affective weight while still retaining a link to certain types of *emanation speech*, in which the crucial aspect is a kind of sound texture created through dialogue that is not necessarily understood word for word (Chion 1994, 172–184). Sturges retains the generalized feel of overlapping dialogue and its rhythmic possibilities but discards the manner in which semantics can surrender to unintelligibility.

Furthermore, Sturges's shooting style is organized in such a manner that dialogue assumes an extraordinary degree of weight, even more than in Wilder and Mankiewicz. Sturges shares little of Wilder's interest in architecture, décor, or specificity of setting. Even when a film is set in a clearly defined location, Sturges will almost invariably drain that setting of its specificity, so that the New York of *Christmas in July* (1940) and the "Connekticut" of *The Lady Eve* (1941) acquire the abstract feeling of the space of a fable. Almost nothing in Sturges is allowed to get in the way of the relationship between the text and an actor speaking that text. His long takes, although typical of a general trend during this period toward increasingly extended shot durations, have less to do with authorial flourish than with permitting a sequence to unfold in a certain (usually quite rapid) rhythm. The actors deliver (sometimes quite breathlessly) page after page of dialogue without a break, as in the long traveling shots through the streets of a small town in *Hail the Conquering Hero* and *The Miracle of Morgan's Creek* (both 1944). Some of his more static long takes (occasionally broken into, and slightly spoiled, with brief cutaways or inserts) seem less punishing, but even here Sturges's staging ideas are very simple. The movements of actors within the frame and their gestures are kept to a minimum, all of this assuring that the spectator will pay maximum attention to the act of speaking.

For all of the apparent anarchy on display in Sturges, then, the actors are also controlled by the overall form of the film—less obviously so than in Lubitsch, but controlled nonetheless. By contrast, the actors in La Cava films like *Stage Door* (1937) or *Unfinished Business* (1941) give the appearance, as a result of shot compositions that are fairly loose and tend to favor the medium-long shot, of being able to move within the spaces of various sequences with a comparative amount of physical and gestural freedom, and often punctuate their performances with casual (and possibly improvised) asides. There is a revealing moment in Sturges's *The Sin of Harold Diddlebock* when Harold Lloyd keeps attempting to make a broad gesture in the midst of delivering an extensive amount of dialogue. Accompanying Lloyd in this sequence is a lion he has on a leash. Every time Lloyd attempts to make this gesture, and presumably distracted by the sight of Lloyd's hand in movement, the lion opens its mouth and snaps in the direction of this hand, causing Lloyd to withdraw the gesture. This apparently unrehearsed moment may also be seen as a paradigmatic one for the function of gesture in Sturges. What is this lion doing, after all, but assuming the role of director, a stand-in for Sturges, keeping the actor's gestures under control in order to assure that maximum attention will be paid to the act of speaking?[3]

A Talking Cinema

Almost anyone who writes on Sturges draws extensively on his biography in order to interpret the films. This approach has produced some insightful work, although sometimes the films are reduced to little more than crude illustrations of what is presumed to be the director's own psychology. My own interest in Sturges's biography has less to do with investigating the specifics of his psychology than with viewing Sturges as a social and cultural subject and looking for these influences on his work. Of particular interest for the concerns of this essay is Sturges's scattered upbringing, alternating principally between France (where he received much of his education—he was fluent in French) and the United States. Sturges may be seen as a kind of émigré director, albeit of a typically (for Sturges) idiosyncratic nature—American-born and a frequent resident, but also regarding America through a kind of long-distance lens.[4] Like the more obvious émigré Wilder, Sturges approaches the English language as an object of fascination, an endless marvel. At the center of Wilder's infatuation with the English language is his love of slang and a kind of hard-boiled American vernacular; both were crucial to his screenplay (written with Charles Brackett) for Howard Hawks's *Ball of Fire* (1941), where they become part of the explicit subject matter of the film when one among a group of professors compiling a dictionary decides to study the slang of band singer Sugarpuss O'Shea (Barbara Stanwyck). Sturges shares this love of the vernacular but in a more far-ranging manner, making films dominated by men who are "ginks" and women who are "cheesecakes" with teeth that are "storefronts." Popular expressions and phrases are repeated but almost invariably with a new spin, acknowledging the clichéd nature of the phrase while just as quickly rewriting it: "You're certainly a sight for lame peepers" or "I've known this boy since he was knee high to a cockroach" or "Posterity is just around the corner."

Furthermore, Sturges films frequently call attention to the forms and structure of language. Characters will sometimes make explicit references to paraphrases and similes or demonstrate an awareness of the rules and forms of the English language, even as they violate them. "Do you get the play on words?" Jimmy MacDonald (Dick Powell) asks his girlfriend Betty Case (Ellen Drew) in *Christmas in July* when he reads aloud his pitiful slogan for a coffee advertisement contest: "If you don't sleep at night, it isn't the coffee. It's the bunk." (She does get the play on words but doesn't think it's funny.) In a Sturges script, talk is subject to rapid-fire alternations between the formal and the vernacular, between a language still tied in some ways to the aristocratic and one that makes use of (to borrow a term from Bakhtin) the experience of the marketplace, in this case the marketplace most often split between that of various ethnic, social, and racial subcultures, on the one hand, and that of the mass media, the world of radio, advertising, and politics on the other. Although the modernity of Sturges's conception of language has, as with so much of the modern impulse, an undeniably urban drive and rhythm to it, even his small towns seem to be affected by this quick method of speaking. As a result, they stand in marked contrast to the clichéd tight-lipped small towns of films like *Mr. Deeds Goes to Town* (Capra, 1936) or *Nothing Sacred* (Wellman, 1937). In *The Good Fairy* (William Wyler, 1935), an early screenplay of Sturges's set in a Lubitsch-like Budapest, we find an aristocratic and near-Shakespearean form of English subjected to parody through the drunken (and lisping) tirade that Dr. Motz (Eric Blore) heaps upon a waiter who attempts to help him descend a small flight of stairs: "Unhand me, varlet, lest I cleave thee with a brisket. Alone I will negotiate yon precipice." English as spoken by the upper-class British becomes not so much a legacy of breeding and birthright (Old World values, after all) as something that can immediately be adopted by Americans through ingenuity and cunning: "I've been English before," says Jean Harrington (Stanwyck) in *The Lady Eve* about her decision to impersonate the upper-class Lady Eve Sidwich. The kings in this world are all Wienie Kings.

Throughout Sturges, language becomes something almost physical, tangible. Sturges's love of alliteration, for example, gives the act of speaking a weight at once ironic and poetic. When the millionaire Charles Pike (Henry Fonda) boards the ocean liner in *The Lady Eve,* his arrival is observed by many of the passengers through a crane shot that moves across them as they comment on Pike's wealth acquired through his family's ale business: "I said Pabst" . . . "It was Pike" . . . "But Mom, it makes me puke" . . . "Puke?" . . . "No, Pike" . . . "Go put on your peekapoo." In the same film, Colonel Harrington's (Charles Coburn) command of aristocratic language (which masks his false aristocracy) is sometimes signaled through his skill in alliterative phrasing, as when he admonishes his daughter Jean, "Let us be crooked but never common," or when he calls Pike "as fine a specimen of the sucker sapien as I've ever seen." But in the same film, the "gink" Muggsy Murgatroyd (William Demarest) shows a similar command in a more vernacular realm: "I'll be a cock-eyed cookie pusher." In *Christmas in July*, advertising is dominated by alliteration, which becomes the primary way of selling a product, of making maximum commercial impact out of language by linking the product with words associated with aristocratic bearing and lineage: Maxford House coffee is Grand to the Last Gulp; Baxter's is The Blue Blood Coffee—It's Bred in the Bean. Sturges even draws upon alliteration to "sell" the titles to three of his own films, *The Miracle of Morgan's Creek, Hail the Conquering Hero*, and, especially, *The Beautiful Blonde from Bashful Bend* (1949).

Likewise, he opts for short rhyming effects and their capacity for strongly implanting language upon the ear of the listener: Pike's Pale, the Ale That Won for Yale, or the titles of John L. Sullivan's films in *Sullivan's Travels*: *Ants in Your Pants of 1939* and *Hey, Hey in the Hayloft*. Even the names of Sturges's protagonists comically emblazon their European origins. Hawks's characters often have names with a simple directness—Dallas, Dude, Feathers, Frenchy, Slim, Chips—nicknames that suggest these people have somehow escaped their origins and transformed themselves into a satisfying vision of self.[5] Sturges, by contrast, engages in a type of branding through language that precludes the possibility of the elegant transcendence of origins that is such a hallmark of Hawks's characters. Sturges's naming is part of a comic impulse indebted to everything from *commedia dell'arte* to Restoration comedy to Dickens, comprising rhymes, alliterations, and innuendoes: Harold Diddlebock, Trudy Kockenlocker, Hilda Gingle-busher, Dr. Zodiac Z. Zippe, Julius Heffelfinger, Formfit Franklin, E. J. Waggleberry, Woodrow Lafayette Pershing Truesmith.

In this and other ways throughout his work, Sturges constantly seeks to control and shape the spoken word, in apparent rebuttal to the "crisis of language" central to much of modernism. However, for Sturges, language in film achieves its power through virtue of being *spoken*, of being delivered in the most colorful, forceful, and public manner possible; he shows none of the interest in language as written text that we find in Wilder and Mankiewicz. If Wilder's and Mankiewicz's protagonists are often writers, Sturges's characters give the impression of barely being able to write a postcard, not so much through ignorance as through temperament. In Sturges, to record a voice (as in Sir Alfred's disastrous attempt to master a recording machine in *Unfaithfully Yours*), to read a text, or to write something down often produces a state somewhere between the traumatic and the ludicrous. The phenomenally wealthy John D. Hackensacker III (Rudy Vallee) in *The Palm Beach Story*, for example, constantly jots down notations of all of the money he spends, for no particular reason: "It's just nonsense, really."

Aside from his screenplay for *The Power and the Glory* (William K. Howard, 1933), a heavy and unrepresentative early effort, Sturges shows little interest in the voiceover narration that was so fashionable in the 1940s, and even flashback films like *The Great McGinty* (1940) and *The Miracle of Morgan's Creek* avoid it. Sturges's characters are not fundamentally narrators or storytellers. They cannot sit still long enough. Instead, language is delivered fast, often on the feet and in motion. The presentation of, or confrontation with, a written text is often a pivotal moment in the development of the narrative, the introduction of a state of disaster. When Sir Alfred receives the documents detailing his wife's supposed infidelity, he responds first by violently ripping them up and then, later, when a house detective delivers another set, burning them in his dressing room. When Charles views a photograph and newspaper clipping of the true identity of his beloved Jean in *The Lady Eve*, a dissolve of the text is superimposed over a close-up of his face, as though the text is deeply marking itself upon his brain. A similar dissolve occurs in *Sullivan's Travels* when the imprisoned Sullivan reads the newspaper report of his own death. It is, in fact, Sullivan's initial encounter with the Steinbeck-like novel *O Brother, Where Art Thou?* and his desire to make a "serious" film of it that precipitate the disaster leading to his prison sentence. All of these written texts become means of containing language, a situation the films must ultimately refuse, as though Sturges were single-mindedly driven to make the passage into a true "talking cinema" that is described by Gilles Deleuze: "The speech-act is no longer connected with the second function of the eye, it is no longer read but heard. It becomes direct, and recovers the distinctive features of 'discourse' which were altered in the silent or written film" (Deleuze 1989, 226).

Modernity and the Death of Laughter

At the center of this refusal of the crisis of language in Sturges is another type of crisis. When Sturges's films began to be screened in Paris after the war, André Bazin detected in them an impulse to destroy the comic genres the filmmaker seemed to be renewing. In relation to *The Sin of Harold Diddlebock,* Bazin argues in *The Cinema of Cruelty* that the film implicitly tells its audience, "Laugh once again and laugh heartily, but it's the last time—because you're laughing at the death of laughter" (1982, 47). Of course comedy by its very nature has historically been a form that deals with much of the same material as tragedy or melodrama, albeit assuming different structures and modes in facing these topics of suffering, pain, and oppression, be they of political, social, or psychological origin. In Sturges, though, and within the context of American cinema of the 1930s and 1940s, we may detect a stronger-than-usual desire simultaneously to renew *and* to exhaust the comic modes within which he is operating. Farber and Poster also recognized this aspect of Sturges, seeing in his work "the reverse side of the uncontrolled American success impulse."[6] This insight suggests that the drive toward speed and fast talk in Sturges has less to do with a simple celebration of American energy than with an exploration of the very real possibility that such a drive will eventually exhaust itself. One talks fast in this world because one has a lot to say *and* because time is running out.

Talking is a matter of both life and death, a paradox unwittingly grasped by Officer Kockenlocker (William Demarest) in *The Miracle of Morgan's Creek* when he declares that the only time a woman *doesn't* feel like talking is when she's dead. The anxiety of failure, of falling from the social and financial ladder as much as rising to the top of it, gives the films their own strongly manic energy (Farber and Poster

1998, 98). Sturges's biographers have noted that a favorite book of the director's was *Two Lifetimes in One: How Never to Be Tired: How to Have Energy to Burn* (an exhausting title in itself), by Marie Beynon Ray, in which the author proclaims the transcendent virtues of energy as central for any success in life (see Jacobs 1992, 276).[7] In *The Miracle of Morgan's Creek,* Trudy Kockenlocker (Betty Hutton) appears to be the very embodiment of this idea when she tells her sister Emmy (Diana Lynn), "You know me. I never get tired." But ultimately, how successful are Sturges's protagonists? How often does their speed, their energy, give them what they desire?

In Sturges we undoubtedly find characters with strong goals superficially consistent with those according to which the protagonist of classical (particularly American) narrative cinema has so often been analyzed: the drive toward social and economic success, often occurring in tandem with the formation of a romantic couple and situated within a cultural environment which, although it may initially pose obstacles, ultimately allows for modifications and transformations of certain basic democratic principles. At the same time, these goals are equally determined by the desire just to survive, simply to "hold your own in this wicked old world" (*The Beautiful Blonde from Bashful Bend*). Characters inhabit a world of energy and speed but also of exhaustion, of tired bodies, fragmented families (usually with only one parent, if any, still alive), and little time for true romance. Even when a couple is formed in a Sturges film, there is almost always something lopsided and implausible about the pairing. Rarely is there a sense of the meeting of equals central to much romantic comedy of the 1930s. Jimmy MacDonald's drive to succeed in *Christmas in July* is also a desire to avoid the mistakes of his father, who was "worn out at 48 and croaked because he couldn't afford a decent doctor." How appropriate, then, that what Jimmy invests his creative energies in as a method of climbing the economic ladder is an advertising slogan for a stimulant. In fact, the most driven characters in Sturges are almost too driven. It is an obsessive drive or desire they possess, as in the quivering, high-strung body of Norval Jones (Eddie Bracken) in *The Miracle of Morgan's Creek,* a body that seems constantly on the verge of spontaneous combustion.

As Eric Bentley has noted, the desire to possess the material world fully, and this often through the extremes of theft or gluttony, is fundamental to the classical comic mode. Thievery and deception abound in Sturges and are often at the very center of the narratives; he gives us a world of impersonations and stolen identities, jewel thieves and card sharks (Bentley 1964, 304–5). These motifs certainly appear in much comedy of this period as well, but arguably the themes of thievery, deception, and impersonation are stronger, clearer, and more extreme in the films Sturges was turning out than in most other American films at this time. The climax of his screenplay for *Diamond Jim* (Edward Sutherland, 1935), for example, involves its title character (Edward Arnold) literally eating himself to death. The mouth not only speaks in Sturges, it also devours. The Sturges world is a world of literal and metaphoric sharp teeth. "How are her teeth?" Jean asks Pike of his imaginary beloved. "You should always pick one out with good teeth. It saves expense later." When Sir Alfred explains what he is aiming for when his orchestra plays *pizzicato con vibrato,* he equates the sound with "a dentist chipping out an old filling."

In Sturges's least popular film of the 1940s, *The Great Moment* (1944), a biographical film about the dentist W.T.G. Morton (Joel McCrea), we find the mouth treated explicitly. The original title of this strange, beautiful film (before it was changed by the studio) was *Triumph over Pain,* a title that one may take as the fundamental impulse behind comedy itself. Sturges's objection to the studio's recutting of the film was that it was "cut for comedy" and that most of its more serious moments were removed (Sturges 1990, 298). But enough of the film survives for us to grasp some of Sturges's intentions for a film that would seem to be something of an anomaly in his work, with its early-nineteenth-century setting and passive female protagonist seemingly far removed from the fast-paced modernity of his other films.[8] *The Great Moment* is a film of breakings, extractions, and amputations, one in which the mouth, the orifice of speaking and devouring, becomes the ultimate source of pain. But it is also a film dominated by something else that emerges from the mouth—laughter—in this case laughter less from the audience watching the film than from characters within it. In *The Great Moment,* laughter and humor are frequently inappropriate: a drunken and corrupt Dr. Jackson (Julius Tannen) jokes about how to deal with dental patients who are screaming in pain (hire an orchestra to drown out their screams); medical students giggle as they are about to observe a surgical operation. But it is also a film in which laughter is tied to violence, to passing out, even to death and oblivion. Laughing gas in this film, used as an anesthetic and administered via a large funnel into the mouth, leads not to unconsciousness but, through inappropriate dosage, violence and destruction when the patients lose control and go on rampages. Morton's own anesthetic, Latheom, is described as "the stream of oblivion that banished all earthly sorrows," and he advertises his practice as one that "Pulls Them Out with a Smile."

The anesthetic element of this film emphasizes the theme of exhaustion in modernity, the degree to which Sturges's protagonists, for all of their drive and speed, run the risk of vitiating themselves and succumbing to wooziness, delirium, or fainting, another side to—a symptom of, and refuge from—this manic and often pain-inducing universe. The last section of *Sullivan's Travels,* in which Sullivan is sent to prison, contains a disturbing amount of violence and physical pain for what is ostensibly a comedy. The significance of the screening of the Disney cartoon for Sullivan and his fellow prisoners has less to do with how comedy can serve as a refuge from pain and suffering than with the refiguring of pain and suffering as slapstick farce. In the excerpt we see of this short, there is no dialogue, only physical comedy in which Pluto, like Sullivan, is the recipient of extreme degrees of violence. Bentley writes that farce supplies the spectator with "the pleasure of hitting one's enemy in the jaw without getting hit back" (Bentley 1964, 297). The prisoners and the members of the African American congregation surrounding them laugh because their pain is transformed and re-imagined, because in this way they are supplied with the imaginary capacity to fight back. "Pain has no memory," Professor Warren (Harry Carey) states in *The Great Moment*. Or, at least, the memory of pain may be eased when it undergoes a metamorphosis into comedy.

In *The Great McGinty* a gangster called the Boss (Akim Tamiroff), who is tied to workings of the government, declares that America is "a land of great opportunity." In his concern with the workings of American institutions and with the concept of the American dream, Sturges has important links with the American comedy directors who precede him: Capra, La Cava, McCarey, and so on. Although claims have been made for the ambivalence with which this earlier generation treats American culture and its institutions, Sturges's mistrust is arguably more extreme and sometimes approaches the explicit. Sturges becomes, in the frequently quoted words of Bazin, "the anti-Capra" (Bazin 1982, 40). In *The Sin of Harold Diddlebock,* Diddlebock makes a drunken speech ostensibly extolling the strengths of the American pioneers, but his paean immediately escalates into a far more scabrous vision of American history:

> That's the trouble with men today. They have no stamina. Look at our forefathers. Look at Washington. Look at Valley Forge. Look at the pioneers. . . . Men were men in those days. . . . They mined the earth and doused the rivers and tamed the wilderness and brought forth peaceful homesteads in the shadow of evil and the echo of thundering herds. And in the final analysis, where are they I ask you? Dead, my friends, deader than a boiled mackerel.

Modernity often proffered appearance for substance, rapidly constructed surface as a currency for social exchange; and in this world of appearances, language itself becomes implicated. As Geraldine Jeffers (Claudette Colbert) instructs her husband (Joel McCrea) in *The Palm Beach Story,* "Don't you know that the greatest men in the world have told lies and let things be misunderstood if it was useful to them? Didn't you ever hear of a campaign promise?" To talk fast is not simply a form of energy and spirit but also a way of selling something, of masking the content of what is being said before the listener has had a chance to absorb the content—or absence thereof. "The trouble with our party is everyone talks too long, all the time," says a politician in *Hail the Conquering Hero.* Even Sturges's proclivity toward outrageous names becomes part of this realm of falseness. A name can be easily appropriated, part of a phony identity that then allows one to move through, alter, and possibly corrupt the world, as when McGinty votes in an important mayoral election under a series of assumed names, from Rufus J. Whiticomb to Dr. Heinrich L. Schutzendorf. "When one's name is Sir Alfred McGlennon Keith, R.F.D. one doesn't have to meet them. One fights them off with a stick," says a successful thief and card sharp (Eric Blore) in *The Lady Eve,* revealing the secret of his success in infiltrating the homes of the wealthy. False and imaginary names dominate this world as much as real ones, from Fuzzy Oldhammer, who went to manual training school in Louisville with Pike (in Jean's imaginary rendering), to Mary Smith of Roaring Falls, Ohio, the name offered to the police by the thief Lee Leander (the great Stanwyck again) in Sturges's script for *Remember the Night* (Mitchell Leisen, 1940): "I never give my real name."[9] In Sturges's America, if you say you are something, the world takes you at your word, in effect desiring the false over the real. "I probably don't look any more like Hilda Swandumper than I look like Swanda Hildumper," says a skeptical Freddie (Betty Grable) in *The Beautiful Blonde from Bashful Bend* as she is about to enter Snake City under a stolen identity. But Freddie is not only accepted by the town, she is told she looks just like her name. Utter a lie and people will believe it and *see* it. (I write these words in the midst of George W. Bush's re-election campaign.)

The basic drive of Sturges's narratives is not toward revelation, confession, and the unveiling of the truth, so central to much of American cinema (and certainly fundamental to Capra). Fascination with the false may explain why his stories so often do not build toward logical culminations but instead scatter in multiple directions or close within themselves before the truth is fully revealed. Within almost every Sturges narrative is another one, hidden or repressed, which could conceivably come forward; thus the images and narrative that unfold before our eyes, for all of their energy and presence, are marked by indeterminacy. One dashes about and speaks quickly because this is effectively an America without a clear ethical center but only, as Bazin notes in relation to *Hail the Conquering Hero*, a set of myths that give it meaning, even though "their power is completely imaginary" (Bazin 1982, 43).[10]

So much of the myth surrounding Sturges's own career confirms this kind of self-exhausting energy in him, a burnt-out case who spent his final ten years unsuccessfully attempting to revive his career and finances. In comparison with the Sturges comedies of the 1940s, American comedy in the 1950s shows a definite slowing down in terms of rhythm and language. Comedy during this period becomes increasingly suburban, from Vincente Minnelli's *Father of the Bride* in 1950 to McCarey's *Rally 'Round the Flag, Boys!* in 1958. Even when set in urban spaces, the films often revolve around family and the domestic scene: *The Marrying Kind* (Cukor, 1952), *The Seven Year Itch* (Wilder, 1955), and much of Frank Tashlin (even if Tashlin did treat the 1950s fascination for the domestic with a decided parodic edge, as in Jayne Mansfield's claims for wanting to be nothing more than a housewife in

The Girl Can't Help It [1956]). It is an increasingly slow world, still verbal but less vernacular (although Tuesday Weld's teenage suburban jive talk in *Rally 'Round the Flag, Boys!* is one important exception to this trend). Even records literally slow down, from 78 to $33^{1}/_{3}$ rpm; and the use of stereophonic sound in films, rather than speeding up the recording of dialogue, seems to contribute to the process of slowness, a kind of basking in the wonder of the separation of sounds and voices across the newer, wider screens. The language of the marketplace is now shaped by the increasingly sophisticated world of electronic home entertainment and television advertising—the subject of Tashlin's *Will Success Spoil Rock Hunter?* (1957). But Tashlin's world of advertising (unlike Sturges's) is dominated by men who are on tranquilizers and undergoing psychoanalysis, while everyone else sits at home glued to the television set. In *Rock-a-Bye Baby* (1958), Tashlin's loose remake of *The Miracle of Morgan's Creek*, we find an old woman so transfixed by the narcotic power of television that she sits in front of it all day long, buying all of the products advertised and obediently following the instructions for their use (see Bukatman 2002, 183–84). The same year in which Farber and Poster published their essay on Sturges, MGM released Minnelli's *The Long, Long Trailer*. This comedy, made in the midst of America's conversion to superhighways and faster automobile transportation, shows us a young married couple (played by the then-reigning monarchs of television, Lucille Ball and Desi Arnaz) traveling the country in an obscenely large mobile home, so weighed down with possessions and domestic "comforts" that it can barely inch its way across the American landscape.[11]

This period of film comedy is often thought of in terms of a decline after the brilliance of the 1930s and early 1940s. I do not share in this view. Rather, I believe 1950s film comedy represents another important historical development. Still, it is difficult to imagine Sturges's sensibility finding a comfortable home in 1950s America. Significantly, the only film he made during this decade was shot in France, *Les Carnets du Major Thompson* (1957).

Near the end of *Unfaithfully Yours,* there is a sequence briefly mentioned earlier in which Sir Alfred attempts and fails to record his own voice on a home recording system. This fumbling I cannot help but read allegorically in relation to Sturges's own failed efforts during the postwar period, an era in which the development of technology seems less kinetically tied to the prewar fascination with speed. The new technology is fundamentally about relaxation, about providing comfort and ease and increased leisure time. In the midst of attempting to master this new recording device, Sir Alfred reads the instructions, which capture the particular irony for Sturges of this moment of transition from the speed of the previous two decades to the more lethargic rhythms of the 1950s: "At 78 rpm the record will play brilliantly for 2 minutes and 56 seconds. At 33$\frac{1}{3}$ rpm it will play nearly 7 minutes but the quality will not be quite so brilliant."

Notes

1. Capra has described Lubitsch as "the complete architect of his films. His scripts were detailed blueprints. . . . Every scene, every look, every camera angle, was designed in advance of photography and he seldom, if ever, deviated from his blueprints in the actual shooting" (Capra 1971, 246). With regard to his one aborted attempt to work for Lubitsch, the producer on *One Hour with You* (1932), Cukor commented, "I admire Lubitsch very much, but he shot things in a highly stylized way that is simply not my own" (Lambert 1972, 43). Lubitsch ultimately assumed control of the project.

2. Rohmer's essay originally appeared in *Les Temps modernes* (September 1948). He lists Sturges as one of the filmmakers responsible for this new development in the use of language.

3. Lloyd later revealed that a principal conflict between him and Sturges was over "business" (physical comedy and gesture) and dialogue. For Sturges, Lloyd's business would "kill the dialogue" (qtd. in Jacobs 1992, 342–43). And Farber and Poster complain that Sturges "has not learned how to get people to use their bodies so that there is excitement merely in watching them move" (1998, 100).

4. Farber and Poster see Sturges's European background as a limitation in a way that I do not. For them, Sturges's European years "prevented his finding a bridge between the two worlds or even a slim principle of relating them in any other way than through dissonance" (1998, 101).

5. Farber has described the type of naming we find in Hawks as "summing up names, they tie a knot around the whole personality, and suggest the kind of bravura signature that underlines itself" (1998, 26).

6. Farber and Poster write: "The first impression one gets from a Sturges movie is that of the inside of a Ford assembly line smashed together and operating during a total war crisis" (1998, 98).

7. Ray's book is also cited in James Curtis's biography but Curtis gives the title as *How Never to Be Tired or Two Lifetimes in One* (1982, 195).

8. The script for *Triumph over Pain* is in Henderson (1995). Henderson performs extensive and valuable work in comparing the various versions of this script with the finished product.

9. Mary Smith is also the name of Jean Arthur's character in the Sturges screenplay for *Easy Living* (Mitchell Leisen, 1937).

10. Bazin's review originally appeared in *L'Ecran français* (May 1949). James Harvey also notes that *The Lady Eve* is marked by "a kind of energetic cruelty" in which the "relentless and systematic humiliation" of Charles Pike at the hands of Jean goes much farther than any other forms of male humiliation at the hands of strong female characters in other comedies of this period, such as *Theodora Goes Wild* (Richard Boleslawski, 1936) and *Bringing Up Baby* (Hawks, 1938) (1998, 570).

11. I am attempting to isolate only very broad trends, of course, and there are some exceptions to the history being sketched out here with regard to film comedy's fixation upon the domestic sphere in the 1950s. A few examples will suffice to suggest a more broad-ranging history of this period: *Pat and Mike* (Cukor, 1952), *Roman Holiday* (Wyler, 1953), *How to Marry a Millionaire* (Jean Negulesco, 1953), *Desk Set* (Walter Lang, 1957), *Designing Woman* (Minnelli, 1957), *Indiscreet* (Stanley Donen, 1958), *Pillow Talk* (Michael Gordon, 1959). Nevertheless, all of them are performed and directed in the slower, more relaxed postwar style even as a few of them attempt to deal with language in relation to the development of technology: the telephone in *Indiscreet* and *Pillow Talk,* the computer in *Desk Set.*

MODERN THOUGHTS

MODERNITY AND CINEMA
A CULTURE OF SHOCKS AND FLOWS
Tom Gunning

"And the more it breaks down, the more it schizophrenizes, the better it works, the American way."

GILLES DELEUZE AND FÉLIX GUATTARI, *ANTI-OEDIPUS*

Elective Affinities: Cinema as an Emblem of Modernity

In the Netherlands, Theo van Doesburg, extraordinary painter of geometric abstraction, revolutionary modern architect, and guiding light of the De Stijl movement, went to the movies in 1917 and saw a slapstick comedy, probably a Keystone film, whose title he gave as *How Nathan Trapped the Villains* and whose proper identification remains unlikely. He wrote to modernist architect J.J.P. Oud, describing the effect of a chase scene, probably reacting to the way editing could instantaneously present closer and farther views of the tumbling slapstick performers: "In an intensity of motion and light you saw people fall away into ever-receding distances, then reappear the next moment. A continuous dying and reviving in the same instant. The end of time and space! The destruction of gravity! The secret of movement in the fourth dimension" (qtd. in Van Beusekom 1997, 234)

In France, Blaise Cendrars, one of the inventors of modern French poetry, author of *Moravagine,* a tale of the global adventures of an escaped lunatic and serial killer, and creator of an extraordinary personal legend (including claims to have instigated the unsuccessful 1905 revolution in Russia and to have directed Hollywood films sometime between 1917 and 1921), declared: "Cinema. Whirlwind of movement in space. Everything falls. We fall in its wake. Like a chameleon, the human mind camouflages itself, camouflaging the universe . . ." (Cendrars 1992, 25)

And here in Russia in 1907 is Andrei Bely, Symbolist poet and author of *Petersburg,* described by Vladimir Nabokov as one of the four great masterpieces of twentieth-century prose, after seeing the British trick film *The Fatal Sneeze*:

> The cinematograph reigns in the city, reigns over the earth. In Moscow, Paris, New York, Bombay, on the same day, maybe at the very same hour, thousands of people come to see a man who sneezes—who sneezes and explodes. The cinematograph has crossed the borders of reality. More than the preachings of scholars and wise men, this has demonstrated to everyone what reality is: it is a lady suffering from a cold who sneezes and explodes. And we, who hold on to her: where are we? (qtd. in Tsivian 1998, 151)

What are we to make of these descriptions of a medium that was supposed during this period to be undergoing a process of standardization, of increased coherence both in its production process and in its narrative form, eventually congealing into what has been described as the classical Hollywood paradigm?[1] Clearly, it would be foolish to claim that, for all their apparent delight in the irrational, these descriptions of the movies indicate that this process of rationalization and narrative coherence evident in feature filmmaking during this era did not take place. But equally clearly, the reception of film is unpredictable and impossible to determine. Given that these are avant-garde artists whose methods involve a process of distortion or defamiliarization, which, as Bely indicates, questions the very nature of reality and, as van Doesburg and Cendrars demonstrate, envisions a systematic disorientation of conventional experiences of space and time, should we assume that the cinema evinced in these rhapsodic descriptions simply formed raw material that these artists refashioned according to their own images and ideals? What they describe, we might claim, is not film as it "truly existed" during this era but their own reformulation of an imagined cinema, an avant-garde cinema, imagined before it was actually created. This is cinema seen through a modernist filter, a cinema of utopian possibility that certain artists of the next decade would try to realize.

But doesn't this view trivialize or even dismiss these passionate and, I would claim, insightful ways of viewing cinema? Are they really irrelevant to the history of cinema, other than as premonitions of the cinema of the 1920s or as footnotes to the history of modernist art and literature? Although it would again be foolish to claim that these panegyrics reflect the experience of the majority of filmgoers in this era, are we sure they are totally irrelevant? How in the world would we confirm this? Was cinema really just neutral material in the hands or consciousness of these artists? Could they just as well have been describing, say, law journals, city directories, or medical textbooks? As historians, we must ask if these descriptions do not in fact illuminate aspects of the cinema as it emerged into the consciousness of intellectuals and artists in the early twentieth century, or even capture aspects of the nature of film as a cultural object in the twentieth century (and perhaps later).

A thorough analysis of such discussions of cinema by avant-garde artists in the years between 1907 and 1921—and there are many others that I could supply, most of them equally fascinating—would overwhelm this essay. But I think we can point out a number of aspects belonging to cinema of this era that triggered this radical enthusiasm. First, cinema emerged as a new form of representation, outside of academic aesthetics and not yet recognized as an art form. Thus, for avant-gardists, the form was not cursed by a hoary tradition of aesthetic principles. Because they offered principles of creation other than traditional ones, a variety of novel products excited avant-garde artists in this era, such as the mass-produced kitchen utensils beloved by Fernand Léger or the automobiles and airplanes that the Futurists pronounced superior to classical sculpture (see Léger 1973, 24–27, and Marinetti 1973, 19–24). Like the centralized assembly of automobiles and airplanes, film's mechanical production increased its distance from the traditional arts. In addition, as a popular art form, film often displayed literally vulgar behavior, outside categories of good taste, as had examples of folk art adapted by avant-garde artists like Wassily Kandinsky or Nataliya Goncharova, or the variety theater championed by both Russian and Italian Futurists, or even the Fantomas novels embraced by Cendrars, Max Jacob, and Juán Gris.

From these comparisons, it appears that the avant-garde primarily valued cinema for what it *was not.* Yet they were also articulating aspects of what cinema *was,* isolating new—and for this generation defining—differences it displayed from other arts: cinema was a machine-based art whose mechanical reproduction made it available to the masses. In valorizing the mechanical nature and popular appeal of the movies, the avant-garde was not simply refashioning cinema in its own image. Although avant-garde works often referred to machines in their imagery or even materials, few works by these artists (architects being, of course, the exception) actually used mechanical processes; and although the utopian aspirations of the Russian Constructivists in the 1920s envisioned widespread popularity, few avant-garde works ever became, or even desired to become, popular.

In granting the originality of avant-garde descriptions of cinema, we should not deny them profound insight into the new medium. Their descriptions of cinema should not be reduced in our estimation to simple avant-gardist caprices, the defamiliarizing of a form of popular entertainment in an all-too-playful manner that can tell us nothing about the way film actually functioned in this early era. Indeed, let us not forget that for the originator of the term, Victor Shklovsky, *defamiliarization* never simply involved distortion, but rather offered an artistic means of rediscovering the nature of the object, of overcoming dulled habitual perception and rendering, as he put it, "the stone stony" (1965, 3–24). Thus, these avant-gardists found something other than simple negation of the traditional arts in the new popular mechanical motion pictures. In all these descriptions motion takes precedence and appears primarily as a destabilizing force. To grasp this, one needs to feel the force of the phrase "motion picture" as an oxymoron, the modifier undermining centuries of practice in which the tableau signified a static composition, a frozen moment, if not utterly an image of repose. An image in motion reintroduced temporal transformation into the field of visual representation, not simply implying it (as did the contorted figures of baroque art), but allowing it to unfold. The radical implications of this new form of representation delighted the representatives of the avant-garde, who found a new world of experience in the action of a comic chase film or the sudden transformations of a trick film.

Traditional, classically founded taste valued the ideal of pictorial beauty as repose. When motion played a role, the artist who rendered it harmonic and balanced fulfilled canons of good taste. As I have indicated elsewhere, the objections first launched against Eadweard Muybridge's images of the horse in motion lay primarily in their unaesthetic nature, their ungainliness and unfamiliarity as images of animal locomotion, contrasting so starkly with the symmetrical images of galloping horses in previous equestrian paintings (see Gunning 2003, 222–72). Even though a number of popular art forms of the nineteenth century sought to add motion to pictures, such as both circular and "moving" (that is, unrolling) panoramas, instantaneous photography, and the dissolving views of the magic lantern, their popular sensationalism kept such forms outside the pale of the respectable arts. The avant-gardists I have quoted not only recognized the potential of film to create new modes but actually experienced this dissolving of traditionally oriented space through film's ability to capture motion and to combine motions into new configurations. I would claim that these avant-gardists recognized both the affinities their experiments shared with the cinema and the differences that separated them. It would be reductive to portray their enthusiasm for the medium as mere narcissistic investment and canny distortion. For the avant-garde in the first years of the twentieth century, cinema stood as an emblem for a revolution they sought to achieve as well in their own practices.

The common ground between the emerging cinema and the avant-garde lay in their crystallization of the novelty of modern experience. To use a terminological differentiation these artists would not have employed, but one that I believe does indeed indicate the major source of their fascination with the cinema, they understood that the cinema was not modernist, but they embraced its modernity. Cinema served as an emblem of a new experience that held utopian possibilities for these artists. The rise of the machine and its transformation of the human environment, as well as the rise of the masses, carried both apocalyptic and millennial possibilities—the possibilities of destruction often heralding the possibilities of renewal. As the harbinger of something new, something transformative, cinema, like other aspects of modern life, sparked an ambivalent reaction among not only artists but also intellectuals and politicians. Cinema, both as a practice and as a force that was understood in a variety of ways, played a central role in the culture of modernity. Given its striking appeal to popular sentiment, its mechanical force and play, its enlivening and contradictory tension between picturing and moving, cinema metaphorised modernity. To deny this claim would be to ignore the key role cinema played as an emblem of modernity, not only for the avant-garde but also for the generation for whom its appearance as part of everyday life was a novelty.

A Demurrer: Constructing a "Modernity Thesis"

Of course, no one can deny this connection, and I don't really think anyone does, in spite of some recent objections raised against the introduction of modernity into discussions of film history, especially of early cinema. It is to this rather strange controversy that I now turn in order to be a little quarrelsome, frankly with the admission that I have never found "quarreling" the best mode of academic discussion. Too much rhetoric of invective and sarcasm—and indeed, pure ego— tends to intervene from both parties, and the argument proceeds *sui generis,* often at the expense of mutual understanding. But recent, repeated publications by Charlie Keil and David Bordwell have made it clear to me that simple statements and clarifications of one's own position do not seem to calm things down, either.[2] My linking (in a number of essays) of my formal description of early cinema before 1907 as a *cinema of attractions* to the shocks of modernity, as described by Walter Benjamin and Siegfried Kracauer, sparked initial critiques by Bordwell and Keil. In subsequent works, I have tried to clarify my ideas, which I thought perhaps had been misunderstood. Bordwell and Keil have mounted an attack on what they both refer to as "the modernity thesis," a term never actually used by any of the scholars they criticize (myself primary among them) but one constructed, indeed, in order to be destroyed. By converting this research project into a "thesis," Keil and Bordwell formulated a claim none of us made: that modernity serves as the all-encompassing explanatory thesis in early film history, excluding other factors, something neither I nor other scholars ever argued, as I will show in the essay that follows. Although their initial critiques helped me to realize the need for further clarity in the discussion of the ways in which early cinema in particular is related to modernity, the more recent forays seem to me to delight primarily in the college debating rhetoric of *reductio ad absurdum* rather than aiming to achieve some mutual understanding through searching for common ground.

As perhaps the most impressive film scholar of his generation, Bordwell helped set the agenda for the new film history, valuing primary research in contextual material (trade journals, professional and technical journals, industry records) and close analysis of the films themselves. These principles guided my own work as well, and I have always felt that we shared goals and methods, even if our interests were not identical. Keil, who completed his dissertation under Bordwell, follows very much in this tradition and has produced important broad investigations of films and their narrative structures in what he refers to as the transitional period (1908–1917). Through a careful analysis of films by several other American film producers from the same period, Keil's work broadens (and basically supports) many of the theses I had formulated about the films D. W. Griffith directed at the Biograph Company, providing a strong sense of the evolutions in narrative style of American films and their relation to the discourse about films found in the trade press of the period.

Ben Singer (2001) and I have tried to indicate that relating early cinema to modernity does not exclude a careful consideration of such factors as efficient industry organization and the development of narrative structures, which both Bordwell and Keil value as scholars (and which the majority of my book on Griffith discussed in detail). Nevertheless, Keil at least has insisted that we are obligated to take a more extreme and absurd position: "Singer is correct when he says no proponent of the modernity thesis isolates modernity 'as the only historical force governing cinema,' but the obvious rejoinder would be that none of them needs to—the collective thrust of their valorization of modernity as the defining cultural moment achieves the result of relegating all other determination to second-class status" (Keil 2004, 54). Keil initially seems to accept Singer's statement—and I have made a similar one—that no scholar has actually claimed that modernity should be treated as *the single* factor in film history (as his and

Bordwell's critiques had seemed to suggest). However, he then declares that, despite our denial, "the collective thrust of their valorization" apparently forces anyone who treats modernity as even a key aspect of film history to posit mere "second-class status" for any other aspect. I have no idea what sort of mania for rank ordering, or mass hysteria, he thinks is operating here, or who, precisely, is succumbing to it. It would seem that even where Singer and I grant the importance of (and practice in our work) traditional film history that Keil valorizes—careful reading of trade journals, description of evolution of narrative forms, consideration of the effects of industry organization—he feels we should be excluded from this common ground.

I frankly doubt that I do not share basic understandings with two such insightful and careful scholars, and suspect that where we disagree it is due less to faulty thinking than to some fundamental differences about the nature of interesting work in cinema and how we see our own research projects. But something in my research project apparently seems to threaten their sense of proper film history. In particular, a rhetorically loaded recent essay by Keil, "'From Here to Modernity': Style, Historiography, and Transitional Cinema," forces me to clear the air with some direct response. I want to clarify one more time what it is that I do, and do not, mean to be saying about the development of narrative cinema and the context of cultural modernity.

Originally, Bordwell (1996, 22–23) pointed out—correctly, I think—that claiming that the historical transformations of modernity brought on "perceptual changes" might well be a misleading way to describe adjustments in behavior and habits of daily life following from shifts in environmental and cultural experiences. Such phrasing could be interpreted as a claim for an evolutionary transformation in human perceptual hard-wiring. (Actually, his articulation of this complaint was a good deal less charitable, but here I rephrase it to emphasize what I found to be a useful criticism.) This seems to me a primarily terminological issue, however, not an argument against the well-attested historical fact that new urban experiences, changes in transportation and communication, and new modes of labor occurred in the latter part of the nineteenth century and transformed the habits of large segments of the population in terms of the way they experienced and negotiated time and space, not as abstract Kantian categories or hard-wired cognitive structures but as material of a historically daily life and labor.

Bordwell indicates a suspicion of a new and vacuous buzzword. I have taken seriously his sense that "modernity" could become an empty concept, and I have tried to give it specificity and trace its effect through concrete mediations (Gunning 1998, esp. 266–68). Only by focusing on its various aspects (as well as on the systematic way in which they interrelate, this being a definitive aspect of modernity) can we seriously discuss its impact in history or its impact on film. In a series of essays, I have discussed the very specific impact of such instances of modernity as the telephone, the railway, and the telegraph on films or sequences within films in terms of narrative and editing strategies (Gunning 1991b, 1994b, 1995b, 1997, 2000b, and 2004). As a term, "modernity" remains a concept, a name for a series of transformations, a general rubric. It should be clear that, as a general term, "modernity" cannot (except as a manner of speaking) exert direct causal effects. In history, discussing causality tends never to be as simple as tracing out one-to-one correspondences between single causes and effects, but rather involves tracing a confluence of causes and influences, some more direct and some more distant. Ultimately, a theory of modernity involves not short-circuiting or ignoring what Keil refers to as "proximate forces" (2004, 52)—the trade press, production companies competing for prestige and a share of the growing marketplace—but rather showing in what ways specific factors relate to the transformations that constitute modernity.

Clearly, this is a big project. That some of my essays proclaiming the connections between cinema and modernity did not simultaneously supply thorough historical and stylistic analyses does not require apology. And I would agree that such analyses must justify referring to modernity as a primary context for cinema. Bordwell and Keil do remind us that in this area much specific work remains to be done. My analyses of *The Lonely Villa* (1909), *The Lonedale Operator* (1911), or *Dr. Mabuse: The Gambler* (*Dr. Mabuse, der Spieler* [1922]) portray specific aspects of modernity, their systematic interrelation, and their connection to basic figures of cinematic narration such as parallel editing. Therefore, I certainly do not think that investigating modernity in relation to film necessarily involves remaining on the level of vague buzzwords. To my knowledge, the only critique of these analyses has been Keil's dismissive indication that *The Lonedale Operator* should not carry weight in this discussion because it is "not typical"—a truly unsubstantiated and untheorized claim (Keil 2004, 60).

I have written that aspects of the cinema of attractions—such as direct confrontation of the audience, brevity of film subjects, a fascination with speed and surprising special effects, a display of novelties, and a lack of sustained temporal and narrative development—corresponded to the new modern environment of shocks as described by Benjamin and others.[3] But I have never claimed that these social and environmental factors on their own constitute a sufficient explanation of all formal aspects of early motion pictures. Anyone who has read my work on Griffith knows that I consider a variety of factors in discussing stylistic change, including economic, technical, industrial, and social factors (such as censorship, control of distribution, industry combinations, modes of exhibition, changing audiences). Keil's recent essay insists that I am simply avoiding "a logical outcome" when I reiterate that I never said modernity on its own and without mediation could explain the stylistic history of film (Keil 2004, 56). The "logic," although clear to him, escapes me; if I think modernity has *an* effect on the formal aspects of the motion picture, must I argue it is the only factor?

Keil also faults me for stating the obvious: that film emerged and developed during the period of modernity, and that it can be related to its historical period. He cannot really deny this claim and instead decides to belittle it, stating, "It is unlikely anyone (even the staunchest of anti-culturalists) would do more than stifle a yawn" when confronted with such a claim (Keil 2004, 54). I am not exactly sure how to approach the dilemma Keil jams me into here: either I am arguing absurdly, *or* I am making an entirely different sort of claim (one he really can't deny), one that is boring and states the patently obvious. (Or perhaps Keil feels I somehow do both.) But there is only so much one can do to try to overcome someone else's boredom, especially given that with boredom it's often impossible to know exactly who is responsible for it.

Clearly, arguments based on yawns should be beyond the pale of serious academic discussion. In fact, I think lists of average shot lengths (such as Keil indeed produces), which to me are not exciting in themselves, become exciting when one discovers something through them, as I think Keil does in his excellent formal analyses of film style in what he calls the transitional era. Likewise, I would claim that the observation (which I hope *is* obvious) that film has an important relation to modernity can become interesting and, for me at least, exciting, depending on the unsuspected connections and interrelations it allows one to explore. This unexceptional and agreed-upon statement must provide the basis for a series of analyses, not a replacement for them.

Any fair account of my writings on early cinema, especially cinema after 1907, would have to acknowledge that I do not claim that modernity and its social effects single-handedly determined stylistic change in film. As I mentioned earlier, Keil contrasts what he feels is the vague nature of my invocations of modernity in film history with his own description of stylistic change, in which he has dealt with "more proximate forces" (Keil 2004, 52). I find this contrast in bad faith. Keil not only knows that my own work deals extensively with this sort of "proximate" material; he has even acknowledged that he has drawn upon my work on Griffith in his own treatment of the transitional period. My book on Griffith (1991a) was one of the first full-length studies of this period of film history to investigate these "proximate forces" in detail; so Keil's vaunting of his own practice as a contrast with my work seems more than a little disingenuous. (In fact, Keil uses, among other things, my calculation of average shot lengths for Griffith's Biograph films.)

I absolutely agree that consideration of these "proximate" factors remains essential to any responsible approach to film history. The factors Keil cites — as well as other "proximate forces," such as patterns of distribution and exhibition, censorship practices, discourse about the cinema in nontrade publications — must always form the foundation of the study of film history. I was part of a pioneering generation that first went into dusty archives to uncover them, and I continue to make use of them. In fact, I have no problem with historians who decide to restrict their research project to these important tasks. But this sort of research need not forbid considerations of broader cultural connections for all scholars. My own speculation about film and modernity came only after such research. No argument for the importance of research into "proximate sources" can justify setting up a shibboleth, and declaring to all other scholars, "Go this far, and no further." Therefore in my book on Griffith, where I discuss extensively the question Keil raises about the stylistic change from the cinema of attractions to the cinema of narrative integration (which was, to be sure, my question before he raised it), I make references to modernity as a secondary aspect of a detailed formal analysis of this stylistic change and a discussion of the "proximate forces," using research undertaken more than a decade before Keil's own.

Therefore, I am basically in agreement with Keil and Bordwell: simple assertions of film's relation to modernity are not the most useful way to account for stylistic change. I am far from saying that reference to modernity has no relevance to changes in film style, but only that it cannot in itself explain change and transformation without a full exploration of mediating aspects and practices. So much for misunderstandings of what my methods and principles have been. But let me try to approach, in a less rhetorical manner, Keil's (and perhaps Bordwell's) major objection to the way I have presented the modernity statement, in the belief that two such fine scholars are not reacting capriciously and that they can help me better articulate my position, especially after I have spent some years thinking it through and testing it with specific case studies. There may well be a central problem they have isolated in my description of early cinema, a problem that I am not sure I have answered sufficiently in my previous response to them.

Keil and Bordwell do seem justified in asking me whether, with the stylistic change from the cinema of attractions, which I have related to modernity as the culture of shocks, modernity ceases to play a role in film stylistics. How do the hallmarks of the cinema of narrative integration (such as the move toward greater continuity, the creation of a different, more indirect address to the spectator, and the dominance of a narratively determined diegesis) relate to modernity? Did cinema after 1907 achieve independence from the shocks of modernity? Or did the broader culture of shock cease to exist after 1907? How does modernity affect cinema after the cinema of attractions? If formal aspects of the cinema of attractions do reflect the culture of shocks that one finds in the avant-garde descriptions of modernity (not only by the artists I quoted above, but also by critical social theorists such as Georg Simmel, Kracauer, and Benjamin), what role does modernity play in the transformation of cinema that occurs *after* 1907, exemplified by the increased narrativization that accompanies attempts to reorganize and systematize the cinema industry? Did modernity cease to be a factor?

Upon reflection, this important query prompts me to rethink and rebalance my account of modernity, without, I admit, the least hope that my complication of an earlier model will prove satisfying to my most devoted critics.

Modernity and Cinema Reconsidered

Depending mainly on critical German social theorists, my description of modernity in relation to the cinema of attractions exemplifies what I might call the avant-garde reception of modernity (and of the cinema), typified by the quotations I cited at the opening of this essay. Describing the cinema of attractions, I emphasized what Marshall Berman might call the "dissolving" aspects of modernity: its discontinuity, its sense of confrontation and shock, its explosive nature, its speed and disorientation (see Berman 1988). But avant-garde and critical thinkers highlighted these aspects partly against more familiar aspects of modernity that they also assumed: an emphasis on systematic organization and rationalization; maximum exploitation of resources; a pervasive reliance on quantification and abstraction. Theorists of modernity such as Simmel, Kracauer, Georg Lukács, and Benjamin wished to reveal the dialectical flip side of the processes of modernity described earlier by Marx and Max Weber and exemplified by such practices as the new factory system, the establishment of worldwide standard time, and Taylorism. Modernity as a culture of shocks constituted the critical underside of modernity as a systematic process of rational and scientific planning. Simmel, Kracauer, Lukács, and Benjamin did not deny the rational and systematic aspects of modernity but revealed that the process of rationalization often entailed chaotic effects (effects that some of them felt had revolutionary potential).

Thus, a thorough account of modernity must include this systematic attempt to contain the energies released by new technologies and means of production. In many ways the organization of Hollywood described in *The Classical Hollywood Cinema* (Bordwell, Staiger, and Thompson, 1985) represents the modernization of the film industry based on models widely adopted in other forms of American industry. Modernity involves systems of containment and control as much as a new, explosive energy. Indeed, critical theories of modernity regard these two aspects as essentially interlinked.

The utopian modernity of the avant-garde constitutes only one aspect of the transformations that established modern life. The dialectical interaction of the forces of chaotic dissolution and those of systematic organization plays an essential role in the analysis of modernity from Marx through Deleuze and Guattari. We could visualize this process as an interaction between the explosive shocks of modernity as motive force and the transformation of these shocks into a regularized and consistent motion, a transformation of shock into flow. The piston in the gasoline motor provides a model: a contained explosion is converted into consistent motion.

Wolfgang Schivelbusch's account of the experience of the railway as an emblem of modernity stresses precisely the interaction of these two aspects (see Schivelbusch 1986, esp. 150–58). The railway perfected a rapid and comfortable mode of transportation, reducing travel time and smoothing the transit for the traveler. Compared with the stagecoach passenger, shaken and bruised along poor roads and subjected to unpredictable travel schedules owing to climatic and geographic conditions, the modern traveler could almost forget how radically briefer and more comfortable the railway journey was. The railway passenger could even read and become absorbed in other mental activities during her voyage. At the same time, however, the increased speed and the capacity to carry large numbers of passengers meant that a train accident, when it did occur, achieved a level of human injury not previously experienced outside of war or industrial accidents. Further, these accidents intervened without warning on the comfortable and relaxed passengers. The systematic train schedule, the rationalization of routes, and the technological perfection of the comfortable journey were haunted by a degree of trauma unimagined up to that time. The culture of shock may have become absorbed by a technology of frictionless flow and rational order, but the possibility of shock still haunted the system as a possibility. This interaction between rationality and surprise defines the dynamic of modernity.

Thus, the transformation in cinema from short, percussive attractions to character- and action-based stories of the one-reel era undertakes a similarly modern transfer from the explosive staccato energy of the attraction to an outgoing, more systematically controlled narrative force. We can trace this transformation by comparing the under-narrativized story films of Georges Méliès with the first narratively dominated genre, the chase film. A Méliès story film sub-ordinates the impulse toward storytelling to an impulse toward at-tractions. Tricks and special effects effectively stop the story in its tracks so that the filmmaker can indulge in a display of spectacle (like the ballet corps that emerges at points in Méliès's longer films to per-form dances with little narrative motivation). The chase film begins to signal a transition from the attractions era by integrating discon-tinuous moments into a continuous and ongoing thrust of action. However, the chase film, while sketching a model of linearity (as Noël Burch indicated [1990, 143–61]), also offers the pure excitement of frenzied actions and frequently displays a succession of caricatured types who rush toward the camera in order to present themselves to the viewer.

Griffith's introduction of parallel editing in the era of narrative integration gave to dramatic sequences an even greater sense of the systematic interrelation of space, time, and action. Yet the device of interruption, so essential to parallel editing, also flirted with derailing the narrative by breaking the natural unfolding of the action with a cut. Keil's claim that the "fragmentary force of editing, which pur-portedly defines the attraction era, is largely vitiated by the move to-wards continuity editing" rather simplifies the transformation of edit-ing during the era of early cinema (2004, 57). Whereas attractions are typified primarily by a lack of editing, by the short single-shot film that directly addresses the audience in a gesture of display, parallel ed-iting (which admittedly does not necessarily constitute the dominant form of editing in all production companies, but is a major device of this era) hardly undermines a sense of fragmentation. Parallel editing, by interrupting action and switching among various strands of the narrative, renders the fragmentary extremely visible—if not visceral. Thus, at least one major form of narrative editing during this period, although certainly different from the autonomy of the shots within the cinema of attractions, nonetheless shows that the development of systematic narration and continuous action could also deliver a sen-sation of shock, of percussive action that is broken and picked up again continually. It is no wonder that Griffith used this figure fre-quently to convey modern devices (such as the railway, telephone, and telegraph) that were essential in new configurations of space and time.

As Ben Singer has insightfully pointed out, thrills as developed in even later action films represented a union of the direct stimulus offered by attractions with the suspense available in narrative form (2001, 202–3, 217–20). To follow my new model of modernity, these later forms of chase or suspense translated the sudden impact of shocks into a kind of shock with duration, a continuous forward motion, often creating a jagged rhythm of stops and starts. The serial film's unique play with narrative closure and suspense through its fragmentary form serves as a perfect example. This dialectical structure of shock and flow also recalls Donald Crafton's description of slapstick comedy as a dialectic of the pie (explosive, show-stopping gags) and the chase (elements of narrative development) (see Crafton 1994). Keil seems to avoid dealing with these genres, seeing them as somehow "atypical" even though their popularity in the era cannot be denied.[4]

As I have always claimed, the new systematic organization through narrative dominance does not eliminate the anarchic energy of the cinema of attraction and modernity; rather it sublates this energy, using and transforming it. In other words, narrative development may be opposed to the form of attractions, but this very dialectical opposition relates it to other key aspects of modernity. Indeed the interaction between narrative forms and the direct stimulus of audiences by thrills provides a fuller sense of the forms of modernity than the simple culture of shocks allows.

But, then, is it true that modernity can be related to anything . . . to attractions and narrative, to shocks and flows, to continuity and discontinuity? And isn't this sort of universal reference therefore meaningless? Am I not simply supplying another, only more dangerous, form of the obvious statement that cinema developed in modern times and therefore can be related to modernity—dangerous, because the statement can be applied to any sort of formal device? This is perhaps a sensible allegation. Yet I doubt that my claim about modernity, the cinema of attractions, and the development of narrative in fact reduces film history and modernity to a night in which all cows appear black. If modernity constitutes the broad social and historical context for cinema, then it seems likely film will relate to modernity in a variety of ways. Properly put, the question should be: What are the proper contexts for cinema history that give us the most complex and thorough view of how cinema operates?

The question of the change between the cinema of attractions and the cinema of narrative integration, and of the relation of this change to modernity needs to be reformulated. The forces I described in my book on Griffith (some of which Keil has further investigated)—new and more systematic organization of the industry in terms of production, distribution and exhibition, and even censorship; a desire to attract a larger middle-class audience; an attempt to promote a more genteel and moral image for the movies; increased production schedules and consequent needs to standardize aspects of the film production—all these remain the major factors behind this change (Gunning 1991a). With Singer's important work on the era of the emergence of the feature and the serial, however, I have also realized that this process (which I once described as the *embourgeoisement* of the cinema) was double-edged (even at points double-faced) (Singer 2001). As Singer makes clear, the courting of a middle-class audience (through narrative) did not lessen a strong desire to hold on to cinema's working-class patrons (who loved thrills). In addition, the adoption of the movies as a widespread form of entertainment contributed to a transformation of middle-class attitudes toward pleasure and leisure-time entertainments. Ultimately, all these factors can be related profitably to a larger sense of modernity, its ongoing dialectic of the generation of novel stimuli and their containment.

Strangely (and, in my opinion, not a little obliquely), Keil warns that the "modernity thesis" risks "sacrificing the fine grained sense of historical change."[5] Does he mean that reference to modernity entails a lack of close analysis? Both Singer's work on melodrama and my essay on *The Lonedale Operator* supply detailed discussions of stylistic devices and their relationship to modernity (none appear in Keil's essay, of course, but it is intended as theoretical—as are many of the essays on film and modernity he refers to, so he can't complain that they lack close analysis). If he claims detailed arguments about the nature of historical change have not been forthcoming, certainly the very essays he cites are attempting that, even if he disagrees with them.

What is it, then, that appears so threatening about references to modernity? Keil concludes his essay with this penultimate sentence, referring to a statement of mine that the relationships between film and modernity must gain specificity and not remain vague analogies: "But rather than responding to that challenge by reconciling their vision of modernity to pre-existing models of film's development, some champions of the thesis appear to be heading in the opposite direction, discrediting previously accepted terms and substituting contentious new concepts of their own" (2004, 63). I hope this is not the call for conformity to "pre-existing models" it seems to be. The implications of this call for submission to authority seem to me disturbing. Wherein lies the preeminent value of "pre-existing" models? Keil seems to be referring to Bordwell, Staiger, and Thompson's extraordinary work, *The Classical Hollywood Cinema*. Among its many virtues, the fact that it is "pre-existing" seems to me trivial. After all, my description of the cinema of attractions pre-exists Keil's critiques—does that pre-existence forbid him the possibility of coming up with his own contentious arguments or new terms? If models are worthwhile, they are worth testing and arguing with.

If quarreling may not be the best mode of scholarly discussion, debate clearly remains a sign of vitality. Such vitality demands that models not persist as static authorities, but rather appear both evolving and mobile—a moving image inherently dynamic, partaking of the sputtering energy of contained explosions that the avant-garde thinkers, embracing the ambivalent possibilities of the machine age, took from the internal combustion engine. André Breton referred to this modern energy with the oxymoron of the "fixed-explosive." Walter Benjamin envisioned it as the "dialectic at a standstill." These formulations channel the contradictory energies of modernity into models for artistic and critical methods. If we cannot recognize these voices from the past as our contemporaries, we must at the very least confront their legacy as well as remain true to it.

I do not feel that the exuberance, this sense of both palpable energies and future possibilities that the cinema offered to talented and bold intellects, should be dismissed. I confess a strong attraction to this aspect of cinema and of modernity, one that I have tried in this essay to balance with other forces, but not to deny. The study of cinema emerged in politically radical cine-clubs and artistic avant-garde journals, searching for a range of possibilities promised by the new medium. Cinema studies, as an academic discipline, needs to avoid becoming a mere embalming process. Undue reverence for "pre-existing models" and suspicion of "contentious new concepts" serve as the very definition of the academic in a pejorative sense. As something of a modernist in my heart, I do not envision the future of film history in this direction.

Notes

This essay is dedicated to Aelia Laelia: "Nec vir nec mulier nec androgyna, nec puella nec juvenis nec anus, nec casta nec meretrix nec pudica, sed omnia sublata."

1. The classic account of the standardization of the American cinema is given in Bordwell, Staiger, and Thompson (1985). A sure-to-be-classic account of this process of transformation is given in Keil (2001).

2. Bordwell first launched a critique of what he calls "the modernity thesis" in Bordwell (1996, 22–29), expanded on it in Bordwell (1997, esp. 139–57), and continues the debate in a yet unpublished manuscript. In addition to Keil (1996), Keil offered his critique in Keil (1998, 123–37). He continues the argument in *Early American Cinema in Transition* (2001). His most recent foray, and the key motivation for my response here, is Keil (2004).

3. This thesis is developed in Gunning (1991b, 1994a, 1994b, 1995b, 1997, 2000b, and 2004) but especially in Gunning (1990). Benjamin's discussion of shock occurs in "The Work of Art in the Age of Its Technological Reproducibility" (of which one version, actually the second, appears in Benjamin [2002, 101–33]; the third version is in Benjamin [2003, 251–83]), and in "On Some Motifs of Baudelaire," in Benjamin (2003, 313–55). Wolfgang Schivelbusch has extended the concept of shock (1979).

4. Keil claims the serial "is not representative of the typical film," whatever that means (2004, 60). He never discusses slapstick.

5. Keil quotes himself from his earlier paper (1996) reiterating this claim (2004, 63).

FILM, MODERNITY, CAVELL
William Rothman

In reflecting on film's relation to modernity and modernism, I find myself endlessly instructed by the writings of Stanley Cavell. On this issue, as on so many matters of concern to film studies, Cavell provides a philosophically sophisticated alternative to views that remain all but unquestioned within the field (see Rothman and Keane 2000).

Within the field of film studies, for example, the main emphasis has been on the aspects of modernity embraced by Futurism—on the kinds of shocks associated with speed and with the power of machines. Thinking of modernity primarily in terms of such shocks seems to support the view that in the silent period it was only the "cinema of attractions" and the avant-garde cinema of the 1920s that fully acknowledged and affirmed modernity. And the emphasis seems to support as well the corollary view that ordinary, popular movies, narrative films that employ the system of "classical" editing to project a continuous world in space and time, tapped into traditional—that is, premodern—modes of representation in a rearguard effort to deny or contain modernity.

As Cavell's writings can help us to recognize, such views channel the concept of modernity to mount yet another campaign to validate the tired old idea, still widely held within the field, that films advance the art of cinema only to the degree that they "subvert" the "illusionist codes" of popular movies. As Cavell reminds us, this idea fails to register the radical implications of Walter Benjamin's understanding of modernity, and of film, which led to his recognition that movies posed a revolutionary problem for traditional criticism and aesthetics (Cavell 2005d, 109). Benjamin's insight was that if movies are accepted as an art, then our concept of art must change. Viewed from this perspective (that is, the denial that movies are a great art of the modern period), the denial of the modernity of movies itself takes on the aspect of a rearguard effort to deny or contain modernity.

If Benjamin's insight is valid, and Cavell does not doubt it is, our persistence in denying the modernity of movies reveals our fear of change. We fear—this is a fear that Benjamin would have us overcome—that our concept of art will become foreign to us. But, as Cavell points out, we also fear that movies would then

> have to be accepted as speaking to our common lives with a depth, as well as an immediacy, no different in principle from the depth of Shakespeare or Dickens or Verdi or Manet; which means acknowledging their revelations of our involvements in the commonest fantasies of romance and of melodrama, and say of the long history of our puzzlements about the legitimacy in what is called marriage. Accepted, I mean, as speaking in terms that we may not elsewhere go beyond, that may reach the limits of our imaginations and intellects, and from which we are accordingly not exempt. As if movies may publicly manifest exactly what we publicly do not discuss. (2005d, 109)

This is a fear that Benjamin himself never overcame. As Cavell notes, the philosopher developed "his famous speculations concerning the technological medium of film ... without consulting a film's idea of itself, or undertaking to suppose that one or another may have such a thing" (Cavell 2005a, 284).

That popular movies "publicly manifest exactly what we publicly do not discuss" is an idea that Cavell fleshes out in *The World Viewed* (1971, 1976) and more fully in *Pursuits of Happiness* (1981), *Contesting Tears* (1996), and *Cities of Words* (2004), and in the essays collected in the volume *Cavell on Film*. These writings provide compelling reasons to be skeptical of the claim that the popular cinema, with its stars and mass audiences, has been peripheral to the development of film as an art. As Cavell argues in "More of *The World Viewed*," the art of film differs from the arts of literature, music, and painting in the modern period. In those arts, the "major experimentalists have generally proven to be the major artists of their period, i.e., their 'experiments' have been central to the development of the art itself, not more or less peripheral attacks upon it" (1979, 218).

In thinking about film's relation to modernity, Cavell's starting point is the fact that film for so long was able—and perhaps is still able—to avoid splitting its works between serious and popular, or between modern and traditional, and to avoid splitting its audience between high and low, or between advanced and philistine. "The movie's ease within its assumptions and achievements . . . is central to its pleasure for us," Cavell writes in *The World Viewed* (1979, 14–15). How, then, was this art able for so long to provide the pleasure it gives to modern human beings like us, a pleasure that cannot be separated from the reasons we care about movies, from what movies are, from their importance to us? If film is seriously to be accepted as an art, as Cavell does not doubt it is, we need to explain how this art was able for so long to avoid the fate of the other great arts in the modern period, how it was able to maintain its popularity as well as its seriousness.

When Cavell asserts that a blatant fact about film—if we accept it as an art—is that it remains "the one live traditional art," he means that film is the one art in the modern period that was able to rest secure in its own tradition (1979, 15). This does not mean that film remained premodern in an age of modern art, for traditional movies are modern, not premodern.

Then is film's unique ability to be both popular and serious in the modern period explained by saying that it is *the* modern art, the one to which modern human beings are naturally responsive? This answer suggests, erroneously, that other arts are *not* still capable of eliciting such responses. And, Cavell adds, it shows a poor view of what is natural, for "if we are seriously to be called 'modern,' one fact about us is that what seems natural to us is not natural, that naturalness, for us, has become a stupendous achievement" (1979, 14).

Is it that film, as is often claimed, has changed the way we see? Cavell concurs with the sense this formulation registers, that movies reflect a radical change of nothing less than human perception as such. But the formulation skips over a prior question: How was film able to achieve this kind of power in our lives? "My thought," Cavell writes, "is that it could not have achieved it unless human perception had already changed, so that the dominance of the moving image (where and when it is dominant) drawn by this change is an indispensable place in which to diagnose it. . . . Film could not have impressed itself so immediately and pervasively on the Western mind unless that mind had at once recognized in film a manifestation of something that had already happened to itself" (Cavell 2005d, 109).

Something has been happening to us at an accelerating rate over the past several centuries, Cavell observes, something "that has produced a sense of distance from the world." As philosophy understands this circumstance, what has been happening to the Western mind is its

> fall into skepticism, together with its efforts to recover itself, events recorded variously in Descartes and Hume and Kant and Emerson and Nietzsche and Heidegger and Wittgenstein. . . . It is in modern philosophical skepticism, in Descartes and in Hume, that our relation to the things of the world came to be felt to hang by a thread of sensuous immediacy, hence to be snapped by a doubt. The wish to defeat skepticism, or to disparage it, has been close to philosophy's heart ever since. (2005d, 116)

The term "skepticism," as Cavell uses it, speaks of a "new—or new realization of—human distance from the world, or withdrawal of the world" (2005d, 116). Beginning with Descartes, modern philosophy interprets this traumatic change in human existence or experience as a limitation in our capacity for knowing the world. But Shakespeare's tragedies and romances, as well as Monteverdi's operas, were already working out, in terms of their own, what philosophy knows as the problematic of skepticism, the terrifying recognition that reason as such, language as such, can no longer be assured of its relation to a world apart from us or to the reality of the passions within us. Such ideas, in Cavell's view, underlie the powers of film, which inherits from opera, as he eloquently puts it, "the flame that preserves the human need, on pain of madness of melancholy, for conviction in its expressions of passion" (2005c, 307). In *The World Viewed,* Cavell describes this cultural trauma, a crisis at once of knowledge and of expression, as the "unhinging of our consciousness from the world." Our subjectivity became interposed between us and our presentness to the world. "Our subjectivity became what is present to us; individuality became isolation" (Cavell 1979, 22).

The World Viewed returns again and again to this unhinging of our consciousness from the world. For Cavell, it is the touchstone of the modern. He locates it at a particular historical moment (the Protestant Reformation; the emergence of capitalism; the birth of opera; the theater of Shakespeare; Descartes's experience of, and response to, skeptical doubt). But he also suggests that it can be located at a particular moment in the life of every modern human being (psychoanalytically, as it were), and that once the unhinging has taken place, it is repeated again and again in that individual's life. The "unhinging of our consciousness from the world" is a historical event and also a mythical event, like the biblical fall from grace, the social contract (or, for that matter, Jacques Lacan's mirror stage). Picture it as a spiritual and psychological and political cataclysm that presents us with a new fact, or a new consciousness of an old fact, about our condition as human beings. We now feel isolated by our subjectivity. It is our subjectivity, not a world we objectively apprehend, that appears present to us. Nor do we objectively apprehend our own subjectivity; our subjectivity, too, appears present to us only subjectively, as if our consciousness has become unhinged from our own subjectivity no less than from the world. This is the modern condition of human perception that film, in Cavell's view, reveals.

The wish that prompted the creation of film as an artistic medium, Cavell argues, is the same wish, intensifying in the West for centuries, that motivated the creation of radically new artistic media in painting and the other great arts. It is the wish to overcome the "unhinging of our consciousness from the world," the wish to escape subjectivity and metaphysical isolation, the wish to "reach this world" and attain selfhood. ("Apart from the wish for selfhood [hence the always simultaneous granting of otherness as well], I do not understand the value of art" [Cavell 1979, 22]: this line could serve as the epigraph of *The World Viewed*.)

In Cavell's view, film and modernist painting exemplify different routes to "reaching this world." Modernist painting "accepts the recession of the world so as to maintain its conviction in its own power to establish connection with reality" (1979, 23). But movies are photographic, and photography maintains the presentness of the world by accepting our absence from it. ("The reality in a photograph is present to me while I am not present to it" [1979, 23].) Film satisfies our wish to "reach this world" by re-creating the world in its own image, re-creating the world *by* creating an image. (The re-created world is literally *in* this image, and this image is, also literally, the world's own; it belongs to the world, it is *of* the world.) Film's route to "reaching this world" is to overcome subjectivity by satisfying, as if by magic, our wish to view, unseen, the world re-created in its own image. The wish to view the world unseen that movies satisfy is the reverse of Faust's or Pygmalion's wish for power over creation. It is the wish not to need power, not to have to bear its burdens, its responsibilities (Cavell 1979, 40).

Viewing a film, we cannot but be invisible to the human beings we are viewing. The medium of film automatically assures our invisibility to them, assures that our feelings will be hidden from them. Because there is nothing they can possibly say or do that would count either as their acknowledging our present feelings or as withholding such an acknowledgment, our feelings make no claims upon these human beings. Similarly, their feelings make no claims upon us. We cannot possibly address an acknowledgment *to* them or withhold an acknowledgment *from* them. Viewing the conclusion of *City Lights* (1931), for example, we know that the Tramp suffers as he desperately searches the eyes of the woman he loves for a sign of her feelings. But we say and do nothing as we view him. In his suffering, the Tramp makes a passionate appeal to the woman in his presence to say or do something to acknowledge him. But the movie screen that separates us from the Tramp automatically ensures that we are not in that woman's place; we are at a distance, displaced from the Little Man who is so desperately appealing to her to return his love.

In viewing films, Cavell writes, "our sense of invisibility is an expression of modern privacy or anonymity, as though the world's projection explains our forms of unknownness and of our inability to know. The explanation is not so much that the world is passing us by, as that we are displaced from our natural habitation within it, placed at a distance from it. The screen . . . makes displacement appear as our natural condition (1979, 40 – 41)." In this passage, Cavell reminds us that modern human beings like us, isolated by our subjectivity, are already all too familiar with the feeling of being trapped within our privacy, unknown, unacknowledged, invisible. (This is the real shock of modernity.) Shrewdly, he sums up the sense of invisibility definitive of modernity by invoking not only our "familiar forms of unknownness" but also the familiar forms of our "inability to know." Our sense that others fail to acknowledge us matches our sense that we fail to acknowledge others. More mysteriously, Cavell also speaks of the world's projection onto the movie screen as *explaining* these modern forms of experience. What can this mean?

We feel that we are placed at such a distance from the world as to render us invisible, but that displacement is not *objectively* our condition; our sense of being invisible is an expression of our *subjectivity*. Our invisibility is a condition we long to overcome, but it is also a condition we impose upon ourselves. Our displacement from our natural habitation within the world is anything but natural, in other words. And yet it is only natural for us to wish to deny our responsibility for it. Such is our fear of change.

When we view a movie, it is objectively the case that we are invisible to the human beings we are viewing. Our displacement from the projected world is not our responsibility; we are displaced from it automatically, through no fault of our subjectivity. The world we inhabit with others is not a mere projection; it exists. But if the existing world were a projection on a screen, we would not be responsible for our displacement. The projection of the world onto a movie screen "explains" our unknownness and our inability to know by turning our unnatural displacement into a natural condition.

We wish to view the world unseen. What we wish to view in this way is everything, the world itself. We wish for the condition of viewing as such, as Cavell puts it (1979, 102). We wish to view the world unseen because that mode of perception feels natural to us. It feels natural to us because we have already become displaced from our natural habitation within the world. It can be taken to be the central claim of *The World*

Viewed that film expresses our displacement as the modern fate of relating to the world by viewing it, by taking views of it. Our way of feeling connected with the world is not so much to look at it as to look *out* at it, as if from behind the self. (An extension of this idea leads Cavell to characterize film as a "moving image of skepticism," a manifestation of our capacity to doubt the existence of the world [1979, 22].)

Cavell's compelling picture of the modern human being looking out at the world from behind the self (as if from behind a camera) is a picture of the self as something interposed, something that interposes itself, between one's true being (one's invisible soul, as it were) and the world. Viewing the world from behind the self, we hide our private fantasies. Indeed, we feel we *must* keep our fantasies hidden for they have become "all but completely thwarted and out of hand" (1979, 102). We keep our fantasies hidden because they have become so widely shared, so public, that we no longer feel that they are ours, and because we feel that our fantasies have become so private, so particular to us, that they cannot be shared at all. We keep our fantasies hidden "as if we could no longer hope that anyone might share them," Cavell writes, "at just the moment that they are pouring into the streets, less private than ever" (1979, 102).

This last line may be read as Cavell's allusion to the fateful period in the late 1960s when he was writing *The World Viewed*: America *was* tearing itself apart then, our thwarted fantasies *were* pouring into the streets. It was a fateful period in the history of film as well, a moment when "conviction in the myths of traditional movies had become lost or baffled, and film was belatedly moving into the modernist environment for so long occupied by the other great arts," as Cavell puts it (1979, 60). But the line may also be read as alluding to the period in the nineteenth century immediately prior to film's emergence, when the new human types that were to become the presiding geniuses of traditional movies were pouring into the streets of Paris—the historical moment of Charles Baudelaire's perception of the modern as the period in which human experience was becoming lost to itself (a perception Ralph Waldo Emerson anticipated in his great essay "Experience").

In *The World Viewed*, Cavell turns to Baudelaire's "The Painter of Modern Life" ("Le Peintre de la vie moderne") to explore the origins of film as a medium of art. He reflects on Baudelaire's way of thinking about the world of his time and the new types who inhabited it—the way these people looked, moved, loved, and thought about the world and themselves. Not only the emergence of film, but film's entire history, Cavell argues, is prophesied by Baudelaire's response to the phenomena of modernity that were all around him. If *these* types of people, *these* ways of moving, *these* clothes, *these* machines, *these* landscapes were not present in the modern world, what would have given us so much as the idea of viewing the world the way we view movies?

"The Painter of Modern Life," the most ambitious of Baudelaire's theoretical statements about art, called for a realization of "the other half of art whose first half is 'the eternal and unchangeable.'" The half Baudelaire wanted, he named "modernity," that which is "ephemeral, fugitive, contingent upon the occasion," the "description of contemporary life," and in particular the "nature of beauty in the present time." In Baudelaire's text, Cavell writes, "the pleasure we derive from the depiction of the present arises not only from the beauty in which [the present] can be attired, but also from its essential quality of being the present" (1979, 41).

Read as art criticism, "The Painter of Modern Life" may well seem perverse or superficial. Baudelaire praises Eugène Delacroix to the skies and fails to recognize what is modern in the paintings of Gustave Courbet and Edouard Manet. As Cavell points out, "the quality of presentness is exactly what Courbet and Manet themselves craved, and in establishing it as it could be established in painting, they were establishing modernist painting" (1979, 41–42). Read, however, as articulating and expressing the wish movies were created to satisfy, Baudelaire's text takes on a prophetic aspect. It presents a veritable catalogue of the phenomena of modernity—new types of objects, of settings, of human beings who inhabit those settings—which, when viewed the way Baudelaire views them, reveal the nature of beauty in the modern world to be ephemeral, fugitive, contingent upon the occasion. "Let me simply recall the titles of his chapters," Cavell writes, "pondering them against our knowledge of cinema: Fashion, The Man of the World, Crowds, The Child, War-Sketches, Pomps and Ceremonies, The Military Man, The Dandy, Cosmetics, Women and Courtesans, Carriages" (1979, 43). "Out of his despair of happiness," Cavell summarizes in a wonderful passage, "out of his disgust with its official made-up substitutes, and out of his knowledge and estrangement from the present and the foreignness of the past (and, I believe, in his experiments with hashish) [Baudelaire] found the wish ... for that specific simultaneity of presence and absence which only the cinema will satisfy" (1979, 42).

The extended discussion of Baudelaire in *The World Viewed* underscores Cavell's conviction that the entire history of movies has been bound up with our wish to overcome the metaphysical isolation that is the condition of human existence in the modern period. Movies originated as a response to this condition. In the course of the history of movies, the condition has not been cured; it has become more intense, or extreme, than ever. The thrust of *The World Viewed* as a whole is that, although film satisfied in a singular way our wish to "reach this world" by neutralizing the need to represent reality in order to connect with it, it also brought the problem of reality "to some ultimate head" (Cavell 1979, 195).

Because our private fantasies have become all but completely thwarted, we hide them. But how can our fantasies not be thwarted if we render them unseen, unseeable? The Clark Gable character in *It Happened One Night* (1934), for example, longs to find a woman with whom he can share the adventurous life of his fantasies. When he finds such a woman, his fantasies are doomed to be thwarted if he fails to acknowledge her as the woman of his dreams. Marrying his private fantasies to the world, as Cavell describes it, is an act this man must perform for himself; no one is in a position to perform it for him. "One's responsibility toward one's desire is to acknowledge it, and acknowledge its object's separateness from you" (1979, 177).

By viewing the world from behind the self, we consign our private fantasies to being thwarted, displace ourselves from our natural habitation within the world. We are responsible for what is unnatural about our condition. That *is* what is unnatural about our condition. Because they *automatically* displace us from the world, take responsibility for our displacement out of our hands, movies relieve us of our unnatural condition. Movies are not escapes *into* our private fantasies; they are reliefs from our private fantasies and their attendant responsibilities, from the fact that our world is *already* drawn by fantasy, as Cavell puts it (1979, 102).

The screen is not a barrier it is possible for us to cross or to sidestep; the medium of film automatically displaces us from the world projected on the screen. Viewing *It Happened One Night,* it is not *possible* for us to marry our own private fantasies to the world we are viewing. Hence it is not possible for us to *fail* to do so. That is why, for modern human beings like us who have become displaced, have displaced ourselves, from our natural habitation within the world, the world projected on the movie screen appears more natural than reality. Movies are able to awaken, or re-awaken, us to the reality of our longing to "reach the world," *The World Viewed* argues. But because it is *by our viewing* them that movies awaken us, they cannot free us from what is unnatural in our condition. Movies can only awaken us to the fact that we long to stop—we must stop—altering the world "illegitimately, against itself," as Cavell puts it (1979, 238). Movies cannot put us in a position to marry our fantasies to the world, as we long to do; they cannot bring the world closer to our heart's desire.

Within the field of film studies, modernism is often thought of as a particular style, or set of stylistic features (self-reflexivity, discontinuity, undermining of narrative causality, and so on). But for Cavell, the essential feature of modernism lies in the condition that the relation between the present practice of an enterprise and the history of that enterprise has become problematic. In Cavell's view, the goal of modernism in an art is not to repudiate that art's history, as is often supposed, but to keep faith with that history in a situation in which doing so requires radically new forms and procedures. Modernism is not a form of skepticism, as is also often supposed; it is a response to skepticism, an effort to overcome it.

In a modernist situation, the difficulty is that of "maintaining one's belief in one's own enterprise," of "making one's present effort become part of the present history of the enterprise" (Cavell 1976, xxii). A modernist artist, dedicated to making an object that will bear the same weight of experience traditionally borne by the objects that constitute the history of that art, "is compelled to find radically new forms and structures that define themselves and their history against one another," as Cavell puts it. Exploring its own medium, defining itself against its past, a modernist work asks itself exactly whether, and under what conditions, its art can survive (Cavell 1979, 72). In modernism, then, "each of the arts becomes its own subject, as if its immediate artistic task is to establish its own existence (1969, xxii).

In one of his most suggestive formulations, Cavell describes modernism in the arts as "the condition of their each yearning for themselves, naming a time at which to survive, they took themselves, their own possibilities, as their aspiration" (Cavell 2005b, 41). Part of what this means, for Cavell, is that in modernism an art has no choice but to assume the condition of philosophy. For it is a defining feature of philosophy—one that distinguishes it from the sciences, for example—that, as Cavell puts it, "philosophy is at all moments answerable to itself, that if there is any place at which the human spirit allows itself to be under its own question, it is in philosophy; that anything, indeed, that allows that questioning to happen *is* philosophy" (qtd. in Conant 1989, 26). (Science is not its own subject, in this sense; it is not a question for science what science is. What philosophy is, however, is a question for philosophy.) The fact that in the modern period film was able for so long to avoid the fate of modernism means, to Cavell, that alone among the great arts film seemed to be free from the imperative to philosophy. And yet, in his reflections on film he discovers that the medium seems "inevitably to reflect upon itself—as though the condition of philosophy were its natural condition" (Cavell 2005b, 41).

More than twenty years ago, in *Hitchcock—The Murderous Gaze*, I wrote:

Hitchcock started with a clear sense of film's traditions and a conviction that film was an art. His achievement, in part, was to create the first films that, fully embracing the medium, reflected seriously on their nature as films. Perhaps we cannot really speak of modernism in regard to an art that was not even born before modernism emerged in painting, music, poetry, and theater. If there is a modernist cinema, however, it begins with Hitchcock, in whose work film attains a modern self-consciousness. (Rothman 1982, 6)

Hitchcock's films are, to be sure, self-conscious demonstrations of, and reflections on, the powers and limits of "the art of pure cinema," as he liked to call it. After my Hitchcock book was published, however,

I realized—and argued in *The "I" of the Camera*—that D. W. Griffith's films were already reflecting seriously on their nature as films. Even Griffith Biograph films like *A Drunkard's Reformation* (1909) and *A House of Darkness* (1913) were exploring, declaring, the powers and limits of film (as distinguished, in particular, from theater and music) (Rothman 1988, 13–15). For that matter, it now seems clear to me that every one of the films the Lumière brothers screened that historic evening in Paris more than a century ago—the train pulling into the station at La Ciotat, the falling wall, the baby's lunch, and so on—perfectly, compellingly, demonstrates or declares some particular feature or condition that made motion pictures different from anything the world had ever seen before. (This is a real train, which could squash us into jelly, yet it is present to us in a way that enables it also to be absent, and enables us to view it without being in its presence. The film frame is contingent; the world extends beyond its limits. The world projected on the screen is free from our control, spontaneous, inherently unpredictable. And so on.) Reflecting seriously on its nature as a film, each one of these "first films" highlighted some particular aspect or aspects of this new kind of image that revealed its potential to satisfy, in an unprecedented way, our wish for the world re-created in its own image.

From the outset, then, film was philosophical as well as modern. But the earliest films were not modern*ist*, as Cavell understands the term, for the simple reason that film at its birth had no artistic tradition of its own. By the mid-1920s, however, in the "Golden Age of Silent Cinema," the art of film surely possessed such a tradition. On the whole, however, I do not think of the filmmakers of the first cinematic avant-garde as modernist. Rather than being compelled to find radically new forms and structures in order to keep faith with film's history as an art, they made films that conformed, stylistically, to modernist works in other arts (above all, painting), disowning or disregarding film's own artistic tradition.

Film began moving into a modernist environment, according to Cavell, only in the years leading up to his writing of *The World Viewed*. This was the period of Alain Resnais's *Hiroshima mon amour* (1959), Jean-Luc Godard's *Breathless* (*À bout de souffle,* 1960), François Truffaut's *Jules et Jim* (1962), Michelangelo Antonioni's *L'Avventura* (1960), Federico Fellini's *8½* (1963), Ingmar Bergman's *Persona*

(1966), and other European films that did seriously question their relation to film's artistic tradition and have a strong claim to being thought of as modernist. Such films seemed to reveal that a conviction in the original myths of movies was becoming "lost or baffled," as Cavell puts it (1979, 50). And yet, successful traditional movies continued to be made in this period. For that matter, they are still being made now, almost a half century after the initial films of the *Nouvelle Vague*.

How is this possible? If traditional movies were already modern, already philosophical, why was modernism in film necessary, or even possible? Why, and how, was film compelled to question its own tradition of self-questioning? And if film was no longer able to avoid the modernist predicament, how was it possible, how *is* it possible, for movies still to be made that are both popular and serious? Are the genres and forms of traditional movies still available to serious filmmakers, or are they not?

A way of approaching these questions—they admit of no simple answers—may perhaps be found in the distinction, reflected on throughout the essays that comprise Cavell's first book, between the traditional and the modern within philosophy. In writing *Must We Mean What We Say?* Cavell found himself unable to say what he meant, to mean what he could say, within the traditional forms of philosophy. Rather than being struck dumb by the modernist situation in which he found himself, Cavell discovered in Ludwig Wittgenstein's *Philosophical Investigations* and in the writings of J. L. Austin (his own professor of philosophy) revolutionary philosophical procedures that enabled him to achieve a radically new medium for saying what he had at heart to say.

In aligning himself with such thinkers, and increasingly with Emerson and his greatest nineteenth-century readers, Henry Thoreau and Friedrich Nietzsche, Cavell declares his commitment to what he takes to be the modern in philosophy. Among the most remarkable of Cavell's discoveries about the genres of romantic comedy and melodrama he studies in *Pursuits of Happiness, Contesting Tears,* and *Cities of Words* is that popular movies like *It Happened One Night* and *Stella Dallas* (1937) are not only philosophical; their ways of thinking are exemplary of what is modern in philosophy, as Cavell's own writing aspires to be. Insofar as they succeed in inheriting Emerson's philosophical perspective, movies are not instruments of pernicious ideology; indeed, they have a revolutionary aspect. For Cavell, then, the perplexing question of the availability to serious filmmakers of the genres and forms of traditional movies cannot be separated from the equally perplexing question of the availability of Emerson's philosophical perspective in our culture, a culture that both fosters and represses it.

Thinking, as Emerson pictures and practices it, has an uncanny affinity with film, with our experience of film. His essays "Behavior" and "Intellect" both highlight the same idea, which they approach from opposite directions—the idea that our behavior and our thinking are so inextricably interwoven that our experience continuously overcomes or transcends the Cartesian opposition between "outer" and "inner," "objective" and "subjective," body and soul, upon which the skeptical problematic hinges. Emerson's Wittgensteinian or Austinian attentiveness to the diversity of the things our eyes do and express—"The eye obeys exactly the action of the mind"; "The eyes of men converse as much as their tongues with the advantage that the ocular dialect needs no dictionary, but is understood all the world over"; "You can read in the eyes of your companion, whether your argument hits him, though his tongue will not confess it"; "There is a look by which a man shows he is going to say a good thing, and a look when he has said it"; "How many furtive inclinations avowed by the eye, though dissembled by the lips"; "There are asking eyes, asserting eyes, prowling eyes; and eyes full of fate"; and so on—puts to shame the pinched, unimaginative view, which so long held sway over film study, that there is such a thing as "the male gaze"—as if there is only one thing that all men never but do with their eyes (and by extension only one thing that the camera is never but doing). When Emerson writes about eyes and gazes the way he does in "Behavior" and "Intellect," he is mining, long before the fact, what has always been for film—and should always have been for film theory—a central, inexhaustible topic.

Emerson anticipates, or originates, the revolution in philosophy that Cavell has taught us to associate with the names "Wittgenstein" and "Austin"—and, I believe we must add, "Cavell." It is a point I have made again and again in my writing (and a point Cavell has made in his own terms, of course): film, in its continuous acknowledgment that human beings are embodied, that they exist in the world, is a privileged exemplar of the overcoming or transcending of Cartesian dualism—a marriage of body and soul. The world we view on film is at once "outer" and "inner." It is like the world we think, as Emerson characterizes it—the objects we see with the mind's vision. And it is like our behavior, what he calls our "manners," which reveals us to others.

Godard once defined film, perhaps ironically, as "truth twenty-four times a second" to register the fact, reflected on at length in *The World Viewed,* that the camera can do nothing but report truly, as it were, whatever is placed in front of it. At the same time, the camera has an astonishing facility that it shares with what Emerson, in a wonderful passage, calls the "mystic pencil" we use to "draw" our dreams.

> As soon as we let our will go, and let the unconscious states ensue, see what cunning draftsmen we are! We entertain ourselves with wonderful forms of men, of women, of animals, of gardens, of woods, and of monsters, and the mystic pencil wherewith we then draw has no awkwardness or inexperience, no meagerness or poverty; . . . the whole canvas which it paints is life-like, and apt to touch us with terror, with tenderness, with desire, and with grief.

The movie camera and projector, the "mystic pencil" with which films are drawn, likewise have "no awkwardness or inexperience, no meagerness or poverty." Their mechanism assures that their whole canvas is not only "life-like," but *real.* And yet, to paraphrase Emerson, films do not *automatically* "touch us with terror, with tenderness, with desire, or with grief." What truth is, in film, and what "mere contrivance"; what it takes to be an artist in the medium of film; what a true filmmaker might be "irresistibly urged to say"; what "forms of nobility and poetry" can "cling" to films; how films can be "useful as Bibles"; what gospel it is that they preach—these are questions for film theory, to be addressed through acts of criticism. Film criticism, as Cavell practices it, is an art that has its own nobilities, its own poetry. And its own truth. That is, it is also philosophy.

Within film studies, it is continually being said that ours is a post-modern age, that we have left modernism behind—as film has, as all the arts have, as the world has. But on what grounds, on what authority,

331

are we to accept it as given that we have been released from our condition as modern human beings, that we no longer believe in art's saving importance, that we no longer wish to master the self's fate, or no longer believe such mastery to be possible? Yielding to skepticism, postmodernism forgoes philosophy. But if the condition of philosophy is film's natural condition, as Cavell suggests, postmodernism must be, for film, an unnatural condition, one that alters the medium "illegitimately, against itself." In truth, there can be only one way to move beyond modernism, as Cavell understands the term: by "reaching this world" and achieving selfhood (hence the always simultaneous granting of otherness as well).

Movies have not made our dreams come true. Yet they have participated in, and affirmed, the quest to overcome or transcend the alienation (from nature, from other people, from ourselves) that is a condition of human existence in the modern period. By helping to keep alive our dream of a radically transformed, more fully human form of life, they still can move us closer to our heart's desire.

WORKS CITED AND CONSULTED

www.acmi.net.au

Adorno, T. W. 2003. "Culture Industry Reconsidered." In *The Audience Studies Reader,* ed. Will Brooker and Deborah Jermyn, 50 – 60. London: Routledge.

Adorno, Theodor W., and Max Horkheimer. 1972. "The Culture Industry: Enlightenment as Mass Deception" (1944). In *Dialectic of Enlightenment,* trans. John Cumming, 120 – 67. New York: Herder and Herder.

Appel, Alfred, Jr. 2002. *Jazz Modernism: From Ellington and Armstrong to Matisse and Joyce.* New York: Alfred A. Knopf.

Astor, Mary. 1967. *A Life on Film.* New York: Dell Publishing.

Bailey, F. G. 1991. *The Prevalence of Deceit.* Ithaca: Cornell University Press.

Baldick, Chris. 1991. *The Concise Oxford Dictionary of Literary Terms.* New York: Oxford University Press.

Barnouw, Dagmar. 1997. *Germany 1945.* Bloomington: Indiana University Press.

Barthes, Roland. 1972. "Operation Margarine." In *Mythologies,* trans. Annette Lavers, 41 – 43. New York: Hill and Wang.

Basinger, Jeanine. 1993. *A Woman's View: How Hollywood Spoke to Women 1930 – 1960.* New York: Alfred A. Knopf.

Bates, Harry. 1940. "Farewell to the Master." *Astounding* (October), 779 – 816.

Bazin, André. 1982. *The Cinema of Cruelty from Buñuel to Hitchcock* (1975). Ed. and with an introduction by François Truffaut. Trans. Sabine D'Estrée with the assistance of Tiffany Fliss. New York: Seaver Books.

Bean, Jennifer. 2002. "Introduction: Toward a Feminist Historiography of Early Cinema." In *A Feminist Reader in Early Cinema,* ed. Jennifer M. Bean and Diane Negra, 1 – 26. Durham: Duke University Press.

Benjamin, Walter. 1985. "The Work of Art in the Age of Mechanical Reproduction." In *Film Theory and Criticism: Introductory Readings,* ed. Gerald Mast and Marshall Cohen, 675 – 94. New York: Oxford University Press.

333

——————. 1997. *Charles Baudelaire: A Lyric Poet in the Era of High Capitalism.* Trans. Harry Zohn. London: Verso.

——————. 2002. *Selected Writings,* vol. 3, *1935–1938.* Ed. Howard Eiland and Michael Jennings. Cambridge, MA: Harvard University Press.

——————. 2003. *Selected Writings,* vol. 4, *1938–1940.* Ed. Howard Eiland and Michael Jennings. Cambridge, MA: Harvard University Press.

Bennett, Tony, Colin Mercer, and Janet Woolacott. 1986. *Popular Culture and Social Relations.* New York: Open University Press.

Bennis, Warren, and Philip Slater. 1968. *The Temporary Society.* New York: Harper and Row.

Bentley, Eric. 1964. *The Life of the Drama.* New York: Atheneum.

Berman, Marshall. 1988. *All That Is Solid Melts into Air: The Experience of Modernity.* New York: Penguin.

Biskind, Peter. 1983. *Seeing Is Believing: How Hollywood Taught Us to Stop Worrying and Love the Fifties.* New York: Pantheon.

Bordwell, David. 1996. *"La Nouvelle Mission de Feuillade;* or, What Was Mise-en-Scene?" *Velvet Light Trap* 37 (Spring), 10–29.

——————. 1997. *On the History of Film Style.* Cambridge, MA: Harvard University Press.

Bordwell, David, Janet Staiger, and Kristin Thompson. 1985. *The Classical Hollywood Cinema: Film Style and Mode of Production to 1960.* New York: Columbia University Press.

Bordwell, David, and Kristin Thompson. 2004. *Film Art: An Introduction.* 7th ed. Boston: McGraw-Hill.

Bouchard, Donald F., ed. 1977. *Language, Counter-Memory, Practice: Selected Essays and Interviews.* Trans. Donald F. Bouchard and Sherry Simon. Ithaca: Cornell University Press.

Branston, Gill. 2000. *Cinema and Cultural Modernity.* Buckingham, UK, and Philadelphia: Open University Press.

Britton, Andrew. 2004. *Katharine Hepburn: The Star as Feminist.* New York: Columbia University Press.

Brophy, Philip. 2001. Interview with Jack Nitzsche. In *Cinesonic: Experiencing the Soundtrack,* ed. Philip Brophy, 1–13. North Ryde, Australia: Australian Film Television and Radio School.

www.buffalohistoryworks.com

Buisseret, David. 2003. *The Mapmaker's Quest.* Oxford: Oxford University Press.

Bukatman, Scott. 2001. "The Artificial Infinite: On Special Effects and the Sublime."

In *Post-war Cinema and Modernity: A Film Reader,* ed. John Orr and Olga Taxidou, 208–22. New York: New York University Press.

——————. 2002. "Terminal Idiocy (The comedian is the message)." In *Enfant Terrible! Jerry Lewis in American Film,* ed. Murray Pomerance, 181–91. New York: New York University Press.

Burch, Noël. 1990. *Life to Those Shadows.* Berkeley: University of California Press.

Butler, Judith. 1999. *Gender Trouble: Feminism and the Subversion of Identity.* New York: Routledge.

Buzard, James. 2001. "Perpetual Revolution." *Modernism/Modernity* 8: 4 (November), 559–81.

Canetti, Elias. 1984. *Crowds and Power.* New York: Farrar, Straus and Giroux.

Capra, Frank. 1971. *The Name Above the Title.* New York: Macmillan.

Carpenter, Niles. 1932. *The Sociology of City Life.* New York: Longmans, Green and Co.

Carroll, Noël Edward. 1976. "An In-Depth Analysis of Buster Keaton's 'The General.'" Ph.D. diss., New York University.

Cavell, Stanley. 1969. *Must We Mean What We Say? A Book of Essays.* New York: Scribner.

——————. 1979. *The World Viewed: Reflections on the Ontology of Film.* Enlarged ed. Cambridge, MA: Harvard University Press.

——————. 2005a. "Concluding Remarks Presented at Paris Colloquium on *La Projection du Monde* (the French translation of *The World Viewed*), University of Paris, 1999." In Rothman, ed., *Cavell on Film,* 281–86.

——————. 2005b. "*North by Northwest.*" In Rothman, ed., *Cavell on Film,* 41–58.

——————. 2005c. "Opera in and as Film." In Rothman, ed., *Cavell on Film,* 305–18.

——————. 2005d. "What (Good) Is a Film Museum? What Is a Film Culture?" In Rothman, ed., *Cavell on Film,* 107–13.

——————. 2005e. "What Photography Calls Thinking." In Rothman, ed., *Cavell on Film,* 115–33.

Cendrars, Blaise. 1992. "The ABC's of Cinema." In *Modernities and Other Writings,* ed. Monique Chefdor, trans. Esther Allen, 23–29. Lincoln: University of Nebraska Press.

Charney, Leo. 1998. *Empty Moments: Cinema, Modernity, and Drift.* Durham: Duke University Press.

Chion, Michel. 1994. *Audio-Vision: Sound on Screen* (1990). Ed. and trans. Claudia Gorbman. With a foreword by Walter Murch. New York: Columbia University Press.

————. 2003. *Eyes Wide Shut*. London: British Film Institute.

Clover, Carol. 1992. *Men, Women, and Chainsaws: Gender in the Modern Horror Film*. Princeton: Princeton University Press.

Cohan, Steve. 1997. *Masked Men: Masculinity and the Movies in the Fifties*. Bloomington: Indiana University Press.

Cohen, Stanley, ed. 1971. *Images of Deviance*. Harmondsworth: Penguin.

Conant, James. 1989. "Introducing Cavell: An Interview with Stanley Cavell." In *The Senses of Stanley Cavell*, ed. Richard Fleming and Michael Payne, 21–34. Lewisburg, PA: Bucknell University Press.

Conley, Tom. 1983. "Vigo Van Gogh." *New York Literary Forum* 5, 153–66.

————. Forthcoming. *Cartographies of Cinema*. Minneapolis: University of Minnesota Press.

Corber, Robert. 1993. *In the Name of National Security: Hitchcock, Homophobia, and the Political Construction of Gender in Postwar America*. Durham and London: Duke University Press.

Coren, Michael. 1993. *The Invisible Man: The Life and Liberties of H. G. Wells*. New York: Atheneum.

Costello, John. 1985. *Virtue under Fire: How World War II Changed Our Social and Sexual Attitudes*. Boston: Little, Brown.

Crafton, Donald. 1994. "Pie and Chase: Gag, Spectacle and Narrative in Slapstick Comedy." In *Classical Hollywood Comedy*, ed. Kristine B. Karnick and Henry Jenkins, 106–19. New York: Routledge.

Cross, Robin. 1981. *The Big Book of B Movies: or, How Low Was My Budget*. New York: St. Martin's.

Curtis, James. 1982. *Between Flops: A Biography of Preston Sturges*. New York and London: Harcourt Brace Jovanovich.

Davenport, Guy. 1985. "Henri Rousseau." *Antaeus* 54 (Spring), 165–80.

Deleuze, Gilles. 1985. *Cinéma 2: L'Image-temps*. Paris: Les Editions de Minuit.

————. 1988. *Foucault*. Trans. Sean Hand. Minneapolis: University of Minnesota Press.

————. 1989. *Cinema 2: The Time-Image*. Trans. Hugh Tomlinson and Robert Galeta. Minneapolis: University of Minnesota Press.

Deleuze, Gilles, and Félix Guattari. 1983. *Anti-Oedipus: Capitalism and Schizophrenia*. Minneapolis: University of Minnesota Press.

Doane, Mary Ann. 2002. *The Emergence of Cinematic Time: Modernity, Contingency, the Archive*. Cambridge, MA: Harvard University Press.

Doherty, Thomas. 1999. *Pre-Code Hollywood: Sex, Immorality, and the Insurrection in American Cinema 1930–1934*. New York: Columbia University Press.

Duncan, Paul. 2000. *Film Noir: Films of Trust and Betrayal*. Harpenden, Herts., UK: Pocket Essentials.

Eckert, Charles. 1991. "The Anatomy of a Proletarian Film: Warner's *Marked Woman*." In *Imitations of Life: A Reader on Film and Television Melodrama*, ed. Marcia Landy, 205–26. Detroit: Wayne State University Press.

Eco, Umberto. 1995. "Eternal Fascism." *Utne Reader* 72 (November–December), 55–59.

Elkins, James. 1997. *The Object Stares Back: On the Nature of Seeing*. San Diego: Harvest-Harcourt.

Elsaesser, Thomas. 1984. "Pathos and Leave Taking: The German Émigrés in Paris during the 1930s." *Sight and Sound* 53: 4 (Autumn), 278–83.

———. 1996. "A German Ancestry to Film Noir? Film History and Its Imaginary." *Iris* 21 (Spring), 129–43.

———. 2003. "Too Big and Too Close: Alfred Hitchcock and Fritz Lang." *The Hitchcock Annual* 12, 1–41.

Erickson, Glenn. 2003. "Savant Review Essay: Things to Come." http://www.dvdtalk.com/dvdavant/s193things.htm.

Farber, Manny, and W. S. Poster. 1998. "Preston Sturges: Success in the Movies." In Manny Farber, *Negative Space: Manny Farber on the Movies*, 89–94. Expanded ed. New York: Da Capo Press.

Fauset, Jessie Redmon. 1990. *Plum Bun* (1928). Boston: Beacon.

Felski, Rita. 2000. "Nothing to Declare: Identity, Shame, and the Lower Middle Class." *PMLA* 115 (January), 33–45.

———. 2003. "Modernist Studies and Cultural Studies: Reflections on Method." *Modernism/Modernity* 10: 3 (September), 501–17.

www.filmsite.org

Fischer, Lucy. 1998. *Sunrise: A Song of Two Humans*. London: British Film Institute.

Flinn, Tom. 1975. "Three Faces of Film Noir: *Stranger on the Third Floor, Phantom Lady,* and *Criss Cross*." In McCarthy and Flynn, eds., *Kings of the Bs*, 155–64.

Foster, Gwendolyn Audrey. 2003. *Performing Whiteness: Postmodern Re/Constructings in the Cinema*. Albany: State University of New York Press.

Foucault, Michel. 1973. *Madness and Civilization: A History of Insanity in the Age of Reason*. Trans. Richard Howard. New York: Vintage.

———. 1975. *The Birth of the Clinic: An Archaeology of Medical Perception*. Trans. A. M. Sheridan-Smith. New York: Vintage.

———. 1977a. "Intellectuals and Power" (a conversation between Michel Foucault and Gilles Deleuze). In Bouchard, ed., *Language, Counter-Memory, Practice*, 205–17.

—————. 1977b. "A Preface to Transgression." In Bouchard, ed., *Language, Counter-Memory, Practice,* 29–52.

—————. 1977c. "Theatrum Philosophicum." In Bouchard, ed., *Language, Counter-Memory, Practice,* 165–96.

—————. 1979. *Discipline and Punish: The Birth of the Prison.* Trans. Alan Sheridan. New York: Vintage.

—————. 1980a. "The Eye of Power" (a conversation with Jean-Pierre Barou and Michelle Perrot). In *Power/Knowledge: Selected Interviews and Other Writings 1972–1977,* trans. Colin Gordon et al., 146–65. New York: Pantheon.

—————. 1980b. *The History of Sexuality,* vol. 1, *An Introduction.* Trans. Robert Hurley. New York: Vintage.

—————. 1980c. "Truth and Power." In *Power/Knowledge: Selected Interviews and Other Writings 1972–1977,* trans. Colin Gordon et al., 109–33. New York: Pantheon.

—————. 1984. *The Foucault Reader.* Ed. Paul Rabinow. New York: Pantheon.

—————. 1987. "The Ethic of Care for the Self as a Practice of Freedom: An Interview with Michel Foucault on January 20, 1984." Trans. J. D. Gauthier, S.J. *Philosophy and Social Criticism* 12: 2–3 (Summer), 112–31.

Fussell, Paul. 1992. *Class: A Guide Through the American Status System.* New York: Touchstone.

Gabbard, Krin. 2004. *Black Magic: White Hollywood and African American Culture.* New Brunswick: Rutgers University Press.

Garber, Marjorie. 1993. "From Dietrich to Madonna: Cross-gender Icons." In *Women and Film: A Sight and Sound Reader,* ed. Pam Cook and Philip Dodd, 16–20. Philadelphia: Temple University Press.

Garnham, Nicholas. 1972. *Samuel Fuller.* New York: Viking Press.

Gemunden, Gerd. N.d. "Gained in Translation: Exile Cinema and the Case of Billy Wilder." Unpublished manuscript.

www.geocities.com

Giddens, Anthony. 1991. *Modernity and Self-Identity: Self and Society in the Late Modern Age.* Stanford: Stanford University Press.

Goffman, Erving. 1974. *Frame Analysis: An Essay on the Organization of Experience.* Cambridge, MA: Harvard University Press.

Gomery, Douglas. 1975. "*They Live By Night* (Nicholas Ray)." In McCarthy and Flynn, eds., *Kings of the Bs,* 185–96.

Gomery, Douglas. 1992. *Shared Pleasures: A History of Movie Presentation in the United States.* Madison: University of Wisconsin Press.

Gorbman, Claudia. 1987. *Unheard Melodies: Narrative Film Music.* Bloomington: Indiana University Press.

Gould, Steven Jay. 1985. *The Flamingo's Smile: Reflections in Natural History.* New York: W. W. Norton.

Gunning, Tom. 1990. "The Cinema of Attractions: Early Film, Its Spectator and the Avant-Garde" (1986). In *Early Cinema: Space, Frame, Narrative,* ed. Thomas Elsaesser and Adam Barker, 56–62. London: British Film Institute.

——————. 1991a. *D. W. Griffith and the Origins of American Narrative Film: The Early Years at Biograph.* Urbana: University of Illinois Press.

——————. 1991b. "Heard Over the Phone: *The Lonely Villa* and the De Lorde Tradition of the Terrors of Technology." *Screen* 32: 2 (Summer), 184–96.

——————. 1994a. "An Aesthetic of Astonishment: Early Film and the [In]Credulous Spectator" (1989). In *Viewing Positions: Ways of Seeing Films,* ed. Linda Williams, 114–33. New Brunswick: Rutgers University Press.

——————. 1994b. "The Whole Town's Gawking: Early Cinema and the Visual Experience of Modernity." *Yale Journal of Criticism* 7: 2 (Fall), 189–201.

——————. 1995a. "Tracing the Individual Body: Photography, Detectives, and Early Cinema." In *Cinema and the Invention of Modern Life,* ed. Leo Charney and Vanessa R. Schwartz, 15–45. Berkeley: University of California Press.

——————. 1995b. "The Whole World Within Reach: Travel Images Without Borders." In *Cinema sans frontiers 1896–1918/Images across Borders: Internationality in World Cinema: Representations, Markets, Influences and Reception,* ed. Roland Cosandey and François Albera, 21–36. Lausanne: Editions Payot.

——————. 1997. "From Kaleidoscope to the X-Ray: Urban Spectatorship, Poe, Benjamin and *Traffic in Souls* (1913)." *Wide Angle* 19: 4 (Fall), 25–63.

——————. 1998. "Early American Film." In *The Oxford Guide to Film Studies,* ed. John Hill and Pamela Church Gibson, 255–71. Oxford: Oxford University Press.

——————. 2000a. "'Animated Pictures': Tales of Cinema's Forgotten Future after 100 Years of Films." In *Re-Inventing Film Studies,* ed. Christine Gledhill and Linda Williams, 316–31. London: Arnold Press.

——————. 2000b. *The Films of Fritz Lang: Allegories of Vision and Modernity.* London: British Film Institute.

——————. 2003. "Never Seen This Picture Before: Muybridge in Multiplicity." In *Time Stands Still: Muybridge and the Instantaneous Photography Movement,* ed. Phillip Prodger, 222–72. New York: Oxford University Press.

——————. 2004. "Systematizing the Electric Message: Narrative Form, Gender, and Modernity in *The Lonedale Operator.*" In *American Cinema's Transitional Era:*

Audiences, Institutions, Practices, ed. Charlie Keil and Shelly Stamp, 15–50. Berkeley: University of California Press.

Hamilton, Marybeth. 1997. *When I'm Bad, I'm Better: Mae West, Sex, and American Entertainment.* Berkeley: University of California Press.

Hansen, Miriam. 2000. "The Mass Production of the Senses: Classical Cinema as Vernacular Modernism." In *Reinventing Film Studies,* ed. Christine Gledhill and Linda Williams, 332–50. London: Oxford University Press.

Hardy, Phil, Tom Milne, and Paul Willemen, eds. 1986. *The Encyclopedia of Horror Films.* New York: HarperCollins.

Harley, J. Brian. 2001. *The New Nature of Maps: Essays in the History of Cartography.* Ed. Paul Laxton. Baltimore: Johns Hopkins University Press.

Harvey, David. 2003. *Paris, Capital of Modernity.* New York: Routledge.

Harvey, James. 1998. *Romantic Comedy in Hollywood, from Lubitsch to Sturges.* New York: Da Capo Press.

Henderson, Brian, ed. 1995. *Four More Screenplays by Preston Sturges.* Berkeley: University of California Press.

Highsmith, Patricia. 1955. *The Talented Mr. Ripley.* New York: Coward-McCann.

hooks, bell. 2000. *Where We Stand: Class Matters.* New York: Routledge.

Horak, Jan-Christopher. 2002. "German Film Comedy." In *The German Cinema Book,* ed. Tim Bergfelder, Erica Carter, and Deniz Gokturk, 29–38. London: British Film Institute.

Houseman, John. 1976. "Lost Fortnight: A Memoir." In *The Blue Dahlia: A Screenplay by Raymond Chandler,* ed. Matthew R. Bruccoli, 7–23. New York: Popular Library.

Hughes, Robert. 1981. *The Shock of the New.* New York: Alfred A. Knopf.

www.infoplease.com

www.inventors.about.com

Israel, Betsy. 2002. *Bachelor Girl: The Secret History of Single Women in the Twentieth Century.* New York: HarperCollins.

Jacob, Christian. 1992. *L'Empire des cartes: Approche théorique à travers l'histoire de la cartographie.* Paris: Albin Michel.

Jacobs, Diane. 1992. *Christmas in July: The Life and Art of Preston Sturges.* Berkeley: University of California Press.

Jacobs, Lea. 1987. "Censorship and the Fallen Woman Cycle." In *Home Is Where the Heart Is: Studies in Melodrama and the Woman's Film,* ed. Christine Gledhill, 100–112. London: British Film Institute.

Jameson, Fredric. 1981. *The Political Unconscious: Narrative as a Socially Symbolic Act.* Ithaca: Cornell University Press.

——————. 1991. *Postmodernism: or, The Cultural Logic of Late Capitalism*. Durham: Duke University Press.

——————. 2002. *A Singular Modernity: Essay on the Ontology of the Present*. London: Verso.

Johnson, James Weldon. 1990. *The Autobiography of an Ex-Colored Man* (1912). New York: Penguin.

Kahn, Ashley. 2000. *Kind of Blue: The Making of the Miles Davis Masterpiece*. New York: Da Capo Press.

Kalinak, Kathryn. 1992. *Settling the Score: Music and the Classical Hollywood Cinema*. Madison: University of Wisconsin Press.

Kaplan, E. Ann, and Ban Wang, eds. 2004. *Trauma and Cinema: Cross-Cultural Explorations*. Hong Kong: Hong Kong University Press.

Karl, Frederick R. 1985. *Modern and Modernism: The Sovereignty of the Author 1885–1925*. New York: Atheneum.

Keil, Charlie. 1996. "Fatal Attractions: The Problems Transitional Cinema Poses for Spectatorship." Paper delivered to the Society for Cinema Studies Conference, Dallas.

——————. 1998. "'Visualized Narratives': Transitional Cinema and the Modernity Thesis." In *Le Cinéma au tournanat du siècle/Cinema at the Turn of the Century*, ed. Claire Dupré la Tour, André Gaudreault, and Roberta Pearson, 123–37. Lausanne and Québec: Éditions nota bene.

——————. 2001. *Early American Cinema in Transition: Story, Style, and Filmmaking 1907–1913*. Madison: University of Wisconsin Press.

——————. 2004. "From Here to Modernity: Style, Historiography, and Transitional Cinema." In *American Cinema's Transitional Era: Audiences, Institutions, Practices*, ed. Charlie Keil and Shelly Stamp, 51–65. Berkeley: University of California Press.

Keniston, Kenneth. 1965. "Morals and Ethics." *American Scholar* 34: 4 (Autumn), 628–34.

Kleinhans, Chuck. 1991. "Notes on Melodrama and the Family under Capitalism." In *Imitations of Life: A Reader on Film and Television Melodrama*, ed. Marcia Landy, 197–204. Detroit: Wayne State University Press.

Kniesche, Thomas W., and Stephen Brockmann. 1994. "Introduction: Weimar Today." In *Dancing on the Volcano: Essays on the Culture of the Weimar Republic*, ed. Kniesche and Brockmann, 1–18. Columbia, SC: Camden House.

Josef Konvitz. 1987. *Cartography in France, 1660–1848: Science, Engineering, and Statecraft*. Chicago: University of Chicago Press.

Kramer, Peter. 2002. "Hollywood in Germany/Germany in Hollywood." In *The German Cinema Book,* ed. Tim Bergfelder, Erica Carter, and Deniz Gokturk, 227–37. London: British Film Institute.

Kyvig, David E. 2002. *Daily Life in the United States, 1920–1939: Decades of Promise and Pain.* Westport CT: Greenwood Press.

Lacan, Jacques. 1978. *The Four Fundamental Concepts of Psycho-Analysis.* Trans. Alan Sheridan. New York: W. W. Norton.

Lambert, Gavin. 1972. *On Cukor.* New York: G. P. Putnam's Sons.

Langer, Lawrence. 2002. "Recent Studies on Memory and Representation." Review of *Words and Witness: Narrative and Aesthetic Strategies of the Holocaust,* by Lea Wernick Fridman; *Traumatic Realism: The Demands of Holocaust Realism,* by Michael Rothberg; *Holocaust Representation: Art within the Limits of History and Ethics,* by Berel Lang; *Spectacular Suffering: Theatre, Fascism, and the Holocaust,* by Vivian M. Patraka; *The Claims of Memory: Representations of the Holocaust in Contemporary Germany and France,* by Caroline Wiedmer; *At Memory's Edge: After-Images of the Holocaust in Contemporary Art and Architecture. Holocaust and Genocide Studies* 16: 1 (Spring), 77–93.

Larkin, Philip. 1985. *All What Jazz: A Record Diary.* New York: Farrar Straus.

Larsen, Nella. 1997. *Passing* (1929). New York: Penguin.

Léger, Fernand. 1973. "Notes on Contemporary Plastic Life." In *Functions of Painting,* ed. Edward F. Fry, trans. Alexandra Anderson, 24–27. New York Viking Press.

Lehman, Peter, and William Luhr. 1977. *Blake Edwards.* Athens: Ohio University Press.

Lherminier, Pierre. 1967. *Jean Vigo.* Paris: Seghers.

Lippit, Akira Mizuta. 2000. *Electric Animal: Toward a Rhetoric of Wildlife.* Minneapolis: University of Minnesota Press.

Luhr, William. 2004. "John Wayne and *The Searchers.*" In *The Searchers: Reflections on John Ford's Classic Western,* ed. Arthur M. Eckstein and Peter Lehman, 75–90. Detroit: Wayne State University Press.

—————. Forthcoming. *Film Noir.* Oxford: Blackwell Publishing.

Lukács, Georg. 1963. *The Meaning of Contemporary Realism.* Trans. John and Necke Mander. London: Merlin.

—————. 1971. *Realism in Our Time: Literature and Class Struggle.* New York: Harper and Row.

—————. 1983. *The Historical Novel.* Lincoln: University of Nebraska Press.

Lyons, Arthur. 2000. *Death on the Cheap: The Lost B Movies of Film Noir.* New York: Da Capo Press.

Madsen, Axel. 1967. "Lang." *Sight and Sound* 36: 3 (Summer), 109–12.

Mangani, Giorgio. 1998. *Il "mondo" di Abramo Ortelio*. Modena: Franco Cosimo Panini.

Mariage, Thierry. 1999. *The World of André Le Nôtre*. Trans. Graham Larkin. Philadelphia: University of Pennsylvania Press.

Marinetti, F[ilippo] T[ommaso]. 1973. "The Founding and Manifesto of Futurism." In *The Futurist Manifestos*, ed. Umbro Apollonio, 19–24. New York: Viking Press.

Marx, Karl. 1978. "Alienation and Social Classes." In *The Marx-Engels Reader*, ed. Robert C. Tucker, 133–35. 2nd ed. New York: W. W. Norton.

Marx, Leo. 1964. *The Machine in the Garden: Technology and the Pastoral Ideal in America*. New York: Oxford University Press.

May, Lary. 2002. *The Big Tomorrow: Hollywood and the Politics of the American Way*. Chicago: University of Chicago Press.

McBride, Joseph. 1982. *Hawks on Hawks*. Berkeley: University of California Press.

McCarthy, Todd, and Charles Flynn, eds. 1975. *Kings of the Bs: Working Within the Hollywood System*. New York: Dutton.

McFadden, Tara Ann. 1996. *Pop Wisdom: A Little Guide to Life*. Philadelphia: Running Press.

McGurl, Tom. 1996. "Making It Big: Picturing the Radio Age in *King Kong*." *Critical Inquiry* 22: 3 (Spring), 415–45.

McIntosh, Mary. 1971. "Changes in the Organization of Thieving." In *Images of Deviance*, ed. Stanley Cohen, 98–133. Harmondsworth: Penguin.

Meisel, Myron. 1975. "Edgar G. Ulmer: The Primary of the Visual." In McCarthy and Flynn, eds., *Kings of the Bs*, 147–52.

http://members.yourlink.net/jgerard/gort/

Metz, Christian. 1974. *Film Language: A Semiotics of the Cinema*. Trans. Michael Taylor. New York: Oxford University Press.

Metz, Walter. 1997. " 'Keep the Coffee Hot, Hugo': Nuclear Trauma in Fritz Lang's *The Big Heat* (1953)." *Film Criticism* 21: 3 (Spring), 43–65.

—————. 2001. "A Very Notorious Ranch, Indeed: Fritz Lang, Allegory, and the Holocaust." *Journal of Contemporary Thought* 13 (Summer), 71–86.

—————. 2004. *Engaging Film Criticism: Film History and Contemporary American Cinema*. New York: Peter Lang.

Meyer, David N. 1998. *A Girl and a Gun: The Complete Guide to Film Noir*. New York: Avon.

Millar, Gavin. 1980. "Samuel Fuller." In *Cinema: A Critical Dictionary: The Major Film-Makers*, ed. Richard Roud, 401–3. London: Secker and Warburg.

Miller, Clive T. 1975. "*Nightmare Alley*: Beyond the Bs." In McCarthy and Flynn, eds., *Kings of the Bs*, 167–83.

Milman, Estera. 2001. *"NO!art" and the Aesthetics of Doom*. Evanston: Northwestern University, Mary and Leigh Block Museum of Art.

Milovanovic, Dragan. 1997. "Dueling Paradigms: Modernist versus Postmodernist Thought." Rev. ed. In Milovanovic, *Postmodern Criminology*. New York: Garland Publishing.

Moi, Toril. 2004. "Ibsen and the Ideology of Modernism." Keynote address, Film and Literature Conference, University of Florida, Tallahassee.

Montaigne, Michel de. 1950. "De la diversion." In Montaigne, *Essais,* vol. 3. Ed. Albert Thibaudet and Maurice Rat. Paris: Gallimard/Pléiade.

Morton, Donald. 1990. "The Cultural Politics of (Sexual) Knowledge: On the Margins with Goodman." *Social Text* 25: 6, 227–41.

Moullet, Luc. 1985. "Sam Fuller: In Marlowe's Footsteps" (1959). In *Cahiers du cinéma: The 1950s: Neo-Realism, Hollywood, New Wave,* ed. Jim Hillier, 145–55. Cambridge, MA: Harvard University Press.

Muller, Eddie. 2001. *Dark City Dames: The Wicked Women of Film Noir*. New York: Regan Books/HarperCollins.

Muller, Tom. 1998. *Dark City: The Lost World of Film Noir*. New York: St. Martin's.

http://naid.sppsr.ucla.edu/coneyisland/articles/1920.htm

Naremore, James. 1998. *More than Night: Film Noir in Its Contexts*. Berkeley: University of California Press.

Nenno, Nancy. 1997. "Femininity, the Primitive, and Modern Urban Space: Josephine Baker in Berlin." In *Women in the Metropolis,* ed. Katharina von Ankum, 141–61. Berkeley: University of California Press.

Nowell-Smith, Geoffrey. 1977. "Minnelli and Melodrama." *Screen* 18: 2 (Summer), 113–18.

—————. 2003. *Luchino Visconti*. London: British Film Institute.

Nye, David E. 1990. *Electrifying America: Social Meanings of a New Technology, 1880–1940*. Cambridge, MA: MIT Press.

Oliver, Kelly, and Benigno Trigo. 2002. *Noir Anxiety*. Minneapolis: University of Minnesota Press.

O'Mahoney, Mike. 2000. "Introduction." In *Art Deco,* ed. Iain Zaczek, 6–15. Bath: Parragon.

Parsons, Talcott. 1951. *The Social System*. Glencoe, IL: Free Press.

Peppis, Paul. 2002. "Rewriting Sex: Mina Loy, Marie Stopes, and Sexology." *Modernism/Modernity* 9: 4 (November), 561–79.

Petro, Patrice. 2002. *Aftershocks of the New: Feminism and Film History*. New Brunswick: Rutgers University Press.

Pilat, Oliver, and Jo Ranson. 1941. *Sodom by the Sea: An Affectionate History of Coney Island*. Garden City, NY: Doubleday, Doran and Co.

Poe, Edgar Allan. 1998. *Selected Tales*. Ed. David Van Leer. Oxford: Oxford University Press.

Polan, Dana. 1986. *Power and Paranoia: History, Narrative, and the American Cinema 1940–1950*. New York: Columbia University Press.

──────. 1994. *In a Lonely Place*. London: British Film Institute.

Pomerance, Murray. 2004. *An Eye for Hitchcock*. New Brunswick: Rutgers University Press.

Popcorn Q. Movies. http://www.planetout.com/pno/popcornq.htm.

Porfirio, Robert. 1988a. *"Decoy."* In Silver and Ward, eds., *Film Noir*, 87.

──────. 1988b. *"They Won't Believe Me."* In Silver and Ward, eds., *Film Noir*, 295–86.

──────. 2002. "Interview with Dore Schary, 1905–1980." In *Film Noir Reader 3*, ed. Robert Porfirio, Alain Silver, and James Ursini, 179–89.. New York: Limelight.

Porfirio, Robert, and Carl Macek. 2002. "Interview with Joseph H. Lewis, 1907–2000." In *Film Noir Reader 3*, ed. Robert Porfirio, Alain Silver, and James Ursini, 67–85. New York: Limelight.

Porter, Eric. 2002. *What Is This Thing Called Jazz? African American Musicians as Artists, Critics, and Activists*. Berkeley: University of California Press.

Rajchman, John. 1988. "Foucault's Art of Seeing." *October* 44 (Spring), 89–117.

Rice, Shelley. 1997. *Parisian Views*. Cambridge, MA: MIT Press.

Riesman, David. 1950. *The Lonely Crowd: A Study of the Changing American Character*. New Haven: Yale University Press.

Roberts, Jim. 1998. "Introduction: Imagistic Information." *Enculturation* 2: 1 (Fall). Available at http://enculturation.gmu.edu/2_1/intro.html.

Robertson, Linda. 2000. "Air Wars: Lone Wolves and Civilized Violence at the Movies and Live from Baghdad." In *Bang Bang, Shoot Shoot! Essays on Guns and Popular Culture*, ed. Murray Pomerance and John Sakeris, 133–46. 2nd ed. Boston: Pearson Education.

Rohmer, Eric. 1989. *The Taste for Beauty*. Trans. Carol Volk. Cambridge: Cambridge University Press.

Rothman, William. 1982. *Hitchcock—The Murderous Gaze*. Cambridge, MA: Harvard University Press.

──────. 1988. *The "I" of the Camera: Essays on Film Criticism, History, and Aesthetics*. Cambridge and New York: Cambridge University Press.

——————, ed. 2005. *Cavell on Film*. Albany: State University of New York Press.

Rothman, William, and Marian Keane. 2000. *Reading Cavell's "The World Viewed": A Philosophical Perspective on Film*. Detroit: Wayne State University Press.

Russell, Catherine. 1995. *Narrative Mortality: Death, Closure, and New Wave Cinemas*. Minneapolis: University of Minnesota Press.

Said, Edward. 2003. *Freud and the Non-European*. London and New York: Verso.

Salles-Gomes, P. E. 1998. *Jean Vigo*. Rev. ed. With an afterword by Paul Ryan. London: Faber and Faber.

Salt, Barry. 1983. *Film Style and Technology: History and Analysis*. London: Starword.

Sarris, Andrew. 1968. *The American Cinema: Directors and Directions 1929–1968*. New York: E. P. Dutton.

Scheib, Richard. 2001. Review of *The Island of Lost Souls*. http://www.moria.co.nz/horror/isllostsouls.htm.

——————. 2003. The Science Fiction, Horror and Fantasy Film Review. http://www.moria.co.nz/sf/justimagine.htm.

Schivelbusch, Wolfgang. 1979. *The Railway Journey: Trains and Travel in the 19th Century*. Urizen Press.

——————. 1986. *The Railway Journey: The Industrialization of Time and Space in the 19th Century*. Berkeley: University of California Press.

——————. 1995. *Disenchanted Night: The Industrialization of Light in the Nineteenth Century*. Berkeley: University of California Press.

——————. 2003. *The Culture of Defeat: On National Trauma, Mourning, and Recovery*. New York: Henry Holt.

Schulz, Juergen. 1978. "Jacobo de' Barbari's View of Venice: Map Making, City Views, and Moralized Geography before 1500." *Art Bulletin* 60: 4 (December), 425–75.

Sharrett, Christopher. 2000. "End of Story: The Collapse of Myth in Postmodern Narrative Film." In *The End of Cinema as We Know It,* ed. Jon Lewis, 319–31. New York: New York University Press.

Shklovsky, Viktor. 1965. "Art as Technique." In *Russian Formalist Criticism: Four Essays,* ed. Lee T. Lemon and Marion J. Reis, 3–24. Lincoln: University of Nebraska Press.

Silver, Alain. 1988. *"Kiss Me Deadly."* In Silver and Ward, eds., *Film Noir,* 156–58.

Silver, Alain, and Carl Macek. 1988. *"Gun Crazy."* In Silver and Ward, eds., *Film Noir,* 116–198.

Silver, Alain, and Elizabeth Ward. 1988. *Film Noir: An Encyclopedic Reference to the American Style*. Revised and expanded ed. Woodstock, NY: Overlook Press.

Simmel, Georg. 2004. "The Metropolis and Mental Life" (1905). In *The City Cultures Reader,* ed. Malcolm Miles and Tim Hall (with Iain Borden), 12–19. 2nd ed. London: Routledge.

Singer, Ben. 2001. *Melodrama and Modernity: Early Sensational Cinema and Its Contexts.* New York: Columbia University Press.

Sloterdijk, Peter. 1987. *Critique of Cynical Reason* (1983). Trans. Michael Eldred. Minneapolis: University of Minnesota Press.

Sobchack, Vivian. 1997. *Screening Space: The American Science Fiction Film.* New Brunswick: Rutgers University Press.

—————. 1998. "Lounge Time: Postwar Crises and the Chronotope of Film Noir." In *Refiguring American Film Genres: Theory and History,* ed. Nick Brown, 129–70. Berkeley: University of California Press.

Stacey, Jackie. 1994. *Star Gazing: Hollywood Cinema and Female Spectatorship.* London: Routledge.

Straw, Will. 1997. "Urban Confidential: The Lurid City of the 1950s." In *The Cinematic City,* ed. David B. Clarke, 110–28. London and New York: Routledge.

Sturges, Preston. 1990. *Sturges on Sturges.* Adap. and ed. Sandy Sturges. New York: Simon and Schuster.

Sturken, Marita, and Lisa Cartwright. 2001. *Practices of Looking: An Introduction to Visual Culture.* Oxford: Oxford University Press.

Sussex, Elizabeth. 1984. "The Fate of F3080." *Sight and Sound* 53: 2 (Spring), 92–97.

Szwed, John. 2002. *So What: The Life of Miles Davis.* New York: Simon and Schuster.

Telotte, J. P. 2001. *Science Fiction Film.* New York: Cambridge University Press.

www.terrypepper.com/lights/closeups/illumination/argand/lewis-lamp.htm

www.the-history-of.net

Thompson, Peggy, and Saeko Usukawa. 1992. *The Little Black and White Book of Film Noir.* Vancouver, B.C.: Arsenal Pulp.

—————. 1996. *Hard Boiled: Great Lines from Classic Noir Films.* San Francisco: Chronicle.

Tomlinson, Gary. 1991. "Cultural Dialogics and Jazz: A White Historian Signifies." *Black Music Research Journal* 11: 2 (Autumn), 229–64.

Tsivian, Yuri. 1998. *Early Cinema in Russia and Its Cultural Reception.* Ed. Richard Taylor. Trans. Alan Bodger. Chicago: University of Chicago Press.

Van Beusekom, Ansje. 1977. "Cinema Militans: Spectators and Authors in the Writings on Film of Theo van Doesburg and Menno ter Braak." Rev. and trans. Tom Gunning. In *In prima dell'autore,* ed. Lorenzo Querisima, 233–42. Udine: Edizioni Forum.

Veblen, Thorstein. 1994. *The Theory of the Leisure Class* (1899). New York: Dover.

Vertov, Dziga. 1984. *Kino-Eye: The Writings of Dziga Vertov.* Ed. Annette Michelson. Berkeley: University of California Press.

Viviani, Christian. 1987. "Who Is Without Sin? The Maternal Melodrama in American Film, 1930–39." In *Home Is Where the Heart Is: Studies in Melodrama and the Woman's Film,* ed. Christine Gledhill, 83–99. London: British Film Institute.

Vogel, Amos W. 1974. *Film as a Subversive Art.* New York: Random House.

Waine, Graham. 1995. *Projection for the Performing Arts.* Oxford: Focal Press.

Warner, Marina. 1993. *L'Atalante.* London: British Film Institute.

Wartenberg, Thomas. 1999. *Unlikely Couples: Movie Romance as Social Criticism.* Boulder, CO: Westview Press.

http://washingtonmo.com/1904/12.htm

Weightman, Gavin. 2003. *Signor Marconi's Magic Box.* Cambridge, MA: Da Capo Press.

Weiss, Allen S. 1989. *The Aesthetics of Excess.* Albany: State University of New York Press.

Widdig, Bernd. 2001. *Culture and Inflation in Weimar Germany.* Berkeley: University of California Press.

Williams, Linda. 1991. "'Something Else Besides a Mother': *Stella Dallas* and the Maternal Melodrama." In *Imitations of Life: A Reader on Film and Television Melodrama,* ed. Marcia Landy, 307–30. Detroit: Wayne State University Press.

Wood, Robin. 1990. "L'Atalante." In *International Dictionary of Films and Filmmakers 1: Films,* ed. Nicholas Thomas, 61–63. Chicago and London: Saint James Press.

———. 2002. *Hitchcock's Films Revisited.* New York: Columbia University Press.

———. 2003. *Hollywood from Vietnam to Reagan and Beyond.* New York: Columbia University Press.

Woolf, Virginia. 1992. *Mrs. Dalloway.* Ed. Stella McNichol. With introduction and notes by Elaine Showalter. London: Penguin Books.

Zelizer, Barbie. 1998. *Remembering to Forget: Holocaust Memory Through the Camera's Eye.* Chicago: University of Chicago Press.

CONTRIBUTORS

Rebecca Bell-Metereau teaches film in the English department at Texas State University and directs the interdisciplinary Media Studies Minor. She is the author of *Hollywood Androgyny* and *Simone Weil on Politics Religion and Society*, and chapters and articles in *BAD: Infamy, Darkness, Evil, and Slime on Screen; Film and Television after 9/11; Ladies and Gentlemen, Boys and Girls; Writing With; Cultural Conflicts in Twentieth Century Literature; Deciding Our Future: Technological Imperatives; Women Worldwalkers: New Dimensions of Science Fiction and Fantasy; College English; Journal of Popular Film and Television;* and *Cinema Journal*.

Steven Alan Carr is an associate professor of communication at Indiana University–Purdue University Fort Wayne and a 2002–2003 Center for Advanced Holocaust Studies Postdoctoral Fellow at the United States Holocaust Memorial Museum in Washington, DC. He is the author of *Hollywood and Anti-Semitism: A Cultural History up to World War II*. His present project, which explores the response of the American film industry to the growing public awareness of the Holocaust, received an award from the National Endowment for the Humanities in 2002.

Tom Conley is a professor of Romance languages and literatures at Harvard University. Author of *The Self-Made Map: Cartographic Writing in Early Modern France*, he has translated Michel de Certeau, *The Writing of History*; Marc Augé, *In the Metro*; and Christian Jacob, *The Sovereign Map* (forthcoming). His essay on Jean Vigo draws on the conceptual material in his forthcoming *Cartographies of Cinema*.

Wheeler Winston Dixon is the James Ryan Endowed Professor of Film Studies, chair of the Film Studies Program, and professor of English at the University of Nebraska, Lincoln. With Gwendolyn Audrey Foster, he is editor-in-chief of the *Quarterly Review of Film and Video*. His newest books as author or editor include *American Cinema of the 1940s: Themes and Variations; Visions of Paradise: Images of Eden in the Cinema; Lost in the Fifties: Recovering Phantom Hollywood; Film and Television after 9/11; Visions of the Apocalypse: Spectacles of Destruction in American Cinema;*

Straight: Constructions of Heterosexuality in the Cinema; and *Experimental Cinema: The Film Reader,* edited with Gwendolyn Audrey Foster. In April 2003, he was honored with a retrospective of his films at the Museum of Modern Art in New York, and his films were acquired for the museum's permanent collection in both print and original format.

Lucy Fischer is a professor of film studies and English at the University of Pittsburgh, where she serves as director of the Film Studies Program. She is the author of seven books: *Jacques Tati; Shot/Countershot: Film Tradition and Women's Cinema; Imitation of Life; Cinematernity: Film, Motherhood, Genre; Sunrise; Designing Women: Art Deco, Cinema, and the Female Form*; and *Stars: The Film Reader* (co-edited with Marcia Landy). Currently, she is editing *American Cinema of the 1920s: Themes and Variations* for Rutgers University Press. She has published extensively on issues of film history, theory, and criticism in such journals as *Screen, Sight and Sound, Camera Obscura, Wide Angle, Cinema Journal, Journal of Film and Video, Film Criticism, Women and Performance, Frauen und Film,* and *Film Quarterly.* Her essays have been anthologized twenty-seven times in volumes of film history, criticism, and/or theory.

Gwendolyn Audrey Foster holds the rank of professor in the Department of English at the University of Nebraska, Lincoln, where she specializes in film studies, cultural studies, and postfeminist critical theory. Her books include *Performing Whiteness: Postmodern Re/Constructions; Identity and Memory: The Films of Chantal Akerman; Experimental Cinema: The Film Reader; Troping the Body: Etiquette, Conduct, and Dialogic Performance*; and *Captive Bodies: Postcolonialism in the Cinema.* Forthcoming is *Class-Passing: Performing Social Mobility in Film and Popular Culture. Performing Whiteness* was cited by the journal *Choice* as "[e]ssential . . . one of the Outstanding Academic Books of the Year" for 2004. Since 1999, Foster has been editor-in-chief of *Quarterly Review of Film and Video.*

Krin Gabbard is a professor of comparative literature and English at the State University of New York at Stony Brook. He is the author of *Black Magic: White Hollywood and African American Culture* and *Jammin' at the Margins: Jazz and the American Cinema,* and the co-author of *Psychiatry and the Cinema.* He is the editor of *Jazz among the Discourses* and *Representing Jazz.* His current project is a cultural history of the trumpet, forthcoming in 2006.

Tom Gunning is Edwin A. and Betty L. Bergman Distinguished Service Professor in the Humanities at the University of Chicago. He teaches in the Department of Art History and the Committee on Cinema and Media. He is the author of *D. W. Griffith and the Origins of American Narrative Film: The Early Years at Biograph* and *The*

Films of Fritz Lang: Allegories of Vision and Modernity, and has published more than one hundred articles, many on early cinema.

Peter Lehman is professor of English at Arizona State University, where he serves as director of the Center for Film and Media Research and director of the Film and Media Studies Program. His edited volume, *Pornography: Film and Culture,* is forthcoming. He is co-author with William Luhr of *Thinking about Movies* (2nd ed.), and author of *Running Scared: Masculinity and the Representation of the Male Body* and *Roy Orbison: The Invention of an Alternative Rock Masculinity.*

William Luhr, a professor of English at Saint Peter's College, is currently completing a book on film noir. His other books include *Raymond Chandler and Film; Thinking about Movies: Watching, Questioning, Understanding* (with Peter Lehman); *The Coen Brother's "Fargo"; "The Maltese Falcon": John Huston, Director; Blake Edwards* (with Peter Lehman); and *World Cinema since 1945.* He is also co-chair of the Columbia University Seminar on Cinema and Interdisciplinary Interpretation.

Joe McElhaney is an assistant professor of film studies at Hunter College–City University of New York. He is the author of *The Death of Classical Cinema: Hitchcock, Lang, Minnelli* and a forthcoming study of Albert Maysles.

Walter Metz is an associate professor in the Department of Media and Theatre Arts at Montana State University–Bozeman, where he teaches the history, theory, and criticism of film, television, and theater. He is the author of *Engaging Film Criticism: Film History and Contemporary American Cinema,* and his articles devoted to the intertextual analysis of film genre, authorship, and adaptation have appeared in *Interdisciplinary Humanities,* the *Journal of Contemporary Thought,* the *Journal of Film and Video, Film Criticism,* and *Literature/Film Quarterly.* He is currently finishing a book on the American films of Fritz Lang.

Patrice Petro is a professor of English and film studies at the University of Wisconsin–Milwaukee, where she is also director of the Center for International Education. She is the author, editor, or co-editor of *Aftershocks of the New: Feminism and Film History; Joyless Streets: Women and Melodramatic Representation in Weimar Germany; Fugitive Images: From Photography to Video; Truth Claims: Representation and Human Rights; Global Cities: Cinema, Architecture and Urbanism in a Digital Age;* and *Global Currents: Media and Technology Now.*

Murray Pomerance is a professor and the chair in the Department of Sociology at Ryerson University, editor of the "Horizons of Cinema" series at State University of New York Press, and co-editor with Lester D. Friedman of the "Screen Decades" series at Rutgers University Press. He is the author of *Magia d'Amore, An Eye for Hitchcock, Johnny Depp Starts Here,* and *Savage Time,* and editor or co-editor of numerous volumes, including *American Cinema of the 1950s: Themes and Varia-*

tions; Where the Boys Are: Cinemas of Masculinity and Youth; and *BAD: Infamy, Darkness, Evil, and Slime on Screen.*

William Rothman is a professor of film studies at the University of Miami. His most recent publication is his edition of *Cavell on Film.* His books include *Hitchcock—The Murderous Gaze, The "I" of the Camera,* and *Documentary Film Classics,* and he is co-author of *Reading Cavell's "The World Viewed."*

Christopher Sharrett is a professor of communication at Seton Hall University. He is the author of *The Rifleman,* the editor of *Crisis Cinema: The Apocalyptic Idea in Postmodern Narrative Film, Mythologies of Violence in Postmodern Media,* and co-editor with Barry Keith Grant of *Planks of Reason: Essays on the Horror Film.* He has contributed to *Cineaste, Kino Eye, Persistence of Vision, Film Quarterly, Journal of Popular Film and Television, Cinema Journal,* and numerous anthologies, including *BAD: Infamy, Darkness, Evil, and Slime on Screen; The New American Cinema; Fifty Contemporary Filmmakers; The Coen Brothers' "Fargo"; Sam Peckinpah's "The Wild Bunch"; Perspectives on German Cinema; The Dread of Difference: Gender and the Horror Film;* and other books.

David Sterritt, longtime film critic of the *Christian Science Monitor* and co-chair of the Columbia University Seminar on Cinema and Interdisciplinary Interpretation, is chairman of the National Society of Film Critics and adjunct professor at the Maryland Institute College of Art. His writing has appeared in many periodicals, including *Cahiers du cinéma,* the *New York Times,* the *Journal of Aesthetics and Art Criticism,* and *Cineaste.* His latest books are *Guiltless Pleasures: A David Sterritt Film Reader* and *Screening the Beats: Media Culture and the Beat Sensibility.*

PHOTO CREDITS

Page 3. The modern experience in *Die Letzte Mann* [The Last Laugh] (F. W. Murnau, Universum Film A. G., 1924). Digital frame enlargement.

Page 15. A ghostly presence of cinema. "Nigeria 1960," © Ed van der Elsken / Nederlands fotomuseum.

Page 19. The illuminated wheel in *Sunrise: A Song of Two Humans* (F. W. Murnau, Fox Film Corporation, 1927). Digital frame enlargement.

Page 38. The darkness from the top of the stairs. Gene Tierney in *Leave Her to Heaven* (John M. Stahl, Twentieth Century Fox, 1945). Courtesy Jerry Ohlinger Archives.

Page 57. The alienated gaze in *Psycho* (Alfred Hitchcock, Shamley/Paramount, 1960). Digital frame enlargement.

Page 74. The fragility of social order in *The Big Heat* (Fritz Lang, Columbia, 1953). Digital frame enlargement.

Page 93. Stella (Barbara Stanwyck) catches a glimpse of how the other half lives in *Stella Dallas* (King Vidor, Howard/Samuel Goldwyn, 1937). Courtesy Jerry Ohlinger Archives.

Page 110. Gort out of control in *The Day the Earth Stood Still* (Robert Wise, Twentieth Century Fox, 1951). Digital frame enlargement.

Page 130. A failure of social critique, *Eyes Wide Shut* (Stanley Kubrick, Hobby/Pole Star/Warner Bros., 1999). Digital frame enlargement.

Page 155. Nature Boy. Dickie Greenleaf (Jude Law) bathes in Tom Ripley's company in *The Talented Mr. Ripley* (Anthony Minghella, Mirage/Miramax/Paramount, 1999). Digital frame enlargement.

Page 175. Retribution on the pitcher's mound in *Experiment in Terror* (Blake Edwards, Columbia, 1962). Digital frame enlargement.

Page 194. The eye of power: *Shock Corridor* (Samuel Fuller, Allied Artists/F&F Productions, 1963). Digital frame enlargement.

Page 211. Frank Abagnale Jr. (Leonardo DiCaprio) prepares to fly high in *Catch Me If You Can* (Steven Spielberg, DreamWorks SKG/Amblin, 2002). Digital frame enlargement.

Page 235. A German vision in Hollywood. Tony Curtis (left) and Jack Lemmon in *Some Like It Hot* (Billy Wilder, Ashton Productions/Mirisch Corporation, 1959). Digital frame enlargement.

Page 253. Getting lost on the map in *L'Atalante* (Jean Vigo, Gaumont-Franco Film-Aubert, 1934). Digital frame enlargement.

Page 273. Discovering oneself through the words of a headline in *Sullivan's Travels* (Preston Sturges, Paramount, 1941). Digital frame enlargement.

Page 297. Modernity and the coordination of activity: *Dr. Mabuse, der Spieler* [Dr. Mabuse, the Gambler] (Fritz Lang, Uco-Film/Ullstein/Universum Film A. G., 1922). Digital frame enlargement.

Page 316. Will the woman in his presence say or do something to acknowledge him? Charlie Chaplin at the conclusion of *City Lights* (Charles Chaplin, United Artists, 1931). Frame enlargement.

INDEX